WEBSTER'S
NEW
ENGLISH
LANGUAGE
DICTIONARY

THE
POPULAR
GROUP

Published by
The Popular Group, LLC
1700 Broadway
New York, NY 10019

Published by arrangement with K DICTIONARIES LTD
http://kdictionaries.com

Publishing Consultant: Charles M. Levine
Design and Composition: Charlotte Staub

FOR K DICTIONARIES
Project Manager: Ilan J. Kernerman
Database Administrator: Vladimír Benko

ISBN: 1-59027-077-0

Printed in the United States of America

9 8 7 6 5 4 3 2

A

a *indef. art.* **1.** one **2.** every **3.** for each

abandon *verb.* **(abandoned, abandoning) 1.** leave someone that you should take care of **2.** leave something where it is —**abandoned** *adj.* —**abandonment** *noun.*

abbey *noun.* a building where monks and nuns live and work

abbot *noun.* a monk who is the head of a monastery

abbreviation *noun.* a shorter way of writing a word

ABC *noun.* the alphabet

abdomen *noun.* the stomach and bowels —**abdominal** *adj.*

abide *verb.* **1.** tolerate (usually used in the negative) **2.** (formal) obey

ability *noun.* the power to do something (plural **abilities**; opposite **inability**)

able *adj.* having the power or skill to do something (opposite **unable**)

aboard *prep. adv.* on a ship, plane or train

abolish *verb.* **(abolished, abolishing)** end or stop something

aboriginal *adj.* concerning the people or things connected to a region (especially Australia) from earliest times

aborigine *noun.* a person who has been living in Australia from earliest times

about *adv.* around

about *prep.* **1.** on the subject of **2.** not exactly; more or less

above *prep.* **1.** just over **2.** higher than; more than —**above** *adv.* (opposite **below**)

—**above all 1.** the most important thing is **2.** more than anything else

abreast *adv.* side by side and facing the same direction

abroad *adv.* **1.** in another country **2.** to another country

absence *noun.* not being there

absent *adj.* not there; not present

absentee *noun.* someone who is not present but should be

absenteeism *noun.* regular absence from work or school

absolute *adj.* complete; total

absolutely *adv.* completely; in every way

absorb *verb.* **(absorbed, absorbing) 1.** take in liquid **2.** learn something **3.** make something a part of yourself

absorption *noun.* **1.** taking in a new group of people into a country, organization, etc **2.** taking in gas, liquid or heat **3.** intense interest in and a lot of attention to something

abstract *adj.* existing as a concept

absurd *adj.* foolish and ridiculous

abuse *noun.* cruelty or wrong use

abuse *verb.* **(abused, abusing) 1.** treat cruelly **2.** use wrongly

academic *adj.* connected with education at a school or college

academy *noun.* a school that teaches special skills

accelerate *verb.* **(accelerated, accelerating)** make something move faster (opposite **slow down**)

accelerator *noun.* the gas pedal of a vehicle

accent *noun.* **1.** a particular way of speaking **2.** the heavy-sounding emphasis on part of a word

accept *verb.* **(accepted, accepting) 1.** take a gift **2.** say **yes** to an offer or invitation **3.** agree with an idea, plan or decision (opposite **reject**)

acceptable *adj.* all right; satisfactory; that you can accept (opposite **unacceptable**)

acceptance *noun.* the act of accepting

access *noun.* the way in

access *verb.* **(accessed, accessing)** (computers) be able to get to certain information stored in a computer

accessible *adj.* able to be reached easily (opposite **inaccessible**)

accessory *noun.* something that is extra and usually helpful but not always necessary

accident *noun.* something bad that happens unexpectedly

accidental *adj.* unexpected; not planned

accidentally *adv.* without meaning to

accommodate *verb.* **(accommodated, accommodating) 1.** have enough space for **2.** give someone a place to sleep

accommodation *noun.* **1.** enough space (no plural) **2.** a place to spend the night (usually plural)

accompaniment *noun.* something that goes along with something else usually to make it better

accompany *verb.* **(accompanied, accompanying) 1.** go with somebody **2.** play a musical instrument together with someone who is singing or playing another instrument

accomplish *verb.* **(accomplished, accomplishing)** get something done; achieve

accomplishment *noun.* something important or difficult that was done

accordance *noun.* agreement (usually used only in the expression **in accordance with**)

accordingly *adv.* in a way that agrees with something that was said or happened

according to *prep.* as someone says or writes

account *noun.* **1.** a bill; a piece of paper that shows how much money you must pay **2.** numbers that show how much money you receive and how much you spend **3.** a description of something that happened; a report

accountant *noun.* someone whose job is to examine the accounts of a business

account executive *noun.* the manager of a client's account, especially in advertising

account *verb.* **(accounted, accounting) 1.** (with **for**) explain what happened to something **2.** (formal) consider

accumulate *verb.* **(accumulated, accumulating) 1.** become more and more **2.** collect something; get more and more of something

accuracy *noun.* exactness

accurate *adj.* exact (opposite **inaccurate**) —**accurately** *adv.*

accusation *noun.* what you are accused of doing

accuse *verb.* **(accused, accusing)** say that someone is guilty

accustom *verb.* **(accustomed, accustoming)** make yourself used to something

ache *noun.* a pain that does not go away quickly

ache *verb.* **(ached, aching)** hurt

achieve *verb.* **(achieved, achieving)** succeed in something difficult — **achievement** *noun.*

achiever *noun.* someone who is successful especially after practicing or hard work

acid *noun.* a sharp, burning chemical

acknowledge *verb.* **(acknowledged, acknowledging) 1.** let someone know that you have received something **2.** say that something is true; admit

acknowledgment *noun.* **1.** letting someone know that you or they received something **2.** admitting something **3.** saying that you are grateful for someone's help

acquaint *verb.* **(acquainted, acquainting)** make familiar; give information

acquaintance *noun.* **1.** (formal) knowing someone or something (no plural) **2.** someone that you have met but do not know well

acquire verb. **(acquired, acquiring) 1.** get or buy something **2.** have or accumulate something

acquisition noun. something you have; possession

acre noun. a measure of land (43,560 square feet or 4,047 square meters)

acrobat noun. a person who can do amazing things with his/her body, especially at a circus

acrobatic adj. connected to what an acrobat does

acrobatics noun. the tricks that an acrobat does in a performance

acronym noun. a name made up of the first letters of other words

across prep. **1.** on the other side of **2.** (also adv.) from one side to the other

act noun. **1.** something that you do **2.** part of a play **3.** a law passed by the law-making body of a nation

act verb. **(acted, acting) 1.** behave **2.** do something **3.** take part in a play

acting noun. the work of being an actor or actress (no plural)

action noun. **1.** something that you do **2.** motion; movement; activity (no plural)

activate verb. **(activated, activating)** bring into use or start

active adj. busy; always doing things — **actively** adv. (opposite **inactively**)

active noun. adj. (grammar; also **active voice**) the **doing** form of the English verb

activism noun. the belief that action, such as demonstrations, is the way to oppose or show support

activist noun. someone active in a political movement

activity noun. **1.** motion; things happening (no plural) **2.** something that keeps you busy (plural **activities**)

actor noun. a person who acts in plays or movies

actress noun. a woman who acts in plays or movies (plural **actresses**)

actual adj. real

actuality noun. truth or reality

actually adv. really; in fact

ad noun. short for **advertisement**

adapt verb. **(adapted, adapting)** make changes so that something is suitable for something else —**adaptable** adj.

adaptability noun. ability to change and be made suitable for a different purpose

adaptation noun. being adapted

add verb. **(added, adding) 1.** put two or more numbers together **2.** put another item on a list **3.** put something more in **4.** say something more

addict noun. someone who is addicted to something

addiction noun. a need or habit that you cannot stop

addictive adj. causing addiction

addition noun. **1.** adding numbers together (no plural) **2.** something that was brought in or attached later

additional adj. **1.** more **2.** more than you have to; extra

additionally adv. as an added thing

address noun. the number of a house or building and the name of the street and town

address verb. **(addressed, addressing)** write an address on an envelope

adequacy noun. being enough

adequate adj. enough —**adequately** adv.

ad hoc adj. (Latin) created for a special purpose

adjacent adj. very close to

adjective noun. (grammar) a word that describes a noun (something or someone); a word that tells what kind

adjourn verb. **(adjourned, adjourning)** stop but not end a meeting, trial, etc

adjudicate verb. **(adjudicated, adjudicating)** (formal) give a judgment regarding a disagreement or a competition

adjudication noun. judgment

3

adjudicator *noun.* judge

adjust *verb.* **(adjusted, adjusting) 1.** make a small change so that something will fit or work properly **2.** become used to a place or situation

adjustment *noun.* **1.** a small change **2.** becoming used to a new place

administer *verb.* **(administered, administering)** manage or direct especially in government or business

administration *noun.* management of a business or government

administrative *adj.* concerning administration

administrator *noun.* someone whose job is to administer

admirable *adj.* deserving praise

admiral *noun.* a rank in the navy

admiration *noun.* a feeling that someone or something is good or beautiful (no plural)

admire *verb.* **(admired, admiring) 1.** have a good opinion of someone **2.** look at something with pleasure

admission *noun.* **1.** saying that you are guilty of doing something wrong; confession **2.** going into a place where you must pay (no plural)

admit *verb.* **(admitted, admitting) 1.** say that you did something that was wrong; confess **2.** let someone into a place

adolescence *noun.* the years between 12 and 18 (no plural)

adolescent *noun.* a young person who is about 12–18 years old; a teenager —**adolescent** *adj.*

adopt *verb.* **(adopted, adopting) 1.** take and raise someone else's child as your own **2.** accept the manners, customs or ideas of other people as your own —**adoption** *noun.* —**adoptive** *adj.*

adorable *adj.* cute and charming

adore *verb.* **(adored, adoring)** love very much —**adoring** *adj.*

adult *noun.* a grown person —**adult** *adj.* —**adulthood** *noun.* (no plural)

advance *noun.* something that you get before the usual time

advance *verb.* **(advanced, advancing)** move forward

advanced *adj.* at a later or more developed stage

advancement *noun.* progress; development; movement to a higher rank

advantage *noun.* something that is good, helpful or useful —**advantageous** *adj.*

adventure *noun.* **1.** action that is new and exciting (no plural) **2.** an exciting and sometimes dangerous event —**adventure** *adj.*

adventurer *noun.* someone who enjoys doing new and sometimes dangerous things

adventurous *adj.* **1.** liking adventure **2.** full of excitement and unusual events **adventurously** *adv.*

adverse *adj.* bad; unfavorable —**adversely** *adv.*

advertise *verb.* **(advertised, advertising)** bring products or services to people's attention, usually on TV or radio or in newspapers

advertisement *noun.* a notice to everyone that you are trying to sell or buy a product or service (short form **ad**)

advertiser *noun.* a person or company that advertises

advertising *noun.* trying to persuade people to buy a certain product (no plural)

advice *noun.* a suggestion about what someone should do (no plural)

advisable *adj.* that is a good idea

advise *verb.* **(advised, advising)** tell someone what to do

adviser, advisor *noun.* someone who helps other people decide what to do

advocate *verb.* **(advocated, advocating)** support; be in favor of

aerial *noun.* a rod or wire used to receive or broadcast radio or TV signals; an antenna

aerobics *noun plural.* a type of physical exercise in which you do a lot of jumping

affair *noun.* 1. concern 2. situation

affairs *noun plural.* business

affect *verb.* **(affected, affecting)** make a difference; influence (the noun is **effect**)

affected *adj.* unnatural; pretended (opposite **unaffected**)

affection *noun.* love; warm feelings

affectionate *adj.* showing love —**affectionately** *adv.*

affidavit *noun.* an official written statement, made under oath, which is used in court

affiliate *noun.* a smaller group or organization that is connected to a bigger one

affiliate *verb.* **(affiliated, affiliating)** associate (with)

afford *verb.* **(afforded, affording)** (usually used only in the expression **can** or **cannot afford**) have enough money, time, etc —**affordable** *adj.*

afraid *adj.* 1. feeling fear; frightened 2. worried; concerned

African *noun.* someone from Africa — **African** *adj.*

African American, African-American *noun.* a black American of African descent —**African-American** *adj.*

after *conj.* later than something else

after *prep.* 1. later than something else 2. following

after *adv.* later

afternoon *noun.* the hours between noon and evening

afterthought *noun.* an idea that comes later

afterward, afterwards *adv.* later

again *adv.* a second time; more than once

—**again and again** repeatedly; many times

against *prep.* 1. opposed to 2. on the opposite side in games or war 3. preventing something 4. on something

—**against the law** forbidden by law; not legal

—**against your will** without your agreeing to it or wanting to do it

age *noun.* 1. the number of years a person has lived; how old someone is 2. a period of your life 3. a period in history or prehistory

age *verb.* **(aged, aging)** become old

aged *adj.* 1. of a certain age 2. old

agency *noun.* 1. an office that works for a larger company 2. a department of the government or an international organization

agenda *noun.* things scheduled to be discussed at a meeting

agent *noun.* a person who takes care of the business of somebody else with other people; a representative

aggression *noun.* the act of starting a war or argument

aggressive *adj.* wanting to start a fight —**aggressively** *adv.*

aggressor *noun.* the person or country starting a quarrel or war

agitate *verb.* **(agitated, agitating)** 1. make someone worried or nervous 2. convince a crowd to act against something 3. shake (usually liquids)

ago *adv.* before now; in the past

agree *verb.* **(agreed, agreeing)** 1. think that an opinion or plan is correct (opposite **disagree**) 2. say that you will do what someone asks you to

agreeable *adj.* pleasant

agreed-upon *adj.* sharing the same opinion

agreement *noun.* 1. having the same opinion (no plural; opposite **disagreement**) 2. saying that something is all right (no plural) 3. a promise or an understanding between two or more people 4. a contract

agricultural *adj.* for or from agriculture **agriculturally** *adv.*

agriculture *noun.* farming; growing crops or raising farm animals (no plural)

5

ahead *adv.* in front

ahead of *prep.* before or earlier than
—**ahead of schedule** earlier than planned
—**ahead of time** early

aid *noun.* **1.** help (no plural) **2.** something that helps you

aid *verb.* **(aided, aiding)** help

AIDS *noun.* Acquired Immune Deficiency Syndrome; a disease that affects the immune system and makes it difficult to fight off infections

aim *noun.* **1.** the ability to hit what you are trying to (no plural) **2.** what you hope to do or achieve

aim *verb.* **(aimed, aiming) 1.** point something at a place or a person **2.** intend or plan to do something

ain't *verb.* (slang) short form of **am not, are not, is not,** etc

air *noun.* what we breathe into our bodies through our nose and mouth

air *verb.* **(aired, airing) 1.** let air into a place **2.** put something outside in the air to make it fresh

air conditioner *noun.* a machine that cools the air

air-conditioning *noun.* a cooling system using air conditioner(s) —**air-conditioned** *adj.*

aircraft *noun.* a machine that flies, such as an airplane (plural **aircraft**)

aircraft carrier *noun.* a warship with a big, flat surface for aircraft to take off from or land on

air force *noun.* the branch of the military that attacks and defends from the air

airline *noun.* a company that owns and operates airplanes

airmail *noun.* sending letters or packages by airplane (no plural)

airplane *noun.* a heavy flying machine (short form **plane**)

airport *noun.* a place where airplanes take off and land (especially for entry to or exit from a country)

aisle *noun.* a passage (walkway) that separates sections of seats

alarm *noun.* **1.** a feeling of danger (no plural) **2.** a bell or buzzer that warns of danger

alarm *verb.* **(alarmed, alarming)** frighten someone

alarm clock *noun.* a clock that rings to wake you up

album *noun.* **1.** a book for keeping photographs or other important things **2.** a long-playing record or CD, or a set of records or CDs **3.** a covering for a record or CD

alcohol *noun.* a strong liquid that can make you drunk or can clean a wound (no plural)

alcoholic *noun.* someone who is addicted to alcoholic drinks

alcoholic *adj.* with alcohol in it

alcoholism *noun.* addiction to alcohol (no plural)

algebra *noun.* a branch of mathematics where letters are used instead of numbers.

alert *verb.* **(alerted, alerting)** warn; make someone aware of possible danger

alertness *noun.* being ready to act (no plural)

alias *noun.* another name you are known by (especially used by criminals)

alias *adv.* otherwise known by

alien *noun.* a foreigner; a being from other worlds —**alien** *adj.*

alienate *verb.* **(alienated, alienating)** make someone become unfriendly

alike *adj.* the same; similar (opposite **different**)

alike *adv.* in the same way; similarly (opposite **differently**)

alive *adj.* living (opposite **dead**)

all *pron.* everyone or everything

all *adj.* **1.** every part of something **2.** every one of something

all *adv.* completely

allegation *noun.* a statement which is not supported by proof

allege *verb.* **(alleged, alleging)** claim without having proof

allergic *adj.* being sensitive to something that can make you sick

allergy *noun.* a sensitivity to something that can make you feel very bad (plural **allergies**)

alley *noun.* a path between buildings (plural **alleys**)

alligator *noun.* a large meat-eating reptile like a crocodile, that lives in rivers and lakes

allocate *verb.* **(allocated, allocating)** put aside (accommodation, money, etc)

allow *verb.* **(allowed, allowing)** **1.** let someone do something; permit **2.** let someone into a place

allowance *noun.* **1.** a certain amount of money that you get regularly without doing work for it **2.** money that you get for a special purpose

alloy *noun.* a mixture of metals to create a new metal

all right *adj. adv.* **1.** words that you can say if you agree to something **2.** words that show that something is allowed **3.** not injured; not harmed; not ill **4.** not bad, but not good either (in conversation = **OK**)

all-round *adj.* able to do many things

allusion *noun.* (formal) a hint about someone or something; speaking about someone in an indirect way

ally *noun.* someone that is on your side in a war, an argument, etc (plural **allies**) —**allied** *adj.*

almost *adv.* nearly; not quite

alone *adv.* **1.** having nobody with you **2.** without help

along *adv.* **1.** forward **2.** with someone

along *prep.* **1.** the whole length of **2.** on

aloud *adv.* using your voice in a way that can be heard; speaking not in a whisper and not silently

alphabet *noun.* the letters for writing a language

alphabetical *adj.* in the order of the alphabet

already *adv.* **1.** before now **2.** before then

also *adv.* too; in addition

altar *noun.* the raised area where religious ceremonies take place

alter *verb.* **(altered, altering)** become different, but still basically remain the same

alteration *noun.* making or becoming different

alternate *verb.* **(alternated, alternating)** do something in turns

alternative *noun.* a choice

alternative *adj.* giving another possibility

although *conj.* in spite of the fact that; though (compare **although he is old** and **in spite of his age**)

altitude *noun.* the height of a thing or place above sea level

altogether *adv.* completely; totally

aluminum *noun.* a lightweight silvery metal

always *adv.* **1.** over and over **2.** at all times **3.** ever since you can remember

am *verb.* the present tense of **to be** with **I** (first person singular) (short form **I'm**)

a.m., A.M. *abbr.* the hours between midnight and noon

amalgamate *verb.* **(amalgamated, amalgamating)** join together groups or businesses

amateur *noun.* someone who performs an activity (such as painting, singing, acting in plays, or taking part in sports) without getting paid for it

amaze *verb.* **(amazed, amazing)** give someone a feeling of great surprise or wonder —**amazing** *adj.* —**amazingly** *adv.*

amazement *noun.* great surprise or wonder (no plural)

ambassador *noun.* someone who represents his/her country in another country

ambition *noun.* **1.** a strong desire to succeed (no plural) **2.** something that you wish very much to do or be

ambitious *adj.* having a strong wish to succeed

ambulance *noun.* a van that takes sick or injured people to the hospital

American *noun.* somebody from the United States —**American** *adj.*

ammunition *noun.* weapons that explode

—**ammunitions depot** *noun.* a place for storing weapons

among, amongst *prep.* **1.** in the middle of many **2.** one of many **3.** between many

amount *noun.* how much of something; sum; quantity (usually with uncountable nouns)

amplifier *noun.* an electrical piece of equipment used to make sounds louder

amuse *verb.* **(amused, amusing) 1.** occupy your attention; entertain **2.** make you smile or laugh

amusement *noun.* entertainment; fun

amusing *adj.* entertaining; funny

an *indef. art.* **1.** one of something **2.** every **3.** for each

analysis *noun.* the careful examination of something (such as a book, chemicals, etc) by dividing it into parts and possibly making a judgment

analyst *noun.* a person, often a scientist, who analyzes

analytical *adj.* using analysis

analyze *verb.* **(analyzed, analyzing)** examine something by dividing it into parts in order to understand it

ancestor *noun.* someone in your family who lived before your grandparents

ancestry *noun.* a person's ancestors

anchor *noun.* a heavy piece of metal that a ship drops down to the bottom of the sea to keep from moving

anchor *verb.* **(anchored, anchoring)** drop an anchor

ancient *adj.* **1.** that happened very long ago; not modern **2.** very old

and *conj.* a word that joins words together to show that there is something more

anesthetic *noun.* a medication used so that you do not have feeling or pain

angel *noun.* **1.** a messenger from God **2.** a very kind, unselfish person

anger *noun.* the strong, unpleasant feeling that you get when someone hurts you or does something terrible

angle *noun.* the space where two lines meet

angrily *adv.* in an angry way

angry *adj.* **(angrier, angriest)** feeling anger

animal *noun.* any living thing that is not a plant

animated *adj.* lively

ankle *noun.* the place where the leg joins the foot

anniversary *noun.* the same date as something that happened in the past (the anniversary of someone's birth is a **birthday**; plural **anniversaries**)

announce *verb.* **(announced, announcing) 1.** give information to the public **2.** say something loudly so that everyone can hear

announcement *noun.* a message to the public

announcer *noun.* someone who reads the news, etc, on TV or the radio

annoy *verb.* **(annoyed, annoying)** bother someone; make someone feel angry or impatient or irritated—**annoyance** *noun.* —**annoying** *adj.*

annual *adj.* **1.** happening every year **2.** of the year

annually *adv.* every year

anonymous *adj.* done by someone whose name is not known

another *adj. pron.* **1.** one more of the same kind **2.** a different one

answer noun. 1. a reply to a question 2. a reply to a letter 3. someone picking up the telephone when you call

answer verb. (answered, answering) 1. reply to a question 2. reply to a letter

ant noun. a small, busy insect

antagonism noun. hatred between groups

antarctic adj. (often **Antarctic**) in or near the South Pole

antenna noun. 1. a rod or wire used to receive or broadcast radio or TV signals; an aerial 2. a sensitive feeler on some insects

anthem noun. the national song of a country

anthropology noun. the scientific study of the human race, including its customs and beliefs

antibiotic noun. a kind of medicine that stops or prevents infections

anticipate verb. (anticipated, anticipating) 1. wait for something to happen 2. think that something will happen; expect —**anticipation** noun.

antics noun plural. silly behavior

antiquated adj. old fashioned; outdated

antique noun. adj. something that was made a long time ago

antique verb. (antiqued, antiquing) make something (like furniture) look antique and so worth more money

antiquities noun plural. things from ancient times

anxiety noun. fear and expectation that something bad may happen

anxious adj. 1. worried; nervous 2. wanting something to happen

anxiously adv. nervously

any adj. 1. (also pron.) some 2. whichever; whatever 3. one (use in questions, negative sentences and with **hardly**; use **some** in positive sentences)

any adv. at all

anybody, anyone pron. 1. somebody 2. a person but no one special

anyhow adv. 1. in spite of that; anyway 2. a word that you can use if you want to get back to the subject

anymore, any more adv. no longer

anyone pron. see **anybody, anyone**

anything pron. 1. something 2. whatever; it doesn't matter what

anytime adv. any time you like

anyway adv. in spite of that; anyhow

anywhere adv. 1. in any place at all; somewhere 2. it doesn't matter where (use **anywhere** in questions and negatives; use **somewhere** in positive sentences)

apart adv. 1. separately 2. away from each other

apartment noun. rooms where someone lives inside a larger building

ape noun. a large monkey without a tail

apologize verb. (apologized, apologizing) say that you are sorry about something that you did

apology noun. saying that you are sorry (plural **apologies**) —**apologetic** adj.

apparent adj. 1. easily seen or understood 2. seeming to be real or true, but not

apparently adv. seemingly; it seems that; appearing to be (opposite **actually**; **really**)

appeal noun. 1. attractiveness 2. asking someone for something 3. a request to do something —**appeal** verb. (appealed, appealing)

appealing adj. attractive; pleasant

appear verb. (appeared, appearing) 1. come into view 2. seem 3. be in a book, on a list, etc 4. act in a play or movie

appearance noun. 1. how someone or something looks 2. coming into view (no plural)

appetite noun. a strong desire for something, usually food

applaud verb. (applauded, applauding) clap your hands to show that you are enjoying something or approve of something

applause *noun.* the clapping of hands to show enjoyment or approval (no plural)

apple *noun.* a round fruit with a smooth skin and small seeds that grows on trees

appliance *noun.* an electrical instrument or machine for personal use

applicable *adj.* relevant

applicant *noun.* someone who asks for a job or acceptance at a school

application *noun.* asking for a job, admission to a school, permission for something, etc

apply *verb.* **(applied, applying)** write to ask for something officially

appoint *verb.* **(appointed, appointing)** choose someone to do a certain job

appointment *noun.* a meeting that you fix in advance

appraise *verb.* **(appraised, appraising)** decide what the worth of something is —**appraisal** *noun.*

appreciate *verb.* **(appreciated, appreciating) 1.** know the value of something **2.** be grateful to someone for something —**appreciative** *adj.* (opposite **unappreciative**)

appreciation *noun.* **1.** knowing the value of something **2.** being grateful to someone for something

apprentice *noun.* someone who is learning a trade with a professional

approach *verb.* **(approached, approaching)** come near someone or something —**approach** *noun.* (plural **approaches**)

appropriate *adj.* right and suitable (opposite **inappropriate**) —**appropriately** *adv.* —**appropriateness** *noun.*

approval *noun.* **1.** saying or thinking that something is good (opposite **disapproval**) **2.** permission

approve *verb.* **(approved, approving)** think or say that something or someone is good (opposite **disapprove**)

approving *adj.* showing approval (opposite **disapproving**)

approximate *verb.* **(approximated, approximating)** (formal) come close to —**approximation** *noun.*

approximately *adv.* not exactly but more or less

Apr. *abbr.* April

April *noun.* the fourth month of the year

apron *noun.* a piece of clothing that you wear over the front of your regular clothes to keep them clean

apt *adj.* **1.** appropriate **2.** likely to behave in a certain way

aptitude *noun.* natural ability, especially in learning

aquarium *noun.* **1.** a glass tank for fish **2.** a building where you can see all kinds of fish

Arabic *noun.* a language spoken especially in the Middle East and North Africa

arbitration *noun.* asking someone to settle a dispute

arbitrator *noun.* someone who settles a dispute

arch *noun.* a curved shape in a building, bridge, etc (plural **arches**)

archaeological, archeological *adj.* of or connected with archaeology

archaeology, archeology *noun.* the study of old buried remains to learn about the past (no plural)

archbishop *noun.* a priest in charge of churches and other bishops of a large area

architect *noun.* someone who plans and designs buildings —**architectural** *adj.*

architecture *noun.* **1.** the designing of buildings (no plural) **2.** the way that buildings are designed

archives *noun.* a place where old documents are kept

arctic *adj.* **1.** relating to the North Pole **2.** very cold —**the Arctic** *noun.*

ardent *adj.* eager

are *verb.* the present tense of the verb **to be** with **we, you** or **they** (short form **we're; you're; they're**)

area *noun.* **1.** a part of the world or of a country; a district; a region **2.** a space for a certain purpose **3.** a neighborhood **4.** a measurement of surface

arena *noun.* a usually closed area for sports or entertainment

argue *verb.* **(argued, arguing) 1.** talk about something and disagree **2.** give reasons for something

argument *noun.* **1.** an angry disagreement **2.** giving reasons for something

arid *adj.* very dry

arise *verb.* **(arose, arisen, arising) 1.** get out of bed (**rise** is more common) **2.** come up

aristocrat *noun.* someone of high social rank; a nobleman or noblewoman

aristocratic *adj.* of high social rank

ark *noun.* **1.** a large ship **2. Noah's Ark** in the Bible, the ship built by Noah

arm *noun.* **1.** the part of the body between the shoulder and the hand **2.** the side rests on some chairs

arm *verb.* **(armed, arming) 1.** get weapons; get ready for war **2.** supply someone with weapons

armchair *noun.* a comfortable chair with rests for your arms

armed *adj.* carrying a weapon (opposite **unarmed**)

armed forces, armed services the army, air force and navy of a country; the military

arms *noun plural.* weapons

army *noun.* **1.** the armed forces; the military **2.** the part of the military that serves on the land, not in the air or on the sea

arose *verb.* past of **arise**

around *prep.* **1.** on all sides of **2.** to the other side of **3.** to all parts of **4.** nearby **5.** making a circle **6.** in different places **7.** in **8.** about; approximately

around *adv.* **1.** facing the opposite way **2.** in many places **3.** on all sides **4.** in all directions **5.** nearby; in the area **6.** in a circle

arrange *verb.* **(arranged, arranging) 1.** make things neat; put things in order **2.** put things in a certain order **3.** make a plan

arrangement *noun.* **1.** the way that something is done **2.** a plan

array *noun.* a collection or display

arrest *verb.* **(arrested, arresting)** take someone prisoner for committing a crime —**arrest** *noun.*

arrival *noun.* coming to a place

arrive *verb.* **(arrived, arriving)** come to a place

arrogant *adj.* proud and unpleasant or rude—**arrogance** *noun.* (no plural)

arrow *noun.* **1.** a thin stick with a point at one end and feathers on the other which you shoot **2.** a sign with a picture in the shape of an arrow

arson *noun.* (legal) starting a fire on purpose

art *noun.* **1.** making things that are beautiful **2.** a skill —**artwork** *noun.*

article *noun.* **1.** a newspaper or magazine report **2.** a thing; an item

artificial *adv.* not real; false

artisan *noun.* a craftsperson

artist *noun.* **1.** someone who paints beautiful pictures **2.** someone who has talent in any of the arts

artistic *adj.* knowing how to make beautiful things

arts *noun plural.* studies connected with literature, language, history, etc, that are taught in a school; the humanities

as *conj. adv.* **1.** (also *adv.*) while; when **2.** because; since **3.** the same way that; like

as *adv. equally*

a.s.a.p., ASAP *abbr.* as soon as possible

ascent *noun.* (formal) the process of climbing to a higher level

ash *noun.* what is left after something burns (plural **ashes**)

ashamed *adj.* feeling shame; embarrassed

Asian *noun.* someone from Asia — **Asian** *adj.*

aside *adv.* **1.** away; to one side **2.** for later use; in reserve **3.** except for; despite

aside *noun.* a remark that is not relevant to the subject

ask *verb.* **(asked, asking) 1.** put a question and seek an answer; try to find out something **2.** make a request

asleep *adj.* sleeping (opposite **awake**)

aspect *noun.* a certain part of an idea

aspire *verb.* **(aspired, aspiring)** (formal) be ambitious **—aspiration** *noun.*

aspirin *noun.* a medicine that reduces fever and pain

ass *noun.* **1.** a donkey **2.** (informal) a fool

assassinate *verb.* **(assassinated, assassinating)** murder a well known person especially for political reasons

assassination *noun.* a (particularly political) murder

assault *noun.* an attack

assault *verb.* **(assaulted, assaulting)** attack violently

assemble *verb.* **(assembled, assembling) 1.** come together **2.** put together

assembly *noun.* a gathering of a particular group of people (plural **assemblies**)

assembly line *noun.* a moving track where a worker handles a certain part of a machine before it continues to the next worker

assert *verb.* **(asserted, asserting) 1.** state something forcefully **2.** insist on your rights **—assertion** *noun.*

assertive *adj.* expressing yourself strongly

assess *verb.* **(assessed, assessing)** decide the value of something (such as for tax purposes) **—assessment** *noun.*

asset *noun.* **1.** something that you own which can be sold to pay debts **2.** a useful skill

assign *verb.* **(assigned, assigning) 1.** tell someone to perform a certain duty **2.** give someone the use of or part of a share in

assignment *noun.* a task

assist *verb.* **(assisted, assisting)** give help

assistance *noun.* help (no plural)

assistant *noun.* someone who has a job helping someone else

associate *noun.* a partner

associate *verb.* **(associated, associating) 1.** connect together **2.** be in the company of someone **—associate with** *verb.* be in the company of

association *noun.* an organized group of people with the same interest

assume *verb.* **(assumed, assuming)** think that something must be true

assumption *noun.* something that is believed to be true even without proof

assurance *noun.* **1.** (formal) a promise **2.** belief in yourself; self-confidence (no plural)

assure *verb.* **(assured, assuring)** promise

asthma *noun.* a disease that makes breathing difficult

astonish *verb.* **(astonished, astonishing)** surprise; amaze

astonishing *adj.* surprising; amazing — **astonishment** *noun.*

astronaut *noun.* someone who travels in a spacecraft; a spaceman or spacewoman

astronomer *noun.* someone whose profession is astronomy

astronomic, astronomical *adj.* **1.** of or for the study of the stars **2.** (informal) tremendous

astronomy *noun.* (no plural) the study of the sun, stars and moon

at *prep.* **1.** a word that tells where (in relation to something else) **2.** near an object, with your legs close to or under **3.** a word that tells when **4.** a word that tells direction **5.** doing something **6.** a word that tells how fast **7.** a word that tells how much (use **at** for a meeting place or location: at home, at the club; use **in** for an enclosed or defined space: in the garage, in an envelope, in Texas)

ate *verb.* past of **eat**

athlete *noun.* someone who is good at sports

athletic *adj.* **1.** connected with sports **2.** good at sports

athletics *noun plural.* sports

Atlantic *adj.* of the Atlantic Ocean

atlas *noun.* a book of maps (plural **atlases**)

atmosphere *noun.* **1.** the gases that surround the Earth **2.** the feeling that a place gives **—atmospheric** *adj.*

atom *noun.* the smallest particle of an element

atomic *adj.* of or coming from atoms

atop *prep.* above

attach *verb.* **(attached, attaching)** fasten one thing to another

attachment *noun.* **1.** something that you add on later **2.** a close relationship; a liking for someone

attack *noun.* **1.** use of violence or violent words **2.** a sudden illness

attack *verb.* **(attacked, attacking) 1.** use violence against someone **2.** say harsh things about someone or something **3.** make someone ill

attacker *noun.* someone who tries to hurt another person

attain *verb.* **(attained, attaining)** reach; achieve

attempt *noun.* a try

attempt *verb.* **(attempted, attempting)** try to do something

attend *verb.* **(attended, attending)** go to a certain place or event; to be present at a meeting, etc

attendance *noun.* **1.** coming to a place or an event **2.** the number of people who come to an event

attendant *noun.* someone who helps customers or the public

attention *noun.* **1.** fixing your thoughts on something **2.** notice; care (no plural)

attentive *adj.* looking and listening

attic *noun.* space under the roof of a house

attitude *noun.* your feeling about something or someone

attorney *noun.* a lawyer

attract *verb.* **(attracted, attracting)** make others want to be with you

attraction *noun.* **1.** a feeling that someone is attractive (no plural) **2.** something that people want to see

attractive *adj.* **1.** good-looking **2.** pleasing; nice; making people want to be with you **3.** tempting; making you think seriously about it

auction *noun.* a public sale where items are sold to the person who offers the most amount of money

audience *noun.* the people who watch or listen to something

audio *noun.* connected with receiving or broadcasting sounds

audit *verb.* **(audited, auditing)** make an official inspection of the accounts of a business

audition *noun.* a test given to a performer before he or she is accepted in a production

auditor *noun.* a person who audits accounts

auditorium *noun.* a large hall with a stage for concerts, plays, etc

Aug. *abbr.* August

August *noun.* the eighth month of the year

aunt *noun.* the sister of one of your parents; the wife of your uncle

aura *noun.* a feeling that seems to surround a person or place

Australian *noun.* someone from Australia **—Australian** *adj.*

authentic *adj.* **1.** genuine; known to be true **2.** in the style of or like the original **—authenticity** *noun.*

author noun. a writer of books, articles, poems, etc

authorities noun plural. the people in control; the government

authority noun. 1. the power to do something 2. control (no plural)

authorize verb. (**authorized, authorizing**) give formal permission for someone to act on your behalf —**authorized** adj. (opposite **unauthorized**)

autobiography noun. a book or a play that someone has written about his/her own life (plural **autobiographies**) —**autobiographical** adj.

autograph noun. someone's signature

automate verb. (**automated, automating**) use machines rather than people to do work in a factory —**automation** noun.

automatic adj. 1. that works by itself 2. that you do without thinking about it

automatically adv. 1. by itself 2. without thinking about it

automobile noun. a car

automotive adj. concerned with vehicles

autumn noun. the season after summer and before winter; fall

auxiliary adj. giving additional help

available adj. 1. that can be gotten or used 2. free; not busy or in use —**availability** noun.

avant-garde noun. adj. artists' and musicians' work that is based on the latest ideas and methods

avenue noun. 1. a wide street 2. a street with trees on both sides

average noun. a middle number that you get by adding two or more numbers and then dividing

average verb. (**averaged, averaging**) have or be an average

average adj. usual; not very good and not very bad

avoid verb. (**avoided, avoiding**) 1. keep away from someone or something 2. take care not to do something

avoidance noun. the act of avoiding

await verb. (**awaited, awaiting**) (formal, literary) wait for

awake verb. (**awoke/awaked, awoken, awaking**) 1. wake up 2. make something begin to happen

awake adj. not sleeping (opposite **asleep**)

award noun. a prize

award verb. (**awarded, awarding**) give, especially as a result of an official decision

aware adj. having understanding; acknowledging —**awareness** noun.

away adv. 1. from this place 2. not here; out 3. at a distance (of); not near 4. in the future 5. in the other direction 6. so that there is none left

awful adj. terrible

awfully adv. very

awhile adv. for a short time

awkward adj. 1. not moving easily; clumsy 2. difficult and embarrassing 3. embarrassed —**awkwardly** adv.

awoke, awoken verb. past and past participle of **awake**

ax, axe noun. a tool with a sharp metal blade and a long handle

B

babe *noun.* **1.** (slang) a girl or young woman **2.** a baby

baby *noun.* a very young child

babysit *verb.* **(babysat, babysitting)** look after a baby or small child when the parents are away

babysitter *noun.* someone who babysits

bachelor *noun.* a man who has never married

back *noun.* **1.** the part that is farthest from the front **2.** the rear part of the body from the buttocks to the neck

back *verb.* **(backed, backing) 1.** support someone or something **2.** move backward

back *adj.* **1.** farthest away from the front **2.** earlier in time; belonging to the past

back *adv.* **1.** behind **2.** in or to the place where something was before **3.** in return

backdrop *noun.* a cloth with scenery painted on it, such as in a theater

backer *noun.* someone who supports an idea, usually by giving money

background *noun.* **1.** the part that is not in front **2.** a person's past

backing *noun.* support or help, usually with money

backlog *noun.* unfinished jobs that should have been done at a certain time but were not and still have to be done

backstage *noun.* behind the stage in a theater

back-up *noun. adj.* a thing or person that can be used instead of or to help; a reserve

backward *adj.* not modern

backward, backward *adv.* the wrong way; from back to front

backyard *noun.* the yard in back of a house

bacon *noun.* smoked meat from the side of a pig

bacteria *noun plural.* tiny living things that cause disease (singular **bacterium**)

bad *adj.* **1.** evil; wrong **2.** misbehaving **3.** disappointing; low; poor **4.** unpleasant; nasty **5.** sad; sorry **6.** not able to do something well **7.** serious; severe

badge *noun.* something that you wear to show what school you go to, what team or group you belong to, etc

badly *adv.* **1.** in a bad way; poorly (opposite **well**) **2.** very much **3.** seriously; severely

—**badly off** *adj.* poor (opposite **well off**)

bag *noun.* **1.** a container with things in it that you can carry **2.** suitcases; baggage; luggage **3.** a purse

baggage *noun.* all the suitcases, bags, etc, that you take with you when you travel (no plural)

bail *noun.* money left by an accused person with the court to guarantee that he/she will appear for trial

bail *verb.* **(bailed, bailing) 1.** pay bail **2.** remove water from a boat

bake *verb.* **(baked, baking)** cook food in an oven

baker *noun.* someone whose job is to bake cakes, bread, rolls, etc

bakery *noun.* a shop where bread, cakes, etc, are made and sold (plural bakeries)

balance *noun.* **1.** the ability to remain steady and not to fall (no plural) **2.** how much money you have in your bank account

balance *verb.* **(balanced, balancing)** make something steady or keep it steady so that it does not fall

balance sheet *noun.* a list of all the money you receive and pay out

balcony *noun.* **1.** an upstairs porch or verandah **2.** a gallery; the seats that are upstairs in a theater

bald *adj.* having no hair on the head

balding *adj.* becoming bald

ball *noun.* **1.** something round that you can throw, kick or hit in games and sports **2.** a big, formal party where everybody dances

ballad *noun.* a (love) song that tells a story

ballerina *noun.* a female ballet dancer

ballet *noun.* a performance where a story is told through dance and music but not singing

balloon *noun.* a soft bag that floats in the air if you blow it up with air or gas

ballot *noun.* a sheet of paper used when voting

ballroom *noun.* a big room used for dancing

ban *verb.* **(banned, banning)** forbid by law —**ban** *noun.*

banana *noun.* a long, yellow, thick-skinned fruit

band *noun.* **1.** a flat, thin strip that you put around something **2.** a group of people who play music together

bandage *noun.* a strip of cloth that you put around an injured part of the body

bandit *noun.* an armed robber who is part of a group that attacks travelers

bang *noun.* a sudden loud noise like an explosion

bang *verb.* **(banged, banging) 1.** make a loud noise by hitting something against something else **2.** get a blow on a part of your body by hitting it against something

banish *verb.* **(banished, banishing)** send someone away as punishment

bank *noun.* **1.** a place where you can keep money and/or borrow money **2.** land along the side of a river or canal

bank account *noun.* an arrangement for keeping money in a bank

banker *noun.* a bank manager or owner

bankrupt *adj.* having no money and unable to repay debts (of a person or company)

bankruptcy *noun.* the state of being bankrupt

banner *noun.* a wide sign, usually of cloth, often carried between two poles

banquet *noun.* a festive, formal dinner, usually in honor of someone

Baptist *noun.* a (Protestant) Christian who believes that someone should be baptized when he/she understands the ceremony, not as an infant

baptize *verb.* **(baptized, baptizing) 1.** put holy water on someone to make him/her a member of a Christian church **2.** give a person a Christian name

bar *noun.* **1.** a long, hard piece of metal or wood **2.** a long piece of chocolate or a whole piece of soap **3.** a kind of restaurant where people buy alcoholic drinks

bar *verb.* **(barred, barring) 1.** put a long piece of metal or wood across an open space to keep something outside or inside **2.** block the way

barbecue *noun.* **1.** a metal grill for cooking meat over an open fire or over charcoal **2.** a meal or a party where people eat food cooked on a barbecue

barbed wire *noun.* metal wire with short, sharp points attached to it

barber *noun.* someone whose job is to cut men's hair

bare *adj.* **1.** not covered **2.** empty

barefoot *adj.* not wearing shoes

barely *adv.* **1.** only just enough **2.** almost not

bargain *noun.* something that you buy very cheaply

bargain *verb.* **(bargained, bargaining)** argue about the price of something

bark *noun.* **1.** the sound made by a dog **2.** the covering of the trunk or a branch of a tree (no plural)

bark verb. (barked, barking) make the sound that a dog makes —**barking** noun. (no plural)

barker noun. a person at an amusement park, circus, etc, who calls out to the crowd to come in

barmaid, barman noun. a person who serves drinks at a bar

barn noun. a building where farm animals live and where some crops are kept

baroque adj. relating to a period in the 17th century in Europe when fashions, architecture and music were very elaborate

barracks noun. a building where soldiers live (singular or plural)

barrel noun. 1. a big container that has round sides and is flat at the top and bottom 2. the long, metal tube of a gun

barricade noun. a wall made of barrels, sandbags, etc, that is put up to prevent anyone from passing

barrier noun. something that stops you from passing

barrister noun. a lawyer in England or Wales who is allowed to appear in the higher courts

base noun. 1. the bottom of something; what something stands on 2. a place where soldiers or sailors live

base verb. (based, basing) provide with a base

baseball noun. 1. a game with two teams of nine players each (no plural) 2. a special kind of ball used in the game of baseball

baseline noun. the line or level used as a base from which to measure

basement noun. the lowest part of a building, usually below ground level

base rate noun. the standard rate of interest that a bank uses in order to give or charge interest

basic adj. the most necessary; beginning (level)

basically adj. with regard to what is basic

basics noun plural. the basic parts of a process or an idea

basilica noun. large Roman Catholic church

basin noun. a round, deep container that can be used for washing

basis noun. the reason behind something; foundation (plural **bases**)

basket noun. a container usually made of straw, plastic or thin strips of wood

basketball noun. 1. a game in which two teams of players throw a ball into a net basket (no plural) 2. a special ball for playing basketball

bass noun. 1. the lowest male singing voice 2. the lowest range of musical notes 3. a type of fish

bastard noun. 1. an illegitimate child (of unmarried parents) 2. a hateful person 3. an unfortunate person

bat noun. a stick that is used for hitting something in some games

bat verb. (batted, batting) 1. hit with a stick as in baseball or cricket 2. blink; show emotion

batch noun. a group of things (plural **batches**)

bath noun. a washing of the whole body

bathe verb. (bathed, bathing) 1. wash someone else 2. clean with water 3. go swimming in the sea, a river or a lake

bathroom noun. a special room where you can wash, bathe and use the toilet

batter noun. 1. a mixture made from flour, water, eggs, etc 2. a person who bats in baseball and cricket

battery noun. a device that stores and provides electricity (plural **batteries**)

battle noun. 1. a fight between opposing people or forces 2. a struggle to overcome something

battle verb. (battled, battling) take part in a battle

battlefield noun. a place where a battle is fought

battleship noun. a very large warship with heavy guns

bay noun. a part of the sea that curves inward at the shore

be verb. (am/are/is, was/were, being, been) 1. a word that tells what something/someone is 2. a word that tells what someone does 3. a word that describes someone or something 4. a word that tells where something is 5. a word that tells how to behave 6. take place; happen

beach noun. a sandy place along the side of the sea; a shore or seashore (plural **beaches**)

beacon noun. a light that guides ships, aircraft, vehicles, etc

bead noun. a small ball with a hole through it for putting on a string or a piece of thread

beam noun. 1. a ray of light 2. a look of joy 3. a radio signal

bean noun. 1. a large seed that we can cook and eat 2. seeds used for making drinks such as coffee and cocoa

bear noun. a large, wild animal that has heavy fur, a thick neck and sharp claws

bear verb. (bore, borne, bearing) 1. carry or support something 2. be able to let something happen without becoming angry, impatient, etc 3. have a baby 4. feel something

beard noun. hair that grows on a man's chin and cheeks

beast noun. a four-footed animal, especially a wild animal

beat noun. a sound that comes repeatedly at regular intervals; rhythm

beat verb. (beat, beating) 1. hit again and again 2. win a game, fight, etc, against someone

beautiful adj. 1. lovely; wonderful to look at 2. pleasing to listen to

beautifully adv. very nicely or well

beauty noun. being beautiful (no plural)

beaver noun. an animal with valuable fur which lives on land and in water

became verb. past of **become**

because conj. for the reason that

become verb. (became, becoming) 1. start to be 2. grow to be something 3. grow to be a certain way 4. attractive on someone

bed noun. 1. a piece of furniture made for sleeping 2. a piece of ground where you grow plants

bedroom noun. a room for sleeping

bedside noun. the area around the bed

bedtime noun. the time when someone usually goes to bed

bee noun. a flying insect that makes honey and can sting

beef noun. meat from a cow (no plural)

been verb. past participle of **be**

beer noun. 1. a bitter alcoholic drink made from grain 2. a glass, bottle or can of beer

beetle noun. an insect with hard, shiny wings covering its body

before adv. in the past

before conj. earlier than some other action

before prep. 1. earlier than something else 2. in front of

beforehand adv. earlier; before something that will happen

beg verb. (begged, begging) 1. ask people for money or food 2. ask someone to do something, with strong feeling

beggar noun. a person who lives by asking people for food or money

begin verb. (began, begun, beginning) start

beginner noun. someone who is just starting to learn something

beginning noun. a start

behalf noun. as a representative of someone

behave verb. (behaved, behaving) act in a certain way

behavior noun. the way that you act at a certain time

behind noun. (informal) the part of the

body that you sit on; the bottom; the buttocks

behind *prep.* **1.** in back of **2.** not as advanced as —**behind** *adj.*

behind *adv.* **1.** in back **2.** not up to where you should be

being *noun.* a human; a person

being *verb.* -ing form of **be**

belief *noun.* what you think is true; believing in something

believable *adj.* something that can be believed (opposite **unbelievable**)

believe *verb.* **(believed, believing) 1.** think that something is true **2.** think that someone is telling the truth

believer *noun.* someone who believes

bell *noun.* something that makes a ringing sound

belly *noun.* (informal) stomach (plural **bellies**)

belong *verb.* **(belonged) 1.** should be in a certain place **2.** feel accepted by people

belongings *noun plural.* things that a person owns

beloved *adj. noun.* (someone who is) dearly loved

below *prep.* lower than

below *adv.* **1.** at a lower place **2.** on a later page (in a book) (opposite **above**)

belt *noun.* a band of plastic, leather, or cloth that you wear around your waist

bench *noun.* **1.** a long seat made of wood or stone **2.** the worktable of a carpenter, shoemaker, etc

bend *noun.* a curve in a road or thing

bend *verb.* **(bent, bending)** make something curve

beneath *prep.* **1.** under **2.** below

benefactor *noun.* a person who gives money for a good purpose

beneficial *adj.* having favorable results

beneficiary *noun.* someone who receives an inheritance or a special advantage

benefit *noun.* **1.** something that does you good **2.** an extra advantage

benefit *verb.* **(benefited, benefiting)** be helpful to

bent *verb.* past tense and past participle of **bend**

bent *adj.* not straight; curved

berry *noun.* a small fruit, usually with seeds (plural **berries**)

beside *prep.* next to; at the side of

besides *prep.* in addition to; as well as

besides *adv.* **1.** also; in addition **2.** anyway

besiege *verb.* **(besieged, besieging) 1.** surround a place with soldiers, police, etc **2.** crowd around

best *adj.* **(good, better, best)** better than any other (opposite **worst**)

best *adv.* **(well, better, best)** better than any way

best seller *noun.* a book which sells very many copies

best-selling *adj.* bought by very many people

bet *verb.* **(bet/betted, betting)** risk money on something that you think will happen

betray *verb.* **(betrayed, betraying)** be disloyal

better *adv.* **(well, better, best)** very well in comparison with someone or something (opposite **worse**)

between *prep.* **1.** after one place or time and before another **2.** more than one price and less than another **3.** among two people **4.** showing a difference

beverage *noun.* a drink (except water)

bewilder *verb.* **(bewildered, bewildering)** be confused by too many things or details —**bewildering** *adj.*

beyond *prep.* farther away than; on the far side of

bias *verb.* **(biased/biassed, biasing)** give a prejudiced and not objective opinion about something —**biased, biassed** *adj.*

Bible *noun.* the holy book of Christians and Jews

bicycle *noun.* a machine with two wheels that you ride by pushing pedals with your feet (also **bike**)

bicycle *verb.* **(bicycled, bicycling)** to use a bicycle as a vehicle

bid *noun.* **1.** an offer to pay a price **2.** a turn in a card game

bid *verb.* **(bid/bade, bidding)** offer a price

bidder *noun.* someone who offers a bid

big *adj.* **1.** large in size **2.** grown up **3.** older **4.** important

—**big deal** *noun. adj.* it's not important

—**big money** *noun.* (informal) a lot of money

bike *noun.* (informal) bicycle

bilateral *adj.* between two sides (people, governments, etc)

bilingual *adj.* knowing how to speak two languages very well

bill *noun.* **1.** a piece of paper that shows how much you must pay for something **2.** a piece of paper money

bill *verb.* **(billed, billing)** ask for payment

billboard *noun.* a large flat surface outdoors where advertising posters are stuck, usually near a road

billing *noun.* **1.** a written announcement for a performance in a theater **2.** preparing and sending bills to customers **3.** the total amount of business done by a company

billion *noun.* a thousand million (1,000,000,000)

billionaire *noun.* someone who has at least one billion dollars, pounds, etc

bin *noun.* a large container, usually with a lid, for storing things or putting garbage in

bind *verb.* **(bound, binding) 1.** tie with rope or string **2.** put a bandage on a wound

binder *noun.* **1.** a machine or person that binds separate pages to create a book **2.** something that makes things stick together **3.** a folder, often with a transparent cover, to hold loose papers together

binoculars *noun plural.* special glasses that make things that are far away look closer and bigger

biographer *noun.* someone who writes a book about the life of someone else

biography *noun.* a book about someone's life

biological *adj.* of biology

biology *noun.* the study of animal and plant life (no plural)

bird *noun.* an animal with feathers and wings that flies and lays eggs

birth *noun.* being born

birthday *noun.* the day of the year when someone was born

birthplace *noun.* the place where someone was born

bit *noun.* **1.** a small piece or amount of something **2.** a little while **3.** a little **4.** (computers) the smallest unit of computer information

bit *verb.* past of **bite**

bite *noun.* **1.** a piece of something that you bite off **2.** a small meal; a snack **3.** a hole in the skin made by a snake or an insect

bite *verb.* **(bit, bitten, biting) 1.** cut into something with your teeth **2.** sting **3.** make a hole with teeth

bitten *verb.* past participle of **bite**

bitter *adj.* **1.** having a strong, unpleasant taste **2.** angry; strongly felt **3.** deeply angry —**bitterly** *adv.* —**bitterness** *noun.*

bizarre *adj.* very strange

black *noun.* **1.** the darkest color **2.** a dark-skinned person of African origin —**black** *adj.*

blackboard *noun.* the dark board in a classroom on which you write with chalk (short form **board**)

blackmail *verb.* **(blackmailed, blackmailing)** threaten to tell something unpleasant about somebody, unless given money or done a favor

black market *noun*. buying or selling things that are forbidden by the law

blade *noun*. the sharp part of a knife, razor, sword, etc

blame *verb*. **(blamed, blaming)** say that someone or something is the cause of something bad (compare with **fault**)

blank *adj*. **1.** empty; with nothing on it **2.** not showing any understanding or feeling

blanket *noun*. something to cover yourself with in bed

blanket *verb*. **(blanketed, blanketing)** cover

blaze *noun*. a bright, strong fire

blaze *verb*. **(blazed, blazing)** burn brightly

blazer *noun*. a kind of jacket (not part of a suit, with no matching trousers or pants)

blazing *adj*. bright and hot

bleach *noun*. a liquid that makes things whiter (plural **bleaches**)

bleach *verb*. **(bleached, bleaching)** make something white

bleed *verb*. **(bled, bleeding)** lose blood

blend *noun*. a mixture

blend *verb*. **(blended, blending)** go together nicely

bless *verb*. **(blessed, blessing) 1.** ask God's help for someone or something; make holy **2.** give thanks for something

blessing *noun*. **1.** a prayer for God's help and care **2.** a prayer of thanks **3.** something that brings you deep happiness

blew *verb*. past of **blow**

blind *adj*. not able to see —**blindly** *adv*.

blindfold *noun*. a piece of cloth that is tied around someone's eyes so that he/she cannot see

blinding *adj*. something (usually very strong light) that makes you unable to see

blindness *noun*. the state of being blind

blinds *noun plural*. something to block light, like a window cover

blink *verb*. **(blinked, blinking)** open and close eyes very quickly

blister *noun*. a swollen place on the skin with water in it

blizzard *noun*. a heavy snowstorm

block *noun*. **1.** a piece of stone, wood, concrete, ice, etc, in the shape of a square or rectangle **2.** the buildings between two streets **3.** something that stops things from passing through a pipe, tube, etc

block *verb*. **(blocked, blocking)** stop someone or something from passing

blockade *noun*. the surrounding of a place to prevent anyone or anything from coming in or going out —**blockade** *verb*. **(blockaded, blockading)**

blond *adj*. having light hair

blonde *noun*. a woman who has blond hair

blood *noun*. the red fluid that flows through the body

blood pressure *noun*. the force with which blood flows through the body

bloodshed *noun*. the killing and wounding of great numbers of people (no plural)

bloody *adj*. **1.** covered with blood **2.** full of killing

bloom *verb*. **(bloomed, blooming)** put out new flowers; blossom

blossom *verb*. **(blossomed, blossoming) 1.** open into flowers; bloom **2.** be unusually beautiful and charming

blouse *noun*. a woman's shirt

blow *noun*. **1.** a hard hit **2.** a shock; a tragedy; a disappointment

blow *verb*. **(blew, blowing) 1.** move air **2.** give a strong push with air **3.** push air into something with your mouth

blue *noun*. the color of the sky on a clear day

blue *adj*. **1.** having the color of the sky on a clear day **2.** (informal) sad

blues *noun plural*. African-American (black) music

bluff *verb*. **(bluffed, bluffing)** trick

someone into thinking that something is true — **bluff** *noun.*

blunt *adj.* not sharp

bluntly *adv.* truthfully but without tact; frankly

blush *verb.* (**blushed, blushing**) become red in the face because of embarrassment

board *noun.* 1. a group of people who run a company or make important decisions 2. a long, flat piece of wood 3. a blackboard 4. meals

board *verb.* (**boarded, boarding**) 1. get meals and a place to sleep for a fixed price 2. get on a plane, ship or train

boarding school *noun.* a school where the pupils both study and live except during holidays

boardroom *noun.* a room where the board of directors meet

boast *verb.* (**boasted, boasting**) 1. tell people how successful you are; brag 2. claim that you can do something better than anyone else

boat *noun.* a small, open ship

body *noun.* 1. the physical part of a person or animal (head, arms, legs, etc) 2. a dead person or animal 3. a group of people with a particular job

bodyguard *noun.* someone whose job is to protect another person

bohemian *adj.* (usually about a writer or artist) not following accepted standards of behavior

boil *verb.* (**boiled, boiling**) 1. begin to turn into steam 2. heat a liquid to the point where it begins to turn into steam 3. cook food in boiling water

boiled *adj.* cooked in boiling water

bold *adj.* without fear; brave

bolt *noun.* 1. a screw without a point at the end 2. a metal bar put across a door to lock it 3. a flash of lightning

bolt *verb.* (**bolted, bolting**) 1. lock 2. run away quickly

bomb *noun.* a container filled with explosives

bomb *verb.* (**bombed, bombing**) attack with bombs

bomber *noun.* an airplane used for dropping bombs

bond *noun.* 1. a commitment 2. a promise to pay somebody an amount of money plus interest

bond *verb.* (**bonded, bonding**) stick two things or people together

bone *noun.* the hard, white inside parts of the body

bone *verb.* (**boned, boning**) take out the bones

bonfire *noun.* a fire that you make outside

bonus *noun.* something, often money, in addition to what was expected

boo *noun.* 1. a sound made by a person to startle someone else 2. a shout of disapproval or disagreement

book *noun.* printed pages fastened together inside a cover

book *verb.* (**booked, booking**) reserve a place on a plane, train, etc, or in a theater or restaurant — **booking** *noun.*

bookcase *noun.* a cabinet or shelves for keeping books

booklet *noun.* a small book, often with instructions or other information

books *noun plural.* business accounts

bookshelf *noun.* a shelf to keep books on (plural **bookshelves**)

bookstore *noun.* a store where books are sold

boom *verb.* (**boomed, booming**) 1. succeed 2. make a very loud noise

boost *verb.* (**boosted, boosting**) lift up or improve — **boost** *noun.*

boot *noun.* a tall, heavy shoe

booth *noun.* a stand at a fair for selling things or for playing games; a small enclosed place that gives someone privacy

border *noun.* 1. the line separating two countries; a frontier 2. an edge that goes all the way around something — **border** *verb.* (**bordered, bordering**)

bore *noun.* someone or something that is not interesting

bore *verb.* **(bored, boring) 1.** be uninteresting **2.** past of **bear** —**bored** *adj.*

boredom *noun.* the state of being bored

boring *adj.* not interesting; dull

born *adj.* having come from a mother's body and starting life

borne *verb.* past participle of **bear** (carry)

borrow *verb.* **(borrowed, borrowing)** take or receive something with the intention of giving it back

borrower *noun.* someone who borrows something

boss *noun.* (informal) the head or manager of a business; the person that you work for; an employer

botany *noun.* the scientific study of plants —**botanic, botanical** *adj.*

both *adj.* this one and that one; the two of something

both *pron.* the two

bother *verb.* **(bothered, bothering) 1.** give trouble to someone; annoy **2.** give yourself trouble

bottle *noun.* a glass or plastic container with a narrow opening at the neck used for holding liquids (milk bottle = a bottle for milk; bottle of milk = a bottle containing milk)

bottle *verb.* **(bottled, bottling)** put into bottles

bottom *noun.* **1.** the lowest part of something **2.** (informal) the part of your body that you sit on; behind

bottom *adj.* the lowest one (opposite top)

bottom line *noun.* **1.** the most important point or result **2.** the amount of money, either profit or loss, at the end of a financial statement

bought *verb.* past tense and past participle of **buy**

boulder *noun.* a large rock

boulevard *noun.* a wide avenue

bounce *verb.* **(bounced, bouncing) 1.** move up and down with small jumps **2.** make something jump up and go down

boundary *noun.* a line between two countries, two pieces of property, etc; a border (plural **boundaries**)

bouquet *noun.* a bunch of flowers

boutique *noun.* a small specialty shop with the latest fashions

bow *noun.* **1.** a knot made by tying a ribbon, string or shoe lace into loops **2.** a curved piece of wood with a string tied tightly to both ends **3.** a piece of wood with tight strings up and down for playing the violin, the cello and some other musical instruments **4.** the act of bending forward

bow *verb.* **(bowed, bowing) 1.** bend the upper half of your body forward to show respect **2.** bend your head forward to show respect or shame

bowl *noun.* a deep, round dish

bowling *noun.* a game in which you knock down wooden pins with a heavy ball (no plural)

box *noun.* a container, usually with square corners (plural **boxes**)

box *verb.* **(boxed, boxing)** fight for sport with thick gloves on

boxer *noun.* **1.** someone who boxes **2.** a type of large dog with short hair

boxing *noun.* a sport in which two men fight with their fists (no plural)

box office *noun.* a place where you can buy tickets to a show or a game

boy *noun.* **1.** a male child **2.** a young man

boyfriend *noun.* the special male friend of a girl or young woman

boyhood *noun.* the time when a boy is a child

bra *noun.* short for **brassiere**

brace *noun.* something that you wear for support

bracelet *noun.* an ornament worn around your arm or wrist

bracket *noun.* a piece of metal or wood that supports a shelf

brackets *noun plural.* punctuation marks, [ ]

brag *verb.* **(bragged, bragging)** tell other people about your successes; boast

braid *noun.* **1.** hair that is divided into parts and then woven together (usually plural) **2.** a decoration of threads twisted together and then sewn on a garment

brain *noun.* the gray material inside your head that you think with

brake *noun.* something for stopping or slowing down a car, train, bicycle, etc —**brake** *verb.* **(braked, braking)**

branch *noun.* **1.** the arm of a tree **2.** an office of a business or organization

brand *noun.* a product made by a particular company (use **make** for cars, machines, etc)

brand name *noun.* the name used to sell a certain brand

brand-new *adj.* completely new; unused

brass *noun.* a metal made by combining copper and zinc

brassiere *noun.* a piece of women's underwear that supports the breasts (short form **bra**)

brave *adj.* not showing fear; courageous

brave *verb.* **(braved, braving)** face danger without showing fear —**bravely** *adv.*

bravery *noun.* courage (no plural)

Brazilian *noun.* someone from Brazil — **Brazilian** *adj.*

breach *noun.* an act of breaking a law, promise, contract, etc

breach *verb.* **(breached, breaching)** break a promise, agreement, etc

bread *noun.* a food made from flour, water and yeast and baked in an oven

breadth *noun.* the distance from one side of a thing to the other; width (see **broad**)

break *noun.* a short period when you stop working

break *verb.* **(broke, broken, breaking) 1.** come apart and become more than one piece by falling or being hit **2.** smash something into pieces by dropping or hitting it —**break-in** *noun.* when someone uses force to enter a building, especially to steal something

breakdown *noun.* **1.** in machinery, a complete stop because something is wrong **2.** the collapse of a process

breakfast *noun.* the morning meal

breakthrough *noun.* a discovery or advancement after much work

breast *noun.* **1.** the part of the female body that gives milk **2.** the upper front part of anyone's body

breath *noun.* air that comes in and out of your nose and mouth

breathe *verb.* **(breathed, breathing)** take air in and let it out through your nose or mouth

breathtaking *adj.* magnificent

breed *noun.* a specific type of a particular kind of animal

breed *verb.* **(bred, breeding)** raise or grow animals or plants

breeder *noun.* someone who breeds animals or plants, usually for sale

breeze *noun.* **1.** a light wind **2.** (slang) something that is easy to do —**breeze** *verb.* **(breezed, breezing)** (informal)

brew *verb.* **(brewed, brewing) 1.** make beer **2.** prepare coffee or tea

brewer *noun.* someone who makes beer

brewery *noun.* a place where beer is produced

bribe *verb.* **(bribed, bribing)** give money or gifts to someone so that the person will do something for you — **bribe** *noun.*

bribery *noun.* the act of bribing someone

brick *noun.* a block of baked clay that is used for building brick *adj.* made of bricks

bride *noun.* a woman on her wedding day

bridegroom, groom *noun.* a man on his wedding day

bridesmaid *noun.* a girl or woman who helps the bride at her wedding ceremony

bridge *noun.* 1. a special road that is built across a river, highway, etc 2. a popular card game (no plural)

brief *adj.* short —briefly *adv.* (shortly means soon, not briefly)

briefcase *noun.* a flat case for carrying papers

briefing *noun.* the act of giving instructions or information

bright *adj.* 1. giving a lot of light 2. strong in color 3. clever; quick to learn —brightly *adv.*

brilliant *adj.* 1. very bright and shining 2. unusually intelligent or clever —brilliance *noun.* —brilliantly *adv.*

brim *noun.* the edge of a cup or a bowl

bring *verb.* (brought, bringing) 1. carry something to a person or a place 2. take someone somewhere

British *noun plural.* the people of Britain —British *adj.*

broad *adj.* wide (opposite narrow)

broadcast *noun.* something that comes to people by TV or radio

broadcast *verb.* (broadcast, broadcasting) send out by TV or radio

broadcaster *noun.* someone whose job is to speak on TV or radio

broaden *verb.* (broadened, broadening) make wider

broadly *adv.* in general

brochure *noun.* an advertising pamphlet

broke *verb.* past tense of break

broke *adj.* (informal) without any money

broken *verb.* past participle of break

broken *adj.* 1. not whole; in pieces 2. not working

broker *noun.* someone who buys and sells stock for clients

bronze *noun.* a metal made by mixing copper and tin

bronze *adj.* made of bronze

broom *noun.* a brush with a long handle that you use for sweeping

brother *noun.* a male with the same parent as you

brother-in-law *noun.* a man who is married to your sister; the brother of your husband or wife (plural brothers-in-law)

brought *verb.* past tense and past participle of bring

brow *noun.* the forehead

brown *noun.* the color of the earth, chocolate, coffee, etc —brown *adj.*

bruise *noun.* a dark-colored mark on the skin from a blow or a bump —bruise *verb.* (bruised, bruising)

brush *noun.* a tool that is made of hairs or nylon and has a handle (plural brushes)

brush *verb.* (brushed, brushing) use a brush for doing a job

brutal *adj.* very cruel —brutality *noun.* —brutally *adv.*

bubble *noun.* a ball of air

bubble *verb.* (bubbled, bubbling) 1. make tiny balls of air 2. be full of life and happy

buck *noun.* (slang) a dollar

buck *verb.* (bucked, bucking) (of a horse) jump and throw the rider

bucket *noun.* a deep container with a handle for holding water, sand, etc; a pail

buckle *noun.* something that fastens a belt or a strap

bud *noun.* a flower that has not opened yet

Buddha *noun.* a statue or picture of the founder of Buddhism

Buddhism *noun.* a religion of India and eastern Asia

Buddhist *noun.* someone who practices Buddhism

budge *verb.* (budged, budging) move a little

budget *noun.* a plan about how you are going to spend your money

budget *verb.* **(budgeted, budgeting)** decide in advance what you will do with a certain amount of money

buffalo *noun.* American bison; a large cow-like animal

buffet *noun.* a meal with many kinds of food that is set out on tables and where people serve themselves

bug *noun.* **1.** an insect **2.** (informal) a germ or virus **3.** a flaw, as in a computer program

build *verb.* **(built, building)** put bricks, stones, concrete blocks, etc, together to make something

builder *noun.* someone whose job is to build houses, etc

building *noun.* a structure with a roof and walls

built *verb.* past tense and past participle of **build**

built-in *adj.* part of something; not separate

bulb *noun.* **1.** something round and made of glass that gives electric light **2.** the round part of some plants that you put into the ground

bulge *verb.* **(bulged, bulging)** swell out of the usual shape; curve outward — **bulging** *adj.*

bulk *noun.* a large amount, mass or size

bull *noun.* a male cow

bulldozer *noun.* a powerful tractor for moving large amounts of earth

bullet *noun.* a small piece of metal fired from a gun

bulletin *noun.* **1.** a news announcement **2.** a printed announcement of news; a notice

bum *noun.* someone who is lazy and uninterested in working

bump *noun.* **1.** a blow or knock when one thing hits against another **2.** a swelling on the body made by knocking against something **3.** an uneven place on the road

bump *verb.* **(bumped, bumping)** hit or knock something against something else by accident

bumper *noun.* a bar of metal or rubber at the front and back of a car to protect it against blows

bumpy *adj.* **(bumpier, bumpiest)** uneven; full of bumps

bun *noun.* a small, round piece of sweet bread

bunch *noun.* **1.** fruit that grows in a group **2.** a group of things of the same kind that are fastened together

bunch *verb.* **(bunched, bunching)** form into bunches

bundle *noun.* a number of things tied or wrapped together

bungalow *noun.* a house with only one floor

bunny *noun.* a child's word for a baby rabbit

bureau *noun.* **1.** a chest of drawers or a large writing desk with drawers **2.** a business or government office that gives information

burger *noun.* short for **hamburger**

burglar *noun.* someone who breaks into a building to steal

burglary *noun.* the crime of forcefully entering a place with the intention of stealing from it

burial *noun.* the service of burying a dead body

burly *adj.* large in size

burn *noun.* an injury made by fire or heat

burn *verb.* **(burned/burnt, burning) 1.** be on fire; be in flames **2.** set something on fire **3.** (use something to) give light or heat **4.** cause injury or damage with fire or heat

burst *verb.* **(burst, bursting) 1.** explode **2.** tear **3.** do something suddenly with force

bury *verb.* **(buried, burying)** put a dead person or animal into a grave

bus *noun.* a large vehicle that carries people from one place to another (plural **buses**)

bush *noun*. **1.** a plant with many branches, something like a small tree (plural **bushes**) **2.** wild, uncultivated land in Australia (no plural)

business *noun*. **1.** commerce; buying and selling (no plural) **2.** a store, company, etc, which people make money from (plural **businesses**)

businesslike *adj*. professional; having qualities that are practical so that a business can succeed

businessman, businesswoman *noun*. (also **businessperson**) a person who is in business

bus stop *noun*. a place where a bus stops to let people get on and off

bust *noun*. **1.** a woman's breasts **2.** (slang) when the police raid a place of criminals

busy *adj*. **1.** having a lot to do **2.** full of activity **3.** in use —**busily** *adv*.

but *conj*. however

butcher *noun*. a person who cuts or sells meat

butler *noun*. the chief male servant

butt *noun*. the end of a smoked cigarette

butter *noun*. a fatty yellow food made from milk

butter *verb*. **(buttered, buttering)** spread butter on a slice of bread, etc

butterfly *noun*. an insect that has wings with beautiful patterns on them (plural **butterflies**)

button *noun*. **1.** something small, usually round, that you pass through a hole to fasten a coat, shirt, etc **2.** a small thing that you press with the fingers to start or stop a machine

button *verb*. **(buttoned, buttoning)** fasten with buttons

buy *verb*. **(bought, buying)** get something by paying money (opposite **sell**)

buyer *noun*. someone whose work is to buy for a department store, a company, etc

buyout *noun*. when someone gains control of a company by buying most of that company's shares

buzz *verb*. **(buzzed, buzzing)** use a buzzer in order to call someone

buzzer *noun*. an electrical bell that makes a buzzing sound

by *prep*. **1.** beside; next to **2.** past **3.** a word that tells who or what did something **4.** not later than **5.** a word that tells how something was made or got done **6.** a word that tells how someone or something got somewhere **7.** a word that tells which author, painter, inventor, etc

bye *interj*. (informal) good-bye

bygone *adj*. (outdated) in the past

by-product *noun*. something that was produced while something else was being made

byte *noun*. (computers) = 8 bits

C

cab *noun.* a car that takes you where you want to go for payment

cabbage *noun.* a round vegetable with large green or red leaves

cabin *noun.* 1. a small, simple house made of wood 2. a room in a ship or an airplane

cabinet *noun.* 1. a closet that is attached to a wall 2. a piece of furniture with shelves and drawers used for keeping or showing things

cable *noun.* 1. a thick rope, wire or chain 2. wires that carry electricity or telephone calls 3. a message sent by telegraph; a telegram

cable *verb.* **(cabled, cabling)** send a telegram

cactus *noun.* a plant that grows in hot, dry places (plural **cactuses** or **cacti**)

cafe *noun.* a restaurant where you can sit and drink coffee or get a simple meal

cafeteria *noun.* 1. a restaurant where you serve yourself and carry the food to a table 2. a canteen in a workplace or school

cage *noun.* a closed space with bars or a box with wires around it for keeping animals or birds

cake *noun.* 1. a sweet food, made from flour, eggs, sugar, etc, that is baked in an oven (no plural) 2. a specific cake

calamity *noun.* a disaster; a misfortune (plural **calamities**)

calculate *verb.* **(calculated, calculating)** use numbers to find the answer to a problem or question **—calculation** *noun.*

calculator *noun.* a small machine that can do calculations

calendar *noun.* a list of the days and months of one year

calf *noun.* a baby cow or the young of some other large animals, such as whales and elephants (plural **calves**)

Californian *adj.* of or from California

call *noun.* 1. a shout 2. the act of using the telephone 3. a short visit 4. the particular cry of a bird or an animal

call *verb.* **(called, calling)** 1. shout to someone 2. use the telephone 3. give someone a name

caller *noun.* a visitor

calm *adj.* 1. quiet; not excited; relaxed 2. without motion

calm *verb.* **(calmed, calming)** make someone quiet or less afraid

calmly *adv.* in a calm way

calorie *noun.* a unit of energy that you get from food

calves *noun.* plural of **calf**

came *verb.* past of **come**

camel *noun.* a large desert animal with one or two humps on its back

camera *noun.* a machine for taking photographs

camouflage *verb.* **(camouflaged, camouflaging)** hide a person, animal or thing by making it look like what is around it

camp *noun.* a place where people live in tents, huts or outdoors **—camp** *verb.* **(camped, camping)**

campaign *noun.* 1. a plan of activities for a special purpose 2. a plan for fighting in a specific area during a war

campaign *verb.* **(campaigned, campaigning)** go on, take part in, or lead a campaign

camper *noun.* 1. someone who goes camping 2. a type of vehicle attached to a car that has beds, a kitchen, etc, where you can live if you go on a camping vacation

campus *noun.* the grounds of a school, college or university (plural **campuses**)

can *verb.* **(could) 1.** be able to **2.** be allowed to **3.** be possible or likely to happen **4.** a word that you use to ask someone for something **5.** know how to (negative **cannot** or **cannot**)

can *noun.* a metal container for keeping food

can *verb.* **(canned, canning)** put in a can

Canadian *noun.* someone from Canada —**Canadian** *adj.*

canal *noun.* a narrow strip of water that is cut through land so that boats or ships can pass or for irrigation

canary *noun.* a small yellow singing bird, often kept as a pet in a cage

cancel *verb.* **(canceled, canceling) 1.** stop a plan **2.** say that you do not want something that you had arranged for —**cancellation** *noun.*

cancer *noun.* a serious illness; a growth in the body which can spread

candidate *noun.* **1.** someone who wants people to vote for him/her **2.** someone who is trying to get a particular job **3.** someone who is taking an examination; an examinee

candle *noun.* a stick made of wax that burns and gives light

candlestick *noun.* a holder for a candle

candy *noun.* **1.** sweet foods made with sugar (no plural) **2.** a piece of candy (plural **candies**)

cane *noun.* **1.** a stick that helps a person walk **2.** the hollow stem of some plants, such as bamboo or sugar

canned *adj.* coming in a can

cannibal *noun.* a person who eats the flesh of another person

cannon *noun.* a big, powerful gun that shoots shells

cannot *verb.* cannot; negative of **can**

canoe *noun.* a light, narrow boat that you move by using paddles

can't *abbr.* = cannot

canteen *noun.* **1.** a place in an office, factory or military base where people buy meals; a cafeteria **2.** a small container used by soldiers, campers, hikers, etc, for carrying water

canvas *noun.* **1.** a strong, heavy cloth that is used for making tents or bags (no plural) **2.** a strong piece of cloth that artists use for oil paintings (plural **canvases**)

canvass *verb.* **(canvassed, canvassing)** ask for votes, orders, etc

canyon *noun.* a deep valley through big rocks

cap *noun.* **1.** a soft hat **2.** a covering for a bottle or tube

capability *noun.* the quality of being good at doing something

capable *adj.* good at doing things

capacity *noun.* the amount or number that can fit into something (no plural)

cape *noun.* **1.** a kind of loose coat with no sleeves **2.** a piece of land that sticks out into the sea

capital *noun.* **1.** the city where the government is located **2.** a large letter of the alphabet **3.** the amount of money that a business has (no plural)

capitalism *noun.* an economic system based on private ownership

capitalize *verb.* **(capitalized, capitalizing) 1.** write with a capital letter **2.** take advantage of

capital punishment *noun.* punishment by death

capsule *noun.* **1.** a compartment that can be sent from a spacecraft **2.** a small container with medicine inside that you swallow like a pill

captain *noun.* **1.** the chief officer of a ship **2.** an officer in the military **3.** the head of a sports team or group

captive *noun.* a prisoner

captivity *noun.* being a prisoner (no plural)

capture *noun.* the act of catching, gaining control or winning

capture *verb.* **(captured, capturing) 1.** catch **2.** take as a prisoner **3.** take control of a place by force

car *noun.* **1.** an automobile **2.** a part of a train which carries passengers

caravan *noun.* **1.** a covered cart or wagon for transporting people, goods, etc **2.** a group of people traveling together

carbohydrate *noun.* the part of a person's diet consisting of sugars and starch

carbon *noun.* an element that is found in all living things and some non-living things, such as diamonds and coal (no plural)

card *noun.* a stiff, thick piece of paper used for messages, in games, etc

cardboard *noun.* heavy, stiff paper used for making boxes and other things (no plural)

cardinal *noun.* a high ranking priest of the Roman Catholic Church

cards *noun plural.* any game that you play with playing cards

care *noun.* **1.** worry; troubles **2.** looking after (no plural) **3.** caution (no plural)

care *verb.* **(cared, caring)** feel concern; have an interest in

career *noun.* someone's profession; the way you make your living

carefree *adj.* without worries

careful *adj.* giving thought to what you do —**carefully** *adv.*

careless *adj.* not careful —**carelessly** *adv.*

career *noun.* someone who takes care of someone else

caretaker *noun.* someone who takes care of someone else

cargo *noun.* things carried by a ship, plane or other vehicle

Caribbean *adj. noun.* the West Indies region in America

caricature *noun.* a picture of, writing about, or imitation of someone whose characteristics are exaggerated so that they become more noticeable and/or funny

caricature *verb.* **(caricatured, caricaturing)** make a caricature

caricaturist *noun.* an artist who draws caricatures

carnation *noun.* a sweet smelling flower that is sold in flower shops

carnival *noun.* a fair or happening of music, entertainment, dancing, food, etc

carpenter *noun.* someone who builds furniture or parts of buildings from wood

carpet *noun.* a covering for a floor; a rug

carriage *noun.* **1.** a wagon pulled by horses **2.** moving things from one place to another **3.** the moving part of a machine that supports other parts

carrier *noun.* **1.** a person or thing that carries things or people from one place to another **2.** someone who can pass on a disease to someone else even though he or she is not sick

carrot *noun.* a long, orange vegetable that grows in the ground

carry *verb.* **(carried, carrying) 1.** walk with something in your arms or in your hands **2.** take something from one place to another **3.** support a weight **4.** have **5.** be able to contain **6.** keep something in your mind

cart *noun.* **1.** a vehicle with wheels that is pulled by an animal **2.** a small vehicle for carrying things, often pushed by hand

cart *verb.* **(carted, carting)** carry something in a cart

carton *noun.* **1.** a box made of thick cardboard **2.** a small, thin cardboard box

cartoon *noun.* **1.** a funny drawing **2.** a movie made with drawings

cartoonist *noun.* someone who draws cartoons

cartridge *noun.* a case that contains something inside

carve *verb.* **(carved, carving) 1.** cut wood or stone into shapes **2.** cut into wood or stone with a sharp tool **3.** cut up meat

cascade *verb.* **(cascaded, cascading)** pour or fall as in a waterfall; arrange things one following the other

case *noun.* **1.** the way things are **2.** an example of something **3.** a legal issue **4.** a large box or container

case *verb.* **(cased, casing)** watch and inspect in order to rob

cash *noun.* money in coins or bills (no plural) **—cash** *verb.* **(cashed, cashing)**

cash flow *noun.* money coming into (income) and going out of (costs) a business

cashier *noun.* **1.** a person who adds up the customers' bills at a store or restaurant **2.** someone who takes and gives out money at a bank; a bank clerk; a teller

casino *noun.* a place for gambling

cassette *noun.* a small plastic case that holds a recording tape

cast *noun.* **1.** the actors and actresses in a play or film **2.** a hard, white covering that keeps a broken bone in place

cast *verb.* **(cast, casting)** throw

castle *noun.* a big, strong building that protected the people inside against attack

castrate *verb.* **(castrated, castrating)** remove the sex organs

casual *adj.* **1.** informal **2.** not planned; accidental **3.** not serious

casually *adv.* informally

casualty *noun.* someone who is killed or seriously injured in war or in an accident (plural **casualties**)

cat *noun.* a small, furry animal that catches mice

catapult *noun.* a slingshot; a small y-shaped stick with a rubber band used to propel stones

catastrophe *noun.* a sudden terrible event; a calamity

catch *verb.* **(caught, catching)** **1.** get and hold in your hands something that is moving **2.** capture **3.** become ill with something **4.** see someone doing something bad **5.** be in time for something **6.** become stuck on something accidentally **7.** hear and understand something

catcher *noun.* in baseball, the player who is stationed behind the batter

catchy *adj.* easy to remember

categorize *verb.* **(categorized, categorizing)** put into categories

category *noun.* a group of similar things

cater *verb.* **(catered, catering)** provide food for an event

cathedral *noun.* a large and important church

Catholic *noun.* a member of the Roman Catholic religion

cattle *noun plural.* cows and bulls

caught *verb.* past tense and past participle of **catch**

cause *noun.* **1.** something or someone that makes something happen **2.** a goal that you struggle for **3.** a reason

cause *verb.* **(caused, causing)** make something happen

causeway *noun.* a raised path or road especially over water or wet ground

caution *noun.* care; attention (no plural)

caution *verb.* **(cautioned, cautioning)** warn about a possible danger

cautious *adj.* **1.** careful **2.** thoughtful; not impulsive **—cautiously** *adv.*

cavalry *noun.* soldiers who fight on horseback (plural **cavalries**)

cave *noun.* a deep hole in the side of a hill or under the ground

cavern *noun.* a large, deep cave

caviar *noun.* a food consisting of the eggs from the sturgeon fish

cavity *noun.* a small hole

CD *abbr.* compact disc

CD player *noun.* a machine that plays compact discs

CD-ROM *abbr.* compact disc read-only memory

cease *verb.* **(ceased, ceasing)** (formal) stop

cedar *noun.* an evergreen tree whose wood is sometimes used to make chests for storing clothes

ceiling *noun.* **1.** the part of a room that is over your head **2.** the highest level of something

celebrate *verb.* **(celebrated, celebrating) 1.** do something to show that a day or an event is special **2.** be joyous because of an important event

celebration *noun.* an occasion for special festivities to mark some happy event

celebrity *noun.* a famous person

cell *noun.* **1.** a tiny unit of living material **2.** a very small room in a prison

cell phone *noun.* a small phone that you can carry around with you (also **cellular phone, mobile phone**)

cellar *noun.* an underground room in a house, usually without windows

cello *noun.* a large stringed musical instrument with a deep sound from the violin family

cellular *adj.* **1.** relating to or having cells **2.** connected with a communication network that is divided into transmission units

cement *noun.* **1.** a gray powder that becomes hard when it is mixed with water **2.** any strong glue

cemetery *noun.* a graveyard; a place where dead people are buried

cent *noun.* a small coin

centennial *noun. adj.* the 100th anniversary of an event; (of) a period of 100 years

center *noun.* **1.** the middle; the mid point **2.** a place where people go to do a particular thing

center *verb.* **(centered, centering)** put something at the mid point

centigrade, Celsius *noun.* a system for measuring temperature, with 0 degrees the freezing point and 100 degrees the boiling point of water (no plural)

central *adj.* in the middle —**centrally** *adj.*

central heating *noun.* a heating system that heats a whole house or building

century *noun.* **1.** a hundred years **2.** a period of a hundred years before or after the birth of Christ

cereal *noun.* food that is made from certain grains

ceremonial *adj.* done according to ceremony

ceremony *noun.* a religious service held on a special occasion or a special way of showing the importance of an event

certain *adj.* **1.** sure **2.** particular **3.** some

certainly *adv.* **1.** surely; without doubt **2.** of course

certainty *noun.* something that is certain

certificate *noun.* a piece of paper that proves something about someone

certify *verb.* **(certified, certifying)** declare that something is true or authentic

chain *noun.* **1.** a row of metal rings that are joined together **2.** a line of anything joined together

chain *verb.* **(chained, chaining)** fasten with a chain

chair *noun.* a piece of furniture that you sit on

chair *verb.* **(chaired, chairing)** be the chairperson of a meeting or committee

chairman, chairwoman *noun.* (also **chairperson**) the person in charge of a meeting or at the head of a committee

chalk *noun.* a stick for writing on a blackboard

challenge *noun.* **1.** something difficult that you want to do well **2.** an invitation to fight or compete

challenge *verb.* **(challenged, challenging) 1.** test **2.** invite someone to fight or play against you **3.** tell someone to do something to show bravery —**challenging** *adj.*

chamber *noun*. an old-fashioned word for a room

champagne *noun*. a kind of French wine

champion *noun*. a winner in a competition —**championship** *noun*.

chance *noun*. 1. opportunity 2. possibility 3. luck

change *noun*. 1. a difference 2. the money that you get back after you pay your bill (no plural)

change *verb*. (**changed, changing**) 1. become different 2. make something different 3. make a difference 4. take a second bus, train, etc

channel *noun*. 1. a narrow opening where the sea passes 2. a TV station 3. a means of communication

channel *verb*. (**channeled, channeling**) direct for a specific purpose

chaos *noun*. a situation with no order or control (no plural)

chapel *noun*. 1. a room or a small building used for worship 2. a small church

chapter *noun*. 1. a part of a book 2. a branch or division

character *noun*. 1. a person's nature; what makes someone special as a person 2. a person in a book, play, movie, etc

characteristic *noun*. what is special about someone or something

characteristic *adj*. typical

characteristically *adv*. typically

characterize *verb*. (**characterized, characterizing**) describe the character or nature of

charade *noun*. 1. something that is clearly untrue or silly 2. a guessing game played by acting out a word or phrase (plural)

charge *noun*. 1. a price 2. an accusation 3. an attack

charge *verb*. (**charged, charging**) 1. demand a price for something 2. put a debt on an account 3. accuse 4. attack; rush forward 5. load with electricity

charitable *adj*. kind and generous

charity *noun*. 1. generosity toward the poor or helpless (no plural) 2. an organization for helping the poor, the sick, etc (plural **charities**)

charm *noun*. 1. some pleasing behavior or quality (no plural) 2. a magic spell

charm *verb*. (**charmed, charming**) behave in a way that pleases people

charming *adj*. pleasing; attractive

chart *noun*. 1. a map 2. a big piece of paper with pictures, diagrams or other information on it

chart *verb*. (**charted, charting**) make a map or chart

charter *noun*. 1. a declaration of the rights and duties of citizens or members of an association 2. a flight, ship, etc, hired for a special purpose — **charter** *verb*. (**chartered, chartering**)

chase *verb*. (**chased, chasing**) run after; try to catch —**chase** *noun*.

chat *verb*. (**chatted, chatting**) 1. have a friendly talk 2. (on the Internet) communicate between two or more people on-line by typing notes to each other —**chat** *noun*.

chatter *verb*. (**chattered, chattering**) talk noisily about unimportant things —**chatter, chattering** *noun*.

cheap *adj*. not expensive; not costing much money —**cheaply** *adv*.

cheat *noun*. a dishonest person

cheat *verb*. (**cheated, cheating**) 1. do something that is dishonest 2. get something from someone dishonestly

check *noun*. 1. examination 2. a piece of paper that you can use for payment instead of cash 3. a small mark that you put beside an item on a list or a correct answer 4. a small square that is part of a pattern

check *verb*. (**checked, checking**) 1. examine to see if something is done or is all right 2. correct an examination or test

checked *adj*. with a pattern of small squares

check-in *noun.* the desk you go to at a hotel, airport, etc, in order to get a room, board a plane, etc
—**check in/into** *verb.* register at a hotel

checkout (counter) *noun.* the place in a supermarket where you pay for what you bought
—**check out** *verb.* leave a hotel

cheek *noun.* 1. one of the sides of your face between your nose and your ears 2. impudence; rude words or behavior

cheer *verb.* **(cheered, cheering)** shout encouragement or approval

cheerful *adj.* generally happy; in a good mood

cheerleader *noun.* someone (usually a girl) who directs cheering at a football game, basketball game, etc, by dancing

cheese *noun.* a solid food made from milk (plural **cheeses**)

chef *noun.* a chief cook in a restaurant or a hotel

chemical *noun.* a substance that is used in or made by chemistry —**chemical** *adj.*

chemist *noun.* 1. a pharmacist 2. someone whose profession is chemistry

chemistry *noun.* the science that studies substances (solids, liquids and gases) and what they do (no plural)

cherry *noun.* a small red fruit with a single hard seed in the middle

chess *noun.* a game for two players with a board and 16 pieces for each player (no plural)

chest *noun.* the part of your body that is between your shoulders and your stomach

chew *verb.* **(chewed, chewing)** grind food between your teeth

chick *noun.* a baby chicken

chicken *noun.* 1. a farm bird that lays eggs 2. the meat of a chicken

chief *noun.* the leader of a tribe

chief *adj.* main; most important

chiefly *adv.* not entirely but mostly

child *noun.* a boy or a girl (plural **children**)

childhood *noun.* the time when a person is a child

childish *adj.* of a child

childlike *adj.* like a child

children *noun.* plural of **child**

chill *noun.* 1. a sharp feeling of coldness (no plural) 2. a shiver 3. an illness; a cold

chill *verb.* **(chilled, chilling)** make something cold

chilled *adj.* made cold

chilly *adj.* 1. unpleasantly cold 2. unfriendly

chime *verb.* **(chimed, chiming)** (make bells) ring

chimney *noun.* a kind of a pipe that carries smoke out of a building

chimpanzee *noun.* a small ape

chin *noun.* the lowest part of your face

china *noun.* delicate cups, plates, etc, made of a kind of oven-baked clay (also called **porcelain**) (no plural) —**china** *adj.*

Chinese *noun.* someone from China; the language of the people in China —**Chinese** *adj.*

chip *noun.* 1. a small piece of something that comes from a bigger piece 2. a flat, round thing used instead of money in some games 3. short for microchip; a small electronic piece used in a computer 4. a small piece of food

chip *verb.* **(chipped, chipping)** break off a very small piece of something by accident

chipped *adj.* with a small piece broken off

chisel *noun.* a tool with a sharp squared end used for cutting stone or wood

chocolate *noun.* a candy made from cocoa

chocolate *adj.* made of chocolate

choice *noun.* 1. a decision between

possibilities **2.** an alternative **3.** a group of things that you can choose from (no plural)

choice adj. the best

choir noun. a group of people who sing together

choke verb. **(choked, choking)** be unable to breathe properly

choose verb. **(chose, chosen, choosing) 1.** make a decision between different possibilities **2.** decide

chop verb. **(chopped, chopping)** cut into small pieces

chopper noun. (informal) a helicopter

chorale noun. **1.** a hymn **2.** a choir — **choral** adj.

chore noun. a usually routine and boring household job

choreographer noun. a person who makes up steps for a dance according to a piece of music

chorus noun. **1.** the part of a song that is repeated **2.** a choir; a group of singers who sing the same piece of music together

Christ noun. the title given to Jesus, the founder of Christianity

christen verb. **(christened, christening) 1.** baptize; make someone a member of a Christian religion **2.** give a name to someone in a church, or to a boat or ship

Christian noun. a believer in Jesus Christ

Christian adj. belonging to the religion that believes in Christ

Christianity noun. the religion based on the teachings of Jesus Christ

Christmas noun. the holiday to celebrate the birth of Christ

Christmas card noun. a greeting that people, especially friends and family, send to each other at Christmas

Christmas tree noun. a tree that Christians decorate at Christmas

chronic adj. **1.** (of a disease) continuing for a long time **2.** (of a person) doing as a habit or for a long time

chronicle noun. a log; (historical) events written down according to the date when they happened

chronicle verb. **(chronicled, chronicling)** make a chronicle

chronological adj. the order of when events happened

chronology noun. an arrangement of events according to when they occurred

chuckle verb. **(chuckled, chuckling)** to laugh quietly and usually not for a long time

chum noun. (informal) a good friend; a pal

church noun. a building where Christians pray

CIA abbr. Central Intelligence Agency

cider noun. an alcoholic drink made from apples

cigar noun. tobacco leaves rolled into a thick tube

cigarette noun. a tube of paper with tobacco in it that some people smoke

cinema noun. the movies as an art or an industry (no plural)

cinematic adj. relating to film making

circle noun. **1.** a round space; a ring **2.** a group of friends or people with the same interests

circle verb. **(circled, circling)** go around and around

circular adj. **1.** with the shape of a circle **2.** moving like a wheel

circulate verb. **(circulated, circulating)** move around from place to place

circulation noun. **1.** the act of moving around from place to place **2.** the number of people who buy a particular newspaper or magazine

circumstances noun plural. the facts of a situation

circus noun. a show with clowns, acrobats and trained animals

citizen noun. **1.** a person who lives in a certain place **2.** a person with full rights and duties in a state or country

citizenship noun. the state of being a citizen

citrus noun. adj. a type of fruit including lemon, lime, orange, grapefruit, etc (plural **citruses**)

city noun. a large town

city hall noun. an office building where the people who govern a city work

civic adj. civil; relating to a citizen

civil adj. 1. civic; belonging to the citizens, but not military or religious 2. coldly polite

civilian noun. someone not in the army, navy, etc

civilization noun. 1. living at a high level of culture; not being savage (no plural) 2. large groups of people who live in a civilized way

civilized adj. having a high level of culture with a system of government and education

civil rights noun plural. the rights of all citizens of a country

civil servant noun. a government employee

civil service noun. all government departments other than the military

civil war noun. a war between the people of one country

claim noun. 1. what someone says is true 2. a right to something

claim verb. (**claimed, claiming**) 1. say that something is true 2. say that you are the owner of something

claimant noun. someone who makes a claim, especially for money

clan noun. a group of families originating from the same ancestor(s) and usually with the same family name

clandestine adj. done in secret; kept secret

clap verb. (**clapped, clapping**) hit your hands together noisily to show that you liked something

clarify verb. (**clarified, clarifying**) make clearer and simpler —**clarification** noun.

clash noun. 1. a fight 2. two different things that happen at the same time

clash verb. (**clashed, clashing**) 1. fight with someone 2. disagree 3. happen at the same time 4. go badly together

clasp noun. something that fastens two things together

class noun. 1. a group of students who study together at school 2. a lesson 3. things that have the same characteristics; a category 4. social level 5. (informal) style; elegance

classic noun. a book or work of art that is so excellent that it never goes out of fashion

classic adj. always in style

classical adj. traditional in style; so excellent that it has lasted for many years

classification noun. the process of classifying

classify verb. (**classified, classifying**) 1. put into classes 2. declare as secret

classmate noun. someone in your class at school

classroom noun. a room where students have their lessons

classy adj. stylish; elegant

clause noun. 1. (grammar) a part of a sentence with its own subject and a verb 2. a part of a document

claw noun. the sharp nail of an animal or a bird

clay noun. heavy, sticky earth that becomes hard when you bake it

clean verb. (**cleaned, cleaning**) make something clean; take dirt off something

clean adj. 1. free from dirt 2. fresh; not yet used

cleaner noun. a person, a tool or a substance that cleans

cleaning noun. the act of making a place clean

cleanliness noun. the state of being clean

cleanse verb. (**cleansed, cleansing**) make completely clean

clear *verb.* **(cleared, clearing)** take things away from

clear *adj.* **1.** easy to see (through) **2.** easy to hear; pure in sound **3.** easy to understand **4.** bright and pure **5.** empty

clearance *noun.* **1.** the act of clearing **2.** the amount of space between an object and something above it

clearly *adv.* **1.** in a way that is easy to see, hear or understand **2.** without doubt

clergy *noun.* priests, ministers, etc

clergyman *noun.* a priest, minister, etc, who performs religious services; a member of the clergy

clerical *adj.* **1.** concerning the work of a clerk **2.** concerning clergymen

clerk *noun.* someone who does office work

clever *adj.* **1.** intelligent **2.** skillful at doing something

cleverly *adv.* done in a skillful way

click *noun.* a small, quick, sharp sound

click *verb.* **(clicked, clicking) 1.** make a small, sharp sound **2.** press the mouse of a computer **3.** be understood **4.** get along well together

client *noun.* a person who pays a professional to do a job

clientele *noun.* customers

cliff *noun.* the high, steep, rocky side of a hill, often at the edge of the sea

climate *noun.* the type of weather a place has

climax *noun.* the highest point in the development of something

climb *verb.* **(climbed, climbing) 1.** move upward by holding on with your hands and your feet **2.** go higher **—climb** *noun.*

climber *noun.* **1.** a person who climbs mountains **2.** a plant that grows by attaching itself to things

cling *verb.* **(clung, clinging)** hang on very tightly

clinic *noun.* a place where people are treated by doctors or dentists, sometimes working as a group

clinical *adj.* connected with a clinic or hospital **—clinically** *adv.*

clip *noun.* a small piece of wire or metal that fastens things together

clip *verb.* **(clipped, clipping) 1.** fasten things together with a metal clip **2.** cut off the ends of something

clique *noun.* a small group of people who keep themselves apart and keep others from joining them

cloak *noun.* **1.** a big, loose piece of clothing without sleeves that you wear like a coat **2.** something that hides or keeps things secret

clock *noun.* an instrument for telling time

clockwise *adj.* moving in the same direction as the hands of a clock

close *verb.* **(closed, closing)** shut

close *adj.* near; within a small distance **—closely** *adv.*

closed *adj.* shut; not open

closet *noun.* a cupboard or small room for hanging your coat or storing things

closure *noun.* the act of closing a business

cloth *noun.* **1.** material made by weaving (no plural) **2.** pieces of material for different purposes

clothes *noun plural.* things that you wear on your body

clothing *noun.* what you wear to cover yourself (no plural)

cloud *noun.* a white mass that floats in the air

cloudy *adj.* with clouds

clown *noun.* an actor, especially in a circus, who makes people laugh

club *noun.* **1.** a group of people who meet regularly to do a certain thing **2.** a heavy stick that is used as a weapon **3.** one of the four symbols on playing cards

club *verb.* **(clubbed, clubbing)** beat someone with a club

clue *noun.* a piece of information that helps find the answer to a problem

clump *noun.* a group of plants or trees

clumsy *adj.* 1. not able to move carefully or attractively 2. not considerate; tactless

clung *verb.* past tense and past participle of **cling**

cluster *noun.* a group of things of the same kind that are close together

cluster *verb.* (**clustered, clustering**) group closely together

clustered *adj.* grouped closely together

clutch *noun.* 1. a tight hold 2. the pedal in a car that separates the gears (no plural)

clutch *verb.* (**clutched, clutching**) hold on tightly to something

clutter *noun.* untidiness; a mess

coach *noun.* 1. one of the passenger cars on a train 2. a comfortable bus for long trips 3. a carriage that is pulled by four or more horses 4. someone who teaches a sport or trains athletes 5. a teacher who gives private lessons; a tutor

coach *verb.* (**coached, coaching**) 1. teach a sport or train athletes 2. prepare pupils for an examination

coal *noun.* 1. a hard, black substance from deep inside the earth (no plural) 2. a piece of coal

coarse *adj.* 1. not smooth or soft; rough 2. vulgar

coast *noun.* the edge of the land along the sea

coastal *adj.* along or on a coast

coaster *noun.* a small flat dish, mat, etc, put under a cup or glass to protect a table

coastguard *noun.* special police who watch the coast

coastline *noun.* the shape of the line along the shore

coat *noun.* 1. a piece of clothing with sleeves and buttons that you wear over everything else 2. the fur of an animal 3. a layer of paint, etc, that covers something

coat *verb.* (**coated, coating**) cover with a layer of something

co-author *verb.* (**co-authored, co-authoring**) write something together with someone else

coax *verb.* (**coaxed, coaxing**) persuade; get (something) by using kindness and gentle encouragement

cob *noun.* the center hard part of corn from where the seeds grow

cobbled *adj.* made of cobblestones

cobblestone *noun.* a medium-sized stone used to pave roads

cock *noun.* a male bird, especially a chicken; a rooster

cocktail *noun.* an alcoholic drink that is made by mixing at least two different types of liquor

cocoa *noun.* 1. a brown powder that comes from the beans of a certain tree 2. a hot drink that people make from cocoa powder

coconut *noun.* a large brown nut that grows on palm trees and has sweet milk inside

COD *abbr.* cash on delivery

code *noun.* 1. a system of secret writing or signs 2. a system of laws or rules

code *verb.* (**coded, coding**) put into code

coffee *noun.* a bitter brown drink that you make from cooking special crushed beans in hot water (no plural)

coffee bar, coffee shop *noun.* a place where you can sit and drink coffee without having a meal

coffin *noun.* a box for a dead person to lie in

coin *noun.* a piece of money that is made from metal

coin *verb.* (**coined, coining**) 1. make coins 2. invent a new word, etc

coincide *verb.* (**coincided, coinciding**) happen at the same time

coincidence *noun.* two things that happen by chance to be the same

coincidentally adv. by coincidence

coke noun. 1. a type of fuel 2. another name for the drug cocaine 3. (**Coke**) shortened version of the trade name Coca Cola

cola noun. a sweet carbonated soft drink

cold noun. 1. lack of heat (no plural) 2. an illness that makes you sneeze and cough

cold adj. 1. not hot or warm; low in temperature 2. unfriendly

coldly adv. in an unfriendly way

collaborate verb. (**collaborated, collaborating**) work together with a partner

collaboration noun. the act of collaborating

collapse noun. loss of strength and the ability to continue doing things

collapse verb. (**collapsed, collapsing**) 1. break into pieces suddenly 2. fall down

collar noun. 1. the part of your shirt that is around your neck 2. a band around the neck of an animal

collate verb. (**collated, collating**) put pages in correct numerical order

collateral adj. something of value used as a guarantee for a loan

colleague noun. a person whom you work with

collect verb. (**collected, collecting**) 1. get from many different people 2. get samples of a certain kind of thing 3. take someone from a certain place 4. gather together

collection noun. 1. taking from many different people or places 2. many different samples of something that belong together

collective noun. a group of people working together

collective noun. (grammar) a noun like "family" or "team" for a group of individuals, and usually taking a singular verb

collector noun. someone who collects a certain type of thing

college noun. 1. a place to continue studying when you finish high school 2. part of a university

collide verb. (**collided, colliding**) 1. hit together violently; crash into something 2. take place at the same time

collision noun. a crash

colon noun. a punctuation mark of two dots (:), usually coming before a list

colonel noun. a high officer in the army

colonial noun. connected to a colony

colonialism noun. having colonies abroad

colonist noun. a person who settled in a colony

colonize verb. (**colonized, colonizing**) set up a colony

colony noun. 1. a country that is under the control of another country 2. people with a certain way of life who live as a group

color noun. 1. what your eye sees when light is broken into parts 2. paint or dye

color verb. (**colored, coloring**) give color to something

colorful adj. full of color

column noun. 1. a tall support for a building, usually made of stone; a pillar 2. a long line of something 3. part of a printed page 4. an article that appears regularly in a newspaper or magazine —**columnist** noun.

comb noun. a tool with teeth for keeping your hair smooth and tidy —**comb** verb.

combat noun. a battle or a struggle

combat verb. (**combated, combating; combatted, combatting**) struggle against something

combination noun. two or more things that are made into one thing or that are used together

combine verb. (**combined, combining**) 1. put two or more things together to make a new thing 2. use two or more things that go well together 3. do more than one thing

come verb. (came, come, coming) 1. move toward 2. arrive 3. go with someone

comeback noun. becoming popular or fashionable again

comedian, comedienne noun. an actor or actress who makes people laugh

comedy noun. a funny play or movie

comfort noun. 1. freedom from need 2. freedom from worry 3. kindness; something that makes another person feel better

comfort verb. (comforted, comforting) try to make someone feel better

comfortable adj. 1. pleasant; making you feel good 2. relaxed; feeling good

comfortably adv. 1. in a way that makes you feel good 2. in a relaxed way 3. without need or worry

comic noun. an actor who tells jokes

comic, comical adj. funny; amusing

comic book noun. a children's magazine that has cartoon pictures

comma noun. a punctuation mark (,)

command noun. an order

command verb. (commanded, commanding) give an order

commemorate verb. (commemorated, commemorating) do something in the memory of

comment noun. what someone says about something

comment verb. (commented, commenting) 1. mention; remark 2. give an opinion

commentary noun. a description of things as they happen

commentator noun. someone in the media who describes events

commerce noun. buying and selling; business; trade

commercial noun. a short TV or radio advertisement

commercial adj. connected with business —**commercially** adv.

commission noun. a percentage of a sale

commission verb. (commissioned, commissioning) ask someone to create something specifically for you

commissioner noun. an official who oversees others; a kind of officer

commit verb. (committed, committing) do something bad

commitment noun. a promise to do something, be faithful to, etc

committee noun. a small group of people who do a particular job

commodity noun. a product

common adj. 1. seen or done often 2. not unusual 3. vulgar 4. belonging to or used by two or more people 5. belonging to everyone

commonly adv. by many people

commonplace adj. found everywhere; ordinary

common sense noun. the ability to do rational and practical things

commonwealth noun. 1. a group of states associated politically 2. (also **the British Commonwealth**) parts of the former British empire that are still connected politically and commercially with the Queen of England and among themselves

communicate verb. (communicated, communicating) tell things to other people

communication noun. 1. sending and receiving messages (no plural) 2. understanding between two people (no plural) 3. something that is communicated

communications noun plural. different ways of sending information and connecting people

communism noun. a political system wherein the state controls production and shares the wealth among its citizens

communist noun. someone who believes in communism

community noun. a group of people who live near each other and share some of the same things

community adj. shared by the people who live in an area

commute verb. (**commuted, commuting**) travel regularly by bus, train, car, etc, to and from work

commuter noun. someone who commutes

compact adj. small in size but containing the essentials

compact disc noun. a high quality recording of music or information on a small, round piece of plastic

companion noun. 1. someone who is with another person 2. someone who lives with another person, to help look after him/her

companionship noun. company

company noun. 1. being with other people (no plural) 2. visitors (no plural) 3. a group of people who work in a business together (plural **companies**)

comparable adj. something you can compare with

comparative noun. (grammar) the form of an adjective or adverb that shows how much two things are alike or different

comparative adj. that can be compared to something else

comparatively adv. by comparing one thing with another

compare verb. (**compared, comparing**) find out or show in what ways or how much two or more things are alike or different

comparison noun. finding out or showing in what ways or how much two or more things are alike or different

compartment noun. 1. a section of a larger thing 2. a small closed room in the car of a train

compass noun. 1. an instrument with a needle that points to the North 2. a tool shaped like a V for drawing circles

compatible adj. suitable; able to live together or be used together

compel verb. (**compelled, compelling**) force someone to do something

compensate verb. (**compensated, compensating**) give money or something else to someone to try to make up for a loss or an injury

compensation noun. 1. payment to make up for a loss or an injury 2. extra payment

compete verb. (**competed, competing**) try to win a race or a contest; try to do better than other people

competence noun. having the skill or ability to do something, but not necessarily excellently (opposite **incompetence**) —**competent** adj. (opposite **incompetent**)

competition noun. 1. a race, a game or a contest 2. trying to do better than other people (no plural)

competitive adj. wanting to win; wanting very much to do better than other people —**competitiveness** noun.

competitor noun. someone who takes part in a race or contest

compile verb. (**compiled, compiling**) collect information from different sources in order to create a list, book, report, etc

complacent adj. a feeling of self-satisfaction even if not deserved

complain verb. (**complained, complaining**) say that something is not the way it should be

complaint noun. 1. what you say is wrong or is bothering you 2. an illness

complement noun. 1. something added to complete something else and make it perfect 2. (grammar) an adjective or noun that gives more information regarding the subject — **complement** verb. (**complemented, complementing**)

complementary adj. making something complete by supplying what is missing

complete verb. (**completed, completing**) finish —**completion** noun.

complete adj. 1. total 2. finished (opposite **incomplete**)

completed adj. with all the information required

completely adv. in every way; totally (opposite **incompletely**)

complex adj. **1.** having many sides to consider **2.** having more than one part

complexion noun. the natural skin color and condition of your face

complexity noun. how complex something is

complicate verb. (**complicated, complicating**) make things more difficult

complicated adj. **1.** complex **2.** difficult to understand

complication noun. **1.** something that makes things more difficult **2.** another illness or medical problem that can come after the first one

compliment noun. something nice that you say about someone

compliment verb. (**complimented, complimenting**) say something nice to someone about him/her

complimentary adj. given free

comply verb. (**complied, complying**) (formal) act according to a demand or rule —**compliance** noun.

component noun. part of a bigger thing, such as a machine, contract, etc

compose verb. (**composed, composing**) make up something new in writing or in music

composer noun. someone who writes music

composition noun. an essay; a piece of music

compound noun. **1.** a combination of two or more chemicals **2.** an area enclosed by a fence with buildings inside

compound adj. having many parts

comprehend verb. (**comprehended**) understand

comprehension noun. understanding

comprehensive adj. including many things or details

comprise verb. (**comprised, comprising**) be made up of

compromise verb. (**compromised, compromising**) settle an argument by each person giving up part of what he/she wanted

compulsive adj. unable to control a desire

compulsory adj. giving no choice; required; not voluntary

compute verb. (**computed, computing**) count; figure out how much

computer noun. a machine that finds answers and stores information

computerize verb. (**computerized, computerizing**) **1.** use a computer (to run a system) **2.** equip an office, etc, with computers

con noun. **1.** an argument against something (opposite **pro**) **2.** (slang, short for **convict**) a prisoner

conceal verb. (**concealed, concealing**) hide something

conceive verb. (**conceived. conceiving**) **1.** become pregnant **2.** form a plan, a concept, etc, in the mind

concentrate verb. (**concentrated, concentrating**) focus your attention on something

concentration noun. **1.** focusing your attention on a certain thing (no plural) **2.** a close gathering

concentration camp noun. a prison camp where large numbers of civilians are forced to live

concept noun. a general idea about something; what you conceive

concern noun. **1.** what interests you **2.** worry **3.** a large business

concern verb. (**concerned, concerning**) **1.** be about **2.** be connected with

concerned adj. worried

concerning prep. about

concert noun. a program of music played in public

concerto noun. a piece of (classical) music for one or more solo instruments together with an orchestra

concession noun. **1.** usually after a discussion, an argument or negotiations, the willingness to agree to do something **2.** something given by the owner to do something

conclude verb. **(concluded, concluding) 1.** bring to an end; come to an end **2.** reach an idea on the basis of facts

conclusion noun. **1.** end **2.** an idea that you reach on the basis of facts —**conclusive** adj.

concrete noun. a hard gray material that is used in buildings and roads

concrete adj. **1.** made from concrete **2.** material; something that can be touched or measured **3.** practical; that can be used

condemn verb. **(condemned, condemning) 1.** say that something is bad in every way **2.** give a decision about punishment in a criminal case

condition noun. **1.** the way something or someone is **2.** something that has to happen before another thing can happen **3.** what is written in a contract; a term

condition verb. **(conditioned, conditioning) 1.** adapt **2.** be trained to act a certain way

conditional adj. **1.** depending on certain things (opposite **unconditional**) **2.** (grammar) saying that something will happen on condition that something else happens, usually using the expression **if** or **unless**

conditions noun plural. the way things around you are; circumstances

condom noun. a soft piece of rubber that a man uses in sexual relations to prevent pregnancy and sexual diseases

condominium noun. an apartment that you own in an apartment house, sharing common property (short form **condo**)

conduct verb. **(conducted, conducting) 1.** lead; guide **2.** manage **3.** lead an orchestra or choir **4.** do or carry out something **5.** pass heat or an electric current

conductor noun. **1.** someone who collects the tickets on a bus or train **2.** someone who directs an orchestra or choir **3.** a guide **4.** something that passes along heat or an electric current

cone noun. **1.** a shape that has a round, flat base at one end and a point at the other end **2.** the fruit of certain trees that have needles

confederation noun. a union created for political or commercial purposes; a league

conference noun. a meeting for the purpose of discussing something

confess verb. **(confessed, confessing) 1.** admit that you did something wrong **2.** (Roman Catholic Church) tell your sins to a priest

confession noun. **1.** saying that you committed a crime **2.** saying something that you feel embarrassed about **3.** the Roman Catholic ceremony of telling your sins to a priest

confide verb. **(confided, confiding)** tell a secret to someone you trust

confidence noun. feeling sure about something or someone

confident adj. sure; certain

confidential adj. **1.** written or spoken in secret and expected to stay secret **2.** entrusted to keep your secrets —**confidentiality** noun.

confidently adv. with confidence

confine verb. **(confined, confining)** be limited, often to a small space —**confinement** noun.

confirm verb. **(confirmed, confirming) 1.** say definitely that a piece of information is true **2.** agree definitely that you have ordered something

confirmation noun. **1.** something that confirms **2.** a religious service when someone becomes a full member of the religion

conflict noun. **1.** a fight; a quarrel **2.** a difference of opinion; disagreement — **conflict** verb. **(conflicted, conflicting)**

conform verb. **(conformed, conforming)** do something or be like everybody/everything else; act according to the rules

confrontation noun. a situation of face-to-face opposition —**confrontational** adj.

confuse verb. **(confused, confusing) 1.** make ideas unclear **2.** mistake one thing for something else

confusing adj. not clear; difficult to understand

confusion noun. **1.** disorder **2.** unclearness

conglomerate noun. a large business with many companies doing or producing many different things

congratulate verb. **(congratulated, congratulating)** tell someone that you are pleased when something good has happened to him/her

congratulations noun plural. good wishes

congress noun. **1.** a meeting of professionals, etc, to discuss ideas and exchange information **2. (Congress)** the law-making body of the United States and also of some other countries —**congressional** adj.

congressman, congresswoman noun. a member of Congress

conjunction noun. (grammar) a word that connects words, phrases, clauses or sentences, such as **and, but, although**

connect verb. **(connected, connecting) 1.** fasten or join two things together **2.** supply with power

connection noun. **1.** a joining together of two things **2.** link **3.** telephone contact **4.** a change of buses, trains, planes, etc, to get where you want to go

conquer verb. **(conquered, conquering)** take over the country of another people by force

conquest noun. conquering a country

conscience noun. a feeling of the difference between right and wrong

conscientious adj. careful and serious about how you do a job

conscious adj. awake; knowing what is happening (opposite **unconscious**)

consciously adv. knowing what you are doing (opposite **unconsciously**)

consciousness noun. knowing what is happening around you (no plural; opposite **unconsciousness**)

consecutive adj. one after another

consensus noun. an opinion that almost everybody agrees on; general agreement

consent verb. **(consented, consenting)** allow someone to do what he/she wants; give your agreement to something —**consent** noun.

consequence noun. a result

consequent adj. resulting; following

consequently adv. as a result

conservation noun. not wasting natural things; protection of the environment (no plural)

conservationist noun. someone who is active in protecting the environment

conservative adj. not liking change

conservatory noun. **1.** a special school for teaching music or drama **2.** a greenhouse for growing plants

conserve verb. **(conserved, conserving)** not waste things that you know will be necessary later

consider verb. **(considered, considering) 1.** think about something seriously **2.** recognize certain facts; take something into account **3.** have an opinion about someone or something

considerable adj. large; significant — **considerably** adv.

considerate adj. thoughtful about the feelings of others

consideration noun. **1.** careful thought (no plural) **2.** thoughtfulness about other people's feelings; tact (no plural) **3.** a fact that you must take into account before you make a decision

considering *prep. conj.* taking into account

consign *verb.* (**consigned, consigning**) send —**consignment** *noun.*

consist *verb.* (**consisted, consisting**) be made up

consistency *noun.* 1. continuing in the same way 2. texture; how stiff a liquid that is mixed with something else is

consistent *adj.* 1. in a regular way 2. continuing in the same way; unchanging —**consistently** *adv.*

consolation *noun.* something that makes you feel better when you are sad or disappointed

console *verb.* (**consoled, consoling**) say kind things to someone who is sad

consolidate *verb.* (**consolidated, consolidating**) 1. merge; combine smaller things into a single bigger one 2. make stronger

consonant *noun.* a letter of the alphabet that is not a vowel

consortium *noun.* the combination of several banks, businesses, etc, for a certain purpose

conspicuous *adj.* standing out from other things; easily seen; attracting attention

conspiracy *noun.* a secret, illegal plan among two or more people; a plot

constant *adj.* without stopping

constantly *adv.* all the time

constitute *verb.* (**constituted, constituting**) 1. make up; form 2. make legal

constitution *noun.* the basic laws of a country

construct *verb.* (**constructed, constructing**) build

construction *noun.* 1. the act of building (no plural) 2. a building

constructive *adj.* helpful; making something better

consul *noun.* a diplomat whose job is to look after the citizens of his/her country in a foreign country

consulate *noun.* the office of a consul

consult *verb.* (**consulted, consulting**) 1. ask for someone's advice about something 2. look up information in an encyclopedia, a dictionary, etc —**consultation** *noun.*

consultant *noun.* an expert adviser

consume *verb.* (**consumed, consuming**) 1. eat or drink, usually in generous amounts 2. use up —**consumption** *noun.*

consumer *noun.* a buyer or user of a product

consumer goods *noun plural.* things that people buy

contact *noun.* 1. the touching of two things 2. communication

contact *verb.* (**contacted, contacting**) reach by telephone

contagious *adj.* catching; (disease) that can be passed on to someone else by contact

contain *verb.* (**contained, containing**) have inside

container *noun.* something that holds other things, such as a barrel, a basket, a box, a can, a carton

contaminate *verb.* (**contaminated, contaminating**) make impure, diseased or dirty —**contamination** *noun.*

contemporary *adj.* belonging to the same time; current; modern — **contemporary** *noun.* (plural **contemporaries**)

contempt *noun.* lack of respect; the feeling that something or someone is worthless (no plural)

content *adj.* satisfied with what you have

contented *adj.* pleased with things; satisfied

contents *noun plural.* things that are inside another thing

contest *noun.* a game or sport that has a winner

contestant *noun.* someone who competes in a contest

context *noun.* what comes before and after a word in a text

continent noun. a mass of land on earth (North America, South America, Africa, Europe, Asia, Australia and Antarctica) —**continental** adj.

continual adj. happening again and again —**continually** adv.

continuation noun. 1. not stopping 2. a new start after something has stopped

continue verb. (**continued, continuing**) not stop; keep on doing something (say either **continue working** or **continue to work**)

continuous adj. without a stop

continuously adv. going on and on without stopping

contraceptive noun. something that is used to prevent pregnancy

contract noun. an agreement

contract verb. (**contracted, contracting**) 1. be made narrower 2. (grammar) be shortened 3. sign an official legal agreement with someone

contraction noun. 1. tightening of a muscle 2. strong pains a woman has just before giving birth 3. (grammar) the shortening of a word or words

contractor noun. someone who enters into a contract, such as to build a house

contradict verb. (**contradicted, contradicting**) 1. say that what someone else says is not true 2. contain conflicting information about something

contradiction noun. two things that do not agree with each other

contradictory adj. containing conflicting information

contrary adj. noun. opposite

contrast noun. a very noticeable difference between two things —**contrast** verb. (**contrasted, contrasting**)

contravene verb. (**contravened, contravening**) break a law; act contrary to

contribute verb. (**contributed, contributing**) 1. give money, clothes, etc, to something you think is important 2. help to make something happen —

contribution noun. —**contributory** adj.

contributor noun. 1. someone who gives money, etc, for something important 2. someone who writes an article, story, poem, etc, for a newspaper or magazine

control noun. 1. restraint; check 2. management 3. a way that something is controlled

control verb. (**controlled, controlling**) 1. have power and responsibility 2. keep someone or something in order

controls noun plural. the instruments that make something work

controversial adj. likely to make people argue

controversy noun. a difference of opinion; an argument (plural **controversies**)

convene verb. (**convened, convening**) call a group together for a meeting

convenience noun. 1. something that makes things easier (opposite **inconvenience**) 2. being convenient (no plural)

convenient adj. 1. helpful; making life easier 2. not causing difficulties —**conveniently** adv. (opposite **inconveniently**)

convent noun. a building or buildings where nuns live

convention noun. 1. a meeting (of professionals) to discuss things of interest; a conference 2. a generally acceptable practice

conventional adj. ordinary; not original; standard (opposite **unconventional**)

conversation noun. when two or more people talk to one another

conversational adj. spoken

converse verb. (**conversed, conversing**) (formal) to talk

convert verb. (**converted, converting**) 1. change into something else 2. change someone's religion

converter noun. a machine that converts iron into steel

convertible *noun.* a car that has a roof that folds down

convey *verb.* **(conveyed, conveying)** make your feeling known

convict *noun.* a person who is in prison for committing a crime

convict *verb.* **(convicted, convicting)** decide in a court of law that a person is guilty of a crime

conviction *noun.* **1.** the decision that someone is guilty **2.** belief

convince *verb.* **(convinced, convincing)** make someone believe or do something by giving reasons; persuade

convincing *adj.* able to make you believe something

cook *noun.* a person whose job is to cook for other people

cook *verb.* **(cooked, cooking)** prepare food by using a stove

cookery *noun.* the art of preparing food

cookie *noun.* a flat, sweet cake

cool *adj.* **1.** a little bit cold **2.** calm; not excited **3.** (slang) great; terrific

cool *verb.* **(cooled, cooling)** become less hot

coop *noun.* a cage for chicken

cooperate *verb.* **(cooperated, cooperating)** work together with other people to get something done —**cooperation** *noun.*

cooperative *adj.* willing to work with and help other people

coordinate *verb.* **(coordinated, coordinating)** cause things or people to work smoothly together —**coordination** *noun.*

coordinator *noun.* someone who coordinates

cop *noun.* (slang) a police officer

cope *verb.* **(coped, coping)** do what you have to do; manage

copper *noun.* a red-brown metal that is sometimes used for making pots, bowls, jewelry, etc

copy *noun.* **1.** more than one example of the same thing **2.** something that looks exactly like something else

copy *verb.* **(copied, copying) 1.** do what someone else does; imitate **2.** write or draw in exactly the same way **3.** make more samples of something **4.** cheat

copyright *noun.* having the exclusive right to sell, produce, print, record, etc, something

coral *noun.* a pinkish or white stone-like material that was once alive in the sea

cord *noun.* **1.** a thick string **2.** an electrical cable that you use in the house

cordial *adj.* (formal) friendly and polite

cordon *noun.* a line of police, soldiers, etc guarding an area or preventing people from passing

core *noun.* the center of a fruit where the seeds are; the hard center of something

cork *noun.* a plug for a bottle that is made from the light-brown outer covering of trees

corn *noun.* large yellow seeds eaten as a vegetable; the plant itself

corner *noun.* a place where two lines, sides, walls, roads, etc, meet; an angle —**corner** *adj.*

coronation *noun.* the ceremony where a queen or king is crowned

Corp. *abbr.* corporation

corporate *adj.* connected to a corporation

corporation *noun.* a large business organization

corps *noun.* **1.** a large army unit **2.** people who act together

corpse *noun.* a dead body, especially of a person

correct *adj.* **1.** without any mistakes **2.** exact

correct *verb.* **(corrected, correcting)** fix a mistake; show what is wrong —**correction** *noun.* —**correctly** *adv.*

correspond *verb.* **(corresponded, corresponding)** be equal to

correspondence *noun.* writing to and receiving letters from someone

correspondent *noun.* **1.** someone who writes letters to someone else **2.** someone who reports news for the media

corridor *noun.* a narrow passage in a building or inside an apartment, with rooms on both sides

corrupt *adj.* dishonest or improper use of power; being bribed —**corrupt** *verb.* **(corrupted, corrupting)** —**corruption** *noun.*

cosmetic *noun.* (usually plural) something to make the skin, hair, etc, more beautiful

cosmic *adj.* found in outer space

cosmopolitan *adj.* containing things or people from all over the world

cosmos *noun.* the whole universe

cost *noun.* the amount of money that you must pay for something —**cost of living** *noun.* how much you have to pay for necessary things —**cost-effective, cost-efficient** *adj.* bringing in the best profits at the lowest cost

cost *verb.* **(cost) 1.** have to pay money **2.** estimate the price to be charged for a job or article

co-star *noun.* a famous actor/actress who plays together with another famous actor/actress in a movie or play

costing *noun.* an estimation of costs

costly *adj.* expensive

costume *noun.* clothes that you wear to look like someone or something else

cot *noun.* a folding bed

cottage *noun.* a small house, especially in the country

cotton *noun.* **1.** a tall plant that has white, puffy balls growing on it **2.** a cloth made from the cotton plant

cotton *adj.* made of cotton

couch *noun.* a long seat where you can sit or lie down; a sofa

cough *verb.* **(coughed, coughing)** make a sharp noise in your throat when air comes out of your lungs suddenly — **cough** *noun.*

could *verb.* **1.** past tense of **can 2.** used instead of **can** in indirect (reported) speech **3.** a word that shows that something might be possible if something else happened **4.** a word that expresses a wish **5.** a polite word to use when you ask for something —**couldn't** *abbr.* = could not

council *noun.* a group of people (usually elected or appointed) who give advice and make decisions

counsel *noun.* **1.** advice **2.** a lawyer representing someone in court

counsel *verb.* **(counseled, counseling)** (formal) advise someone

count *noun.* **1.** the act of adding numbers for a specific reason **2.** a nobleman in some European countries

count *verb.* **(counted, counting) 1.** say numbers in order **2.** find out how many things or how much money you have **3.** be important **4.** have value

countable noun *noun.* (grammar) a noun that has a plural form and can take **a** or **an** before it

countdown *noun.* counting backward (usually to one), such as before sending a rocket into space

counter *noun.* **1.** a long narrow table in a store, bank, etc, that separates the workers from the customers **2.** a long, narrow table with stools on one side where you can sit and eat

counter- *prefix.* part of a word meaning **against** or **opposed to**

counteract *verb.* **(counteracted, counteracting)** lessen the effects of something

counter-attack *verb.* **(counter-attacked, counter-attacking)** attack in reply to an attack on you

counterpart *noun.* someone or something that does the same thing but in a different system

countess *noun.* a noblewoman (plural **countesses**)

countless *adj.* too many to count

country *noun.* **1.** the land of a nation **2.** a people **3.** the land outside the city (no plural)

country *adj.* in the country

countryside *noun.* the open land outside the city

county *noun.* a large area of local government

couple *noun.* two people who are married or live together

coupon *noun.* a small, printed piece of paper that you can tear off and use instead of money or to receive a service

courage *noun.* the ability to control fear; bravery (no plural)

courageous *adj.* brave

courier *noun.* a messenger

course *noun.* **1.** forward movement **2.** the direction or path that something moves in **3.** an arranged set of lessons **4.** part of a meal **5.** a piece of land for a sport with movement in one direction

court *noun.* **1.** a building where lawyers argue cases **2.** a space that has markings for a certain sport **3.** the king and queen and the people around them

court *verb.* **(courted, courting)** (of a man) pay special attention to a woman hoping she will marry him

courteous *adj.* having good manners; polite

courtesy *noun.* politeness; good manners

courthouse *noun.* a building where law courts are located

courtroom *noun.* a room inside a court where a judge sits and listens to lawyers arguing a case

courtship *noun.* special behavior of a male animal to attract the female

courtyard *noun.* an open space behind a building or between buildings

cousin *noun.* the child of your aunt or uncle

cove *noun.* a small bay

covenant *noun.* a formal agreement

cover *noun.* **1.** something you put over something else **2.** the outside of a book —**coverage** *noun.*

cover *verb.* **(covered, covering) 1.** put something over something else **2.** lie everywhere on something **3.** include **4.** pay for **5.** be about something **6.** report something **7.** get as far as

covering *noun.* something that covers

cow *noun.* a farm animal that gives milk, eats grass and says **moo**

coward *noun.* someone without courage. —**cowardly** *adj.*

cowboy *noun.* a man who looks after the cattle on a ranch

crab *noun.* a sea animal that has ten legs, with a body covered by a flat shell

crack *noun.* **1.** a line where a surface is broken **2.** a sharp noise **3.** (slang) a very dangerous drug made of cocaine (no plural)

crack *verb.* **(cracked, cracking) 1.** break something open sharply **2.** break something partly but not completely **3.** break a code

cracker *noun.* a flat, dry baked food that is not sweet and can be salty

crackle *verb.* **(crackled, crackling)** make a series of sharp cracking sounds

cradle *noun.* a small bed for a baby

craft *noun.* **1.** work that is done with the hands and needs a lot of skill **2.** a boat, ship, airplane or spaceship (no plural)

craftsman, craftsperson *noun.* someone who makes things with his/her hands (plural **craftsmen, craftspersons, craftspeople**)

craftsmanship *noun.* the art or skill of a person who produces something with his/her hands

crafty *adj.* clever in a dishonest way

cram *verb.* **(crammed, cramming) 1.** stuff something into something else **2.** (informal) study intensively for a test at the last minute

crammed adj. too full

crank noun. 1. an L-shaped handle used for turning something 2. (slang) a person with unusual ideas and behavior 3. (slang) a bad-tempered person

crash noun. 1. a serious accident in which two things collide 2. an airplane accident

crash verb. (**crashed, crashing**) 1. hit violently together with something else 2. hit something violently and break into pieces 3. (computers) stop working

crate noun. a large wooden box for packing and storing things

crawl verb. (**crawled, crawling**) 1. walk on your hands and knees 2. move by pulling your body along the ground 3. move very slowly

crayon noun. a soft, colored stick that you draw or color pictures with

craze noun. a very popular fashion which lasts for a short time

crazy adj. 1. out of your mind; not rational 2. unusual and silly

creak verb. (**creaked, creaking**) make a noise like a door that needs oil or old wooden stairs

cream noun. 1. the thick part of milk 2. a soft white substance to put on your body

creamy adj. soft and smooth

create verb. (**created, creating**) 1. make something new 2. make something happen

creation noun. 1. a specific new thing 2. (**Creation**) the creation of the universe by God

creative adj. having the imagination to make new and original things

creativity noun. the power to be creative (no plural)

creator noun. someone who creates something new

creature noun. a living animal or person

credit noun. 1. respect; recognition (no plural) 2. a way of buying now and paying later (no plural) 3. something to be proud of

credit verb. (**credited, crediting**) 1. add money to an account 2. postpone payment 3. believe

credit card noun. a plastic card that you can use instead of cash

creditor noun. who someone owes money to

credit rating noun. the history of how someone handled paying his/her debts in the past in order to decide if he/she can get a new loan

creek noun. a small river of water; a narrow body of water going from a lake or sea into land

creep verb. (**crept, creeping**) 1. move by dragging your body along or close to the ground 2. move very quietly and slowly—**creepy** adj.

crept verb. past tense and past participle of **creep**

crew noun. a group that works together

crib noun. a baby's bed with bars on the sides to protect the baby from falling

cricket noun. 1. an insect that makes a loud noise by rubbing its wings together 2. a game in which players try to hit a ball with a bat (no plural)

cried verb. past tense and past participle of **cry**

cries noun. plural of **cry**

crime noun. 1. all acts that are against the law (no plural) 2. an act that is against the law

criminal noun. someone who committed a crime —**criminal** adj.

cripple noun. someone who is unable to use his/her legs or arms —**crippled** adj. —**crippling** adj.

crisis noun. 1. a time of serious trouble 2. a turning point in a situation

crisp adj. hard and crunchy

criterion noun. a standard on which a decision or judgment is made (plural **criteria**)

critic noun. someone who writes his/her

opinion of books, movies, plays or concerts

critical *adj.* **1.** extremely serious **2.** a time of crisis **3.** giving an opinion that something is bad —**critically** *adv.*

criticism *noun.* **1.** the expression of opinions about something **2.** saying negative things about someone or something (no plural)

criticize *verb.* **(criticized, criticizing) 1.** give opinions on something **2.** say negative things about someone or something

critique *noun.* a review of a book, movie, etc

crocodile *noun.* a large reptile with many teeth that lives in a lake or a river and also on land

crook *noun.* someone who lives by cheating other people

crooked *adj.* **1.** not straight **2.** dishonest; cheating

crop *noun.* what a farmer grows and harvests in one season

crops *noun plural.* plants or plant products, such as grain, fruit and vegetables

cross *noun.* two lines that go through each other like this (+) or like this (x)

cross *verb.* **(crossed, crossing)** go from one side to the other

cross *adj.* angry; in a bad mood

cross-country *adj.* across open fields

crossing *noun.* **1.** a place where you are allowed to cross a road **2.** a place where a railroad track passes

crossroads *noun plural.* a place where two roads meet; a junction

crosswalk *noun.* a pedestrian crossing

crow *noun.* a kind of large black bird

crowd *noun.* **1.** a large number of people together in one place **2.** (informal) the group of people who are your friends —**crowd** *verb.* **(crowded, crowding)**

crowded *adj.* full of people

crown *noun.* the headdress that kings and queens wear

crown *verb.* **(crowned, crowning)** place a crown on the head of a new king or queen

crucial *adj.* extremely important; necessary

cruel *adj.* bad; liking to make others suffer —**cruelly** *adv.* —**cruelty** *noun.*

cruise *noun.* a vacation or pleasure trip on a ship that continues for a number of days

cruise *verb.* **(cruised, cruising) 1.** sail for pleasure in an unhurried way **2.** have a car, plane, etc, go at a steady rate

cruiser *noun.* a kind of warship smaller than a battleship

crumb *noun.* a tiny piece that breaks off bread or cake

crumble *verb.* **(crumbled, crumbling) 1.** break apart into crumbs **2.** fall apart

crumple *verb.* **(crumpled, crumpling)** make something full of wrinkles by crushing it

crunch *verb.* **(crunched, crunching)** make a noise with your teeth when you eat something hard

crush *verb.* **(crushed, crushing)** cause damage by pressing with strong force —**crushed** *adj.*

crust *noun.* **1.** the hard outside of bread **2.** a hard covering that forms over something

crutch *noun.* a stick that can support you for walking

cry *noun.* **1.** a call of fear, surprise, etc **2.** a bird call (plural **cries**)

cry *verb.* **(cried, crying) 1.** make a sound like a baby; weep **2.** shout

crystal *noun.* **1.** a transparent mineral **2.** very high quality glass **3.** the shape of certain small grain-like things that were formed by nature **4.** the clear covering on the face of a watch

cub *noun.* the young of a bear, a lion, a tiger and certain other wild meat-eating animals

Cuban *adj.* from Cuba

cube *noun.* **1.** a solid thing that has six

equal square sides **2.** in mathematics, the third power of a number —**cubic** *adj.*

cuckoo *noun.* a bird that lays eggs in other birds' nests

cucumber *noun.* a long green-skinned vegetable used in salads and for making pickles

cuddle *verb.* **(cuddled, cuddling)** hold very close and lovingly

cuddly *adj.* **(cuddlier, cuddliest; more cuddly, most cuddly)** soft and nice to hug

culinary *adj.* connected to food, or used in the kitchen

cult *noun.* **1.** a group of people who worship in a special way **2.** admirers of a public figure (pop singer, politician, etc) who make a kind of idol out of the person

cultivate *verb.* **(cultivated, cultivating)** prepare the soil and grow crops

cultivated *adj.* not wild

cultivation *noun.* the growing of crops on prepared soil (no plural)

cultural *adj.* improving the mind; educational

culture *noun.* the beliefs, customs, art, etc, of a particular group of people

cultured *adj.* **1.** well educated and with good manners **2.** caused to grow under artificial conditions and not by nature

cunning *adj.* clever at getting what you want and deceiving others

cup *noun.* **1.** a small, round container with a handle on one side that you drink from **2.** a prize in a competition

cupboard *noun.* a closet or cabinet

curator *noun.* someone who is in charge of (an art) exhibition in a museum

curb *noun.* the outside edge of a sidewalk

cure *noun.* something that gets rid of an illness

cure *verb.* **(cured, curing)** make someone well from an illness

curiosity *noun.* **1.** wanting to know things (no plural) **2.** something strange and unusual (plural **curiosities**)

curious *adj.* **1.** eager to learn **2.** wanting to know something **3.** strange; unusual

curl *noun.* **1.** a ring of hair **2.** a thing that has the shape of a spiral

curl *verb.* **(curled, curling)** make something into the shape of curls —**curly** *adj.*

currency *noun.* the money that is used in a country

current *noun.* **1.** a rapid movement of water or air **2.** the flow of electricity

current *adj.* new; recent

currently *adv.* happening now

curriculum *noun.* a syllabus; the course of study in a school (plural **curricula** or **curriculum**)

curse *noun.* **1.** something magical that brings harm **2.** violent, abusive language

curse *verb.* **(cursed, cursing) 1.** use violent, abusive language **2.** say magic words to bring harm to someone

cursor *noun.* the symbol on a computer screen that indicates where data can be typed

curtail *verb.* **(curtailed, curtailing)** shorten; limit; make less than originally planned

curtain *noun.* **1.** a piece of cloth over a window **2.** the heavy piece of material in front of the stage

curve *noun.* a bend; a rounded line

curve *verb.* **(curved, curving)** have the shape of a curve

curved *adj.* having the shape of a curve; not straight

cushion *noun.* a pillow for leaning against or sitting on

custom *noun.* something that almost everyone in a certain culture does

customary *adj.* usual; according to custom

customer *noun.* someone who buys in a certain place

customize *verb.* **(customized, customizing)** make or change especially for one person according to his/her request

customs *noun plural.* **1.** a place or department that checks bags and packages that come into and go out of a country **2.** money that you have to pay to bring certain things into a country

cut *noun.* **1.** an injury from a sharp instrument **2.** an opening made by a sharp instrument

cut *verb.* **(cut, cutting) 1.** break into two or more pieces with a sharp instrument **2.** remove a small piece of something from a bigger piece **3.** make something shorter **4.** wound yourself with something sharp
—**cut up** *verb.* cut into small pieces

cutback *noun.* a reduction that was planned

cut-rate, cut-price *adj.* sold at a rate lower than the regular price

cute *adj.* charming and sweet

cutlery *noun.* (no plural) knives, forks and spoons

cutting *noun.* a piece cut from a newspaper

cutting edge *noun.* the newest and most advanced point

CV *noun.* = curriculum vitae

cycle *noun.* **1.** something that happens again and again in nature **2.** a bicycle; a motorcycle —**cycle** *verb.* **(cycled, cycling)**

cycling *noun.* riding a bicycle

cyclist *noun.* someone who rides a bicycle or a motorcycle

cyclone *noun.* a very violent wind, whose center is calm, that turns quickly in a circle

cynic *noun.* a sarcastic and negative person who believes that selfishness is the only reason why people do things —**cynicism** *noun.*

cynical *adj.* being sarcastic and negative

D

dabble verb. **(dabbled, dabbling)** work at something but not in a serious manner

dad, daddy noun. a loving name for a father

daily adj. adv. noun. every day

dairy noun. a place on a farm or a company that makes milk, butter, cheese, etc —**dairy** adj.

dam noun. a wall built to prevent the flow of water from a river

damage noun. harm or injury (no plural)

damage verb. **(damaged, damaging)** cause harm

damages noun plural. (law) money that the court decides someone must pay to someone else for harm caused to the second person

dame noun. 1. old fashioned slang word for a woman 2. a British rank of honor (title) given to a woman

damp adj. a little bit wet

dance noun. 1. a special kind of movement, usually to music 2. a party for the purpose of dancing

dance verb. **(danced, dancing)** move in a special way, usually to music —**dancing** noun. adj.

dancer noun. someone who dances

danger noun. 1. a chance that something harmful will happen to you (no plural) 2. something harmful that may happen

dangerous adj. harmful —**dangerously** adv.

dangle verb. **(dangled, dangling)** 1. hang loosely so that it can swing 2. offer something attractive with hopes of getting a certain result

Danish noun. the language spoken in Denmark
—**Danish** adj. from Denmark; characteristic of Denmark

dare verb. **(dared, daring)** 1. challenge a person to do something (dangerous) in order to prove he/she is brave 2. show you are angry at someone else because of something he/she has done

dark noun. where or when there is no light (no plural)

dark adj. 1. without light 2. not light in color 3. almost black in color —**darkly** adv. —**darkness** noun.

darling noun. a name that you can use for someone you love

darling adj. charming; very cute

dash noun. 1. a quick run 2. just a little 3. a short line (-) used to separate words (also called **hyphen**)

data noun plural. information; facts

database noun. a large amount of information arranged in a computer that users can access and process

date noun. 1. the day, month and year 2. (informal) an appointment, usually with someone of the opposite sex for romantic reasons

date verb. **(dated, dating)** 1. put a date on something 2. decide how old something (archaeological) is 3. go out with someone

daughter noun. a person's female child

daughter-in-law noun. your son's wife (plural **daughters-in-law**)

dawn noun. the early morning when the sun comes up

day noun. a period of 24 hours

daydream noun. pleasant thoughts that come into your mind as if in a dream

daylight noun. light from the sun (no plural)

daytime noun. adj. the hours between dawn and dark (no plural)

dead adj. no longer living

deadline noun. a time when something must be finished

deaf *adj. noun.* not able to hear

deafen *verb.* **(deafened, deafening)** make deaf for a short time

deal *noun.* an agreement

deal *verb.* **(dealt, dealing)** hand out cards in a game

dealer *noun.* someone who buys and sells something

dealership *noun.* a place that sells a certain product

dean *noun.* in some universities, someone in charge of a department or someone who deals with the behavior of the students

dear *noun.* a word that you can use for someone you love

dear *adj.* **1.** loved **2.** cute; charming **3.** a beginning for a letter, before the person's name

dearest *noun. adj.* a word that you can use when speaking or writing to someone you love very much

death *noun.* the end of life

debatable *adj.* doubtful; perhaps not true

debate *noun.* **1.** a civilized difference of opinion; a formal discussion **2.** something up for discussion **—debate** *verb.* **(debated, debating)**

debit *noun.* a record of money owed or spent; a charge in someone's account **—debit** *verb.* **(debited, debiting)**

debt *noun.* money that you owe someone

debtor *noun.* a person or a company that owes money

debut *noun.* a first appearance in public

Dec. *abbr.* December

decade *noun.* a period of ten years

decay *verb.* **(decayed, decaying) 1.** rot **2.** get to a low level **—decay** *noun.*

deceive *verb.* **(deceive, deceiving)** lie; trick someone **—deceit** *noun.*

December *noun.* the last month of the year

decency *noun.* respect; going according to acceptable social standards

decent *adj.* **1.** of behavior that does not cause shame or shock **2.** enough **3.** (informal) kind; nice

deception *noun.* tricking someone

deceptive *adj.* misleading

decide *verb.* **(decided, deciding) 1.** choose to do something **2.** choose among two or more things

decipher *verb.* **(deciphered, deciphering)** break a code; read or understand something unclear, such as a code or handwriting

decision *noun.* something that you have thought about and chosen to do **—decision-making** *noun.*

decisive *adj.* **1.** showing seriousness in wanting something **2.** unquestionable **3.** leading to a certain result

deck *noun.* **1.** the wooden floor out-of-doors on a boat or ship where you can walk **2.** a pack of playing cards

declaration *noun.* an official statement

declare *verb.* **(declared, declaring)** announce something firmly

decline *verb.* **(declined, declining) 1.** go from better to worse **2.** refuse **3.** slope downward **—decline** *noun.*

decor *noun.* furniture, decorations, etc, of a room, restaurant, stage, etc

decorate *verb.* **(decorated, decorating)** use pretty or colorful things to make a place look beautiful **—decorative** *adj.*

decoration *noun.* something that you use to make a place look pretty

decrease *verb.* **(decreased, decreasing) 1.** become less **2.** make smaller or less **—decrease** *noun.*

dedicate *verb.* **(dedicated, dedicating) 1.** give for a particular purpose or cause **2.** write in a book, sing a song, etc, that it is in honor of someone else **—dedication** *noun.*

dedicated *adj.* hard-working toward a purpose; committed

deduce *verb.* **(deduced, deducing)** come to a conclusion or form an opinion based on knowledge; infer

deduct verb. (deducted, deducting) subtract from a total

deduction noun. 1. a process where general principles are used in order to reach a conclusion 2. a certain amount of money that is taken away

deep adj. going down a long way — **deep** adv.

deeply adv. very much

deer noun. a grass-eating animal that has horns on its head and runs fast (plural **deer**)

default noun. 1. a failure to pay debts 2. failure to take part in a contest 3. in a computer, the instruction that tells it to perform in a certain way unless the user gives new instructions

defeat verb. (defeated, defeating) win a victory over; beat —**defeat** noun. — **defeated** adj.

defect noun. something wrong — **defective** adj.

defend verb. (defended, defending) 1. protect from harm 2. argue in support of

defendant noun. someone against whom a legal action is brought

defender noun. 1. a person who defends an idea; a lawyer who defends a person in court 2. in sports, someone who defends the goal area

defense noun. 1. the act of defending 2. the arguments used to defend someone in court 3. protection — **defensive** adj.

defer verb. (deferred, deferring) postpone; delay

deficit noun. an amount that is less than what is necessary

define verb. (defined, defining) 1. give the meaning of a word 2. explain qualities or characteristics of something

definite adj. clear and firm (opposite **indefinite**)

definitely adv. without doubt

definition noun. meaning

definitive adj. that is the final word on a subject

defraud verb. (defrauded, defrauding) cheat

degree noun. 1. a measurement for heat 2. a measurement of an angle 3. a university or college title to show that you have studied there and passed examinations

delay verb. (delayed, delaying) put off until a later time; postpone —**delay** noun.

delegate noun. someone who is sent to a conference as a representative

delegate verb. (delegated, delegating) 1. give power to someone for a limited time 2. appoint as representative

delegation noun. a group of delegates

delete verb. (deleted, deleting) take out something that someone has written

deliberate verb. (deliberated, deliberating) think about or discuss seriously before making a decision

deliberate adj. intentional; planned

deliberately adv. on purpose

delicacy noun. a rare and expensive food

delicate adj. 1. easily broken 2. finely made 3. small and pretty 4. sensitive; needing tact —**delicately** adv.

delicious adj. very tasty; having a wonderful smell

delight noun. someone or something that gives you pleasure

delighted adj. very pleased

delightful adj. charming; giving pleasure

deliver verb. (delivered, delivering) bring something to someone —**delivery** noun.

delta noun. 1. the fourth letter of the Greek alphabet 2. the area near the mouth of a river that is shaped like the Greek letter delta

deluxe adj. luxurious; of high quality; elegant

demand verb. (demanded, demanding) say that someone must have or do something —**demand** noun.

demobilize *verb.* **(demobilized, demobilizing)** release soldiers after army service

democracy *noun.* (a country with) government that is elected by the people

democrat *noun.* **1.** someone who believes in democracy **2.** **(Democrat)** a supporter or member of the Democratic Party

democratic *adj.* belonging to, or characteristic of, democracy

demonstrate *verb.* **(demonstrated, demonstrating) 1.** show how something works **2.** show strong feeling about something by going out into the street with other people —**demonstrator** *noun.*

demonstration *noun.* **1.** a showing of how something works **2.** a show of strong feeling for or against something by a group of people

den *noun.* **1.** a home of certain wild animals **2.** a comfortable room in a house, for relaxing, watching TV, etc

denomination *noun.* **1.** the value of a certain coin or bill **2.** a religious category

dense *adj.* **1.** difficult to see or go through **2.** (slang) stupid

dent *noun.* *verb.* **(dented, denting)** (make) a small hollow

dental *adj.* connected with the teeth

dentist *noun.* someone who takes care of people's teeth

deny *verb.* **(denied, denying) 1.** say you did not do something; declare untrue **2.** refuse to allow —**denial** *noun.*

deodorant *noun.* a cosmetic that you put under your arms so that you will smell good

depart *verb.* **(departed, departing)** leave —**departure** *noun.*

department *noun.* a part of a big organization such as a government, a university, a company, etc, that deals with a specific thing —**departmental** *adj.*

department store *noun.* a large store that has different departments for different kinds of things

depend *verb.* **(depended, depending) 1.** happen only under certain conditions **2.** rely on; be supported by

dependable *adj.* that can be relied on

dependence *noun.* a great need for something or someone

dependent *adj.* **1.** depending on someone else for food, clothing, etc **2.** that will be decided on —**dependent** *noun.*

depict *verb.* **(depicted, depicting)** describe or show

deposit *noun.* **1.** money that you put in the bank **2.** paying part of the money for something immediately and the rest later

deposit *verb.* **(deposited, depositing)** put money in your bank account

depot *noun.* **1.** a storage place **2.** a small bus station

depreciate *verb.* **(depreciated, depreciating)** fall in value

depreciation *noun.* loss of value

depress *verb.* **(depressed, depressing) 1.** cause to feel sad **2.** cause to be less active

depressed *adj.* feeling very sad for a long time —**depressing** *adj.*

depression *noun.* **1.** a continued period of little business activity **2.** the mental state of being depressed

deprive *verb.* **(deprived, depriving)** take something from someone; stop someone from having something —**deprived** *adj.*

depth *noun.* how deep something is; how far something is from the top

deputy *noun.* **1.** an official who is next in rank or is in charge when someone is away **2.** someone who is appointed by a sheriff to help him

derive *verb.* **(derived, deriving)** get something from something else

dermatologist *noun.* a doctor who is an expert in skin diseases

descend verb. (**descended, descending**) go down

descendant noun. a person who has a historical family connection with somebody

describe verb. (**described, describing**) tell what something is like or the way something happened —**description** noun. —**descriptive** adj.

desert noun. a large area of dry land without water or plant life

deserted adj. abandoned; without anyone inside

deserve verb. (**deserved**) ought to have something; earn

design noun. **1.** a drawing that shows how to make something **2.** a plan **3.** a pattern

design verb. (**designed, designing**) make a plan; invent —**designer** noun.

desire noun. something that you want strongly

desire verb. (**desired, desiring**) (formal) want something very badly —**desirable** adj. (opposite **undesirable**)

desk noun. a table where you sit to write

desktop adj. using a small computer

despair noun. loss of hope or confidence —**despair** verb. (**despaired, despairing**)

desperate adj. ready to do anything because of loss of hope —**desperately** adv. —**desperation** noun.

despise verb. (**despised, despising**) feel contempt for

despite prep. without letting something bad stop you; in spite of (despite the bad weather, without **of**; in spite of the bad weather, with **of**)

dessert noun. something sweet at the end of a meal

destination noun. the place where someone or something in going

destroy verb. (**destroyed, destroying**) do damage that cannot be fixed

destruction noun. the act of destroying or being destroyed —**destructive** adj.

detail noun. a particular fact (where, when, what color, how big, etc) about something —**detail** verb. (**detailed, detailing**)

detain verb. (**detained, detaining**) keep a person from going

detect verb. (**detected, detecting**) notice or discover something —**detection** noun. —**detector** noun.

detective noun. someone whose job is to investigate crimes, etc

detergent noun. a powder or liquid for washing clothes, dishes, etc

determine verb. (**determined, determining**) form a decision; find out exactly —**determination** noun.

devaluation noun. the reduction in value of something (usually the exchange rate of currencies)

develop verb. (**developed, developing**) **1.** become bigger **2.** make bigger or more advanced **3.** discover and work on something **4.** use chemicals on a film to bring out the photograph

developer noun. **1.** someone who builds on land with hopes of making a profit **2.** a chemical used to develop photographs

development noun. **1.** becoming bigger (no plural) **2.** making bigger (no plural) **3.** a new fact, event or discovery —**developmental** adv.

device noun. a small, useful instrument

devil noun. the spirit of evil

devise verb. (**devised, devising**) cleverly invent or plan something

devote verb. (**devoted, devoting**) set aside for a person or purpose

devotion noun. loyalty; great affection for a person or cause

dew noun. drops of water that form on cool surfaces during the night

diagnose verb. (**diagnosed, diagnosing**) examine in order to find the reason for a (health) problem

diagnosis noun. a doctor's decision

about what illness you have (plural **diagnoses**)

diagonal *noun. adj.* (a straight line) going from one corner to the opposite one of a square or rectangle

diagram *noun.* a design on paper that explains how something is made or how it works

dial *noun.* **1.** the round disk at the front of a telephone **2.** the button on a radio or a measuring instrument **3.** the face of a clock or watch

dial *verb.* (**dialed, dialing; dialled, dialling**) make a phone call

dialect *noun.* a variety of a language, used in a certain area of a country or by a certain group of people

diamond *noun.* **1.** a precious stone that reflects light **2.** one of the red shapes on a playing card

diaper *noun.* a basic piece of clothing worn by a baby that is made of absorbent material, drawn up between its legs and fastened at the waist

diaper *verb.* (**diapered, diapering**) put a diaper on a baby

diary *noun.* a private book that you write in

dice *noun plural.* small cubes marked with dots to indicate numbers that is used in games

dictate *verb.* (**dictated, dictating**) say something aloud for someone else to copy

dictator *noun.* a ruler who has complete power

dictionary *noun.* a book that gives you the spelling, definition (and other information) of words

did *verb.* past of **do**
—**didn't** *abbr.* = did not

die *verb.* (**died, dying**) come to the end of life

diesel *noun.* a heavy fuel used in certain engines

diet *noun.* **1.** what you eat **2.** a plan for losing weight

diet *verb.* (**dieted, dieting**) be on a diet, in order to lose weight —**dieter** *noun.*

differ *verb.* (**differed, differing**) **1.** not to be like something else in character, quality, etc **2.** disagree

difference *noun.* what is not the same

different *adj.* **1.** not the same **2.** more than one —**differently** *adv.*

differentiate *verb.* (**differentiated, differentiating**) distinguish; show or identify differences

difficult *adj.* **1.** not easy; hard **2.** hard to deal with

difficulty *noun.* **1.** trouble; the need for effort (no plural) **2.** a problem

diffuse *verb.* (**diffused, diffusing**) spread out evenly in all directions —**diffusion** *noun.*

dig *verb.* (**dug, digging**) take earth out of the ground

digest *verb.* (**digested, digesting**) **1.** change food in the stomach so that the body can use it **2.** understand new and difficult information —**digestive** *adj.*

digestion *noun.* what the body does to change food into a form it can use (no plural)

digital *adj.* showing only the numbers

dignified *adj.* calm and formal

dignity *noun.* calm formality; self-respect

dilemma *noun.* a situation where you have to make a difficult choice

diligence *noun.* hard work to get what you want (no plural)

diligent *adj.* serious and hard-working

dilute *verb.* (**diluted, diluting**) make a liquid weaker by adding another liquid to it —**dilution** *noun.*

dim *adj.* **1.** not bright **2.** not clear **3.** not intelligent

dim *verb.* (**dimmed, dimming**) make a light less bright

dime *noun.* a coin worth ten cents (one tenth of a dollar)

dimension *noun.* **1.** the measurement

of one direction in space **2.** a side of a problem

diminish *verb.* **(diminished, diminishing)** become less; become smaller

dimly *adv.* **1.** not brightly **2.** not clearly

din *noun.* loud and unpleasant noise (no plural)

dine *verb.* **(dined, dining)** (formal) have dinner

diner *noun.* a simple restaurant

dining room *noun.* the room where people eat

dinner *noun.* the largest meal of the day

dinosaur *noun.* a very large prehistoric animal

dip *noun.* something tasty and soft that you can put crackers, celery sticks, etc, into

dip *verb.* **(dipped, dipping)** put something into liquid and take it out again

diploma *noun.* a certificate that proves you have completed your studies and passed the tests at a certain school

diplomat *noun.* an official representative of his/her country abroad

diplomatic *adj.* **1.** concerning being a diplomat **2.** tactful; skilled in dealing with people

direct *adj.* **1.** straight through; without stopping **2.** straight; honest

direct *verb.* **(directed, directing) 1.** show someone which way to go **2.** coordinate or supervise a process, event, project, etc

direction *noun.* way

directions *noun plural.* instructions

directly *adv.* **1.** straight through; without stopping **2.** right away

director *noun.* **1.** a manager **2.** someone who directs actors in the making of plays or films

directory *noun.* a book that contains lists, usually in alphabetical order

dirt *noun.* anything that makes something unclean (mud, dust, etc)

dirty *adj.* **1.** unclean **2.** nasty; unkind — **dirty** *verb.* **(dirtied, dirtying)**

disability *noun.* a handicap

disabled *adj.* not being able to do something because of a physical or mental limitation

disadvantage *noun.* something that makes things more difficult (opposite **advantage**)

disadvantaged *adj.* lacking basic economic and social conditions thought of as necessary to be part of society

disagree *verb.* **(disagreed, disagreeing)** have a different opinion (opposite **agree**)

disagreement *noun.* **1.** a difference of opinion (no plural) **2.** an argument

disappear *verb.* **(disappeared, disappearing)** no longer be seen (opposite **appear**) —**disappearance** *noun.*

disappoint *verb.* **(disappointed, disappointing)** not do what someone hoped you would

disappointed *adj.* sad because something wasn't good enough —**disappointing** *adj.* —**disappointment** *noun.*

disapprove *verb.* **(disapproved, disapproving)** think that something is wrong or bad —**disapproval** *noun.*

disaster *noun.* **1.** a large and terrible happening **2.** a terrible event in someone's life

disastrous *adj.* terrible

disbelief *noun.* inability to believe something even if you see it

disc, disk *noun.* **1.** something that is round and flat **2.** a record (for playing music)

discharge *verb.* **(discharged, discharging) 1.** dismiss; fire **2.** send home **3.** send out gas, smoke, etc

disciple *noun.* a follower of a religious leader

discipline *verb.* **(disciplined, disciplining) 1.** train a person or an animal to obey **2.** punish —**discipline** *noun.* (no plural) —**disciplinary** *adj.*

disclosure *noun.* something that is made known, especially a secret

disco, discotheque noun. a place where people dance to music

discomfort noun. the state of being uncomfortable

discontinue verb. **(discontinued, discontinuing)** stop something that used to happen regularly

discount noun. money that is taken off the price of something; reduction —**discount** verb. **(discounted, discounting)**

discourage verb. **(discouraged, discouraging)** make someone feel that he/she is not good enough for something; take away confidence

discover verb. **(discovered, discovering)** 1. be the first to find something 2. find out something

discovery noun. finding something for the first time

discreet adj. tactful; careful in what you say or do so that you do not insult (opposite **indiscreet**) —**discreetly** adv.

discrepancy noun. no similarity; lacking agreement

discrete adj. separate; distinct

discriminate verb. **(discriminated, discriminating)** 1. see a difference between 2. treat someone differently (better or worse) —**discrimination** noun. —**discriminatory** adj.

discuss verb. **(discussed, discussing)** talk about something —**discussion** noun.

disease noun. an illness

disgrace verb. **(disgraced, disgracing)** bring shame on —**disgrace** noun. —**disgraceful** adj.

disguise noun. something that changes the way someone or something looks

disguise verb. **(disguised, disguising)** change the way someone or something looks to hide the real thing

disgust noun. a sick feeling that you get when you see or hear something nasty

disgust verb. **(disgusted, disgusting)** make someone feel sick —**disgusting** adj.

dish noun. 1. a plate or bowl 2. a particular food

dishonest adj. intending to cheat or lie (opposite **honest**) —**dishonesty** noun. (no plural; opposite **honesty**)

dishwasher noun. a machine that washes dishes

disillusioned adj. disappointed because you have lost your belief in something

disk noun. 1. something that is round and flat 2. a computer accessory used for storing information 3. a disc

dislike verb. **(disliked, disliking)** feel that something or someone is unpleasant (opposite **like, enjoy**)

dismantle verb. **(dismantled, dismantling)** take apart

dismay noun. a feeling of disappointment and discouragement

dismiss verb. **(dismissed, dismissing)** 1. allow to leave 2. send away from a job 3. refuse to think about something —**dismissal** noun.

disobedience noun. not doing what you are told to do (no plural; opposite **obedience**) —**disobedient** adj. (opposite **obedient**)

disobey verb. **(disobeyed, disobeying)** not do what you are told to do (opposite **obey**)

disorder noun. 1. a mess; untidiness; confusion (no plural) 2. rioting in the streets (no plural) 3. something that is wrong with the mind or the body

disorganized adj. without order or organization (opposite **organized**)

dispatch verb. **(dispatched, dispatching)** send out

dispense verb. **(dispensed, dispensing)** 1. give something to a number of people 2. prepare medication according to a prescription

display verb. **(displayed, displaying)** show —**display** noun.

displease verb. **(displeased, displeasing)** annoy someone

displeased (with) adj. not satisfied; not happy about something

disposable adj. intended to be used once and then thrown away

dispose verb. **(disposed, disposing)** throw away; get rid of **—disposal** noun.

disproportionate adj. without proportion; too much or too little in relation to something else **—disproportionately** adv.

disprove verb. **(disproved, disproving)** prove something to be untrue

dispute noun. a disagreement; a quarrel

dispute verb. **(disputed, disputing)** disagree with; challenge

disqualify verb. **(disqualified, disqualifying)** declare unsuitable or unable **— disqualification** noun.

disregard verb. **(disregard, disregarding)** pay no attention to

disrupt verb. **(disrupted, disrupting)** disturb; interrupt; cause disorder

dissatisfied adj. unhappy about something; displeased

dissatisfy verb. **(dissatisfied, dissatisfying)** displease **—dissatisfaction** noun.

dissertation noun. a (long) written work done in order to get a high academic degree

dissolve verb. **(dissolved, dissolving)** melt completely in a liquid

dissuade verb. **(dissuaded, dissuading)** persuade not to do something

distance noun. how far it is from one point to another

distant adj. **1.** far away **2.** not closely related in the family

distillery noun. a factory where alcoholic drinks (especially whiskey) are produced

distinct adj. **1.** clear; easy to see, hear or understand **2.** separate; different

distinction noun. **1.** a clear difference **2.** a mark of quality, honor or fame

distinctive adj. clearly marking someone or something as particular to that person or thing

distinctly adv. clearly

distinguish verb. **(distinguished, distinguishing)** see or make a difference

distinguished adj. **1.** well known for his/her work **2.** looking very dignified

distort verb. **(distorted, distorting) 1.** tell facts incorrectly **2.** twist; give an unusual shape to

distract verb. **(distracted, distracting)** take your mind off what you are doing

distress noun. misery; suffering (no plural)

distress verb. **(distressed, distressing)** cause sadness and suffering

distribute verb. **(distributed, distributing)** give out or send out something **— distribution** noun.

distributor noun. **1.** a person or company that distributes something **2.** a car part that sends electricity to the spark plug

district noun. a division of a country or city for a certain purpose

distrust verb. **(distrusted, distrusting)** think that someone may not be honest (opposite **trust**)

disturb verb. **(disturbed, disturbing)** interrupt your thinking, sleeping or conversation; bother someone

disturbance noun. **1.** something that bothers you **2.** a lot of noise made by people shouting and fighting

ditch noun. a narrow channel in the earth for carrying water

dive verb. **(dived/dove, diving) 1.** jump into water with your head and arms first **2.** go under water **—dive** noun.

diver noun. someone who wears special clothes to dive

diverse adj. showing a variety **—diversity** noun. (plural **diversities**)

diversify verb. **(diversified, diversifying)** make a variety **—diversification** noun. **—diversified** adj.

divert verb. **(diverted, diverting)** change the direction of

divide *verb.* **(divided, dividing) 1.** separate into two or more parts **2.** separate something into two or more parts **3.** find out how many times one number will go into another number

dividend *noun.* an amount of the profits of a company that is given to shareholders

division *noun.* **1.** something that separates two things **2.** the separating of something into parts (no plural) **3.** finding out how many times one number goes into another number (no plural) **4.** a part of a larger thing **5.** a group of units in the army —**divisional** *adj.*

divorce *noun.* the end of a marriage by law —**divorce** *verb.* **(divorced, divorcing)** —**divorced** *adj.*

dizzy *adj.* **(dizzier, dizziest)** feeling that things around you are spinning and you may fall

dizzy *verb.* **(dizzied, dizzying)** make dizzy; cause to be confused

DJ *noun.* disc jockey; someone who plays records or CDs as a job

do *verb.* **(did, done, doing) 1.** perform or carry out an action **2.** have a job, a profession or an occupation **3.** make a difference **4.** make progress **5.** a helping verb used to form questions and negatives in the simple tenses **6.** a word that says something very strongly **7.** a verb that replaces another verb that has already been used (**he, she, it** use **does** in the present simple tense)

dock *noun.* a place where ships come for loading, repair, etc

dock *verb.* **(docked, docking) 1.** moor a ship at a harbor pier **2.** the joining of spaceships together in space

doctor *noun.* **1.** someone who has a license to practice medicine; a physician **2.** someone who has a PhD (the highest academic degree) from a university in a certain subject

document *noun.* an official paper with important information —**document** *verb.* **(documented, documenting)**

documentary *noun.* a film that gives information about a particular subject (plural **documentaries**)

documentation *noun.* papers that prove that something is correct

dodge *verb.* **(dodged, dodging)** get out of the way of something

doe *noun.* a female deer or rabbit

does *verb.* see **do**

doesn't *abbr.* = does not

dog *noun.* an animal that people keep as a pet or guard

dogmatic *adj.* believing without question that your opinions are totally right for everyone

dole *noun.* money given to the unemployed by the government

doll *noun.* a toy that looks like a person

dollar *noun.* the unit of money used in the U.S., Canada and some other countries; $

dolly *noun.* a child's word for doll

dolphin *noun.* a sea mammal of high intelligence that swims in groups

domain *noun.* **1.** area of interest, activity or knowledge **2.** (computers) an Internet address (also **domain name**)

dome *noun.* a roof that is high and round

domestic *adj.* **1.** connected with the home or the family **2.** trained to live with people; not wild

dominant *adj.* **1.** strong; powerful **2.** the most important

dominate *verb.* **(dominated, dominating)** have control over

domination *noun.* rule over another

domino *noun.* **1.** a flat, black piece with white dots that is used in a game **2.** a game that is played with **dominoes** (plural)

donate *verb.* **(donated, donating)** give money, food, clothing, time, blood, etc, to something that you think is important —**donation** *noun.*

done *verb.* past participle of **do**

donkey *noun.* **1.** an animal like a small horse that is used for riding or carrying heavy things **2.** a fool

donor *noun.* someone who donates something

don't *abbr.* = do not

door *noun.* a board or panel that you can open or shut to go into a room, closet, etc.

doorbell *noun.* a bell or buzzer that you ring if you want someone to answer the door

doorway *noun.* the entrance to a building or a room, where the door opens

dormitory *noun.* a building where live-in students sleep (plural **dormitories**; short form **dorm**)

dose *noun.* a specific amount of something that someone must take at one time

dot *noun.* a point —**dot** *verb.* **(dotted, dotting)**

double *noun.* someone who looks exactly like someone else

double *verb.* **(doubled, doubling) 1.** make twice the size or twice as much **2.** become twice as big or twice as much **3.** use two of something

double *adj.* **1.** twice the amount **2.** having two parts **3.** for two people **4.** appearing twice

doubt *noun.* uncertainty

doubt *verb.* **(doubted, doubting)** think that something is probably not true or may not happen

doubtful *adj.* **1.** not likely to happen **2.** having a feeling of uncertainty — **doubtfully** *adv.*

dough *noun.* a thick mixture of flour and water used for making bread and cake

dove *noun.* a bird like a pigeon with a soft call

down *adv.* **1.** from the top toward the bottom **2.** from a higher place to a lower place **3.** to the ground

down *adj.* **1.** sad **2.** (computers) not working

down *prep.* **1.** from a higher place to a lower one **2.** along

down *noun.* soft under feathers of geese or ducks, used to make warm blankets and clothing

downgrade *verb.* **(downgraded, downgrading) 1.** move a person to a lower level job in a company **2.** make something seem unimportant

downhill *adv.* **1.** sloping toward the bottom of a hill **2.** (slang) easier

down payment *noun.* a deposit; part of a payment

downpour *noun.* a sudden heavy rain

downright *adv. adj.* absolute; complete (usually refers to something negative)

downstairs *adv. adj.* on or to a lower floor (opposite **upstairs**)

downtown *noun.* the center of the city

downtown *adj. adv.* located in or going to the center of the city

downward *adj.* going toward a lower place

downward, downwards *adv.* toward the bottom (opposite **upward(s)**)

doze *verb.* **(dozed, dozing)** sleep lightly for a little while

dozen *noun.* twelve of something

draft *noun.* **1.** a first copy of something that you write, such as a composition or a speech **2.** requiring people to serve in the armed forces

draft *noun.* a cold wind inside a room

draft *verb.* **(drafted, drafting) 1.** write a draft **2.** require to serve in the armed forces

drag *verb.* **(dragged, dragging) 1.** pull something along the ground **2.** move very slowly

dragon *noun.* a big, imaginary animal found in stories

drain *noun.* a pipe that carries dirty water away

drain *verb.* **(drained, draining) 1.** flow away through a pipe or a channel **2.** let something become dry **3.** make something drier by taking away the liquid

drama *noun.* **1.** a play **2.** excitement; tension; conflict (no plural)

dramatic *adj.* **1.** exciting; impressive **2.** connected to dramas **—dramatically** *adv.*

dramatist *noun.* an author of plays

dramatize *verb.* **(dramatized, dramatizing) 1.** make into a play **2.** present something or react to a situation in an exaggerated and dramatic way

drank *verb.* past of **drink**

drape *noun.* the way a material falls or how a cloth is cut

drastic *adj.* extreme; very serious

drastically *adv.* severely

draw *noun.* a situation where nobody wins or loses

draw *verb.* **(drew, drawn, drawing) 1.** make a picture with a pencil, crayon, chalk, etc **2.** pull something **3.** pull or take something out of something else

drawback *noun.* a disadvantage

drawer *noun.* a type of box that you can pull out from a desk, cupboard, cabinet, etc

drawing *noun.* **1.** making pictures with a pencil, crayon, etc (no plural) **2.** a picture that is made with a pencil, crayon, etc

drawn *verb.* past participle of **draw**

dread *noun.* a feeling of terrible fear about something that may happen (no plural) **—dread** *verb.* **(dreaded, dreading)**

dreadful *adj.* terrible

dream *noun.* **1.** pictures and thoughts that come into your mind while you are sleeping **2.** something that you wish for and think about constantly

dream *verb.* **(dreamed/dreamt, dreaming) 1.** see pictures and images in your mind while you are sleeping **2.** have a hope or wish that you think about constantly **—dreamer** *noun.*

dreamy *adj.* **1.** unclear (thoughts); more in the imagination than connected to real life **2.** (slang) wonderful

dreary *adj.* **(drearier, dreariest)** dull; boring; without excitement or color

dress *noun.* **1.** a piece of clothing that women or girls wear that has an attached top and a skirt **2.** the kind of clothing that people wear in a certain place or for a particular event (no plural)

dress *verb.* **(dressed, dressing) 1.** put on clothes **2.** wear a certain kind of clothes **3.** put clothes on someone else

dressing *noun.* a bandage on a wound or a burn

dressing room *noun.* a special room for changing clothes

dressing table *noun.* a small, low bedroom table with a mirror

drew *verb.* past of **draw**

dried *verb.* past of **dry**

dried *adj.* with all the liquid taken out

drift *verb.* **(drifted, drifting)** float on water or air

drill *noun.* **1.** a tool or machine that makes holes **2.** an exercise that is done again and again

drill *verb.* **(drilled, drilling) 1.** make a hole by using a drill **2.** train people to do something so that they do it perfectly

drink *noun.* **1.** any liquid that you take into your mouth **2.** something alcoholic

drink *verb.* **(drank, drunk, drinking) 1.** take liquid into your mouth **2.** take something alcoholic into your mouth

drip *verb.* **(dripped, dripping)** fall or allow to fall drop by drop **—dripping** *adj. adv.*

drive *noun.* **1.** a car trip **2.** energy and ambition (no plural) **3.** a small street **4.** an organized effort to collect money, clothes, etc, for something **5.** part of a computer **6.** see driveway

drive *verb.* **(drove, driven, driving) 1.** make a motor vehicle move **2.** go somewhere in a car **3.** take someone

65

someplace by car **4.** make someone do something bad —**driving** noun. adj.

driven verb. past participle of **drive**

driver noun. someone who drives a car, bus, etc

driveway noun. a small private path for a car beside or in front of a house (also **drive**)

drizzle noun. a very light rain (no plural)

drop noun. **1.** a very small amount of liquid **2.** a fall in the amount of something, such as temperature, price, etc

drop verb. (**dropped, dropping**) **1.** fall **2.** let something fall **3.** become lower

drought noun. a long period of dry weather

drove verb. past of **drive**

drown verb. (**drowned, drowning**) **1.** die in water because you cannot breathe **2.** kill someone or something with water

drug noun. **1.** a medicine **2.** a dangerous substance that makes changes in your body and your mind —**drug** verb. (**drugged, drugging**)

drugstore noun. a store that sells medicines, cosmetics and some other things

drum noun. a musical instrument that you beat on with your hands or with sticks —**drum** verb. (**drummed, drumming**)

drummer noun. someone who plays the drums

drunk noun. someone in a drunken condition

drunk verb. past participle of **drink**

drunk adj. out of control because of drinking too much alcohol

drunken adj. under the influence of alcohol

dry adj. **1.** not wet; having no water in it **2.** not rainy

dry verb. (**dried, drying**) **1.** become dry **2.** make something become dry

dryer, drier noun. a machine for drying something

duchess noun. a noblewoman; the wife of a duke (plural **duchesses**)

duck noun. a bird with short legs that swims and sometimes lives on farms

duck verb. (**ducked, ducking**) **1.** bend down quickly to avoid being hit (in the head) by something **2.** push under water for a short time

dude noun. (slang) a city man

due adj. **1.** that must be paid or returned **2.** expected

dues noun plural. money paid to an organization in order to be a member

duel noun. a formal fight using swords or guns to settle an argument or a point of honor

duet noun. a song or a piece of music for two people

dug verb. past tense and past participle of **dig**

duke noun. a nobleman

dull adj. **1.** not bright **2.** not interesting; boring **3.** not strong

duly adv. as expected; properly

dumb adj. **1.** not able to talk **2.** (informal) stupid

dummy noun. **1.** a doll that looks like a person **2.** an object that looks like another thing but is not **3.** (slang) someone stupid

dump verb. (**dumped, dumping**) **1.** put something down in a careless way **2.** throw away —**dump** noun.

dune noun. a low sand hill

duplicate verb. (**duplicated, duplicating**) make an exact copy of something; repeat

durable adj. long-lasting; strong

duration noun. (formal) the time that something lasts

during prep. **1.** for the whole time of **2.** at some point in time

dusk noun. evening; the time when it begins to get dark (no plural)

dust noun. dirt that is like dry powder

dust verb. (**dusted, dusting**) wipe away dust

dusty *adj.* **(dustier, dustiest)** covered with dust

Dutch *noun.* the language or people of the Netherlands (Holland) **—Dutch** *adj.*

duty *noun.* **1.** whatever you must do **2.** a tax that you must pay for bringing something into a country (plural **duties**)

duty-free *adj.* without duty

dwarf *noun.* **1.** a person, animal or plant that does not grow to the usual size **2.** a tiny person in a fairy tale

dwell *verb.* **(dwelled/dwelt, dwelling)** live **—dweller** *noun.*

dwindle *verb.* **(dwindled, dwindling)** become less

dye *noun.* something that changes the color of cloth, hair, paper, egg shells, etc **—dye** *verb.* **(dyed, dyeing) — dyed** *adj.*

dynamic *adj.* full of energy

dynamics *noun.* the science that deals with the movement of matter or objects

dynamite *noun.* a powerful explosive

dynasty *noun.* a family line of kings and queens

E

each *adj. pron.* **1.** every one of a certain group **2.** for every one separately

each other *pron.* two people doing or feeling the same thing one to the other

eager *adj.* **(more eager, the most eager)** wanting very much to do something —**eagerness** *noun.*

eagerly *adv.* excitedly; enthusiastically

eagle *noun.* a large, powerful bird

eagle-eyed *adj.* having very sharp eyesight

ear *noun.* the part of the body that hears

earache *noun.* a pain in the ear

earl *noun.* a high ranking British nobleman

early *adj. adv.* **1.** near the beginning of something **2.** before the usual time.

earn *verb.* **(earned, earning) 1.** get money for work that you do **2.** deserve something good

earring *noun.* a piece of jewelry for your ear

earsplitting *adj.* extremely loud and piercing (sound)

earth *noun.* **1.** (usually **Earth**) the planet that we live on **2.** soil; the ground **3.** (sometimes **Earth**) the world

earthquake *noun.* a strong sudden movement of the ground

ease *noun.* the ability to do something without difficulty

ease *verb.* **(eased, easing) 1.** make less difficult **2.** become less tense **3.** move carefully into a different position

easel *noun.* a board covered with a piece of canvas that artists use for painting

easily *adv.* with no trouble

east *noun.* one of the four directions (north, south, east and west) —**east** *adj.*

east *adv.* toward the east

Easter *noun.* a Christian holiday

eastern *adj.* **1.** in the east **2.** of the east

eastward, eastwards *adv.* toward the east

easy *adj.* **(easier, easiest)** not difficult

easy chair *noun.* a soft, comfortable armchair

easygoing *adj.* with a relaxed attitude toward life

eat *verb.* **(ate, eaten, eating)** take food into your body —**eater** *noun.*

eccentric *adj.* behaving in a strange manner that is not acceptable by social standards

echo *noun.* a sound that comes back to you (plural **echoes**) —**echo** *verb.* **(echoed, echoing)**

eclectic *adj.* not following or using one specific system, method, style, etc, but a combination of many different ones

eclipse *noun.* the disappearance of all or part of the moon when the shadow of the Earth falls on it

ecology *noun.* the relationship of living things to their surroundings (no plural) —**ecological** *adj.* —**ecologically** *adv.* —**ecologist** *noun.*

economic *adj.* **1.** connected with trade, business and finance **2.** profitable

economical *adj.* **1.** not expensive to use **2.** not wasting money, time or energy —**economically** *adv.*

economics *noun.* the study of how countries produce goods and make money (used with a singular verb)

economist *noun.* someone who specializes in economics

economize *verb.* **(economized, economizing)** spend less money

economy *noun.* **1.** the financial and industrial system of a country **2.** the careful use of money

ecstasy noun. a feeling of great joy (plural **ecstasies**)

edge noun. 1. the line where something ends 2. the sharp cutting line of a blade

edge verb. **(edged, edging)** 1. put a decoration, such as lace, fringes, etc, on the outer part of something 2. move slowly with small movements

edgy adj. nervous and easily angered

edit verb. **(edited, editing)** prepare for printing, broadcast, etc, by deciding what should be included and what should not in addition to correcting mistakes

edition noun. all the copies of a newspaper, magazine or book that are published at one time

editor noun. 1. someone who makes changes in a text before it is published or shown 2. someone who is responsible for what to print or show in a book, magazine, newspaper, TV program, etc

editorial noun. adj. an article that the editor of a newspaper or magazine writes to give his/her own opinion

editor-in-chief noun. the editor responsible for the work of other editors of a publishing house, newspaper, etc

educate verb. **(educated, educating)** 1. teach or train someone in a school 2. teach children what is right and what is wrong, what they may or may not do, etc

educated adj. having formal teaching or training

education noun. teaching that you receive in school, etc —**educational** adj.

effect noun. what happens because of something else; a result

effect verb. **(effected, effecting)** make happen as a result

effective adj. bringing good results — **effectiveness** noun.

effectively adv. in fact even if it doesn't seem so

efficiency noun. the ability to do something well, quickly and without a waste of time and energy (opposite **inefficiency**)

efficient adj. working well, quickly and without waste (opposite **inefficient**) — **efficiently** adv. (opposite **inefficiently**)

effort noun. hard work; trying hard

egg noun. something round with a shell that the mother bird lays and the baby bird comes out of

Egyptian noun. adj. from Egypt

eight noun. adj. the number 8

eighteen noun. adj. the number 18

eighteenth noun. adj. = 18th

eighth noun. adj. = 8th

eightieth noun. adj. = 80th

eighty noun. adj. the number 80

either adj. 1. one of two 2. one and the other of two; each

either pron. one or the other of two

either...or conj. one or the other of two

elaborate verb. **(elaborated, elaborating)** add more information or details

elaborate adj. with a lot of details

elbow noun. the place where the upper part of your arm joins with the lower part

elder adj. noun. the older of two people (also **older** for people and things; opposite **younger**)

elderly adj. noun. a polite word for **old**

eldest adj. noun. the first-born; the oldest of three or more people (also **oldest** for people and things; opposite **youngest**)

elect verb. **(elected, electing)** choose by voting

election noun. choosing a leader by voting

elective adj. 1. filled or chosen by voting 2. optional

electric adj. working by electricity

electrical adj. 1. working by electricity; electric 2. connected with electricity — **electrically** adv.

electrician *noun.* someone who repairs the wiring in a building or electrical appliances

electricity *noun.* the energy that comes through electrical wires (no plural)

electric shock *noun.* the shock that you get if an electric current runs through your body

electronic *adj.* using devices that control electricity going through a radio, TV, computer, etc —**electronically** *adv.*

electronics *noun.* the study of or making things that work electronically

elegant *adj.* stylish and tasteful —**elegance** *noun.* (no plural) —**elegantly** *adv.*

element *noun.* **1.** a basic chemical substance that is found in nature **2.** a small amount of something **3.** one part of something larger

elementary *adj.* for beginners

elementary school *noun.* a primary school for the first six to eight years of education; a grade school

elephant *noun.* a very large animal that lives in Africa and Asia

elevator *noun.* a kind of cage in a building for carrying people from one floor to another

eleven *noun. adj.* the number 11

eleventh *noun. adj.* = 11th

elicit *verb.* (**elicit, eliciting**) get information from someone, usually after some effort

eligible *adj.* fitting the necessary requirements in order to be chosen — **eligibility** *noun.*

eliminate *verb.* (**eliminated, eliminating**) get rid of

elite *noun.* a group that considers itself to be the best; the highest class

elm *noun.* a large tree with broad leaves

else *adv.* **1.** more; in addition **2.** other

elsewhere *adv.* in a different place

e-mail, email *noun.* **1.** a message sent electronically by computer **2.** the system of electronic mail (no plural)

e-mail email, *verb.* (**e-mailed, e-mailing**) send mail, documents, etc, electronically by computer

embargo *noun.* an official order forbidding trade with another country

embark *verb.* (**embarked, embarking**) get on a plane or a ship to take a trip (opposite **disembark**)

embarrass *verb.* (**embarrassed, embarrassing**) make someone feel uncomfortable or ashamed

embarrassing *adj.* making you feel uncomfortable among other people

embarrassment *noun.* being embarrassed

embassy *noun.* a building where a group of diplomats represent their own country in another country (plural **embassies**)

embrace *verb.* (**embraced, embracing**) put your arms around someone — **embrace** *noun.*

emerald *noun.* **1.** a precious green stone **2.** a very green color —**emerald** *adj.*

emerge *verb.* (**emerged, emerging**) come out

emergency *noun.* a sudden dangerous situation which needs attention immediately (plural **emergencies**) —**emergency** *adj.*

emigrant *noun.* someone who leaves his/her own country to live in another country (an **immigrant** is someone who has come from another country)

emigrate *verb.* (**emigrated, emigrating**) leave your own country to go and live in another country —**emigration** *noun.*

emotion *noun.* **1.** an inner feeling **2.** a show of strong feeling

emotional *adj.* **1.** showing strong feeling **2.** causing people to show strong feeling —**emotionally** *adv.* (opposite **unemotionally**)

emperor *noun.* the ruler of an empire

emphasis *noun.* special attention given to something

emphasize verb. **(emphasized, emphasizing) 1.** point out the importance of something **2.** make something stand out in a picture or on a page

emphatic adj. said with force or emphasis

empire noun. a group of countries under the control of one strong country

employ verb. **(employed, employing)** have as a worker

employee noun. someone who works for someone else

employer noun. someone who has other people working for him/her

employment noun. **1.** a regular job **2.** something to do

empress noun. (plural **empresses**) a woman who rules an empire

empty adj. **1.** having nothing inside **2.** without people or traffic **3.** with no writing on it; blank

empty verb. **(emptied, emptying)** remove everything from inside — **emptiness** noun. (no plural)

empty-handed adj. without anything

emulate verb. **(emulated, emulating)** do as well as (or better than) someone else

enable verb. **(enabled, enabling)** make possible

enchant verb. **(enchanted, enchanting) 1.** use magic on someone or something **2.** charm and delight someone

enchanted adj. under a magic spell

enchanting adj. charming and delightful

enclave noun. a country or a group of people that is wholly within the boundaries of another country or majority group

enclose verb. **(enclosed, enclosing)** put something inside something else

enclosure noun. **1.** a place that is surrounded by a fence or wall **2.** something put inside an envelope along with a letter

encore noun. **1.** the call by an audience for a performer to give an additional performance **2.** the additional performance by a performer, especially a musician

encounter noun. a sudden meeting (usually unpleasant)

encounter verb. **(encountered, encountering) 1.** meet a problem or danger **2.** meet someone unexpectedly

encourage verb. **(encouraged, encouraging)** give support, approval, or confidence (opposite **discourage**) — **encouragement** noun.

encouraging adj. **1.** giving confidence and support **2.** bringing hope

encyclopedia noun. a book or set of books that gives information on many different subjects — **encyclopedic** adj.

end noun. **1.** the place where something finishes **2.** the last of something **3.** the tip of something

end verb. **(ended, ending)** be the last point; finish something

endanger verb. **(endangered, endangering)** put into a situation that may cause harm

ending noun. the way something finishes

endless adj. without an end

endlessly adv. without stopping

endorse verb. **(endorsed, endorsing) 1.** show support **2.** sign your name on the back of a check in order to receive cash for it

endorsement noun. **1.** your signature on the back of a check to enable it to be paid into your account **2.** a public statement of support or approval

endurance noun. (no plural) the ability to suffer pain or to keep going under hard conditions

endure verb. **(endured, enduring) 1.** be able to suffer or to survive under hard conditions **2.** be able to bear something

enemy noun. someone who wants to

harm you (plural **enemies**) —**enemy** adj.

energetic adj. strong and active; full of energy

energy noun. 1. the power that makes things move 2. the ability to be active and get things done

enforce verb. (**enforced, enforcing**) make sure a law is carried out — **enforceable** adj. —**enforcement** noun.

engage verb. (**engaged, engaging**) give work to someone

engagement noun. 1. a promise to marry someone 2. an appointment with someone

engine noun. 1. a machine that gives power to a vehicle or another machine; a motor 2. the locomotive of a train

engineer noun. someone who designs bridges and roads (= a civil engineer); someone who designs machines (= a mechanical engineer)

engineering noun. the science of the design and building of roads, bridges, machines, etc (no plural)

English noun. 1. the language of the U.S., Britain, Australia, etc, 2. the people of England
—**English** adj. of or relating to the English language or England

Englishman, Englishwoman noun. a man or woman from England (plural **Englishmen, Englishwomen**)

engrave verb. (**engraved, engraving**) to cut in stone, wood, metal, etc

enjoy verb. (**enjoyed, enjoying**) get pleasure from something —**enjoyable** adj.

enjoyment noun. pleasure that you receive from something

enlarge verb. (**enlarged, enlarging**) make bigger —**enlargement** noun.

enormous adj. 1. very big; huge 2. great

enormously adv. very

enough adj. adv. as much as necessary

enrichment noun. something added to make it a better quality or more — **enrich** verb. (**enriched, enriching**)

ensemble noun. 1. a group of musicians playing together 2. a set of things, especially clothes, which go together in order to make a single effect

ensure verb. (**ensured, ensuring**) make sure; promise; guarantee

entail verb. (**entailed, entailing**) involve; include what is necessary in order to get a certain result

enter verb. (**entered, entering**) 1. come in 2. become a member of or a student of

enterprise noun. 1. a way of organizing business projects 2. a plan that is difficult and/or challenging

enterprising adj. marked by an energetic spirit and willingness to experiment

entertain verb. (**entertained, entertaining**) 1. amuse; give someone a good time 2. have guests —**entertaining** adj. —**entertainment** noun.

entertainer noun. a performer

enthusiasm noun. strong interest and eagerness —**enthusiast** noun. —**enthusiastic** adj. —**enthusiastically** adv.

entire adj. whole; complete

entirely adv. completely

entirety noun. (formal) as a whole unit

entitle verb. (**entitled, entitling**) give someone rights to something

entitlement noun. the official right to receive something

entourage noun. people who accompany an important person

entrance noun. the place where you go in (opposite **exit**)

entry noun. 1. a way in (plural **entries**) 2. permission to come in (no plural)

envelope noun. a paper cover for a letter

envious adj. wishing that you were like someone else or had what someone else has; feeling envy

environment *noun.* **1.** all the world around us **2.** your family and neighborhood

environmental *adj.* relating to the environment

environmentalist *noun.* someone who supports environmental issues

envy *verb.* **(envied, envying)** wish you were more like someone else or had what someone else has —**envy** *noun.* (no plural)

epic *adj.* full of action; having heroic characteristics; bigger than life

epidemic *noun.* an illness that attacks many people

episode *noun.* **1.** one of several parts (of a radio or TV program) **2.** an incident

equal *noun.* someone who is as good as someone else

equal *adj.* the same

equal *verb.* **(equaled)** be the same as — **equality** *noun.* (no plural)

equalize *verb.* **(equalized, equalizing)** make equal; spread out evenly

equally *adv.* so that everyone has the same amount

equation *noun.* a mathematical statement that uses an equal(s) sign (=) to show that two quantities or formulas are equal

equator *noun.* an imaginary line around the center of the earth

equestrian *adj.* of or for horseback riding

equip *verb.* **(equipped, equipping)** give someone the tools and other things that he/she needs

equipment *noun.* the tools and other things that you need for something

equity *noun.* a share in a company that does not earn interest (plural **equities**)

equivalent *adj.* equal in value, amount, meaning, etc, to something else

era *noun.* a set period of time in history

erase *verb.* **(erased, erasing)** rub out something written

erect *adj.* straight; not curved

erect *verb.* **(erected, erecting)** build

errand *noun.* something that you have to do outside the house often for someone else

error *noun.* a mistake

erupt *verb.* **(erupted, erupting)** explode with fire coming out

escape *verb.* **(escaped, escaping) 1.** succeed in getting free **2.** leak from a pipe **3.** manage to avoid —**escape** *noun.*

escort *verb.* **(escorted, escorting)** go with someone —**escort** *noun.*

especially *adv.* most of all; in particular

espionage *noun.* spying; secretly finding out the secrets of another country, business, group, etc)

essay *noun.* a written composition

essence *noun.* the most important thing; a part extracted from something

essential *adj.* very necessary; vital

essentially *adv.* in reality, even if it does not appear so

establish *verb.* **(established, establishing) 1.** set up **2.** find out for certain that something is true

establishment *noun.* **1.** setting something up (no plural) **2. (the Establishment)** the people in society who are in control (and usually resist change)

estate *noun.* **1.** a large piece of land that one person owns **2.** a person's property and possessions

esteem *noun.* (formal) respect

esthetic *adj.* pleasing; having beauty; understanding beautiful things

estimate *noun.* a rough calculation

estimate *verb.* **(estimated, estimating) 1.** judge the value of something **2.** calculate how much something will probably cost **3.** make a calculation of how long something will take

estimation *noun.* an opinion

eternal *adj.* lasting forever; without an end —**eternity** *noun.*

ethics *noun plural.* a set of principles stating what is right and wrong

ethnic *adj.* of a certain nation, race, tribe, etc

ethnicity *noun.* belonging to a certain race, nationality, etc

ethos *noun.* the beliefs guiding a person or group

EU *abbr.* the European Union; an economic and political organization of many European countries

eucalyptus *noun.* a tall tree that produces a strong smelling oil used in some medications

euro *noun.* the money unit of the European Union

European *noun. adj.* someone or something from Europe; belonging to Europe

evacuate *verb.* **(evacuated, evacuating)** move all the people from a place — **evacuation** *noun.*

evade *verb.* **(evaded, evading)** avoid; find a way not to do something (especially unpleasant) —**evasion** *noun.*

evaluate *verb.* **(evaluated, evaluating)** calculate the cost or the results of something

evaluation *noun.* a judgment of the value of someone or something

eve *noun.* the evening before an event or a holiday

even *adj.* **1.** flat and smooth **2.** the same; equal **3.** that can be divided by two

even *adv.* **1.** a word that makes something that you say stronger **2.** a word that shows that something was unexpected

evening *noun.* the time when the sun goes down and it begins to get dark — **evening** *adj.*

evenly *adv.* in a stable way; equally

event *noun.* **1.** an important happening **2.** something that is arranged

eventual *adj.* happening in the end, as a result

eventuality *noun.* a possible event

eventually *adv.* in the end; after some time; after a while

ever *adv.* at any time

every *adj.* each one; of every person or thing in a group

everybody *pron.* **1.** each person **2.** all the people

everyday *adj.* for ordinary use; not for special occasions

everyone *pron.* everybody

everything *pron.* **1.** all the things **2.** all

everywhere *adv.* in all the places (opposite **nowhere**)

evidence *noun.* proof (no plural)

evident *adj.* clear

evidently *adv.* apparently

evil *noun.* **1.** that which is bad; wickedness (no plural) **2.** bad or harmful things

evil *adj.* very bad; wishing to do harm

evolution *noun.* a slow process of change, from simpler to more complicated forms

exact *adj.* **1.** correct in every detail **2.** accurate

exactly *adv.* in every detail

exaggerate *verb.* **(exaggerated, exaggerating)** make something seem bigger or more important than it really is —**exaggeration** *noun.*

exaggerated *adj.* more than in reality

exam *noun.* short for **examination**

examination *noun.* **1.** a test of what someone knows **2.** a careful look at something

examine *verb.* **(examined, examining)** **1.** test what someone knows **2.** look closely at **3.** ask questions to find out what someone knows or if he/she is telling the truth

example *noun.* **1.** one of something **2.** something that shows how to do something

exceed *verb.* **(exceeded, exceeding)** go beyond; be more than

excel *verb.* **(excelled, excelling)** be very good at something

excellence *noun*. being very good (no plural)

excellent *adj*. very good

except (for) *prep*. but not

exception *noun*. something that is not included

exceptional *adj*. 1. unusual; not ordinary 2. better than usual

exceptionally *adv*. unusually

excessive *adj*. too much

excessively *adv*. going beyond the reasonable amount

exchange *noun*. giving one thing or person in return for another

exchange *verb*. **(exchanged, exchanging)** 1. give something and receive something in return 2. bring something back to a store and take something else instead

exchange rate *noun*. the value of one country's money compared to the value of another country's money

excite *verb*. **(excited, exciting)** make someone feel strong emotions — **excitedly** *adv*. —**excitement** *noun*. (no plural) —**exciting** *adj*.

exclaim *verb*. **(exclaimed, exclaiming)** say something suddenly or in surprise

exclude *verb*. **(excluded, excluding)** leave or keep someone or something out (opposite **include**) —**excluding** *adj*. (opposite **including**)

exclusive *adj*. limited to one group or person; not shared with everyone — **exclusively** *adv*.

excursion *noun*. a trip, usually made with others, for pleasure

excuse *noun*. a reason for doing something wrong or not doing something you should have

excuse *verb*. **(excused, excusing)** forgive

execute *verb*. **(executed, executing)** 1. kill someone as a punishment 2. carry out a plan —**execution** *noun*.

executive *noun*. a manager —**executive** *adj*.

exempt *verb*. **(exempted, exempting)** free someone from a certain duty, payment, etc

exercise *noun*. 1. activity that keeps you strong (no plural) 2. special body movements that someone repeats to make some part of the body strong 3. an activity that helps you learn something; a drill

exercise *verb*. **(exercised, exercising)** repeat special body movements to be strong

exhaust *noun*. the gas that comes out of an engine of a car, etc

exhaust *verb*. **(exhausted, exhausting)** 1. make someone very tired 2. use something up

exhausting *adj*. very tiring

exhaustion *noun*. 1. having no strength left 2. using something up

exhibit *verb*. **(exhibited, exhibiting)** show something that you have done

exhibition *noun*. a show of a certain type of thing

exile *noun*. 1. being sent away from your country by force (no plural) 2. someone who lives in another country against his/her wishes

exile *verb*. **(exiled, exiling)** force a person or a group of people to leave a country

exist *verb*. **(existed, existing)** 1. be; be real 2. continue living

existence *noun*. being; reality (no plural)

exit *noun*. the place where you leave from (opposite **entrance**) —**exit** *verb*. **(exited, exiting)**

exotic *adj*. unusual and striking

expand *verb*. **(expanded, expanding)** become bigger

expansion *noun*. an increase in size or importance

expansive *adj*. friendly and talkative

expect *verb*. **(expected, expecting)** 1. believe that something is going to happen 2. wait for something or someone **3.** think someone will do something —**expectation** noun.

expedition noun. a long journey for a certain purpose

expel verb. **(expelled, expelling)** force someone to leave a school, a club, a team, etc

expenditure noun. the spending of money

expense noun. **1.** the price or cost of something (no plural) **2.** something that costs money

expensive adj. costing a lot of money; costly

experience noun. **1.** what someone has done and learned from (no plural) **2.** something that happened to someone —**experience** verb. **(experienced, experiencing)** —**experienced** adj.

experiment noun. a test or trial to see what happens

experiment verb. **(experimented, experimenting)** try something to see what will happen —**experimental** adj. —**experimentally** adv.

experimentation noun. the making of experiments

expert noun. someone with special knowledge, training or skill —**expert** adj.

expertise noun. expert knowledge or skill (no plural)

expire verb. **(expired, expiring)** (of something that lasts a certain length of time) come to the end and become invalid

explain verb. **(explained, explaining) 1.** tell what something means **2.** give a reason for something; try to make clear

explanation noun. telling how to do something or how something works

explode verb. **(exploded, exploding)** burst violently, making a loud noise

exploit verb. **(exploited, exploiting) 1.** use something **2.** use something for your own advantage **3.** use something wrongly or cruelly for your own advantage —**exploitation** noun.

exploration noun. a long journey to discover things about a place

explore verb. **(explored, exploring) 1.** travel to a place to discover things about it **2.** find out about something

explorer noun. someone who travels to a place to explore it

explosion noun. a sudden, violent bursting

explosive noun. a substance that explodes —**explosive** adj.

export verb. **(exported, exporting)** send goods out of the country (opposite **import**) —**export** noun. (opposite **import**)

exporter noun. a person, company, or country that exports

expose verb. **(exposed, exposing) 1.** uncover; leave unprotected **2.** make known **3.** let light fall on film

exposition noun. a major show of products, etc

express adj. fast

express verb. **(expressed, expressing) 1.** say something in words **2.** show an emotion —**expressive** adj.

expression noun. **1.** a phrase; a number of words that go together and have a special meaning **2.** a look on someone's face

expressly adv. especially

expressway noun. a wide, open road where you can travel fast; a freeway

exquisite adj. extremely beautiful

extend verb. **(extended, extending) 1.** reach or continue **2.** make longer **3.** (formal) give

extension noun. a telephone line connecting a number of rooms in the same building

extensive adj. **1.** large in area, amount, etc **2.** having an effect on many things or parts —**extensively** adv.

extent noun. **1.** amount **2.** limit

exterior noun. the outside —**exterior** adj. (opposite **interior**)

external adj. on or for the outside (opposite **internal**)

extinct *adj.* no longer in existence; no longer active —**extinction** *noun.*

extinguish *verb.* **(extinguished, extinguishing)** put out a fire, a cigarette or a light

extra *adj.* more; additional

extra *adv.* very

extract *noun.* **1.** a part of something longer, usually written or spoken **2.** a product obtained by extracting from something else

extract *verb.* **(extracted, extracting)** take something out of something else, usually with difficulty

extraordinary *adj.* very unusual or strange

extravaganza *noun.* a very spectacular show

extreme *adj.* **1.** very great **2.** not moderate

extremely *adv.* very

extremist *noun.* someone whose political or religious beliefs are not moderate

eye *noun.* what we see with

eyebrow *noun.* lines of short hair above the eyes

eye-catching *adj.* attracting your attention

eyelash *noun.* one of the short hairs at the edge of the eyelid (plural **eyelashes**)

eyelid *noun.* the covering that moves up and down over the eye

eyesight *noun.* seeing (no plural)

F

fable *noun.* a short story that teaches some kind of lesson

fabric *noun.* material; cloth made from woven threads

fabricate *verb.* **(fabricated, fabricating)** make up a false story

fabulous *adj.* terrific; wonderful

facade *noun.* 1. the front of a building 2. an insincere show of feeling

face *noun.* the front part of the head

face *verb.* **(faced, facing)** 1. be or stand opposite something or someone 2. deal with something unpleasant

facial *adj.* of or for the face

facility *noun.* 1. an ability 2. something done easily 3. a place where you can do things

facing *prep.* opposite

facsimile *noun.* 1. an exact copy of a book, picture, etc 2. a fax

fact *noun.* something that is true or real

faction *noun.* a group within a larger group, usually in a political party

factor *noun.* one of a group of things that makes something happen

factory *noun.* a place where a certain type of thing is made (plural **factories**)

factual *adj.* based on fact

faculty *noun.* 1. a power connected with the mind 2. the teachers in a school 3. a department in a university that includes similar subjects

fad *noun.* a changing fashion

fade *verb.* **(faded, fading)** 1. lose color; become lighter or paler 2. become less loud —**faded** *adj.*

fail *verb.* **(failed, failing)** try but not succeed

failure *noun.* 1. not succeeding in what you are trying to do (no plural) 2. someone or something that has not succeeded

faint *verb.* **(fainted, fainting)** suddenly collapse and not know what is happening

faint *adj.* 1. very weak 2. feeling ill and dizzy —**faintly** *adv.*

fair *noun.* 1. a big outdoor festival with amusements and places to buy things 2. a special market for selling or advertising a particular kind of thing

fair *adj.* 1. right and honest (opposite **unfair**) 2. not so good and not so bad 3. (weather) bright, sunny 4. (skin) pale 5. (hair) light-colored

fairly *adv.* in a way that is just

fairness *noun.* being fair (no plural)

fairy *noun.* a little imaginary person who can do magic things (plural **fairies**)

fairy tale *noun.* a story about fairies or other magical things

faith *noun.* 1. belief and trust (no plural) 2. religion

faithful *adj.* loyal

faithfully *adv.* truly; honestly

fake *noun.* something not real that fools people

fake *adj.* false; not real

fake *verb.* **(faked, faking)** make an exact copy in order to fool people

falcon *noun.* a large bird that kills animals and eats their flesh

fall *noun.* 1. a drop from a high place to a lower place 2. becoming lower or less 3. loss of power (no plural) 4. the season after summer and before winter; autumn

fall *verb.* **(fell, fallen, falling)** 1. drop from a high place to a low place 2. become lower 3. come down from above 4. lose power

false *adj.* 1. not true 2. artificial; not real

falsely *adv.* wrongly; unjustly

falsify *verb.* **(falsified, falsifying)** change in order to give untrue information

fame *noun.* being known and recognized by a lot of people (no plural)

familiar *adj.* 1. known to someone 2. known by most people

familiarity *noun.* knowing something or someone very well and feeling comfortable with it

family *noun.* 1. parents and their children 2. animals or plants that belong to the same group —**family** *adj.*

famine *noun.* little or no food for a long time in a region, with many people dying

famous *adj.* well known

famously *adv.* very well; excellently

fan *noun.* 1. an enthusiastic supporter of a sports team, a performer, etc 2. something that makes the air move to make it cooler

fan *verb.* (**fanned, fanning**) use a fan

fanatic *noun.* someone with extreme ideas who believes that his/her ideas are the only truth

fanatical *adj.* too extreme; too enthusiastic

fan club *noun.* a group of fans who organize to support a singer, etc

fancy *noun.* 1. something that you imagine to be true 2. a daydream

fancy *verb.* (**fancied, fancying**) 1. think for a moment that something is true 2. want to have or do something

fancy *adj.* very decorated (opposite **plain, simple**)

fantastic *adj.* amazing; wonderful; unbelievable

fantasy *noun.* 1. a fancy; a dream 2. something that a person imagines is true but is not —**fantasy** *adj.*

far *adj.* (**farther, farthest; further, furthest**) 1. distant; not near 2. other

far *adv.* (**farther, farthest; further, furthest**) not near; a long distance from somewhere

faraway *adj.* distant

fare *noun.* money that you pay to travel on a plane, bus, train, etc

Far East *noun.* eastern Asia

farewell *noun.* (literary) goodbye

farm *noun.* a piece of land for raising animals or crops

farm *verb.* (**farmed, farming**) keep a farm; work the land

farmer *noun.* someone who farms

farmhouse *noun.* the main house on a farm, where the farmer lives

farther *adv. adj.* (also **further**) more far

fascinate *verb.* (**fascinated, fascinating**) attract and keep someone's interest — **fascinating** *adj.* —**fascination** *noun.*

fashion *noun.* a way that people dress or do things at a certain time

fashion *verb.* (**fashioned, fashioning**) make or shape something, especially with your hands

fashionable *adj.* being in fashion

fast *noun.* not eating or drinking

fast *verb.* (**fasted, fasting**) not eat or drink

fast *adj.* quick

fast *adv.* 1. quickly 2. firmly (opposite **slowly**)

fasten *verb.* (**fastened, fastening**) 1. make something stay closed 2. attach one thing to another

fast food *noun.* food, such as hamburgers, that is prepared and served quickly

fat *noun.* 1. something white that is found under the skin of animals, which is meant to keep them warm 2. an oily substance used in cooking

fat *adj.* (**fatter, fattest**) having a lot of flesh on your body (opposite **thin**)

fatal *adj.* 1. ending in death 2. bringing ruin

fate *noun.* 1. the power that seems to make things happen; destiny (no plural) 2. what will happen to someone

father *noun.* a male parent

father-in-law *noun.* the father of your husband or wife (plural **fathers-in-law**)

fatigue *noun.* great tiredness

fatigue *verb.* (**fatigued, fatiguing**) make someone tired

fatty adj. having a lot of fat

fault noun. something that is bad about someone or something

faulty adj. having defects

fawn noun. a deer younger than one year old

fax noun. 1. a machine for transmitting or receiving documents electronically over a telephone line 2. a document transmitted through a fax machine

fax verb. (**faxed, faxing**) send documents by fax

FBI abbr. Federal Bureau of Investigation

fear noun. a feeling that something bad is going to happen —**fear** verb. (**feared, fearing**)

fearful adj. full of fear; not brave

fearless adj. without fear; brave

feasible adj. 1. that can be done 2. that can be believed —**feasibility** noun.

feast noun. 1. a celebration with a lot of eating and drinking 2. a religious festival

feast verb. (**feasted, feasting**) eat large amounts of food that you enjoy

feat noun. an action requiring great skill, courage or strength

feather noun. what grows from a bird's skin

feature noun. an important part of something

feature verb. (**featured, featuring**) include in a movie, show, book, etc

Feb abbr. February

February noun. the second month

federal adj. of a group of states that are united by one government

federation noun. a group of organizations, labor unions, etc, that have united

fee noun. the amount of money that you must pay for a service or for being a member of an organization, etc

feeble adj. (**feebler, feeblest**) very weak

feed noun. special food for animals

feed verb. (**fed, feeding**) 1. give food 2. eat (used for animals) —**feeder** noun.

feedback noun. information given back to makers of a product, those who gave a course, etc, by the users or participants

feel verb. (**felt, feeling**) 1. learn by touching 2. sense that something is touching you 3. have a sense of being well, ill, cold, hot, dizzy, etc 4. have an emotion

feeling noun. 1. the ability to learn by touching (no plural) 2. a sense of something about your body 3. an emotion about yourself 4. an intuition about something (no plural)

feelings noun plural. emotions

feet noun. plural of **foot**

fell verb. past of **fall**

fellow noun. a man

fellow adj. of the same clan or situation as you

felt verb. past tense and past participle of **feel**

female noun. one of the sex that has babies; a girl or woman (opposite **male**)

female adj. of the female sex (opposite **male**)

feminine adj. 1. like or suitable for a girl or woman 2. (grammar) relating to a certain group of words (opposite **masculine**)

feminism noun. feminist beliefs

feminist noun. someone who is active in trying to get equal rights for women

fence noun. something that you put around an open place to keep something in or out

fence verb. (**fenced, fencing**) 1. put a fence around something 2. fight with thin swords (as a sport)

fern noun. a green plant with feathery leaves

ferocious adj. very fierce and violent

ferry noun. a boat that takes passengers across the water (plural **ferries**)

fertile *adj.* **1.** able to produce plants **2.** able to have children

fertilizer *noun.* something you put in the ground to help plants grow **—fertilize** *verb.* **(fertilized, fertilizing)**

festival *noun.* **1.** a religious celebration; a feast **2.** a big musical or theatrical meeting that takes place regularly

festive *adj.* special, as if for a holiday

festivity *noun.* a joyful celebration

fetch *verb.* **(fetched, fetching)** go and bring something

feud *noun.* a bitter quarrel that lasts a long time, often between families.

fever *noun.* body temperature that is above normal

feverish *adj.* **1.** feeling as if you have fever **2.** wildly excited

few *adj.* **(fewer, fewest)** not many (use with uncountable nouns; opposite **many, a lot (of))**

fiasco *noun.* a total failure (of an event)

fiction *noun.* stories that someone makes up **—fictional** *adj.*

fictitious *adj.* untrue

fiddle *verb.* **(fiddled, fiddling) 1.** play the violin **2.** falsify figures, accounts, etc

field *noun.* **1.** a piece of land for growing crops **2.** a piece of land for a special purpose **3.** a profession; an area of interest

fielder *noun.* a baseball or cricket player who plays in the field

fierce *adj.* **1.** savage and dangerous; ferocious **2.** strong

fiercely *adv.* **1.** in a frightening way **2.** strongly and bravely

fiery *adj.* **1.** full of violent feelings **2.** like fire

fifteen *noun. adj.* the number 15

fifteenth *noun. adj.* = 15th

fifth *noun. adj.* = 5th

fifties *noun.* the years from 1950 to 1959

fiftieth *adj.* = 50th

fifty *noun. adj.* the number 50

fig *noun.* a tree bearing small sweet soft fruit; this tree's fruit

fight *noun.* a struggle; a quarrel

fight *verb.* **(fought, fighting) 1.** use violence with your body or with weapons **2.** quarrel **3.** struggle for or against something

fighter *noun.* **1.** someone who struggles for something **2.** a fast military plane

figure *noun.* **1.** a diagram or illustration **2.** a human or animal shape **3.** the shape of the human body **4.** a person in history or in a story **5.** a sign that shows a number **6.** a number; an amount

figure *verb.* **(figured, figuring) 1.** appear **2.** represent something in a drawing **3.** consider; believe **4.** occur; take part in

figures *noun plural.* arithmetic

file *noun.* **1.** a cardboard folder for keeping papers in order **2.** a collection of information about someone or something **3.** information in a computer **4.** a small tool for making things smooth **5.** a line of people

file *verb.* **(filed, filing) 1.** (also **file away**) put a piece of paper into a file **2.** make something smooth

fill *verb.* **(filled, filling) 1.** put something inside something else **2.** become or make full **3.** place something inside a hole in a tooth to prevent further decay

fillet *noun.* a piece of fish or meat without bones

filling *noun.* **1.** something special inside certain types of food (such as chocolate, pies, sandwiches, etc) **2.** material placed inside a hole in a tooth to prevent further decay

film *noun.* **1.** special paper that you put into a camera to take photographs (no plural) **2.** a movie

film *verb.* **(filmed, filming)** take a photograph or make a movie, TV show, etc

film-maker noun. someone who makes movies, for example a movie director or producer

film star (also **movie star**) noun. a famous actor or actress

filter noun. something that lets liquids or gas pass through and holds back what is not needed —**filter** verb. (**filtered, filtering**)

filthy adj. very dirty (**filthier, filthiest**)

final adj. last

finale noun. the last part of a concert or show

finalize verb. (**finalized, finalizing**) bring to an end; complete

finally adv. 1. at last 2. lastly

finals noun plural. 1. the last examinations of the year 2. the last games in a championship match

finance noun. the management of money in a business, government, etc (no plural)

finance verb. (**financed, financing**) pay for something

finances noun plural. matters related to money

financial adj. connected with money — **financially** adv.

financier noun. someone who lends or controls large amounts of money

find noun. something valuable or useful that is discovered

find verb. (**found, finding**) 1. discover where someone or something is 2. discover something by chance 3. solve a problem 4. have a judgment about something 5. give a judgment in court

finder noun. someone who finds something, usually by accident

fine noun. money that you have to pay for breaking a law or a rule

fine verb. (**fined, fining**) make someone pay a fine

fine adj. 1. good 2. bright and pleasant 3. elegant and expensive 4. very thin 5. in very tiny pieces 6. delicate; breaking easily 7. well

finely adv. 1. very small 2. elegantly

finger noun. one of the five parts of your hand

fingernail noun. the nail on one of your fingers

fingerprint noun. a mark found on a smooth surface that was left by a finger and may be used by the police to help identify criminals

fingertip noun. the end of your finger

finish noun. 1. the end of something (no plural) 2. polish (plural **finishes**)

finish verb. (**finished, finishing**) 1. complete 2. stop 3. eat everything

finite adj. having a limit (opposite **infinite**)

Finnish noun. the language of Finland —**Finnish** adj. of or from Finland

fire noun. 1. burning with flames (no plural) 2. burning for a certain purpose 3. burning that is out of control

fire verb. (**fired, firing**) 1. shoot with a gun 2. force someone to leave his/her job

fireman, firefighter noun. someone whose job is to put out dangerous fires (plural **firemen**)

fireplace noun. an opening in a wall for making a fire in the house

firewood noun. wood used as fuel

fireworks noun plural. explosives that make a loud noise and shoot beautiful patterns into the air

firm noun. a business; a company

firm adj. 1. hard; solid; strong 2. not likely to change 3. showing strongly that you mean what you say 4. steady —**firmly** adv.

first pron. adj. before all others; = 1st

first adv. 1. before anyone else 2. the earliest time that 3. in the first place

first aid noun. basic medical treatment for a sick or injured person before the doctor comes

first-hand adj. coming directly from the source

firstly adv. in the first place

fiscal *adj.* connected to taxes and/or public money

fish *noun.* a cold-blooded animal that lives in water (plural **fish** or **fishes**)

fish *verb.* (**fished, fishing**) catch fish

fisherman, fisherwoman *noun.* someone whose job is catching fish (plural **fishermen, fisherwomen**)

fist *noun.* a tightly closed hand

fit *noun.* **1.** a short period of laughing, etc, which you cannot control **2.** the way something fits

fit *verb.* (**fitted, fitting**) be the right size

fit *adj.* **1.** good enough; suitable (opposite **unfit**) **2.** healthy and strong

fitness *noun.* **1.** being the right person or thing for something **2.** physical health

five *noun. adj.* the number 5

fiver *noun.* (informal) a five-dollar bill or five-pound note

fix *verb.* (**fixed, fixing**) **1.** repair; mend **2.** prepare **3.** arrange **4.** set a time for something **5.** set something in place so that it doesn't move

fixture *noun.* something that is fixed in place in a building

flag *noun.* a piece of cloth with a symbol or picture on it

flagrant *adj.* (of a crime, scandalous behavior, etc) very obvious and not paying attention to the law, society, customs, etc

flair *noun.* a natural ability

flake *noun.* a small, thin chip of something

flame *noun.* a fire that burns brightly

flamenco *noun.* a dance (and music) typical of Spain

flank *noun.* the side of an animal that is between the ribs and hip

flap *noun.* a flat piece that folds over something else

flash *noun.* **1.** a sudden, sharp light **2.** an important news bulletin

flash *verb.* (**flashed, flashing**) send out a sudden burst of light

flashlight *noun.* a lamp with a battery that you can take with you in the dark

flat *adj.* level; smooth; without hills or bumps

flat *adv.* **1.** in a flat position **2.** completely

flatly *adv.* **1.** in a dull way **2.** absolutely

flatter *verb.* (**flattered, flattering**) try to make someone like you by saying nice things about him/her that are not necessarily true

flaw *noun.* **1.** a defect that is sometimes not immediately noticeable **2.** something that lessens the value

flawed *adj.* imperfect; defective; containing mistakes

flea *noun.* a very small insect that lives on animals

fled *verb.* past of **flee**

fledgling *noun.* **1.** someone without experience **2.** a young bird —**fledgling** *adj.*

flee *verb.* (**fled, fleeing**) run away

fleet *noun.* **1.** a group of warships **2.** a group of buses, ships, etc, that belong to one company

fleeting *adj.* lasting for a very short time; disappearing fast

flesh *noun.* the soft part of the body between the bones and the skin (no plural)

flew *verb.* past of **fly**

flexibility *noun.* the ability to bend or change

flexible *adj.* **1.** easy to bend and stretch **2.** easily changed

flicker *verb.* (**flickered, flickering**) go on and off —**flickering** *adj.*

flier, flyer *noun.* **1.** someone who flies **2.** a page of advertisements given out in the street or put into mailboxes

flight *noun.* **1.** flying (no plural) **2.** a trip on an airplane **3.** stairs or steps that go from one floor to another **4.** running away (no plural)

fling *verb.* (**flung, flinging**) throw

flip *verb.* (**flipped, flipping**) **1.** throw up

(especially a coin) in the air 2. (slang) go crazy

flirt verb. (**flirted, flirting**) behave in a playful way to attract sexually

float verb. (**floated, floating**) 1. stay on top of water or some other liquid 2. stay up in the air (opposite **sink**)

flock noun. 1. a group of birds 2. a group of sheep or goats that belong to one owner

flood noun. water that covers the land —**flood** verb. (**flooded, flooding**) — **flooded** adj.

floor noun. 1. the bottom of a room where we walk (opposite **ceiling**) 2. a story (in a building)

floppy adj. soft; without stiffness to keep something upright

floral adj. relating to or of flowers

flour noun. a soft, white powder made from wheat, corn, etc (usually no plural)

flourish verb. (**flourished, flourishing**) 1. be successful 2. grow well

flow verb. (**flowed, flowing**) move smoothly, like water —**flow** noun.

flower noun. the colored part of a plant which has the seeds in it

flower verb. (**flowered, flowering**) bloom

flowing adj. hanging gracefully

flown verb. past participle of **fly**

flu noun. an illness with high fever (short for **influenza**; no plural)

fluctuate verb. (**fluctuated, fluctuating**) not be steady; move up and down; constantly and frequently change — **fluctuation** noun.

fluent adj. able to speak smoothly and freely

fluff noun. soft loose airy material from wool or similar material —**fluffy** adj.

fluid noun. something that can flow; a liquid —**fluid** adj.

flung verb. past and past participle of **fling**

flush verb. (**flushed, flushing**) get rid of water

flute noun. a musical instrument that you hold at the side and blow through

flutter verb. (**fluttered, fluttering**) 1. move delicately in the air 2. move something back and forth or up and down quickly and delicately

fly noun. a buzzing insect that flies (plural **flies**)

fly verb. (**flew, flown, flying**) 1. use wings for staying in the air 2. travel by plane or helicopter 3. run quickly 4. be the pilot of a plane or helicopter 5. make something go up into the air and stay there

FM abbr. (radio) frequency modulation

focus noun. 1. the point at which you see an image most sharply 2. the center of attention or interest

focus verb. (**focused, focusing**) bring an image into focus so that it is clear and sharp —**focal** adj.

foe noun. (literary) an enemy

fog noun. a low cloud; a thick mist — **foggy** adj. (**foggier, foggiest**)

fold verb. (**folded, folding**) bend one part of something on top of another part

folder noun. a soft cardboard cover for papers

folding adj. able to be folded

folk noun. people

folklore noun. the beliefs, stories and customs of a particular people (no plural)

folks noun plural. (informal) family

follow verb. (**followed, following**) 1. come after 2. go after 3. go along 4. understand 5. take an interest in

follower noun. a supporter; a believer

following adj. next

fond adj. loving

food noun. things that you eat (usually a collective noun)

food processor noun. an electrical appliance used in the kitchen, usually with interchangeable blades, that chops, mixes or slices food

foodstuff *noun.* food; material used a s food (usually in the plural only)

fool *noun.* someone who is stupid or doesn't have good sense

fool *verb.* **(fooled, fooling) 1.** make someone believe something that is not true; deceive **2.** joke

foolish *adj.* silly; not wise

foot *noun.* **1.** the part of the body that you stand on (plural **feet**) **2.** the bottom (no plural) **3.** a measurement of length (plural **feet**)

football *noun.* **1.** a game with 11 players on each side (no plural) **2.** a special ball that is used for playing football

footnote *noun.* a note at the bottom of the page in a book

footprint *noun.* a mark left by a foot on a soft surface such as sand or mud

footstep *noun.* the sound of someone walking

footwear *noun.* things that people wear on their feet (like shoes, sandals)

for *prep.* **1.** a word that tells who will receive something **2.** a word that tells what to do with something **3.** a word that tells why **4.** a word that tells how much **5.** a word that tells how long **6.** a word that tells how far **7.** as a help to **8.** as an alternative to **9.** a word that tells where you are going **10.** a word that shows support **11.** a word that shows contrast with what you expect **12.** a word that tells whom you mean **13.** a word that tells what activity

for *conj.* because (used in formal writing but not in speaking)

forbid *verb.* **(forbade, forbidden, forbidding)** not allow (opposite **allow, permit**)

force *noun.* **1.** physical power; strength **2.** a group of people who have a certain power

force *verb.* **(forced, forcing) 1.** make someone do something against his/her will **2.** use strength to do something

forceful *adj.* strong; powerful —**forcefully** *adv.*

forecast *verb.* **(forecast, forecasting)** say what you think is going to happen —**forecast** *noun.*

forefront *noun.* the leading position; the most forward part

foreground *noun.* the part of a picture that is nearest the viewer; the most noticeable part

forehead *noun.* the part of the face between the hair and the eyes

foreign *adj.* from a different country

foreigner *noun.* someone who comes from a different country

foreman, forewoman *noun.* **1.** a worker in a factory who has authority over other workers but is not a manager **2.** the spokesperson for a jury

foresee *verb.* **(foresaw, foreseen, foreseeing)** predict; imagine what is likely to happen —**foreseeable** *adj.*

foresight *noun.* the ability to imagine what the future will bring (opposite **hindsight**)

forest *noun.* a place with a lot of trees; a big woods

forever, for ever *adv.* without end; always

forge *verb.* **(forged, forging) 1.** make false copies of something; fake **2.** shape metal by heating and hammering

forgery *noun.* **1.** (the crime of) forging (no plural) **2.** a fake

forget *verb.* **(forgot, forgotten, forgetting) 1.** not remember **2.** not think about something anymore

forgive *verb.* **(forgave, forgiven, forgiving)** not be angry with someone for what he/she did

forgiveness *noun.* the act of being forgiven; willingness to forgive

forgot, forgotten *verb.* past tense and past participle of **forget**

fork *noun.* **1.** a tool for eating with points at the end **2.** a tool for gardening with a long handle and points at the end **3.** a place where a road divides in two different directions

form *noun.* **1.** a particular shape **2.** kind; type **3.** a printed paper with spaces for writing information

form *verb.* **(formed, forming) 1.** make a shape **2.** organize **3.** begin to develop

formal *adj.* according to strict rules or customs (opposite **informal, casual**)

formally *adv.* very politely and correctly

format *noun.* the general plan, arrangement or shape of something

format *verb.* **(formatted, formatting) 1.** arrange a page of text in a certain way **2.** prepare a computer disk for storing data

formation *noun.* **1.** development **2.** arrangement; organization **3.** structure

former *noun.* the first of two things (opposite **(the) latter**)

former *adj.* past

formerly *adv.* in the past

formidable *adj.* difficult to deal with or overcome

formula *noun.* **1.** a statement of a scientific or mathematical rule **2.** a list of ingredients in a medication or other chemical substance **3.** a recipe

formulate *verb.* **(formulated, formulating)** say in an exact and clear way

fort *noun.* a strong building or group of buildings for military defense

forth *adv.* (literary) forward

forthcoming *adj.* **1.** going to come in the near future **2.** (informal) coming forward; ready

fortieth *noun. adj.* = 40th

fortress *noun.* a large fort

fortunate *adj.* lucky (opposite **unfortunate**)

fortunately *adv.* luckily (opposite **unfortunately**)

fortune *noun.* **1.** a lot of money **2.** luck

forty *noun. adj.* the number 40

forum *noun.* a place or meeting where public matters can be discussed

forward *noun.* a front-line player in certain team games, like football

forward *adj.* toward the front

forward *verb.* **(forwarded, forwarding)** send a letter on to someone's new address

forward, forward *adv.* **1.** toward the front **2.** to the future

fossil *noun.* a part or a footprint of a prehistoric animal that has become hard, like stone

foster *verb.* **(foster, fostering) 1.** help to develop **2.** take a child from another family into your home and care for her/him

fought *verb.* past tense and past participle of **fight**

foul *noun.* **1.** a ball that is outside the limits in certain sports **2.** doing something that is against the rules of a sport

foul *adj.* **1.** dirty; horrible **2.** bad; filthy **3.** evil **4.** unpleasant

found *verb.* **(founded, founding)** start to build something; establish

found *verb.* past tense and past participle of **find**

foundation *noun.* **1.** the beginning of something (no plural) **2.** the strong bottom part of a building

founder *noun.* someone who creates or establishes something

fountain *noun.* a structure that has a stream of water coming out of it

four *noun. adj.* the number 4

fourteen *noun. adj.* the number 14

fourteenth *noun. adj.* = 14th

fourth *noun. adj.* = 4th

fox *noun.* a wild animal with a thick tail and reddish-brown fur (plural **foxes**)

foyer *noun.* an entrance hall, especially of a theater or hotel

fraction *noun.* **1.** a small part of something **2.** a number that is not a whole number

fracture *noun.* a break in a bone — **fracture** *verb.* **(fractured, fracturing)**

fractured *adj.* broken

fragile *adj.* delicate; easily broken

fragment *noun.* a small piece of something larger

fragment *verb.* **(fragmented, fragmenting)** break into fragments —**fragmentation** *noun.*

fragrance *noun.* 1. a pleasant smell 2. a perfume —**fragrant** *adj.*

frail *adj.* weak; in delicate health

frame *noun.* 1. a border of wood or metal around something 2. the border around someone's glasses with parts to go over the ears —**frame** *verb.* **(framed, framing)**

framework *noun.* the basic supporting structure of a bridge, building, budget, plan, etc

franc *noun.* the former currency of many French-speaking countries, like France, Belgium, Luxembourg, etc (now changed to the **euro**)

frank *adj.* open and honest in what you say

frankly *adv.* honestly speaking

frantic *adj.* in a panic; emotionally out of control —**frantically** *adv.*

fraud *noun.* dishonesty; cheating people —**fraudulent** *adj.*

freak *noun.* 1. something with an abnormal form, that is very unusual or unexpected 2. (slang) an enthusiast 3. someone who looks strange or acts strangely

free *adj.* 1. not under the control of anyone else 2. not costing anything 3. not busy

free *verb.* **(freed, freeing)** allow someone or something to leave prison or slavery

freedom *noun.* 1. being free (no plural) 2. the right to do or have something

freelance, freelancer *noun.* someone who works independently for several employees

freelance *verb.* **(freelanced, freelancing)** work as a freelance

freely *adv.* without restrictions

freeway *noun.* an expressway; a toll free highway; a fast road without intersections

freeze *verb.* **(froze, frozen, freezing)** 1. become solid 2. put something in a cold place to make it solid 3. feel very cold

freezer *noun.* a machine that keeps food frozen

freight *noun.* cargo; goods carried by truck, train, ship, or airplane

freighter *noun.* a ship or plane that carries freight

French *noun.* the people or language of France —**French** *adj.*

Frenchman, Frenchwoman *noun.* a French person (plural **Frenchmen, Frenchwomen**)

frequency *noun.* 1. how often or the rate something happens or is repeated 2. the number of radio waves per second a particular radio signal is broadcast

frequent *adj.* happening or doing something often

frequently *adv.* often (opposite **infrequently, seldom, rarely**)

fresh *adj.* 1. recently picked or produced 2. not frozen or canned 3. not salty (water) 4. clean 5. new —**freshly** *adv.* —**freshness** *noun.*

freshman *noun.* a first year student in a high school or college

freshwater *noun.* not salt water

friar *noun.* a male member of a Christian order who lives in poverty and travels around teaching Christianity

Friday *noun.* the sixth day of the week

fridge *noun.* a machine for keeping food cold (short for **refrigerator**)

fried *adj.* cooked in a pan in hot oil, margarine or butter

friend *noun.* someone whom you feel close to and trust

friendly *adj.* 1. open and easy to talk to 2. (of an animal) tame and liking people

friendship *noun.* being friends; a feeling that you can talk to and trust someone

fright *noun.* sudden fear (no plural)

frighten *verb.* **(frightened, frightening)** make someone suddenly afraid

frightened *adj.* afraid

fringe *noun. adj.* **1.** decorative threads around the edges of a scarf, curtain, etc **2.** the edge of a place **3.** people or events that are not part of accepted society

fro *adv.* backward and forward

frog *noun.* a small, green, jumping animal that lives in water and on land

from *prep.* **1.** a word that tells who gave or sent something **2.** a word that tells where something starts **3.** a word that tells where someone lives or was born **4.** a word that tells what time something starts **5.** a word that tells at what distance **6.** a word that tells the reason why **7.** a word that shows the lowest number **8.** a word that tells what something is made of **9.** a word that tells you that something is separate

front *noun.* **1.** the forward part (no plural; opposite **back**) **2.** the side where the entrance is (no plural; opposite **back**) **3.** where a war is fought —**front** *adj.* (opposite **back**)

frontier *noun.* a border between two countries

frost *noun.* a thin, white covering of ice on the ground and the leaves in very cold weather

frosty *adj.* very cold; unfriendly

frown *noun.* an expression of anger or worry on your forehead in which the eyebrows come together

frown *verb.* **(frowned, frowning)** have an expression on your face that shows that you are angry or worried

froze, frozen *verb.* past tense and past participle of **freeze**

frozen *adj.* **1.** solid from cold; turned into ice **2.** kept fresh in a freezer **3.** feeling very cold

fruit *noun.* the part of a plant that has the seeds, and is usually sweet and good to eat (usually a collective noun, like **food**)

fruit *adj.* made with fruit

fruitful *adj.* successful; with positive results

frustrate *verb.* **(frustrated, frustrating) 1.** cause to have angry, dissatisfied and disappointing feelings due to a lack of success **2.** prevent someone from succeeding —**frustrated** *adj.* —**frustrating** *adj.* —**frustration** *noun.*

fry *verb.* **(fried, frying)** cook in a pan in hot oil, margarine or butter

frying pan *noun.* a shallow pan for frying food, such as fish or eggs

ft. *abbr.* (measurement) feet or foot

fuel *noun.* something that gives power, light or heat when it burns (plural **kinds of fuel**) —**fuel** *verb.* **(fueled, fueling)**

full *adj.* **1.** holding all that it can (opposite **empty**) **2.** not able to eat any more **3.** complete

full-time *adj.* during all the working hours; not doing anything else

fully *adv.* completely; totally

fun *noun.* enjoyment; a good time (no plural)

fun *adj.* enjoyable

function *noun.* **1.** what something is supposed to do **2.** an important party or other social event

function *verb.* **(functioned, functioning)** work properly

functional *adj.* **1.** practical **2.** in working condition

fund *noun.* a supply of money for a certain purpose —**fund** *verb.* **(funded, funding)**

fundamental *adj.* basic

fundamentally *adv.* in every way that really matters

fundraising *noun.* collecting money for a specific cause

funeral *noun.* a ceremony for burying someone who has died

funky adj. 1. (usually relating to jazz music) in a direct, simple unsophisticated manner 2. fashionable and unusual

funnel noun. 1. a narrow tube for pouring liquids, etc 2. a chimney on a ship

funny adj. 1. making you laugh 2. strange

fur noun. the thick hair that covers an animal (no plural) —**fur** adj.

furious adj. extremely angry

furiously adv. angrily; wildly

furnace noun. 1. a closed-in fire for producing hot water or steam 2. a closed space for melting metals or glass

furnish verb. (**furnished, furnishing**) 1. supply with furniture 2. supply something

furnished adj. containing furniture

furniture noun. tables, chairs, sofas, beds, etc (no plural; use **a piece of furniture**)

furry adj. (**furrier, furriest**) from fur or like fur

further adv. 1. a longer way 2. a longer time

further adj. more; additional (preferred instead of **farther**)

furthermore conj. in addition; moreover

furthest noun. (also **farthest**) the most far

fury noun. 1. extreme anger 2. wildness

fuse noun. a small electrical wire which burns when there is something wrong with the electricity

fuss noun. worry or trouble over small things (no plural) —**fuss** verb. (**fussed, fussing**)

fussy adj. (**fussier, fussiest**) caring too much about every small thing

futile adj. useless because it won't succeed

future noun. 1. the time that will be (no plural) 2. the things that will happen to a particular person —**future** adj.

futuristic adj. dealing with the future

G

gable *noun.* the upper end of a wall with three corners that joins a slanting roof

gadget *noun.* a small tool, usually for household use

gag *noun.* **1.** a piece of cloth over your mouth that keeps you from talking or screaming **2.** (slang) a joke

gage *noun.* = gauge

gaily *adv.* in a cheerful, happy way

gain *noun.* profit (opposite **loss**)

gain *verb.* (**gained, gaining**) **1.** get or learn something useful **2.** get more of something (opposite **lose**)

gale *noun.* a strong wind

gallery *noun.* **1.** a building or a special room for showing pictures **2.** a balcony

gallon *noun.* a measurement for liquids

gallop *verb.* (**galloped, galloping**) (of horses) run very fast

gamble *verb.* (**gambled, gambling**) risk money in a game of chance

gambler *noun.* someone who gambles

gambling *noun.* playing games for money (no plural)

game *noun.* **1.** anything that you play according to certain rules **2.** animals or birds hunted for food or as a sport (lions, elephants, etc)

games *noun plural.* a sports competition

gang *noun.* **1.** an organized group of criminals **2.** an organized group of young people who do violent things **3.** a group of people who are doing the same job **4.** a group of friends; the people that you go around with

gangster *noun.* a member of an organized gang of criminals

gap *noun.* a space between two things

garage *noun.* **1.** a place where cars are repaired **2.** a special part of a house for keeping a car

garbage *noun.* **1.** the waste from your house that you throw away; trash; rubbish (no plural) **2.** meaningless words on a computer screen

garden *noun.* a piece of land by a house for growing flowers, bushes, etc

garden *verb.* (**gardened, gardening**) work in a garden

gardener *noun.* someone who works in a garden —**gardening** *noun.* (no plural)

gardens *noun plural.* a public park

garlic *noun.* a plant with a strong smell that is used for giving food a special taste (no plural)

gas *noun.* **1.** a substance like air (plural **gases** or **gasses**) **2.** a fuel that is used for cooking, heating, etc (no plural) **3.** short for **gasoline**

gas *verb.* (**gassed, gassing**) **1.** provide gas **2.** kill or wound with gas

gas mask *noun.* a face covering that fits over the head and has a filter to keep out poisonous gases

gasoline *noun.* a flammable liquid that comes from petroleum and is used as fuel in cars, aircraft, etc

gasp *verb.* (**gasped, gasping**) breathe with difficulty

gas station *noun.* a place where you can buy gasoline for your car, and check the oil, water, etc

gate *noun.* a door in a fence

gather *verb.* (**gathered, gathering**) **1.** come together; assemble **2.** collect a lot of one thing

gathering *noun.* a meeting or a party

GATT *abbr.* General Agreement on Tariffs and Trade

gauge *noun.* **1.** an instrument for measuring the amount of something, such as gasoline in a car **2.** an estimate of the amount or nature of something — **gauge** *verb.* (**gauged, gauging**)

gave *verb.* past tense of **give**

gay *adj.* 1. (informal) homosexual 2. happy; joyful; cheerful

gaze *noun.* a long look

gaze *verb.* **(gazed, gazing)** look for a long time at something

GDP *abbr.* gross domestic product

gear *noun.* 1. a set of wheels with teeth in a machine 2. equipment (no plural)

gearing *noun.* the parts of a machine that move by using gears

geese *noun.* plural of **goose**

gel *noun.* 1. a semi-liquid substance used for beauty products 2. something that is of the consistency between solid and liquid

gem *noun.* a precious stone

gender *noun.* 1. (technical) the biological division between the sexes; male or female 2. (in grammar) the masculine, feminine, or neuter class of words

gene *noun.* the biological unit that passes on what you receive from each parent

general *noun.* a very high officer in the army

general *adj.* 1. for everyone 2. without details 3. usual

generalize *verb.* **(generalized, generalizing)** 1. make a statement that does not go into detail 2. form a conclusion that applies to everything/everyone by using only a small amount of information **—generalization** *noun.*

generally *adv.* usually

general public *noun.* people in general; ordinary people; everyone

generate *verb.* **(generated, generating)** produce; cause to happen

generation *noun.* 1. approximately 20–30 years from when parents have children until these children themselves are capable of having their own children 2. people born at more or less the same time

generator *noun.* a machine that supplies electricity

generosity *noun.* kindness; willingness to share with other people (no plural)

generous *adj.* 1. kind; liking to give to other people 2. big **—generously** *adv.*

genetic *adj.* connected with genes

genetics *noun.* the study of genes

genius *noun.* a brilliant or especially talented person (plural **geniuses**)

genocide *noun.* the deliberate extermination of a people

genre *noun.* a category, style or form in writing, music or art

genteel *adj.* aristocratic; not vulgar or rude; having polite manners

gentle *adj.* **(gentler, gentlest)** soft; not rough **—gently** *adv.*

gentleman *noun.* 1. a man who is polite and considerate 2. a man

genuine *adj.* 1. real; not an imitation; not fake 2. sincere; honest

genuinely *adv.* really; truly

geography *noun.* the study of the earth's surface, mountains, countries, etc (no plural) **—geographic, geographical** *adj.*

geology *noun.* the study of the history of the earth through rocks and fossils (no plural) **—geological** *adj.*

geometry *noun.* the branch of mathematics that studies the relationship of lines and angles (no plural) **—geometric, geometrical** *adj.* **—geometrically** *adv.*

Georgian *adj. noun.* 1. in the style of the period 1714–1811 in Britain 2. someone from Georgia (a country in southeastern Europe; a southern state in the U.S.); the language spoken in Georgia

germ *noun.* a microscopic organism that causes illness

German *noun.* the language or people of Germany **—German** *adj.*

gesture *noun.* 1. a movement of a part of the body to express meaning 2. an action which is done to show friendship, etc **—gesture** *verb.* **(gestured, gesturing)**

get *verb.* **(got, gotten, getting) 1.** become **2.** receive **3.** arrive **4.** have something **5.** buy something **6.** catch an illness **7.** take someone or something from a place **8.** (informal) understand or hear something **9.** cause someone else to do a job for you

getaway *noun.* **1.** an escape **2.** a secluded vacation spot

ghetto *noun.* **1.** in Europe, the section of a town where Jews had to live **2.** a crowded section of a city where minority groups live

ghost *noun.* the spirit of a dead person which appears as a real human being (in stories, etc)

ghostly *adv.* full of ghosts; looking like a ghost

giant *noun.* **1.** (in stories) a very big person who is cruel and frightening **2.** a person or an animal that is unusually big

giant *adj.* unusually big (opposite **dwarf**)

giddy *adj.* feeling unbalanced

gift *noun.* something that you give to someone; a present

gifted *adj.* talented; very clever

gig *noun.* (informal) a work engagement for a performer, especially musicians

gigantic *adj.* unusually big; huge; enormous

giggle *noun.* a high, silly laugh

giggle *verb.* **(giggled, giggling)** laugh in a silly way

gilt *adj.* with a thin covering of gold

gimmick *noun.* a trick or item that is used to attract people's attention especially when advertising something else.

ginger *noun.* a spice that is used in cooking and baking

girl *noun.* a female child or a young woman

girlfriend *noun.* **1.** a girl or woman who is the special friend of a boy or man **2.** any female friend

give *verb.* **(gave, given, giving) 1.** hand something to someone **2.** allow someone to have **3.** cause to have **4.** provide **5.** make a command **6.** organize and present

glad *adj.* **(gladder, gladdest)** happy about something; pleased —**gladly** *adv.*

glamour *noun.* attractiveness; being sparkling and exciting —**glamorous** *adj.*

glance *noun.* a quick look at something

glance *verb.* **(glanced, glancing)** take a quick look at something

gland *noun.* an organ in the body that produces substances used by the body or released from it

glare *noun.* **1.** a bright light that shines strongly on something **2.** an angry stare at someone —**glare** *verb.* **(glared, glaring)**

glass *noun.* **1.** a hard, clear, breakable substance used for windows (no plural) **2.** something that you drink from that does not have a handle (plural **glasses**)

glass *adj.* made of glass

glasses *noun plural.* something that you wear to help you see better; eyeglasses

glee *noun.* a feeling of joy; delight (especially because of a success)

glide *verb.* **(glided, gliding)** move smoothly, without appearing to make an effort

glider *noun.* an aircraft without an engine

glimmer *noun.* a small irregular light

glimpse *noun.* a short look —**glimpse** *verb.* **(glimpsed, glimpsing)**

globe *noun.* **1.** anything that is round like a ball **2.** a map of the earth that is painted on a round ball

gloom *noun.* **1.** a feeling of sadness or depression **2.** near darkness

gloomy *adj.* **1.** sad **2.** making you feel sad

glorious *adj.* **1.** deserving to be famous

and honored **2.** splendid; beautiful **3.** wonderful and exciting

glory *noun.* **1.** a reason for pride **2.** great beauty **3.** fame

glossy *adj.* **(glossier, glossiest)** with a shiny, smooth finish

glove *noun.* a covering for the hand

glow *verb.* **(glowed, glowing)** give light and heat without a flame —**glow** *noun.*

glue *noun.* a substance that sticks things together

glue *verb.* **(glued, gluing)** stick things together

GM *abbr.* general manager

GNP *abbr.* gross national product

go *noun.* a turn at something

go *verb.* **(went, gone, going) 1.** move from one place to another **2.** enter a place **3.** leave a place **4.** lead somewhere **5.** do something (go + verb + -ing) **6.** take a walk or a ride **7.** do something regularly **8.** become **9.** make progress **10.** (of a song) have certain words or a certain melody

go-ahead *noun.* confirmation to do something

goal *noun.* **1.** what you hope to do **2.** the space between two posts that a ball or puck has to go through

goalkeeper, goalie *noun.* the player who guards the goal

goat *noun.* a small animal with horns and a beard

god *noun.* any being that people think has control over nature

God *noun.* the creator of the universe in the Christian, Jewish, and Muslim religions

goddess *noun.* a female god (plural **goddesses**)

goes *verb.* third person singular present simple of **go**

going *verb.* present participle and gerund of **go**

gold *noun.* a shiny, yellow metal that is worth a lot of money

gold *adj.* made of gold

golden *adj.* gold in color

golden age *noun. adj.* **1.** a time of success and achievement **2.** the age of people after they retire (= senior citizens)

goldfish *noun.* a small orange colored fish that is kept as a pet

golf *noun.* an outdoor game in which you use a long stick to hit a ball into a hole in the ground

golf *verb.* **(golfed, golfing)** play golf

golfer *noun.* a golf player

gone *verb.* past participle of **go**

good *adj.* **1.** done well **2.** able; capable **3.** working the way it should **4.** behaving nicely **5.** fun **6.** pleasant **7.** interesting **8.** still usable **9.** of high quality

good *noun.* **1.** what is helpful **2.** the right thing to do

good *interj.* an exclamation of pleasure

goodbye *interj.* what you say when leaving or being left by someone

good day *noun.* a greeting that means hello or goodbye

good-looking *adj.* attractive

good-natured *adj.* kind; friendly; cheerful

goodness *interj.* an exclamation of surprise

good night *noun.* what you say when leaving someone (or as the answer) at night, especially before going to bed

goods *noun plural.* **1.** things that someone sells **2.** what someone owns

goose *noun.* a big water bird with a long neck that is very tasty to eat (plural **geese**)

gorgeous *adj.* very beautiful

gorilla *noun.* a large African ape

gossip *noun.* **1.** conversation about the details of other people's lives **2.** critical things that people say about other people but which may not always be true —**gossip** *verb.* **(gossiped, gossiping)**

got *verb.* the past tense and past participle of **get**

Gothic *adj. noun.* **1.** an architectural style in Europe in the 12th-16th centuries **2.** in the style of writing that was popular during the 18th century about scary places **3.** a type of printing with thick pointed letters

gourmet *noun. adj.* **1.** someone who knows a lot about and enjoys food and wine **2.** food that is suitable for such a person

govern *verb.* **(governed, governing)** rule a country

governess *noun.* a woman who lives with a family and educates the children (plural **governesses**)

government *noun.* the group of people controlling the affairs of a country

governor *noun.* the head of a state or a province

gown *noun.* **1.** a long dress **2.** something that you wear over your other clothes for a special purpose

grab *verb.* **(grabbed, grabbing)** take something quickly by force —**grab** *noun.*

grace *noun.* **1.** a beautiful way of moving (no plural) **2.** a short prayer said before or after a meal

graceful *adj.* **1.** moving in a beautiful way **2.** elegant —**gracefully** *adv.*

gracious *adj.* kind and considerate

grade *noun.* **1.** the mark for a test or a course **2.** the particular year that you are in at school **3.** a way of showing how good something is

grade *verb.* **(graded, grading) 1.** give marks for a test or for a course **2.** arrange things according to size, quality, etc

gradual *adj.* slow; step by step; not sudden

gradually *adv.* slowly; step by step

graduate *noun.* someone who graduated from a particular school

graduate *verb.* **(graduated, graduating)** complete your studies successfully at a certain school

graduation *noun.* a ceremony for students who successfully complete their studies at a particular school

grain *noun.* **1.** a seed of a food plant **2.** a tiny piece of something hard **3.** (no plural) the seeds of a food plant

gram *noun.* a measure of weight

grammar *noun.* the rules of a language

grammar school *noun.* elementary school

grammatical *adj.* correct according to grammar

grand *adj.* **1.** splendid; elegant **2.** wonderful **3.** trying to impress; too proud

grandchild *noun.* the child of your son or daughter (plural **grandchildren**)

granddaughter *noun.* the daughter of your son or daughter

grandfather *noun.* the father of your father or mother

grandma *noun.* a loving name for grandmother

grandmother *noun.* the mother of your father or mother

grandpa *noun.* a loving name for grandfather

grandparent *noun.* the father or mother of one of your parents

grandson *noun.* the son of your son or daughter

grandstand *noun.* rows of seats under a roof where people sit to watch a sport

granite *noun.* a hard gray stone used in building

granny, grannie *noun.* a loving name for grandmother

grant *noun.* money that someone gets from a government or an institution to be used for a certain purpose

grant *verb.* **(granted, granting)** (formal) give what someone asks for

grape *noun.* a small, round, juicy fruit that you can eat or use for making wine —**grape** *adj.*

grapefruit *noun.* a large, yellow fruit

grapevine *noun.* **1.** a plant on which grapes grow **2.** an unofficial way for news to get around

graph noun. a chart with lines that shows the connection between different things

graphic adj. 1. clearly described or shown 2. concerned with drawing, printing, lettering, etc —**graphically** adv.

graphics noun. the art and/or process of producing graphs, diagrams, drawings, etc

grasp noun. 1. the way you hold something 2. your understanding of something (no plural)

grasp verb. (**grasped, grasping**) 1. hold something tightly 2. understand something

grass noun. 1. the green plants that make up a lawn (no plural) 2. any kind of low green plant that horses, cows or sheep eat (plural **grasses**)

grass roots noun. adj. the ordinary members of an organization (not the leaders); ordinary people

grassy adj. (**grassier, grassiest**) covered with grass

grate verb. (**grated, grating**) rub something into small pieces or strips —**grated** adj.

grateful adj. feeling thankful toward someone

gratefully adv. in a way that shows that you are thankful

gratitude noun. being grateful (no plural)

grave noun. a hole in the earth where a dead person is buried

grave adj. very serious

gravely adv. seriously

graveyard noun. a place where dead people are buried; a cemetery

gravity noun. the force that keeps things on the ground and makes them fall to the ground (no plural)

gravy noun. the juice that comes from meat when it is cooking (plural **gravies**)

gray noun. a combination of the colors black and white —**gray** verb. adj.

grease noun. 1. animal fat 2. something oily like jelly that keeps machine parts working smoothly

grease verb. (**greased, greasing**) to put grease on something

greasy adj. (**greasier, greasiest**) fatty and sticky

great adj. 1. very large in amount or degree 2. very important 3. very special and excellent 4. (informal) wonderful —**greatly** adv. —**greatness** noun.

greed noun. a strong desire for more money, possessions, food, etc, than you need (no plural) —**greedy** adj. (**greedier, greediest**)

Greek noun. adj. the language or people of Greece
—**Greek** adj. of or from Greece

green noun. the color of grass and leaves

green adj. 1. of the color green 2. not yet ripe 3. (informal) inexperienced

greenhouse noun. a building with plastic or glass walls for growing plants under controlled conditions (plural **greenhouses**)

greens noun plural. green vegetables, such as cabbage, lettuce, etc

greet verb. (**greeted, greeting**) 1. say **Hello** to someone 2. welcome someone

greeting noun. 1. the first words that you say when you meet someone 2. the first words of a letter 3. good wishes

grenade noun. a small bomb

grew verb. past of **grow**

greyhound noun. a type of tall, slim and fast dog, used for racing and hunting

grief noun. deep sadness; sorrow (no plural; opposite **joy**)

grievance noun. a complaint against someone; a protest

grievous adj. very severe

grill noun. 1. part of a stove or a similar part for grilling 2. a set of bars for cooking quickly on fire or charcoal **3.** grilled food

grill *verb.* **(grilled, grilling)** cook meat over or under a direct flame; broil

grin *noun.* a big smile showing that you are pleased about something

grin *verb.* **(grinned, grinning)** smile widely

grind *verb.* **(ground, grounding) 1.** chop up into a fine powder **2.** cut up by putting through a machine with holes **3.** rub one thing against another, making a crushing noise **4.** make something sharp by rubbing something against it

grinder *noun.* a grinding machine

grip *noun.* a tight hold on something

grip *verb.* **(gripped, gripping)** hold on to something tightly

gripping *adj.* very exciting; holding your attention

gritty *adj.* covered with small bits of sand, stone, etc

groan *noun.* a long, deep sound of suffering, pain or disapproval **—groan** *verb.* **(groaned, groaning)**

grocer *noun.* someone who owns or operates a store that sells food

groceries *noun plural.* foods and other things on sale in a grocery or supermarket

grocery *noun.* a store that sells food in packages, cans, etc

groovy *adj.* (slang) marvelous

grope *verb.* **(groped, groping)** use your hand to try and find your way

gross *adj.* **1.** very obviously bad or wrong **2.** total (including all sums before taxes are deducted) **3.** (slang) disgusting

gross domestic product *noun.* GDP; the value of all the products and services produced in a country in one year excluding foreign investments

ground *noun.* **1.** the surface of the earth (no plural) **2.** a piece of land for a special purpose, such as parade ground **3.** the earth itself (no plural)

ground *adj.* **1.** made into a powder **2.** put through a meat grinder

ground *verb.* past tense and past participle of **grind**

grounds *noun plural.* **1.** a reason **2.** the land surrounding a building

group *noun.* **1.** a number of people or things together **2.** a small number of people who do a certain thing together

group *verb.* **(grouped, grouping) 1.** form yourselves into a group **2.** make groups out of things that go together

grove *noun.* an area were a group of citrus trees were planted

grow *verb.* **(grew, grown, growing) 1.** become taller or bigger **2.** become **3.** become more **4.** produce plants or crops **5.** let your hair get longer **6.** become longer

grower *noun.* **1.** a producer of agricultural crops **2.** how a plant grows

growl *verb.* **(growled, growling)** make a low, threatening sound in your throat

grown *adj.* finished growing

grown *verb.* past participle of **grow**

grown-up *noun. adj.* a person who is no longer a child; an adult

growth *noun.* **1.** becoming bigger (no plural) **2.** something that grows on the skin or inside the body

grub *noun.* (slang) food

grubby *adj.* **(grubbier, grubbiest)** dirty

grudge *noun.* a feeling of anger, dislike, etc, that you have against someone for a long time; a grievance

grumble *verb.* **(grumbled, grumbling)** complain in a quiet but angry way

grunge *noun.* (slang) dirt; filth

guarantee *noun.* **1.** a promise **2.** a written promise from a company

guarantee *verb.* **(guaranteed, guaranteeing) 1.** make a promise **2.** promise a buyer that the company will take responsibility

guard *noun.* **1.** a person who protects someone or something **2.** someone who keeps people from escaping from a place **3.** a group of guards (no plural) **4.** something that protects against harm

guard *verb.* **(guarded, guarding)** protect someone or something from harm

guardian *noun.* a person who is legally responsible for a child who has no parents

guerilla, guerrilla *noun. adj.* a fighter who does not belong to an official army unit and often fights behind the lines

guess *noun.* an answer or opinion you are not sure of (plural **guesses**)

guess *verb.* **(guessed, guessing) 1.** give an answer you hope is right but you are not sure **2.** suppose

guest *noun.* **1.** someone who comes to visit **2.** someone who stays at a hotel

guidance *noun.* advice or help to others about what to do or how to deal with difficult situations

guide *noun.* **1.** someone who shows the way to a place **2.** a book that gives information about how to do something —**guide** *verb.* **(guided, guiding)**

guidelines *noun plural.* informal rules or instructions on how something should be done

guild *noun.* a society for people who have the same interests

guilt *noun.* the feeling that you have done something bad (no plural)

guilty *adj.* **1.** feeling that you have done something bad **2.** having broken the law

guinea pig *noun.* a small animal often used in medical experiments

guise *noun.* (formal) an outer appearance

guitar *noun.* a musical instrument with six strings that singers often play

guitarist *noun.* a guitar player

gulf *noun.* a small part of the sea which is almost completely surrounded by land

gullible *adj.* easily fooled

gulp *verb.* **(gulped, gulping)** take a large swallow of food or drink

gum *noun.* **1.** the pink flesh above and below your teeth **2.** chewing gum (no plural)

gun *noun.* a weapon that shoots bullets

gunman *noun.* an armed person, especially one who is a criminal or a terrorist (plural **gunmen**)

gush *noun.* a strong flow

guts *noun plural.* (slang) courage; bravery

gutter *noun.* a small channel at the side of the road or the edge of a roof for taking rain water away

guy *noun.* (informal) a man; a fellow

gym *noun.* **1.** gymnasium **2.** physical education

gymnasium *noun.* a building or large room for sports and physical exercise

gymnastics *noun.* a sport including physical exercises

gypsy *noun.* a member of a people who live in caravans and move from place to place (plural **gypsies**)

H

habit *noun.* something that you do again and again without thinking about it

habitat *noun.* the natural home of an animal or plant

habitual *adj.* 1. usual 2. having a habit

had *verb.* past and past participle of **have**; had + past participle of verb = past perfect tense
—**hadn't** *abbr.* = had not

haggle *verb.* (**haggled, haggling**) argue over a price

hail *noun.* frozen rain; ice that falls from the sky (no plural) —**hail** *verb.* (**hailed, hailing**)

hair *noun.* 1. what grows on your head (no plural) 2. one of the threads that grows on the bodies of animals and people

haircut *noun.* 1. the way that your hair is cut 2. the cutting of your hair

hairdresser *noun.* someone whose job is cutting and arranging hair; a barber (only for men)

hairy *adj.* 1. having a lot of hair 2. (slang) frightening

half *noun. pron.* one of the two equal parts of something (plural **halves**) — **half** *adj. adv.*

half-hearted *adj.* not enthusiastic

half-price *adj. adv.* an item on sale for 50% of its original price

halfway *adv.* the middle distance between two points

hall *noun.* 1. a large room for a particular purpose 2. a passage between rooms

hallmark *noun.* 1. the mark on gold or silver to prove that it is truly gold or silver of a certain quality 2. a distinguishing feature

Halloween *noun.* a holiday celebrated on October 31st when it was thought that ghosts and spirits come out

hallway *noun.* a long passage with rows of doors on both sides; a corridor

halt *noun.* a stop

halt *verb.* (**halted, halting**) stop walking or driving

halve *verb.* (**halved, halving**) cut into two equal parts

halves *noun.* plural of **half**

ham *noun.* salted or smoked meat from a pig

hamburger *noun.* a flat, round piece of ground meat, usually served as a sandwich inside a round roll

hammer *noun.* a tool with a long handle and metal head that is used for hitting nails —**hammer** *verb.* (**hammered, hammering**)

hand *noun.* 1. the part of your body that you hold things with 2. the pointer on a clock or a watch 3. a worker on a farm or in a factory 4. help (no plural)

hand *verb.* (**handed, handing**) pass something; give

handbag *noun.* the bag that a woman carries with her to hold money, cosmetics, etc (same as **purse** or **pocketbook**)

handful *noun.* 1. what you hold in your hands 2. only a few

hand grenade *noun.* a small bomb that someone throws by hand

handicap *noun.* something that makes it difficult to do well —**handicap** *verb.* (**handicapped, handicapping**) —**handicapped** *adj.*

handkerchief *noun.* a square piece of cloth for blowing your nose

handle *noun.* the part of a thing that you hold in your hand

handle *verb.* (**handled, handling**) 1. touch something with your hands 2. manage; deal with; control 3. take care of

handout noun. 1. something given for free 2. a flier; information given out

handshake noun. shaking someone's hand when you meet, say goodbye, etc

handsome adj. 1. attractive; good-looking (usually for a man) 2. generous

handwriting noun. the way that someone writes

handwritten adj. written by hand, not typed or photographed

handy adj. 1. useful 2. close by; easy to get to 3. good at doing things by hand

hang verb. (hung/hanged, hanging) 1. fix something at the top so that the lower part is loose 2. be fixed at the top, with the rest loose 3. kill someone by putting a rope around the person's neck and tying the other end to something high up

hanger noun. 1. a thin bar with a hook at the top to hang your clothes on 2. a garage for airplanes

hangover noun. a feeling of illness the morning after a person drinks too much alcohol

hang-up noun. (informal) something that someone is worried about all the time

happen verb. (happened, happening) take place

happening noun. 1. any event 2. a big event

happy adj. (happier, happiest) 1. having pleasant experiences 2. glad; joyful 3. satisfied —**happily** adv. (opposite **unhappily; sadly**) —**happiness** noun. (no plural; opposite **unhappiness; sadness; sorrow**)

harass verb. (harassed, harassing) annoy constantly

harbor noun. a place where ships are safe; a port

hard adj. 1. firm; not soft 2. difficult 3. full of troubles 4. not gentle or forgiving

hard adv. 1. with a great deal of effort 2. to a strong degree

hardback noun. adj. a book with a stiff cover (opposite **paperback**)

hard currency noun. money that is used in international trade; money that can be easily exchanged with the money of other countries and does not lose value

harden verb. (hardened, hardening) 1. become hard 2. make something hard (opposite **soften**)

hardly adv. almost not at all

hardship noun. difficult conditions

hardware noun. 1. tools and equipment made of metal 2. the electronic and electric parts of a computer (not the programs)

hare noun. a kind of large rabbit

harm noun. damage; injury (no plural)

harm verb. (harmed, harming) do damage or injury

harmful adj. (more harmful, most harmful) causing damage; dangerous

harmless adj. not dangerous

harmony noun. 1. notes of music that sound well together (plural **harmonies**) 2. agreement (no plural) —**harmonious** adj.

harness noun. leather straps for controlling or fastening a horse (plural **harnesses**)

harp noun. a large musical instrument with many metal strings on a big frame

harsh adj. 1. rough and unpleasant 2. strict; cruel 3. cold and hard to live through —**harshly** adv.

harvest noun. the gathering in of a crop

harvest verb. (harvested, harvesting) gather in ripe fruit, vegetables, etc

has verb. 1. third person, singular, present simple of **have** 2. a helping verb in the present perfect tense —**hasn't** abbr. = has not

haste noun. hurry; rush (no plural)

hastily adv. quickly; in a hurry

hasty adj. (hastier, hastiest) done quickly

hat noun. something that you wear on your head

hatch *verb.* **(hatched, hatching)** come out of an egg

hate *verb.* **(hated, hating)** feel strong dislike or anger (opposite **like; love**) — **hate** *noun.* (no plural; opposite **love**)

hatred *noun.* (also **hate**) total dislike or anger of a particular thing

haul *verb.* **(hauled, hauling)** drag or pull something heavy

haulage *noun.* **1.** a business of transporting things by road **2.** the charge for hauling something

haunt *verb.* **(haunted, haunting) 1.** come back over and over **2.** be visited by a ghost or spirit

haunted *adj.* believed to have ghosts

haunting *adj.* staying in your mind

have *verb.* **1.** belonging to someone **2.** be part of someone or something **3.** do something **4.** be sick with something; feel pain **5.** experience something **6.** eat or drink something **7.** used as a helping verb in the present perfect tense

—**haven't** *abbr.* = have not

hawk *noun.* a large meat-eating bird that hunts small animals and birds

hay *noun.* grass that is dried and used for feeding horses and cattle (no plural)

hay fever *noun.* an illness that is like having a cold but is caused by an allergy (no plural)

hazard *noun.* a danger —**hazardous** *adj.*

haze *noun.* a thin mist (no plural)

he *pron.* a man or boy

—**he'd** *abbr.* **1.** = he would **2.** = he had

—**he'll** *abbr.* = he will

—**he's** *abbr.* **1.** = he is **2.** = he has

head *noun.* **1.** the part of the body above the neck **2.** the brain **3.** the front part or the top of something **4.** someone at the top of something

head *verb.* **(headed, heading)** be at the top or in front of something

headache *noun.* a pain in the head

heading *noun.* the title of an article; the words at the top that tell what the article is about

headlight *noun.* one of the two lights in the front of a car

headline *noun.* the title of an article in a newspaper —**headline** *verb.* **(headlined, headlining)**

head-on *adj.* in a way that is exactly opposite

headphones *noun plural.* ear pieces that fit over your head for listening to a radio

headquarters *noun.* the place from which something is controlled (plural and singular; *abbr.* **HQ**)

heads *noun.* one side of a coin, usually with a head stamped on it

head start *noun.* an advantage over other people

headway *noun.* progress; advancing in order to get good results

heal *verb.* **(healed, healing) 1.** become well again **2.** make someone well again —**healer** *noun.*

health *noun.* the condition of the body or the mind (no plural)

healthy *noun.* **(healthier, healthiest)** in good health (opposite **unhealthy**)

heap *noun.* **1.** a pile **2.** (informal) a lot of

heap *verb.* **(heaped, heaping)** make a pile of things

hear *verb.* **(heard) 1.** receive sound through your ears **2.** learn about something

hearing *noun.* **1.** the ability to hear; the sense that enables you to be aware of sounds (no plural) **2.** how far away someone can hear something (no plural) **3.** a chance to explain yourself

heart *noun.* **1.** the organ that supplies blood to your body **2.** the center of someone's feelings **3.** courage **4.** the center of something **5.** one of the sets of playing cards

heartache *noun.* sadness and worry (no plural)

heart attack noun. a serious illness in which the heart stops working properly

heartbeat noun. a movement of the heart

heartbreak noun. terrible disappointment and sadness

heartfelt adj. truly felt

hearth noun. a fireplace

hearty adj. 1. strong and healthy 2. friendly

heat noun. high temperatures; hotness (no plural; opposite **cold**)

heat verb. **(heated, heating)** make something hot

heated adj. full of anger and excitement

heater noun. an instrument for heating a place or heating water

heath noun. an open area of land that is overgrown with wild plants and bushes

heating noun. a system for warming your house, office, etc

heave verb. **(heaved, heaving)** throw something heavy

heaven noun. 1. the sky 2. in some religions, the happy place where good people go after they die

heavenly adj. 1. connected with the sky 2. connected with the religious idea of heaven 3. (slang) completely wonderful

heavily adv. 1. slowly and with difficulty 2. more than usually so

heavy adj. 1. having a lot of weight 2. having a certain weight 3. strong 4. more than the usual; hard to bear 5. serious and boring

heavy-duty adj. strong; made to last a long time

heavy-handed adj. 1. clumsy 2. unkind or unfair

heavyweight noun. a boxer who is in the highest weight category

hectic adj. full of excited activity

hedge noun. a row of bushes at the edge of a yard

hedgehog noun. a small animal that is covered with needles, like a small porcupine

heel noun. 1. the back part of a foot 2. the part of a shoe or boot that is under the heel of your foot

hefty adj. 1. big and strong 2. large in amount

height noun. 1. how tall someone or something is (no plural) 2. being high up

heir noun. someone who gets the money and possessions of a person who dies

held verb. past tense and past participle of **hold**

helicopter noun. an aircraft with big, revolving blades on top

hell noun. 1. in some religions, a terrible place where bad people go after they die (opposite **heaven**) 2. cruel conditions or misery 3. an exclamation of anger or disappointment

hello interj. what you say when you meet someone whom you know or when you make or receive a phone call

helmet noun. a round metal hat that protects your head

help noun. 1. aid 2. something that makes life easier

help verb. **(helped, helping)** do something to make things easier for another person

helper noun. someone who helps

helpful adj. 1. willing to help 2. being of help

helping noun. a portion of food

helpless adj. not knowing what to do or how to take care of yourself —**helplessly** adv.

hem noun. the edge of a piece of material that you fold and sew neatly

hemisphere noun. 1. half of the earth (especially when relating to the equator as the dividing line between north and south) 2. either of two halves of the brain

hen *noun.* **1.** a female chicken (a male chicken = **rooster, cock**) **2.** any female bird

hence *adv.* (formal) therefore

her *adj.* belonging to a girl or woman (the possessive form of **she**) (compare with **hers**)

her *pron.* a word that means a girl or a woman (the object form of **she**) (plural **them**)

herb *noun.* a plant with a pleasant smell that is used in cooking or in medicines —**herbal** *adj.*

herd *noun.* a group of certain grass-eating animals

here *adv.* **1.** in or at this place **2.** to this place **3.** at this point

heresy *noun.* a religious belief not according to the official religion

heritage *noun.* traditions, ways of life and values passed on by society from one generation to another

hero *noun.* **1.** a man or boy who is very brave **2.** the most important male character in a story or play

heroic *adj.* very brave

heroin *noun.* a very dangerous habit-forming drug (no plural)

heroine *noun.* **1.** a very brave woman or girl **2.** the main female character in a story or play

heroism *noun.* great courage (no plural)

hers *pron.* (the possessive pronoun of **she**) belonging to a woman or girl (plural **theirs**)

herself *pron.* **1.** a word that shows that it is the same woman or girl **2.** without help **3.** a word that tells emphatically who did something

hesitant *adj.* uncertain about whether to do something

hesitate *verb.* (**hesitated, hesitating**) start to do something and then stop because you are uncertain

hesitation *noun.* uncertainty about doing something (no plural)

heterogeneous *adj.* made up of different kinds (opposite **homogeneous**)

heterosexual *adj.* attracted to the opposite sex

hey *interj.* said to attract someone's attention or when you are annoyed

heyday *noun.* a time of great success and wealth

hi *interj.* hello

hide *verb.* (**hid, hidden, hiding**) **1.** stay somewhere where you cannot be seen **2.** put something in a place where nobody will find it **3.** keep as a secret —**hiding** *noun.* (no plural)

hi-fi *noun.* high-fidelity sound equipment

high *adj.* **1.** tall **2.** far from the ground **3.** how far something is from the ground **4.** important; senior **5.** more than the usual **6.** near the top of a scale

high *adv.* far above the ground (opposite **low**)

highland *noun.* mountainous land; relating to the Highlands of Scotland

highlight *verb.* (**highlighted, highlighting**) pick out something as important

highly *adv.* very

Highness *noun.* a title for a royal person

high-profile *noun.* something that attracts a lot of attention

high-quality *adj.* made from the best things

high school *noun.* secondary school

highway *noun.* a main road

hijack *verb.* force the driver of a plane or other vehicle to go where you tell him/her to (**hijacked, hijacking**)

hijacker *noun.* someone who hijacks a vehicle

hike *noun.* a long walk

hike *verb.* (**hiked, hiking**) take a long walk in the country

hilarious *adj.* very funny; making someone laugh a lot

hill *noun.* **1.** a low mountain **2.** a piece of ground that is higher than the rest

hilly *adj.* full of hills

him *pron.* (object of **he**) a word that means a man or boy (plural **them**)

himself *pron.* **1.** (reflexive of **he**) a word that means the same man or boy **2.** a word that tells emphatically who did something **3.** without help

hind *adj.* back (used only for four-legged animals)

hinder *verb.* **(hindered, hindering)** slow someone or something down; prevent someone's or something's advance or development

hindsight *noun.* understanding what should have been done only after something already happened

Hindu *noun. adj.* someone who believes in or something connected to the major religion of India, which states that a person is born again with different social ranks

hinge *noun.* a small piece of metal that joins two things together and lets one swing

hint *noun.* **1.** a small piece of information that gives a clue to an answer **2.** an indirect way of telling something **3.** helpful advice

hint *verb.* **(hinted, hinting)** give information in an indirect way

hip *noun.* the place where your leg joins the side of your body

hippie *noun.* a young person who dresses and behaves in unconventional ways

hire *verb.* **(hired, hiring) 1.** give work to someone **2.** rent something for a short period —**hire** *noun.* (no plural)

his *adj.* (the possessive form of **he**) belonging to a man or boy (plural **their**)

his *pron.* (the possessive pronoun of **he**) belonging to a man or boy (plural **theirs**)

Hispanic *noun. adj.* people from Central or South American countries

hiss *verb.* **(hissed, hissing)** make a sound like a snake —**hissing** *noun. adj.*

historian *noun.* someone whose profession is the study of history

historic *adj.* **1.** memorable; that will be remembered in the future **2.** very important in history

historical *adj.* connected with history — **historically** *adv.*

history *noun.* **1.** a study of the past (no plural) **2.** past events (plural **histories**) **3.** the past events of a person's life (plural **histories**)

hit *noun.* **1.** a blow with the hand or with an instrument **2.** something or someone who is very popular

hit *verb.* **(hit, hitting) 1.** strike with your hand or with an instrument **2.** bump against something with force

hitch *verb.* **(hitched, hitching)** get a ride by standing by the roadside

hi-tech *noun. adj.* high-technology

hitherto *adv.* until now; until then

hive *noun.* where bees live

hoard *verb.* **(hoarded, hoarding)** save and not use, often secretly

hoarse *adj.* having a rough voice because of a sore throat

hobby *noun.* something that you do for enjoyment (plural **hobbies**)

hockey *noun.* a game in which two teams of players try to hit a ball with a curved stick

hog *noun.* a male pig raised for meat

hold *noun.* a grip on something

hold *verb.* **(held, holding) 1.** have or take something in your hands or arms **2.** have inside; contain **3.** be strong enough to carry a certain weight **4.** keep something for someone **5.** organize an event **6.** have a job, etc

holder *noun.* **1.** someone who has a title, property, money, land, etc **2.** something that holds something else

hole *noun.* a space; a gap; an open place in something

holiday *noun.* **1.** a special day that people celebrate **2.** a day or days when you don't work or go to school; a vacation

hollow *adj.* empty inside

holocaust *noun.* large-scale destruction of human lives

—the Holocaust *noun.* the massacre of Jews and other people in Europe in Nazi concentration camps during the Second World War

holy *adj.* **1.** connected with God; sacred **2.** very religious

home *noun.* **1.** the place where someone lives **2.** where a person comes from

home *adv.* to the place where you live

homeless *adj.* not having a place to live

homelessness *noun.* the state of being homeless

home-made *noun.* made at home; not bought from a store

homesick *adj.* missing a person or a place so strongly that you feel depressed

homestead *noun.* a house and land around it, especially a farm, that is lived in by a family

homework *noun.* lessons or assignments that you have to do at home (no plural)

homogeneous *adj.* all or everyone the same (opposite **heterogeneous**)

homosexual *noun. adj.* a person who is attracted to members of her/his own sex; gay

honest *adj.* **1.** not likely to cheat you **2.** truthful; not a lie (opposite **dishonest**)

—honestly *adv.* (opposite **dishonestly**)

honesty *noun.* being honest (no plural; opposite **dishonesty**)

honey *noun.* **1.** the sweet food that bees make **2.** (informal) a word that men or women use to talk to the person that they love (no plural)

honeymoon *noun.* a trip that a newly married couple go on just after the wedding

honorary *adj.* **1.** a rank, degree, etc, given without going through the ordinary process of getting that rank, degree, etc **2.** holding a position without being paid for it

hood *noun.* **1.** a head covering that is attached to a jacket, coat or sweater **2.** the covering of the front of the car where the motor usually is

hoof *noun.* the hard foot of a horse, etc

hook *noun.* **1.** a curved piece of metal or plastic **2.** one part of a fastener

hook *verb.* **(hooked, hooking) 1.** catch something on a hook **2.** fasten with a hook

hooligan *noun.* a rough and violent young man

hoot *noun.* **1.** the call of an owl. **2.** the sound of a car horn

hop *noun.* **1.** a short jump on one foot **2.** a short journey by airplane, often a stage on a long flight

hop *verb.* **(hopped, hopping) 1.** jump on one leg **2.** move in small jumps like a rabbit

hope *noun.* **1.** the wish that something will happen the way you want to **2.** a reasonable chance of something happening (no plural)

hope *verb.* **(hoped, hoping)** wish very much for something to happen

hopeful *adj.* **1.** having hope **2.** giving reason to hope; encouraging

hopefully *adv.* **1.** with hope **2.** if things work out well

hopeless *adj.* very bad; without hope — **hopelessly** *adv.*

horizon *noun.* the line where the sky meets the sea

horizontal *adj.* going from side to side, not up and down (opposite **vertical**) **horizontally** *adv.* (opposite **vertically**)

hormone *noun.* a chemical substance in the body that affects the functions of the cells

horn *noun.* **1.** a sharp point that sticks out of the head of certain animals **2.** a musical instrument that you blow **3.** an instrument in a car, bus, etc, that makes a noise to warn people

horrible adj. 1. very unpleasant 2. terrible; very bad and cruel

horrify verb. (horrified, horrifying) cause fear or shock

horror noun. shock and fear —**horror** adj.

horse noun. a large, strong animal that you can ride and that sometimes works on a farm

horseback noun. adj. on a horse's back

horseshoe noun. a U-shaped piece of iron nailed onto the foot of a horse

horticulture noun. the science of growing flowers, fruit and vegetables — **horticultural** adj.

hose noun. a rubber or plastic pipe for watering or washing something

hospital noun. a place where doctors and nurses take care of sick or injured people

hospitality noun. friendly and generous treatment of guests (no plural)

hospitalize verb. (hospitalized, hospitalizing) keep someone in the hospital

host noun. 1. a person who receives guests 2. a presenter on a radio or a TV show

host verb. (hosted, hosting) entertain guests; introduce participants in a TV or radio show

hostage noun. someone who is taken prisoner in exchange for something

hostel noun. a place where students or travelers can get rooms and meals inexpensively

hostess noun. a woman who receives guests at home or organizes a social event

hostile adj. very unfriendly; enemy — **hostility** noun.

hot adj. 1. very warm (opposite **cold**) 2. very sharp and spicy

hot dog noun. a long sausage in a bread roll (also **frankfurter**)

hotel noun. a building with rooms for travelers or tourists to stay in

hound noun. a kind of dog used for hunting

hour noun. 1. 60 minutes 2. the time for a particular activity

hourly adj. every hour

house noun. a building where people live (usually meant for one or two families)

household noun. the people who live in a house

household adj. household expenses include groceries, electric bills, gas bills, etc

housekeeper noun. someone whose job is taking care of another person's house

housekeeping noun. the management of a house including cleaning, cooking, shopping, etc

housewife noun. 1. a woman who takes care of her house and family 2. a woman who stays at home to do housework and takes care of the family, etc, but does not work outside (plural **housewives**)

housework noun. work connected with taking care of a house and the people who live in it (no plural)

housing noun. 1. places to live 2. conditions in which people live

housing development noun. a group of houses built by one builder

hover verb. (hovered, hovering) be able to stay in the air in one place

how adv. 1. in what way; by what means 2. in what condition 3. the way that 4. an exclamation of surprise

however conj. 1. even so; in spite of that fact 2. on the other hand; in contrast

however adv. no matter how

howl noun. the sound that a dog or a wolf makes when it cries loudly

hub noun. 1. the center of activity 2. the center of a wheel

hug verb. (hugged, hugging) put your arms around someone to show love — **hug** noun.

huge adj. very big; enormous (opposite **tiny**)

hum *noun.* the noise that a bee makes (no plural)

hum *verb.* **(hummed, humming) 1.** sing with your lips closed **2.** make a noise like a bee

human *noun. adj.* a person, not an animal; of people

human being *noun.* a person; a human

humanitarian *adj.* trying to help people and improve their lives

humanity *noun.* the human race; all the human beings

human race *noun.* all the human beings (no plural)

human resources *noun plural.* skills and abilities of people

human rights *noun plural.* the freedoms and rights that all people should have

humble *adj.* **1.** low in rank or social position **2.** having a low opinion of yourself

humid *adj.* very damp

humidity *noun.* (no plural) the amount of water in the air

humiliate *verb.* **(humiliated, humiliating)** make someone feel ashamed in front of other people

humiliation *noun.* the feeling of being humiliated

humor *noun.* the ability to be funny or see things as funny

humorous *adj.* funny; amusing

hump *noun.* a big, round lump

hundred *noun. adj.* the number 100

hundredth *noun. adj.* = 100th; number 100

hung *verb.* past and past participle of **hang**

Hungarian *noun* the language spoken in Hungary; a person from Hungary —**Hungarian** *adj.* of or from Hungary

hunger *noun.* **1.** the need for food **2.** a strong need

hungry *adj.* **(hungrier, hungriest)** wanting food

hunk *noun.* **1.** a thick piece of something, especially food **2.** (slang) a good-looking, muscular man

hunt *verb.* **(hunted, hunting)** kill wild animals for food or for sport —**hunting** *noun. adj.* (no plural)

hunter *noun.* someone who hunts

hurricane *noun.* a terrible storm with strong winds

hurry *verb.* **(hurried, hurrying) 1.** move or act very quickly **2.** try to make someone do something faster —**hurry** *noun.* —**hurried** *adj.*

hurt *verb.* **(hurt, hurting) 1.** cause pain or damage; injure **2.** feel pain **3.** be unkind to someone

husband *noun.* the man that a woman is married to

hush *verb.* **(hushed, hushing)** make someone be quiet

hut *noun.* a small, simple house with only one room

hydrogen *noun.* a chemical substance that is lighter than air and has no smell or color

hygiene *noun.* rules and practices for keeping healthy

hypothesis *noun.* a guess, assumption or idea that suggests an explanation; a theory that has not been tested or proven (plural **hypotheses**)

hypothetical *adj.* based on an imaginary situation, a suggestion, or something that has not been proved

hysteria *noun.* **1.** nervous excitement **2.** dangerously excited behavior in a crowd

hysterical *adj.* **1.** panicky and unreasoning **2.** excited and dangerous

I

I *pron.* (first person subject singular) the person who is speaking; myself (plural we)
—**I'd** *abbr.* **1.** = I would **2.** = I had
—**I'll** *abbr.* = I will; I shall
—**I'm** *abbr.* = I am
—**I've** *abbr.* = I have

ice *noun.* **1.** water that is frozen (no plural) **2.** something cold and sweet made from water and syrup

ice *verb.* **(iced, icing)** put icing on a cake

iceberg *noun.* a massive piece of ice floating in the ocean where only a small part is above water

ice cream *noun.* a soft, sweet, cold food made from cream

iced *adj.* **1.** with icing **2.** made cold

ice hockey *noun.* hockey played on ice by players wearing ice skates (no plural)

icing *noun.* a sweet covering for a cake

icon *noun.* **1.** a picture or statue of a holy person **2.** a famous person who represents something important **3.** a small graphic sign on a computer screen that if clicked on by a computer mouse makes the computer do something

icy *adj.* **1.** covered with ice **2.** very cold

ID *abbr.* identification (documents)

idea *noun.* **1.** a new thought that comes into your mind **2.** a picture in the mind; a concept

ideal *noun.* an example or an idea that seems perfect

ideal *adj.* perfect

ideally *adv.* if conditions were perfect

ideals *noun plural.* high standards or principles

identical *adj.* exactly the same

identification *noun.* **1.** ID; a piece of paper that shows who you are —**identification card 2.** telling who someone is **3.** a sense of having the same feelings and problems as someone else

identify *verb.* **(identified, identifying)** know or tell who someone is

identity *noun.* who someone is (plural identities)

idiom *noun.* a group of words which have a special meaning when they are used together

idiot *noun.* a person who is stupid or does something foolish

idle *adj.* **1.** standing still; not moving **2.** lazy —**idle** *verb.* **(idled, idling)**

idly *adv.* with nothing to do

idol *noun.* **1.** a person or thing greatly admired and loved **2.** a statue prayed to as a god

if *conj.* **1.** on condition that **2.** supposing something that is not true **3.** supposing that something had happened or had not happened **4.** whenever **5.** whether; supposing that something may or may not happen

ignorant *adj.* **1.** not knowing anything **2.** not knowing about a specific thing

ignore *verb.* **(ignored, ignoring)** refuse to pay attention to something that you know about —**ignorance** *noun.*

ill *adj.* sick; not feeling well

illegal *adj.* against the law (opposite legal) —**illegally** *adv.*

illiterate *adj.* not able to read and write; not literate

illness *noun.* **1.** being ill; being sick (no plural) **2.** a disease; a specific sickness (plural **illnesses**)

illogical *adj.* not logical

illuminate *verb.* **(illuminated, illuminating)** give light to

illuminating *adj.* giving new information about something

illusion *noun.* something that you think is true but is not

illustrate *verb.* **(illustrated, illustrating)** **1.** draw pictures for a book **2.** make something clearer by drawing a picture, map, by giving an example, etc

illustrated *adj.* having pictures with the text

illustration *noun.* **1.** a drawing in a book **2.** an example

image *noun.* **1.** a picture in your mind **2.** what you see in a mirror or a camera **3.** a person who looks very much like someone else **4.** a figure that is made to look like someone **5.** the way that other people see someone **6.** the picture that you see on TV or in a photograph

imaginable *adj.* that can be imagined

imaginary *adj.* in the mind; not real (opposite **real**)

imagination *noun.* **1.** the ability to see things in your mind or make things up **2.** thinking that you see, hear or feel something that is not there (no plural)

imaginative *adj.* having a strong imagination

imagine *verb.* **(imagined, imagining) 1.** see pictures or situations in your mind **2.** think that you see, hear or feel something that is not there **3.** suppose

imbalance *noun.* usually a noticeable and undesirable difference between two things (opposite **balance**)

imitate *verb.* **(imitated, imitating)** copy the way that someone else does something

imitation *noun.* **1.** copying the way that someone else does something **2.** something made to look like something else; a false copy —**imitation** *adj.*

immature *adj.* not mature; not acting the way expected of someone at a certain age

immediate *adj.* done or needed right away

immediately *adv.* right away; now

immensely *adv.* to a very large degree

immigrant *noun.* someone who comes to a different country to make a new life there

immigration *noun.* coming to another country to live (**emigration** (from) = leave a country; **immigration** (to) = come to a country) —**immigration** *adj.*

immune *adj.* protected against/to

impact *noun.* **1.** the force that is there when one thing hits another thing **2.** the strong influence one thing (such as an idea, invention, happening, etc) has on someone or something

impact *verb.* **(impacted, impacting) 1.** have an effect on; affect **2.** hit; collide with

impaired *adj.* weak

impartial *adj.* not biased; not favoring either side

impatience *noun.* without patience

impatient *adj.* **1.** not wanting or not able to wait (opposite **patient**) **2.** not tolerant —**impatiently** *adv.* (opposite **patiently**)

impeccable *adj.* perfect; without a fault

imperative *noun.* (grammar) the command form of a verb

imperial *adj.* **1.** connected to an empire or its ruler **2.** relating to a British standard of weights and measures

impersonal *adj.* **1.** cold and unfriendly; without personal feelings **2.** (grammar) without a subject or with a meaningless expression like "it"

impersonate *verb.* pretend to be another person **(impersonated, impersonating)**

implant *verb.* **(implanted, implanting)** fix deeply in the mind or body

implement *verb.* **(implemented, implementing)** carry out —**implementation** *noun.*

implication *noun.* **1.** involvement (usually with a negative meaning) **2.** something that was suggested (implied) but not actually stated

implicit *adj.* **1.** unquestioning **2.** understood even though not directly (implicitly) stated

imply verb. (**implied, implying**) suggest; hint at

import noun. something that is brought into a country (opposite **export**)

import verb. (**imported, importing**) bring things into a country from another country

important adj. 1. having value or the power to make a difference 2. powerful —**importance** noun. (no plural) — **importantly** adv.

importer noun. a person, company or country that imports goods from other countries

impose verb. (**imposed, imposing**) 1. officially charge a tax 2. cause additional work or take unfair advantage of

impossible adj. that cannot happen; that cannot be done (opposite **possible**) —**impossibility** noun.

impound verb. (**impounded, impounding**) (formal) officially take until someone claims

impoverished adj. made poor; without money

impractical adj. not good in basic matters (opposite **practical**)

impress verb. (**impressed, impressing**) fix a strong positive image in the mind of someone else

impression noun. feelings or reactions that you have for something

impressionist noun. an artist who does not paint detail but uses small strokes of color to make forms

impressive adj. making a strong positive impression

imprint noun. a mark left in or on something

imprison verb. (**imprisoned, imprisoning**) put a person in prison or some other place that he/she cannot leave —**imprisonment** noun.

improbable adj. having only a very small chance of happening; not likely to happen (opposite **probable**)

improper adj. not acceptable or suitable according to social customs (opposite **proper**)

improve verb. (**improved, improving**) become or make better

improvement noun. a situation that is becoming or has become better (no plural)

improvise verb. (**improvised, improvising**) 1. make up music on the spot 2. make something with things on hand, often because of an unexpected situation

impulse noun. a sudden desire to do something —**impulsive** adj.

in prep. adv. 1. inside 2. a word that tells which place 3. a word that tells direction 4. a word that tells when 5. a word that tells when something will happen 6. a word that tells what someone is wearing 7. a word that tells how 8. a word that tells what was used 9. a word that tells you what language 10. a word that tells what someone does 11. at home or at the place where you work 12. popular

inability noun. not being able to do something (no plural; opposite **ability**)

inaccurate adj. not correct; not exact (opposite **accurate**)

inactive adj. passive; quiet (opposite **active**) —**inactively** adv.

inadequacy noun. not being good enough; a shortcoming; a defect (plural **inadequacies**)

inadequate adj. not enough (opposite **adequate, sufficient**)

inappropriate adj. not suitable; not the right thing (opposite **appropriate; suitable**)

inaugurate verb. (**inaugurated, inaugurating**) hold a special ceremony to start something (a term of presidency, a new service, a period of time, etc)

incapable adj. not having the capacity to

incentive noun. something that makes someone want to do something else

inception *noun.* (formal) the beginning of something

inch *noun.* a measurement of length (plural **inches**)

incident *noun.* a happening; an event

incidental *adj.* happening by the way and not as the main event

incidentally *adv.* by the way

inclined *adj.* have a tendency

include *verb.* (**included, including**) **1.** have as part of a total; contain **2.** be part of a total **3.** add someone or something as part of the total (opposite of 2 and 3 **exclude**)

including *prep.* having as a part (opposite **excluding**)

inclusive *adj.* that includes this last item as well

income *noun.* the money that someone earns

income tax *noun.* money that the government takes from your income

incoming *adj.* something coming in

incompetence *noun.* not having the skill or ability to do something (opposite **competence**) —**incompetent** *adj.* (opposite **competent**)

incomplete *adj.* **1.** not enough; not sufficient **2.** not finished; not whole (opposite **complete**) —**incompletely** *adv.* (opposite **completely**)

incomprehensible *adj.* that cannot be understood (opposite **comprehensible**)

inconvenience *noun.* trouble; difficulty (opposite **convenience**)

inconvenience *verb.* (**inconvenienced, inconveniencing**) cause difficulties; bother

inconvenient *adj.* causing difficulty — **inconveniently** *adv.* (opposite **conveniently**)

incorporate *verb.* (**incorporated, incorporating**) include as part of something else (usually larger) —**incorporation** *noun.*

incorrect *adj.* wrong (opposite **correct**) —**incorrectly** *adv.*

increase *noun.* growth; becoming more or bigger

increase *verb.* (**increased, increasing**) **1.** become more or bigger **2.** make something bigger —**increasingly** *adv.*

incredible *adj.* impossible to believe; unbelievable

incredibly *adv.* extremely

incur *verb.* (**incurred, incurring**) get, have or bring upon yourself

incurable *adj.* something that cannot be cured

indeed *adv.* **1.** a word that makes stronger what someone says **2.** truly; certainly

indefinite *adj.* **1.** not clear; vague **2.** without limit

indefinite article *noun.* (grammar) the words **a** or **an**

indefinitely *adv.* without limit

independence *noun.* **1.** the state of not being dependent on or being controlled by anyone; freedom **2.** the desire or ability to do things by yourself (no plural)

independent *adj.* **1.** free **2.** able to do things by yourself

independently *adv.* **1.** by yourself **2.** separately

in-depth *adj.* thorough

index *noun.* a list of names, places, subjects, etc, in alphabetical order (plural **indexes**) —**index** *verb.* (**indexed, indexing**)

Indian *noun. adj.* **1.** someone or something from India **2.** a former name for a Native American

indicate *verb.* (**indicated, indicating**) **1.** show signs of something **2.** show something by giving a sign **3.** make something clear

indication *noun.* **1.** a sign **2.** what you say to make something clear —**indicator** *noun.*

indigestion *noun.* an uncomfortable feeling in the stomach and intestines because the body is not able to digest food that was eaten

indirect *adj.* not straight

indirectly *adv.* not straight; by hinting

indiscreet *adj.* not discreet

individual *noun.* one; a person

individual *adj.* for each one separately

individualism *noun.* the belief that the freedom and rights of a single person are the most important values of society

individually *adv.* separately; by yourselves; one by one

indoor *adj.* inside a building (opposite **outdoor**)

indoors *adv.* inside a building (opposite **outdoors**)

indulging *adj.* pampering; allowing someone to have whatever he/she wants

industrial *adj.* having a lot of factories; related to industry

industrialist *noun.* the owner of a factory or industrial company

industrialize *verb.* (**industrialized, industrializing**) develop industries

industry *noun.* 1. the production of goods (no plural) 2. the production of a certain thing (plural **industries**) 3. any type of trade

inefficient *adj.* wasting time and energy (opposite **efficient**) —**inefficiently** *adv.* (opposite **efficiently**)

inevitable *adj.* something that cannot be prevented or stopped —**inevitably** *adv.*

inexpensive *adj.* not costing much; cheap (opposite **expensive**)

inexperienced *adj.* new at doing something; without experience (opposite **experienced**)

infancy *noun.* the time when someone is a baby

infant *noun.* a baby

infect *verb.* (**infected, infecting**) 1. pass on an illness that is caused by germs to someone 2. cause a wound, cut or sore to develop an infection —**infected** *adj.*

infection *noun.* 1. an illness 2. a part of the body that has become infected

infectious *adj.* passing from one person to another

infer *verb.* (**inferred, inferring**) conclude from facts or reasoning; understand even though not told directly

inferior *adj.* not as good as something or someone else

infinite *adj.* 1. without end 2. too many to be counted

infinitely *adv.* very (much)

infinitive *noun. adj.* (grammar) the basic form of the verb (to + base form)

infirmary *noun.* a place in a school, camp, etc, where you receive medical treatment (plural **infirmaries**)

inflate *verb.* (**inflated, inflating**) fill something with air

inflation *noun.* prices going up continually (no plural)

inflexible *adj.* firm and unbending; refusing to change (opposite **flexible**)

influence *noun.* the power that someone or something has in order to affect someone or something else

influence *verb.* (**influenced, influencing**) 1. have the power to make someone do what you want 2. have the power to change in some way

influential *adj.* having influence; with influence

influx *noun.* a sudden inflow of a large amount of something

inform *verb.* (**informed, informing**) tell; give information —**informative** *adj.*

informal *adj.* not according to strict rules; casual (opposite **formal**) —**informally** *adv.*

information *noun.* data; facts (no plural; use **a piece of information**)

informer *noun.* someone who gives information to the police for payment

infringe *verb.* (**infringed, infringing**) (formal) go against —**infringement** *noun.*

ingenious *adj.* showing inventiveness and cleverness

ingredient *noun.* a part of something

inhabit *verb.* **(inhabited, inhabiting)** live in a certain place

inhabitant *noun.* a person or animal who lives in a certain place

inhabited *adj.* lived in

inherit *verb.* **(inherited, inheriting)** 1. receive money or property from a dead person 2. receive a characteristic from one side of the family or the other —**inheritance** *noun.*

in-house *adj. adv.* something done within an organization

inhuman *adj.* very cruel (opposite **human**)

initial *noun.* each of the first letters of a name

initial *adj.* the first; the earliest

initial *verb.* **(initialed, initialing)** sign your initials

initially *adv.* at first

initiate *verb.* **(initiated, initiating)** be responsible for starting something

initiation *noun.* a ceremony to introduce someone into an organization

initiative *noun.* 1. the ability to use your judgment and make decisions by yourself (no plural) 2. an act of initiating something

inject *verb.* **(injected, injecting)** use a needle to put liquid into something

injection *noun.* using a needle to put liquid into something

injunction *noun.* (law) an official order form the courts not to do something

injure *verb.* **(injured, injuring)** hurt

injured *adj.* hurt

injury *noun.* 1. harm; damage (no plural) 2. a wound (plural **injuries**)

injustice *noun.* 1. unfairness; a wrong judgment of/about someone (no plural) 2. an act of unfairness (opposite **justice**)

ink *noun.* a dye that is used for writing

inland *adj.* not near the coast; placed inside a country

inlet *noun.* a stretch of water going from a sea inland

inn *noun.* a small, old-fashioned hotel

inner *adj.* 1. the part that is inside (opposite **outer**) 2. private; inside the mind

inner city *noun.* the part of a city near the center

inning *noun.* one of the periods in the game of baseball or cricket when each team has a turn to play

innocence *noun.* not being guilty (no plural)

innocent *adj.* 1. not guilty 2. having no experience in life 3. harmless —**innocently** *adv.*

innovate *verb.* **(innovated, innovating)** introduce new ideas —**innovation** *noun.* —**innovative** *adj.*

innovator *noun.* someone who innovates

input *noun.* information; anything that is put in

input *verb.* **(input/inputted, inputting)** put data into computers

inquire *verb.* **(inquired, inquiring)** ask about something

inquiry *noun.* 1. a question about something 2. an investigation in which you ask people questions

insane *noun. adj.* (opposite **sane**) 1. sick in the mind; crazy; mad 2. mad; irrational

insanity *noun.* being insane; madness (no plural)

insect *noun.* a small animal with six legs and no bones

insecure *adj.* 1. not safe 2. not feeling safe 3. not sure of yourself —**insecurity** *noun.*

insert *verb.* **(inserted, inserting)** put something inside another thing —**insertion** *noun.*

inside *noun.* the inner part of something

inside *adv.* 1. into something 2. indoors

inside *prep.* in something else (opposite **outside**)

insignificant *adj.* not important

insist verb. (**insisted, insisting**) 1. be firm about something 2. say something repeatedly because someone does not believe you

insolvent noun. adj. someone, a company, etc, that does not have enough money to pay his/her/its debts (opposite **solvent**)

inspect verb. (**inspected, inspecting**) 1. look closely at something 2. check to see that someone or something is working well

inspection noun. 1. a close look at something 2. a check to see that someone or something is working well

inspector noun. 1. someone who checks up on schools, hospitals, restaurants, etc, to see if things are the way that they should be 2. a police officer who investigates crimes

inspiration noun. the urge and ability to produce creative work; the force behind the urge to create

inspire verb. (**inspired, inspiring**) give inspiration

install verb. (**installed, installing**) put something new in place so that you can use it

installation noun. putting a new thing in its place

instance noun. a case of something

instant noun. moment

instant adj. very quick

instantly adv. immediately

instead adv. in place of something

instinct noun. knowing how to do something without thinking about it

instinctive adj. by instinct —**instinctively** adv.

institute noun. an organization or group that exists for a special purpose

institution noun. a large building for a special purpose

instruct verb. (**instructed, instructing**) 1. teach someone to do something 2. order someone to do something

instruction noun. 1. teaching a practical thing (no plural) 2. an explanation of how to do a certain thing

instructive adj. giving information

instructor noun. someone who teaches people how to do something; a teacher

instrument noun. 1. a tool used especially for delicate or scientific work 2. something that you play on to make music

instrumental adj. 1. for musical instruments and not for voices 2. helpful in bringing about something

insufficient adj. not enough (opposite **sufficient**) —**insufficiently** adv.

insult noun. a cruel thing that someone says to you

insult verb. (**insulted, insulting**) say unkind things to a person; hurt someone's feelings —**insulting** adj.

insurance noun. a contract with a company to which payments are made so that in case something happens to you or to your property that company will give you an amount of money according to the contract (no plural)

insure verb. (**insured, insuring**) 1. buy insurance to cover a particular kind of damage or injury 2. make sure

insurer noun. a person or a company that sells insurance

intangible adj. something that cannot be touched but can be sensed

integrate verb. (**integrated, integrating**) join together two or more groups or things

integrated adj. joined together (opposite **segregated**)

integration noun. joining together of different groups (no plural; opposite **segregation**)

integrity noun. honesty; honor; morality (no plural)

intellectual adj. using or needing the power of reason —**intellectual** noun. —**intellectually** adv.

intelligence noun. 1. the ability to think

and understand **2.** information gathering; spying

intelligent *adj.* clever; having the ability to think and understand

intend *verb.* **(intended, intending)** mean to do something; plan

intense *adj.* extreme or concentrated in quality; having feelings or opinions that are very strong and fierce —**intensify** *verb.* **(intensified, intensifying)**

intensive *adj.* **1.** giving a lot of information in a short time; concentrated **2.** deep and complete

intensive care *noun.* special care in a hospital for seriously ill patients

intent *noun.* a purpose; an aim

intention *noun.* what someone intends to do

intentional *adj.* on purpose; meaning to do something (opposite **unintentional**)

intentionally *adv.* on purpose (opposite **unintentionally**)

interact *verb.* **(interacted, interacting)** have an effect on one another; communicate with one another —**interaction** *noun.*

interactive *adj.* **1.** acting on one another **2.** relating to the exchange of information between a computer and its user

interest *noun.* **1.** the wish to know more about something **2.** extra money that you pay for money that you borrow (no plural) **3.** a hope to get some kind of benefit

interest *verb.* **(interested, interesting)** make someone want to know more about a particular thing

interesting *adj.* **1.** able to hold your attention **2.** making you want to know more about something

interfere *verb.* **(interfered, interfering)** try to take part in someone else's affairs without being invited

interference *noun.* **1.** taking an unwanted part in someone else's

affairs **2.** radio noise, TV lines, etc, that spoil listening or watching

interior *noun.* the inside of something (opposite **exterior**)

intermediary *noun.* a person who brings two parties together in order for them to reach an agreement

intermediate *adj.* in the middle; between elementary and advanced

intermission *noun.* the short time between parts of a play, a concert, etc

internal *adj.* **1.** on the inside of the body **2.** having to do with what happens inside your own country (opposite **external**)

international *adj.* concerning more than one country —**internationally** *adv.*

Internet *noun.* an international network for passing information by way of computer communication

interpret *verb.* **(interpreted, interpreting)** **1.** understand the probable meaning of something **2.** use your own way of understanding a piece of art, a poem, etc **3.** translate from one language into another —**interpretation** *noun.* —**interpreter** *noun.*

interrupt *verb.* **(interrupted, interrupting)** **1.** start to talk while someone else is talking **2.** stop someone or something while they are doing something else

interruption *noun.* stopping someone or something for a short time

intersection *noun.* the place where something meets and crosses something else

interval *noun.* **1.** a time between two things **2.** a space between two things

interview *noun.* a meeting at which someone has to answer questions — **interview** *verb.* **(interviewed, interviewing)** —**interviewer** *noun.*

intimidating *adj.* impressive; frightening, especially if someone or something threatens

into *prep.* **1.** to the inside of something **2.** from one thing to another

intolerable *adj.* something that is too hard, painful or difficult to bear

intolerant *adj.* not willing to accept something (behavior, religion, etc) different than what you believe —**intolerance** *noun.* (opposite **tolerance**)

intonation *noun.* (language) the way something is spoken, with a rise or fall of the voice, that sometimes changes the meaning of the sentence

intrigue *noun.* secret plotting

introduce *verb.* (**introduced, introducing**) **1.** tell who someone is **2.** (with **into**) bring in something new

introduction *noun.* **1.** telling who someone is **2.** (with **into**) bringing in something new (no plural) **3.** something written at the beginning of a book before the text; a preface; a foreword

intuition *noun.* knowing something without having to think about it (no plural) —**intuitive** *adj.*

invade *verb.* (**invaded, invading**) attack something by entering it

invalid *noun.* someone who is too ill to live a normal life

invalid *adj.* not true; not acceptable (opposite **valid**)

invasion *noun.* an attack on enemy territory

invent *verb.* (**invented, inventing**) **1.** make something for the first time **2.** make something up in your mind

invention *noun.* something that someone invented

inventive *adj.* having the ability to think in a new and different way

inventor *noun.* someone who invents something

inventory *noun.* stock; (a list of) all the products in a place that are available for sale and/or are stored somewhere

inversion *noun.* **1.** changing the order or position of something so that it is different from usual **2.** a weather condition where air is coolest near the ground

invest *verb.* (**invested, investing**) put money into something in the hope that you will get more money back

investigate *verb.* (**investigated, investigating**) try to discover the facts about something —**investigation** *noun.* —**investigator** *noun.*

investment *noun.* money put into something

investor *noun.* someone who invests money

invisible *adj.* that cannot be seen

invitation *noun.* asking someone to come to a party, wedding, etc

invite *verb.* (**invited, inviting**) **1.** ask someone to come to a party, wedding, etc **2.** ask someone to visit you

invoice *noun.* a list of services and/or products supplied and at the same time a request for payment

involve *verb.* (**involved, involving**) **1.** concern someone; have something to do with someone **2.** include as a necessary part; require

involved *adj.* **1.** busy with **2.** necessary; included —**involvement** *noun.*

inward, inwards *adv.* toward the inside

iodine *noun.* something you put on a cut to prevent infection (no plural)

IQ *noun. adj.* intelligence quotient; a measurement of intelligence

Irish *noun.* the language or people of Ireland
—**Irish** *adj.* of or from Ireland

iron *noun.* **1.** a strong, hard metal found in nature (no plural) —**iron** *adj.* **2.** an instrument for making clothes smooth

iron *verb.* (**ironed, ironing**) press clothes to make them smooth

ironing *noun.* things that need to be ironed (no plural)

irony *noun.* the use of words to mean the opposite of their usual meaning

irregular *adj.* **1.** not following the usual rules **2.** not at the usual times

irrelevant *adj.* not connected to the subject

irresponsible *adj.* careless; not to be trusted (opposite **responsible**) —**irresponsibly** *adj.*

irrigate *verb.* **(irrigated, irrigating)** supply water to crops, fields, etc

irrigation *noun.* watering dry land

irritable *adj.* short-tempered; quick to get angry

irritate *verb.* **(irritated, irritating)** **1.** annoy someone; get on someone's nerves **2.** make a wound worse

irritating *adj.* annoying

is *verb.* **1.** third person singular present simple of **be 2.** is + verb + -ing = present progressive
—**is not** *abbr.* = is not

Islam *noun.* the Muslim religion, established by the prophet Muhammad — **Islamic** *adj.*

island *noun.* **1.** a piece of land with water around it **2.** a raised place that resembles an island, in the middle of a road, where someone can wait for traffic to pass before crossing the rest of the road

isle *noun.* an island (used in names of islands or in poetry)

isolate *verb.* **(isolated, isolating)** put apart; separate

isolated *adj.* alone; away from other things —**isolation** *noun.*

issue *noun.* **1.** something that people discuss and argue about **2.** a problem **3.** something that is published at intervals

issue *verb.* **(issued, issuing) 1.** put out a newspaper, stamps, coins, etc **2.** say or print something in public **3.** provide people with something

it *pron.* **1.** a word for a thing **2.** a word that is often used for an animal **3.** a word that tells the time, day, month, year or season **4.** a word that leads to the real subject of the sentence **5.** a word that tells about the weather **6.** a word that tells who **7.** word that tells how far something is or how long it takes to get there (plural **they, them**)
—**it'll** *abbr.* = it will
—**it is** *abbr.* = it is; it has

Italian *noun. adj.* someone or something from Italy; the language spoken in Italy

itch *noun.* an annoying feeling on the skin that makes you want to scratch (plural **itches**)

item *noun.* an article; one of various things

itinerary *noun.* a plan for a journey (plural **itineraries**)

its *adj.* belonging to it (plural **their**; **it is** = it is, **its** = belongs to it)

itself *pron.* **1.** (reflexive) a word that means the same one or thing **2.** a word that tells emphatically what thing

ivory *noun.* **1.** the stuff that elephants' tusks are made of, something like bone **2.** the color of ivory, a kind of yellowish white

J

jack *noun*. **1.** a tool for lifting a car off the ground **2.** a playing card between 10 and Queen

jacket *noun*. a short coat

jackpot *noun*. all the money bet in a game of cards, chance, etc, or the biggest prize won from a slot machine

jade *noun*. *adj*. a green stone that is not transparent and is used in jewelry or for carving figures; bright green (color).

jail *noun*. prison; a place of punishment for someone who is convicted of a crime **—jail** *verb*. **(jailed, jailing)**

jam *noun*. **1.** something thick and sweet made from fruit that is spread on bread **2.** a crowd that cannot move easily **—jam** *verb*. **(jammed, jamming)**

jammed *adj*. **1.** crowded; full **2.** stuck

January *noun*. the first month of the year

Japanese *noun*. the language or people of Japan **—Japanese** *adj*.

jar *noun*. a glass container with a wide mouth for holding food

jargon *noun*. specialized vocabulary used by a group of people who are connected in the same field

jaw *noun*. either one of the two bones that form your mouth and hold your teeth

jazz *noun*. music with a strong beat

jealous *adj*. wanting something or someone all to yourself

jealousy *noun*. feeling jealous; envy (no plural)

jeans *noun*. trousers made from a strong cloth called denim (plural; also **a pair of jeans**)

jeep *noun*. (trademark) an open car that can travel in difficult conditions

jeer *verb*. **(jeered, jeering)** laugh at someone disrespectfully; make fun of someone

jelly *noun*. **1.** a sweet food made of fruit and sugar which you can spread on bread, like jam but without fruit pieces and usually clear **2.** a semi-solid, fruity dessert

jerk *noun*. **1.** a strong, quick pull **2.** a sudden bumpy motion **3.** (slang) a stupid person

jerk *verb*. **(jerked, jerking) 1.** pull something hard and suddenly **2.** move in a bumpy way

jerky *adj*. **(jerkier, jerkiest)** bumpy and uneven

jersey *noun*. **1.** warm clothing for the upper part of your body **2.** a fine knitted material for clothes (plural **jerseys**) **—jersey** *adj*.

jest *noun*. a joke

jet *noun*. **1.** a very fast airplane **2.** a strong, fast stream of something that is forced out of a small opening

jet *verb*. **(jetted, jetting)** travel by jet — **jet** *adj*.

Jew *noun*. a member of the Jewish people; a person whose religion is Judaism **—Jewish** *adj*.

jewel *noun*. **1.** a small, beautiful stone that is worth a lot of money **2.** a piece of jewelry made from jewels

jeweler *noun*. someone who knows about and sells jewelry

jewelry *noun*. ornaments that you wear, like necklaces, bracelets or earrings (no plural)

jingle *noun*. a catchy tune or phrase used to promote something

jingle *verb*. **(jingled, jingling)** make a light, high sound like small bells

job *noun*. **1.** work that you do for money **2.** a particular piece of work

jobless *adj*. unemployed

jockey *noun*. someone who rides a horse in a race

jog verb. **(jogged, jogging)** run slowly at a regular speed

jogging noun. a sport in which a person runs slowly at a regular speed

join verb. **(joined, joining)** 1. come together 2. fasten two things together 3. connect between two things 4. do something with someone 5. become a member of something 6. take part in activity

joint noun. a place where two bones come together

joint adj. concerning two or more people together —**jointly** adv.

joke noun. 1. a short, funny story 2. a trick

joke verb. **(joked, joking)** make a joke or say something as a joke

joker noun. 1. someone who jokes a lot 2. in a deck of cards, a wild card without a specific value

jolly adj. cheerful

jolt verb. **(jolted, jolting)** 1. shake or awaken roughly 2. move with big bumps

jot down verb. **(jotted, jotting)** write something down quickly

journal noun. 1. a newspaper or magazine for a special purpose 2. a diary

journalism noun. the profession of collecting, writing and editing material that is meant to be published in a newspaper and/or magazine

journalist noun. someone whose job is to write for a newspaper —**journalistic** adj.

journey noun. a trip

journey verb. **(journeyed, journeying)** travel

joy noun. 1. a feeling of happiness; gladness (no plural) 2. something that gives great pleasure (opposite **sadness, sorrow**)

joyful adj. 1. very happy 2. making very happy —**joyous** adj.

jubilee noun. the 50th anniversary of an event; a special anniversary

Judaism noun. the Jewish religion

judge noun. 1. a person who sits in a court-room and decides cases 2. someone who decides the winner of a competition

judge verb. **(judged, judging)** 1. decide if something is right or wrong 2. decide if something is good or bad 3. decide who the winner of a contest will be

judgment, judgement noun. 1. the ability to act sensibly (no plural) 2. the decision of a judge 3. a decision if something is right or wrong 4. an opinion about the value or quality of something (no plural)

judicial adj. related to a judge's decision or to a court of law

jug noun. a round container with a handle, a short neck and no lip

juggle verb. **(juggled, juggling)** keep a number of things moving in the air at the same time

juice noun. the liquid from fruit

juicy adj. **(juicier, juiciest)** full of juice

July noun. the seventh month

jumbo adj. (informal) extra large in size

jump noun. a leap in the air

jump verb. **(jumped, jumping)** 1. make a small leap into the air with both feet 2. move suddenly from excitement, surprise or fear 3. go up sharply —**jump to conclusions** reach a conclusion too quickly, before you have all the facts

jumper noun. a sleeveless dress that is worn over a blouse

junction noun. a place where roads, railroad lines, rivers, etc, meet; an intersection

June noun. the sixth month of the year

jungle noun. adj. a thick forest in hot, rainy countries

junior adj. 1. younger 2. less important; lower in rank 3. (also **Jr**) the younger when two men have the same name

junk noun. old worthless stuff that just takes up space (no plural)

juror noun. someone who is serving on a jury

jury noun. 1. a group of people who are

chosen to hear and decide a case in court **2.** a group of people who decide the winner of a contest

just *adj.* fair and right (opposite **unjust, unfair**)

just *adv.* **1.** only **2.** exactly **3.** by a little bit **4.** a little while ago; before **5.** at this moment

justice *noun.* **1.** fairness and rights (no plural; opposite **injustice**) **2.** the law (no plural) **3.** a title for a judge

justified *adj.* right and reasonable (opposite **unjustified**)

justify *verb.* **(justified, justifying)** give a reason that tells what you or someone else did was right —**justifiable** *adj.* — **justifiably** *adv.* —**justification** *noun.*

jut *verb.* **(jutted, jutting)** stick out in comparison to something else

juvenile *adj.* connected with children or teenagers (opposite **adult**) —**juvenile** *noun.*

juvenile delinquency *noun.* criminal behavior by people under adult age

juvenile delinquent *noun.* a criminal who is under adult age

K

K *abbr.* **1.** (computers) kilobyte **2.** one thousand

kangaroo *noun.* a large gray or brown animal from the mouse family, native to Australia, with a strong thick tail and large back feet that help it jump

karate *noun.* a fighting skill developed in East Asia that uses kicking, hitting and throwing your partner, sometimes used for self-defense

keen *adj.* **1.** very sharp **2.** strong **3.** very intelligent —**keenly** *adv.*

keep *verb.* **(kept, keeping) 1.** look after; take care of **2.** have for your own **3.** hold for a while **4.** have **5.** write in something regularly **6.** stay a certain way **7.** make something or someone stay a certain way **8.** do what you said that you would **9.** take up someone's time **10.** keep (on) + verb + -ying = continue

keeper *noun.* **1.** someone who is responsible for something or someone **2.** someone who owns something

kennel *noun.* a small house for a dog

kept *verb.* past tense and past participle of **keep**

kettle *noun.* a special pot with a spout and a handle on top for boiling water

key *noun.* **1.** a metal instrument for opening locks **2.** one of the small parts of a piano, a typewriter or other keyboard that you press with your finger **3.** something that helps you understand something **4.** a set of answers **5.** in music, a set of notes that go together

keyboard *noun.* a set of keys on a piano, a typewriter, a computer, etc

keynote *noun.* the most important issue of a conference, a discussion, etc

khaki *noun. adj.* a kind of greenish brown color

kick *noun.* a blow with the foot

kick *verb.* **(kicked, kicking) 1.** strike with your foot **2.** move your legs around with force

kid *noun.* **1.** a young goat **2.** (informal) a child

kid *verb.* **(kidded, kidding)** (informal) joke

kidnap *verb.* **(kidnapped, kidnapping)** steal someone usually in order to get money for returning that person —**kidnapping** *noun.*

kidney *noun.* one of a pair of organs of the body that gets rid of liquid waste

kill *verb.* **(killed, killing) 1.** cause death **2.** end something **3.** hurt; be painful; bother

killer *noun.* someone or something that kills

kilo *noun.* short for **kilogram**

kilogram *noun.* = 1,000 grams (about 2.2 pounds) (short form **kg**)

kilometer *noun.* = 1,000 meters (about 0.6 miles) (short form **km**)

kin *noun.* (a collective term for) relatives; family

kind *noun.* sort; type; having many things that are the same

kind *adj.* **1.** (person) good-hearted; generous; helpful; caring **2.** nice (of something that someone does for another person)

kindergarten *noun.* a school for younger children, usually ages 5 and 6

kindly *adv.* in a kind way

kindness *noun.* being kind (no plural; opposite **unkindness**)

king *noun.* **1.** the ruler of a country who belongs to a royal family **2.** the most important piece in chess

kingdom *noun.* a country that is ruled by a king

kingfisher *noun.* a kind of bird that feeds on fish

kiosk *noun.* an open shop in a train station, airport, etc, or outdoors that sells newspapers, candy, etc

kiss *noun.* a touch of the lips to show love or affection (plural **kisses**)

kiss *verb.* **(kissed, kissing)** touch someone with your lips to show love or affection

kit *noun.* 1. a set of equipment for a special purpose 2. a set of parts that can be put together

kitchen *noun.* the room where you cook food, wash the dishes, etc

kite *noun.* a thing made of paper with a long tail that you can fly

kitten *noun.* a very young cat

kitty *noun.* (informal) an amount of money collected by a group of workers, students, friends, etc, for a special purpose

knack *noun.* the natural ability to do something; talent

knee *noun.* the joint in the middle of your leg where your leg bends

kneel *verb.* **(knelt, kneeling)** go down on your knees

knelt *verb.* past tense and past participle of **kneel**

knew *verb.* past tense and past participle of **know**

knife *noun.* a tool with a sharp blade for cutting things with (plural **knives**)

knight *noun.* 1. a title that a king or queen gives to someone for his achievements 2. a noble soldier in the Middle Ages who wore a protective metal suit (armor) in battle 3. a chess piece with the shape of a horse's head

knit *verb.* **(knitted or knit, knitting)** make something from yarn using two long needles —**knitting** *noun.* (no plural)

knives *noun.* plural of **knife**

knob *noun.* 1. something round that you turn to open a door or pull to open a drawer 2. a control button on a machine

knock *noun.* 1. the sound of something hitting against something else 2. a blow

knock *verb.* **(knocked, knocking)** 1. hit something to make a noise 2. give someone a blow

knockout *noun.* 1. (slang) a very attractive woman 2. a blow that knocks someone (usually a boxer) out

knot *noun.* 1. the place where string, ribbon, rope, etc, is tied to keep something in place 2. a place where something gets twisted together 3. a measurement of speed for a ship

knot *verb.* **(knotted, knotting)** fasten something by tying a knot

know *verb.* **(knew, known)** 1. have information in your mind or memory 2. be sure about something 3. be acquainted with someone 4. be familiar with something 5. recognize

knowledge *noun.* 1. what a person knows 2. information

knowledgeable *adj.* knowing a lot about something

known *adj.* 1. that everyone knows 2. famous

known *verb.* past participle of **know**

knuckle *noun.* the joint in the middle of your finger

Koran *noun.* the holy book of the Muslims

Korean *noun. adj.* someone or something from Korea; the language spoken in Korea

kudos *noun.* praise and honor (singular)

Kuwaiti *noun. adj.* someone or something from Kuwait

L

L *abbr.* **1.** the Roman numeral 50 **2.** large size (clothes) **3.** learner-driver

lab *abbr.* short for **laboratory**

label *noun.* a sticker or a piece of cloth with information on it

label *verb.* **(labeled, labeling)** put a label on something

labor *noun.* hard work, usually physical
—**labor relations** *noun.* the relationship between workers and management
—**labor-saving** *adj.* lessening the physical work needed

labor *verb.* **(labored, laboring)** work hard

laboratory *noun.* a building or room where scientists or students of science work (short form **lab**)

laborer *noun.* someone who earns money by doing physical work

lace *noun.* **1.** a decorative piece of material made of delicate threads in a net-like weave that is often almost transparent **2.** a string used to close the opening of shoes, a shirt, etc

lack *noun.* shortage or absence
—**lack of** not having any or not having enough of a certain thing

lack *verb.* **(lacked, lacking)** not to have something or not to have enough of it

ladder *noun.* something that you climb to get to a higher place

laden *adj.* **1.** heavily loaded **2.** very full of problems/troubles

lady *noun.* **1.** a woman **2.** a woman who is especially elegant and charming **3.** (Lady) the title for the wife or daughter of some British noblemen

ladybug *noun.* a small red beetle with black spots on its back

lag *verb.* **(lagged, lagging)** be slower than everyone else

lager *noun.* a type of light beer

lagoon *noun.* a wide body of (salty) water

from the ocean that is almost completely surrounded by sand, rocks, etc

laid *verb.* past tense and past participle of **lay**

laid-back *adj.* easy-going; relaxed and not formal

lain *verb.* past participle of **lie** (down)

lake *noun.* a large body of (fresh) water with land around it

lamb *noun.* **1.** a young sheep **2.** the meat of a young sheep (no plural)

lame *adj.* not able to walk properly because of an injury, etc

lamp *noun.* an instrument that gives light

lamppost *noun.* a pole that holds a street light

lampshade *noun.* a covering for a lamp to make the light softer

land *noun.* **1.** the earth (no plural) **2.** the ground; soil; property (no plural) **3.** a country

land *verb.* **(landed, landing)** come from the air to the ground (opposite for an airplane **take off**)

landfill *noun.* waste that is buried between layers of soil in order to fill a low area

landing *noun.* **1.** the coming in of a plane **2.** a flat place at the top of a flight of stairs

landlady *noun.* a woman who owns a house or rooms that people can rent

landlord *noun.* a man who owns a house or rooms that people can rent

landmark *noun.* something that helps you recognize or remember a place

landscape *noun.* a wide view of the land

landscape *verb.* **(landscaped, landscaping)** make an area look attractive by planting bushes, lawns, etc

landslide *noun.* **1.** the falling of earth

and rocks from the side of a hill or mountain **2.** a very large victory in an election

lane *noun*. **1.** a narrow street **2.** one line of traffic on a road

language *noun*. **1.** a system of words and grammar **2.** communicating with words (no plural) **3.** the particular words that someone uses (no plural)

lantern *noun*. a lamp with a glass covering over an open flame

lap *noun*. **1.** the part of your legs that you can put things on when your are sitting **2.** in a race, one time around the track

lap *verb*. **(lapped, lapping)** drink like an animal

laptop *noun*. a portable computer with all the basic features of a full-sized computer that works on batteries and which you can carry in a small case

larceny *noun*. (law) theft; robbery

large *adj*. big in size or amount (opposite **small**)

largely *adv*. mostly

large-scale *adj*. elaborate; big; extensive

laser *noun*. a very narrow beam of light that can cut through different types of material, used in medical operations, for creating images in the sky, etc

last *noun. adj. adv*. **1.** at the end; after all the others **2.** the final one or ones **3.** the final one or ones up to now **4.** the one before this

last *verb*. **(lasted)** **1.** continue; go on **2.** be enough **3.** stay in good condition **4.** stay alive

lasting *adj*. continuing for a very long time; permanent

last-minute *adj*. just before the event

latch *noun*. a fastener for a door, gate or window

late *adj*. **1.** no longer early **2.** coming at an hour that is no longer early **3.** after the usual or expected time **4.** coming at the end of a certain time

lately *adv*. recently (use the present perfect tense)

late-night *adj*. happening or occurring late at night

later *adv*. afterward

latest *adj*. the most recent; the newest

Latin *noun*. the language of the ancient Romans which is no longer spoken and is the basis for the French, Spanish, Italian, Portuguese and Romanian languages —**Latin** *adj*.

latter *adj*. the second part (opposite **former, first, earlier**)

laugh *noun*. **1.** the act of laughing **2.** a particular way of laughing

laugh *verb*. **(laughed, laughing)** make a sound that people usually make after hearing or seeing something funny
—**laugh at** *verb*. **1.** laugh because something is funny **2.** make fun of
—**laugh your head off** laugh very much

laughter *noun*. laughing; laugh (no plural)

launch *noun*. **1.** the act of launching **2.** a type of motor boat

launch *verb*. **(launched, launching)** **1.** send a spacecraft, a missile, etc, into the air **2.** send a ship or boat into the water for the first time **3.** start something

laundry *noun*. **1.** clothes that need to be washed or have just been washed (no plural) **2.** a place where laundry is washed

laureate *noun*. someone who receives a very high academic honor

lava *noun*. the hot liquid that flows down when a volcano erupts (no plural)

lavatory *noun*. a bathroom; a toilet

law *noun*. **1.** a rule made by a government that everyone must obey **2.** the profession of being a lawyer (no plural)

law-abiding *adj*. keeping or respecting the laws

law and order *noun*. respect for the law; living without breaking laws

law court, court of law noun. the place where legal cases are heard by judges

lawful adj. by law

lawless adj. without law

lawman noun. a policeman; a law enforcement officer

lawn noun. a stretch of closely cut grass that borders a house

lawsuit noun. the bringing of a case to court

lawyer noun. attorney; someone whose job is to give advice about the law and to represent people in a court of law

lay verb. (**laid, laying**) 1. put something or someone on top of something 2. produce an egg 3. past of **lie**, as in lie down
—**lay a hand on** harm
—**lay off** 1. fire from a job 2. (slang) don't touch; stop
—**lay your hands on something** find what you are looking for

layabout noun. someone who avoids work; a lazy person

layer noun. one of a number of things on top of each other —**layer** adj.

layout noun. (technical) the design of an apartment, house, etc, or in newspapers, magazines, etc, the way a page is designed

lazy adj. 1. not wanting to work 2. not doing work —**lazily** adv. —**laziness** noun.

lb. abbr. pound

lead noun. 1. being ahead of your opponents 2. a kind of heavy, gray metal 3. the black writing material in the middle of a pencil 4. a chain or strap for walking a dog; a leash

lead verb. (**led, leading**) 1. be in front and give directions 2. use a rope, strap or your hand to bring someone somewhere 3. show where something is by walking in front 4. be the way to get to a certain place 5. be the first in a race 6. be ahead of others

leader noun. 1. the head of a country 2. someone who leads a group of people

leadership noun. 1. the people who are in charge of a group or an organization 2. the ability to take responsibility as a leader (no plural)

leading adj. 1. ahead of everyone else 2. the most important

leaf noun. one of the green parts that grow from the branch of a tree or the stem of a plant (plural **leaves**)

leaflet noun. a small booklet with information or advertising in it

league noun. a group of sports teams

leak noun. a hole through which liquid, air or gas gets out

leak verb. (**leaked, leaking**) 1. have a leak in it 2. get through a leak

lean verb. (**leaned or leant, leaning**) 1. put your weight against something 2. bend over something 3. put part of your body outside something

leaning noun. a tendency; an inclination

leap noun. a big jump

leap verb. (**leaped/leapt, leaping**) take a big jump

learn verb. (**learned/learnt, learning**) 1. get knowledge 2. get knowledge by studying or practicing 3. hear or read about something

learner noun. someone who is learning something

lease noun. a contract which states that someone can use an apartment, a car, etc, for a period of time for a certain fee —**lease** verb. (**leased, leasing**)

least noun. adj. adv. (**little, less**) the smallest in size or amount (use **fewest** with countable nouns; opposite **most**)

leather noun. animal skin that is used for making shoes, bags, etc (no plural)

leave verb. (**left, leaving**) 1. go away from a place 2. quit school, a job, an organization, etc 3. not take something or someone with you 4. forget to take something 5. put something somewhere 6. not change the way that something is **7.** let something remain **8.** not do something until later **9.** make it possible for someone to get your property or money when you die

leave noun. a vacation from work; a holiday

leaves noun. plural of **leaf**

lecture noun. **1.** a talk that someone gives for the purpose of teaching something **2.** a scolding

lecture verb. **(lectured, lecturing) 1.** teach a subject at a college or university **2.** give a lecture **3.** scold

led verb. past tense and past participle of **lead**

ledge noun. a narrow shelf

leeway noun. a margin of freedom; some extra time or space, especially when interpreting a law, for mistakes or for getting somewhere

left noun. **1.** opposite of right **2.** (political, often **Left**) those who support socialism or social change and social welfare —**left** adj. adv.

left verb. past and past participle of **leave**

left-hand adj. the one on the left

left-handed adj. using the left hand for writing, cutting, etc

leftist noun. adj. a supporter of the left in politics (opposite **rightist**)

leg noun. **1.** the part of your body that you stand on **2.** what a piece of furniture stands on

legal adj. **1.** allowed by law **2.** connected with the law —**legally** adv.

legality noun. being permitted by law

legalize verb. **(legalized, legalizing)** make something legal

legend noun. an old story that may or may not be true

legendary adj. **1.** coming from a legend **2.** famous and admired

legislate verb. **(legislated, legislating)** pass laws

legislation noun. a set of laws or the act of passing laws

legislative adj. having the function of making laws

legitimate adj. **1.** reasonable; acceptable **2.** according to law **3.** born to parents who are legally married

leisure noun. time when you can do what you want (no plural)

leisurely adv. unhurried; slow

lemon noun. a fruit with a thick yellow skin and sour juice —**lemon** adj.

lemonade noun. a drink made from lemon juice, water and sugar (no plural)

lend verb. **(lent, lending)** give something to someone for a period of time; let someone use something of yours (opposite **borrow**)

lender noun. someone who lends something

length noun. **1.** how long something is **2.** a measurement of the long side of something

lengthen verb. **(lengthened, lengthening)** make longer (opposite **shorten**)

lens noun. a special piece of glass that helps you see better (plural **lenses**)

lent verb. past tense and past participle of **lend**

less adj. adv. **(little, less, least)** not as much as (use **fewer** with countable nouns)

less pron. not so much

less prep. minus; not counting

lessen verb. **(lessened, lessening) 1.** become less **2.** make less (opposite **increase**)

lesson noun. **1.** a period of time for learning something with a teacher **2.** something that you learn from experience

lessons noun plural. homework

let verb. **(let, letting) 1.** allow someone to do something **2.** allow something to happen **3.** allow someone to live in your house, apartment, etc, for payment; rent

—**let's** abbr. = let us; I suggest we ...

letter noun. **1.** one of the signs of the alphabet **2.** a message in writing

lettuce noun. a vegetable with thin wide crisp green leaves used in salads

level noun. **1.** a line which you can use for measuring how high something is **2.** how high something is **3.** how advanced something is

level verb. **(leveled, leveling)** destroy buildings or other structures

level adj. smooth, flat and not sloping

lever noun. a bar or other tool that you use for lifting heavy things

leverage noun. **1.** power or influence **2.** the act of using a lever or the advantage gotten by using a lever

lexical adj. (technical) of or about words

liability noun. (law) responsibility

liabilities noun plural. debts

liable adj. **1.** likely to do something **2.** legally responsible

liar noun. someone who tells lies

libel noun. (law) something (often a lie, gossip, etc) that is published about someone (usually famous) which makes others think badly of that person

liberal adj. **1.** open-minded; willing to consider new ideas **2.** generous **3.** not strict **4.** (politics) moderate; holding a center position

liberalism noun. moderation in politics; a center position (neither Left nor Right)

liberate verb. **(liberated, liberating)** make free —**liberation** noun.

liberty noun. **1.** freedom (no plural) **2.** freedom to do a certain thing

librarian noun. someone who works in a library

library noun. **1.** a room or building where a collection of books is kept for people to use or borrow **2.** a collection of books, records, films, etc

lice noun. Plural of **louse**

license noun. **1.** a written piece of paper which shows that you have permission to do or have something **2.** a piece of paper which shows that you are allowed to practice a certain profession; a certificate —**license** verb. **(licensed, licensing)**

lick verb. **(licked, licking) 1.** pass your tongue over something **2.** drink by moving your tongue quickly

lid noun. a cover for a pot, box, can, jar, etc

lie noun. something that someone says which is false —**lie** verb. **(lied, lying)**

lie verb. **(lay, lain, lying) 1.** not stand or sit; stretch out your body **2.** be on something flat

life noun. **1.** what makes animals and plants different from earth, stones and other things (no plural) **2.** being alive **3.** the time between birth and death **4.** the way someone lives **5.** energy

life cycle noun. the different stages a living thing passes through during its lifetime

life expectancy noun. the number of years that someone is expected to live

life imprisonment noun. serving a sentence in prison for the rest of your life

lifeless adj. **1.** dead **2.** without living things **3.** dull; without energy **4.** boring; without activity

lifeline noun. **1.** a rope extended to someone to help rescue him/her **2.** a rope attached to a diver or swimmer to prevent him/her from drowning

life-saving adj. **1.** the skills needed to save people from drowning **2.** something that will save lives

life sentence noun. life imprisonment; a sentence by a court to imprisonment for life

lifestyle noun. the way someone chooses to live

lifetime noun. the years that you are alive

lift noun. **1.** an elevator **2.** a ride that someone gives you

lift verb. **(lifted, lifting)** pick something up

lift-off *noun*. the start (launch) of a rocket into space —**lift-off** *verb*. **(lifted-off, lifting-off)**

light *noun*. **1.** the opposite of darkness (no plural) **2.** a thing that makes it possible to see, such as an electric lamp **3.** a traffic signal

light *verb*. **(lit/lighted, lighting) 1.** give light to a place **2.** make something start burning

light *adj*. **1.** not bright or dark in color **2.** without much weight **3.** gentle; not strong

light bulb *noun*. a round piece of glass with an electric wire which gives light

lighten *verb*. **(lightened, lightening) 1.** give light to **2.** make a color less strong **3.** make something less heavy or difficult

lighter *noun*. a small instrument that you can use to make a flame

light-hearted *adj*. cheerful; not serious

lighthouse *noun*. a tall building on a coast with a flashing light to guide ships

lighting *noun*. **1.** the amount of light in a room **2.** an electrical system of giving light (no plural)

lightly *adv*. gently

lightning *noun*. a flash of light in the sky that comes before thunder (no plural)

lightweight *noun*. a boxer weighing up to 135 pounds (61 kg) —**lightweight** *adj*.

like *prep*. **1.** the same as **2.** in the same way as

like *verb*. **(liked, liking) 1.** have kind feelings toward someone; enjoy being with someone **2.** enjoy eating something **3.** enjoy doing something (opposite **dislike**)

likeable, likable *adj*. pleasant; easy to like

likelihood *noun*. probability

likely *adj*. **(likelier/more likely, likeliest/most likely)** probable (opposite **unlikely**)

likeness *noun*. similarity; being the same

likes *noun plural*. the things that you like

likewise *adv*. the same thing

liking *noun*. love; fondness (no plural)

limb *noun*. a person's arm or leg

limerick *noun*. a usually humorous poem with five lines in each verse where the first two lines are long, the next two lines are short and the last line is long

limit *noun*. **1.** an edge that forms a boundary **2.** the most that is allowed or possible

limit *verb*. **(limited, limiting)** not allow more than a certain number or amount

limitation *noun*. something that keeps you from doing something or doing any better

limited *adj*. not very large; with restrictions

limits *noun plural*. boundaries

limousine *noun*. a big, expensive, luxurious car that usually has a private driver (short form **limo**)

limp *verb*. **(limped, limping)** walk unevenly —**limp** *noun*.

line *noun*. **1.** a long mark that goes from one point to another **2.** a long mark that goes from side to side on a piece of paper **3.** words that are written next to each other on a page **4.** a long mark that separates two things **5.** a row of people waiting for something; a queue **6.** a row **7.** a boundary in sports **8.** a cord, rope, wire, etc **9.** a telephone connection

line *verb*. **(lined, lining) 1.** be all along both sides of something **2.** put lines on something **3.** put an additional piece of cloth inside a dress, skirt, etc

linear *adj*. **1.** made of or referring to lines **2.** referring to the measurement of length

lined *adj*. **1.** having lines **2.** having wrinkles **3.** having a lining

linen *noun.* **1.** a cloth used for making sheets, tablecloths, etc (no plural) **2.** towels, sheets, pillow cases, tablecloths, etc

liner *noun.* **1.** a big passenger ship **2.** a pencil for making lines around your eyes

lines *noun plural.* what an actor has to say in a play

lingerie *noun.* women's underwear and nightgowns (no plural)

linguist *noun.* **1.** someone who knows foreign languages **2.** someone who studies language or languages

lining *noun.* a piece of cloth on the inside of clothing

link *noun.* **1.** part of a chain **2.** a connection

link *verb.* **(linked, linking) 1.** connect two things **2.** join two things

lion *noun.* a large meat-eating wild cat native to Africa and South Asia

lip *noun.* one of the two outer parts of the mouth

lipstick *noun.* color that women put on their lips to look pretty

liquid *noun.* something that flows; something that is not solid or gas — **liquid** *adj.*

liquidate *verb.* **(liquidated, liquidating) 1.** turn assets into cash in order to repay debts **2.** (slang) kill

liquidation *noun.* the process of closing a business by selling its assets

liquidator *noun.* the official who carries out the liquidation of a business

liquidity *noun.* having money or something that can easily be sold

liquor *noun.* highly alcoholic drink

list *noun.* words or names that you write one below the other

list *verb.* **(listed, listing)** write down or have on a list

listen *verb.* **(listened, listening) 1.** try to hear things **2.** do what someone suggests; pat attention

listener *noun.* **1.** someone who listens

2. someone who listens to a program

lit *verb.* past tense and past participle of **light**

liter *noun.* a measurement of liquid

literal *adj.* **1.** exact; actual; not idiomatic **2.** very exact; word for word

literally *adv.* **1.** exactly; actually **2.** used to make a forceful impression for the emotional effect

literary *adj.* referring or connected to literature

literature *noun.* **1.** written works that have value as art **2.** books, articles, etc, on a particular subject (no plural)

litigation *noun.* (law) taking a complaint to a court of law

litter *noun.* **1.** bits of paper and other trash scattered around (no plural) **2.** things that are not in their places (no plural) **3.** a group of baby animals that are born together

litter *verb.* **(littered, littering)** scatter things or leave trash all over the place

little *noun. pron.* not much; a very small amount

little *adj.* **1.** small **2.** young **3.** younger

little *adv.* **(less, least)** not much

live *verb.* **(lived, living) 1.** have life **2.** have a home **3.** exist; continue life **4.** spend your life in a certain way **5.** stay in people's minds

live *adj.* **1.** living **2.** referring to a program that is shown or given as it happens

livelihood *noun.* **1.** the way that someone earns money **2.** the money that a person earns

lively *adj.* full of energy or activity

lives *noun.* plural of **life**

livestock *noun.* animals, such as cattle, sheep, pigs, etc, that live on a farm

living *noun.* **1.** the money you need to live on **2.** the way that someone lives (no plural)

living *adj.* alive at this time

living room *noun.* salon; the main room of the house, where people sit together

load *noun*. **1.** something that you carry **2.** the weight that something can hold

load *verb*. **(loaded, loading) 1.** pile something onto something else **2.** take on passengers **3.** put bullets in a gun, rifle, etc (opposite for 1., 2., and 3. **unload**) **4.** put data into a computer's memory

loaded *adj*. **1.** too full **2.** (of a gun, etc) having bullets in it **3.** having too much work to do **4.** (slang) having too much money

loaf *noun*. something that is cooked or baked in a mass (plural **loaves**)

loan *noun*. money or an object that someone lends to another person

loan *verb*. **(loaned, loaning)** lend

lobby *noun*. **1.** the large entrance of a hotel or public building **2.** an organized group that puts pressure on a government for a certain purpose

lobbyist *noun*. a member of a pressure group who tries to persuade the government to support certain issues

local *adj*. in or of a certain place

local *noun*. a train or bus that stops at every small station

local government *noun*. the people who run a town, district, etc

locality *noun*. a neighborhood or district

locally *adv*. in a particular area

locate *verb*. **(located)** find

location *noun*. the place where something is

lock *noun*. **1.** an instrument for keeping something closed or fastened **2.** a bunch of hair

lock *verb*. **(locked, locking) 1.** close a door, drawer, etc, with a key so that other people cannot open it **2.** fasten something with a lock so that it cannot move or be stolen **3.** put jewels, money, important papers, etc, in a locked place **4.** be stuck **5.** become fastened (opposite **unlock**) **—locked** *adj*. (opposite **unlocked**)

locker *noun*. a small cupboard or cabinet for keeping your things

locker room *noun*. a room in a sports center, etc, where people change their clothes and put them in lockers

locomotive *noun*. a railroad engine

locust *noun*. a flying insect native of Africa and Asia that flies in groups and destroys crops by eating them

lodge *noun*. a wooden house in the mountains for hunters, skiers, etc

lodge *verb*. **(lodged, lodging)** pay to live in a room in someone else's house

lodger *noun*. someone who pays to live in a room in another person's house; a roomer

lodgings *noun plural*. a place to live, usually for money

lofty *adj*. **1.** high **2.** thinking that you are of a higher level than someone else **3.** big and impressive

log *noun*. a piece of the trunk of a tree that has been cut down

logger *noun*. someone who cuts down trees

logic *noun*. **1.** the ability to think rationally **2.** a way of reasoning **3.** sense (no plural) **—logical** *adj*. (opposite **illogical**) **—logically** *adv*.

logistics *noun plural*. **1.** the necessary planning and organization required in order to get a big operation together **2.** organizing the movement of military troops **—logistic, logistical** *adj*.

logo *noun*. a company trademark; a small design that represents a company and helps people identify that company

lone *adj*. single; solitary; with no other person

lonely *adj*. **1.** (unhappily) alone; lonesome **2.** without people; deserted; remote **—loneliness** *noun*. (no plural)

long *verb*. **(longed, longing)** want something very much

long *adj*. **1.** not short **2.** lasting a lot of time **3.** far from one place to another

4. having a certain length **5.** lasting a certain time

long *adv.* a lot of time

long-distance *adj. adv.* covering a long distance

longevity *noun.* long life (no plural)

longing *noun.* a strong desire

long-range *adj.* covering a long distance or time

long-standing *adj.* being in existence for a long time

long-term *adj.* for a period of a long time

look *noun.* **1.** the action of looking (no plural) **2.** appearance (no plural) **3.** expression

look *verb.* **(looked, looking) 1.** use your eyes **2.** search **3.** appear

lookout *noun.* **1.** alertness for something, usually by the act of watching **2.** a guard or watchman or the place where a guard or watchman is stationed

looks *noun plural.* your appearance

loop *noun.* tie something with a string, rope, etc, by folding it back on itself

loop *verb.* **(looped, looping)** make a loop

loophole *noun.* a way to avoid legally what a law, etc, requires

loose *adj.* **1.** not firm **2.** not tight **3.** not fastened **4.** free

loosen *verb.* **(loosened, loosening)** make less tight

loot *noun.* goods that are stolen (no plural)

loot *verb.* **(looted, looting)** steal things in large amounts

lord *noun.* **1.** a British nobleman **2.** a complete master

lose *verb.* **(lost, losing) 1.** not be able to find something you had **2.** no longer have something you had before **3.** not win a game, battle, election, etc **—lose (someone)** to have someone close to you die

loser *noun.* **1.** someone who loses **2.** someone who is not successful because of his/her personality

loss *noun.* **1.** not having something that you had before (no plural) **2.** the money that you lose **3.** not winning a game **4.** the death of a loved one

lost *adj.* **1.** not knowing where you are **2.** missing

lot *noun.*: **a lot (of), lots of 1.** a large amount (of something) **2.** very much **3.** often

lotion *noun.* a liquid that you put on your skin

lottery *noun.* a raffle; the drawing of numbered tickets which were sold in advance in order to receive a prize

loud *adj. adv.* with a big sound **—loudly** *adv.*

loudspeaker *noun.* **1.** the part of a radio, hi-fi, etc, that the sound comes out of **2.** an instrument that is used to make your voice louder

lounge *noun.* a public room or hall where someone can relax

lounge *verb.* **(lounged, lounging)** spend time in a lazy, doing-nothing way

louse *noun.* a tiny insect that passes from one person's head to another and causes itching (plural **lice**)

lousy *adj.* (slang) bad; poor

lovable *adj.* charming; easy to love

love *noun.* **1.** a deep feeling of affection for someone (no plural) **2.** someone that you love

love *verb.* **(loved, loving) 1.** have a deep feeling of affection for someone **2.** like something very much (opposite **hate**)

lovely *adj.* **1.** beautiful **2.** pleasant

lover *noun.* **1.** the person someone has a sexual relationship with **2.** someone who likes something very much

loving *adj.* showing love **—lovingly** *adv.*

low *adj.* **1.** not far from the ground or the floor **2.** not loud **3.** soft **4.** not expensive **5.** not enough **6.** (of temperatures) not high

lower *adj.* referring to the bottom one

of two things; near the bottom of something (opposite **upper**)

lower *verb.* **(lowered, lowering)** bring or take something down

low-paid *adj.* not getting a high salary

loyal *adj.* faithful

loyalty *noun.* faithfulness to someone or something (no plural)

luck *noun.* the good or bad things that happen to someone (no plural)

lucky *adj.* **1.** having luck **2.** bringing luck

lucrative *adj.* making you a lot of money; profitable

ludicrous *adj.* ridiculous; laughable

luggage *noun.* suitcases, trunks, boxes, etc, that you travel with; baggage

lukewarm *adj. adv.* (of liquids) only slightly warm

lump *noun.* **1.** a hard piece of something **2.** a hard swelling

lunatic *noun.* a mad person; someone with crazy ideas

lunatic *adj.* mad; crazy

lunch *noun.* a light meal in the middle of the day

lunchtime *noun.* the time when lunch is usually eaten

lung *noun.* one of the two sack-like organs in the chest of an animal or human body that is used for breathing

lure *noun.* something that attracts; artificial bait used to attract fish in the sport of fishing

lush *adj.* thick and plentiful, especially of plants

luxurious *adj.* **1.** expensive, good and comfortable **2.** very comfortable; with luxuries

luxury *noun.* **1.** expensive and comfortable living (no plural) **2.** something expensive that you don't really need but which gives you pleasure (plural **luxuries**) —**luxury** *adj.*

lying *verb.* see **lie**

lynch *verb.* **(lynched, lynching)** hang someone without a trial in court

lyric *adj.* (of a poem) expressing strong personal emotions

lyrics *noun plural.* words to a song

M

M *abbr.* the Roman numeral 1000; medium size

ma *noun.* = mother

MA, M.A. *abbr.* Master of Arts

ma'am *noun.* = Madam

machine *noun.* an instrument with more than one part that does a job

machine gun *noun.* a gun that fires bullets one after another without stopping

machinery *noun.* (no plural) **1.** all the machines in a factory **2.** all the working parts of one type of machine

mad *adj.* **1.** crazy; insane **2.** angry

Madam *noun.* a respectful way of talking to a woman that you do not know

made *verb.* past tense and past participle of **make**

madman *noun.* a person with a sick mind (plural **madmen**)

madness *noun.* an illness of the mind (no plural)

Mafia *noun.* a secret organization of violent criminals dealing in all kinds of illegal activities like drugs, gambling, etc

magazine *noun.* **1.** a weekly or monthly newspaper **2.** the part of a gun which holds the bullets

magic *noun.* **1.** special powers that can make strange and unnatural things happen, like turning a person into a frog **2.** tricks of a magician, like finding a coin in someone's ear —**magic, magical** *adj.*

magician *noun.* **1.** someone who has the power to make unnatural things happen **2.** someone who entertains by doing magic tricks

magistrate *noun.* a type of judge, such as for non-serious crimes

magnate *noun.* a powerful and very rich businessperson

magnet *noun.* a piece of iron that attracts other pieces of iron —**magnetic** *adj.*

magnificent *adj.* grand; splendidly beautiful

magnify *verb.* (**magnified, magnifying**) make something look bigger

magnitude *noun.* (no plural) **1.** bigness **2.** greatness in size or importance **3.** brightness of a star

mahogany *noun.* a hard reddish-brown type of wood coming from trees from West India or Africa used in furniture making (plural **mahoganies**)

maid *noun.* a woman who cleans someone else's house for pay

mail *noun.* the letters, bills, etc, that you send or receive (no plural)

mail *verb.* (**mailed, mailing**) send through the mail; put into a mailbox or bring to a post office

mailbox *noun.* **1.** a closed metal box where people put the letters they want to send **2.** a small box for receiving mail

main *adj.* the most important

mainframe *noun.* a large and powerful computer that is able to do many things at the same time and that many people can use at the same time

mainland *noun.* a big land mass without its islands

mainly *adv.* more than anything else

mainstream *noun.* the beliefs held by the majority of people

maintain *verb.* (**maintained, maintaining**) **1.** keep something in good condition **2.** keep up a certain level or speed **3.** claim —**maintenance** *noun.* (no plural)

majesty *noun.* used when talking to or about a king or queen

major *noun.* (**majored, majoring**) **1.** an

army officer one rank above a captain **2.** the main subject studied at university —**major** verb. **(majored, majoring)**

major adj. **1.** serious **2.** important (opposite **minor**)

majority noun. most of the people or things (plural **majorities**; opposite **minority**)

make verb. **(made, making) 1.** build something with your hands **2.** prepare something **3.** cause something to happen **4.** cause someone to feel a certain way **5.** force someone to do something **6.** produce something **7.** (math) be equal to

maker noun. someone who makes things

male noun. a man or boy; the sex that does not give birth to young ones — **male** adj. (opposite **female**)

malice noun. wishing to harm or upset someone

mall noun. a large shopping center housed in one building, usually with a lot of parking space nearby

mama noun. mother

mammal noun. any animal whose young drink milk from the mother's body

mammoth noun. a prehistoric hairy animal that resembled an elephant

man noun. **1.** an adult male human being (plural **men**) **2.** all human beings **3.** any person (man or woman)

man verb. **(manned, manning)** supply people to do a job

manage verb. **(managed, managing) 1.** be able to deal with problems **2.** run a business or other organization **3.** control people or animals

management noun. **1.** the people who control a business **2.** the way that someone runs a business or other organization (no plural)

manager noun. someone who controls a company, restaurant, etc —**managerial** adj.

mandate noun. the power given by the people who chose a government, etc, to act in certain way

mandatory adj. compulsory; that must be done or obeyed

manifest adj. very clear and obvious

manipulate verb. **(manipulated, manipulating) 1.** handle or operate skillfully **2.** control and/or influence for your own advantage by using unfair methods

mankind noun. all the people in the world (no plural)

manly adv. having qualities that are thought to be typical of a man

manner noun. **1.** the way that someone does something (no plural) **2.** the way in which something happens (no plural) **3.** the way that someone talks to other people

manners noun plural. the way of behaving with other people

manor noun. a big house with land surrounding it

manpower noun. the number of workers needed for a certain job or type of job

mansion noun. a large, elegant house

manual noun. a small book of instructions

manual adj. by hand, not by machine — **manually** adv.

manufacture verb. **(manufactured, manufacturing)** produce something with machines —**manufacture** noun. (no plural)

manufacturer noun. a producer of manufactured goods

manuscript noun. a book or piece of writing (usually that is handwritten or typed) before being published

many adj. pron. **(more, most)** a lot of; a large number (use **many** with countable nouns; use **much** with uncountable nouns)

map noun. a drawing that shows part of the surface of the earth with mountains, oceans, rivers, streets, etc

maple *noun.* a tree in North America whose sap is made into syrup and whose leaf is on the Canadian flag

marathon *noun.* 1. a race that is 24 miles 385 yards or 42 kilometers long 2. any event that carries on for a long time

marble *noun.* 1. a hard, light-colored stone that is used for special buildings, statues and tombstones (no plural) 2. a small colored glass ball used in the game of **marbles** —**marble** *adj.*

marbles *noun plural.* a game that children play with marbles

march *verb.* (**marched, marching**) walk in a special, firm way like a soldier

March *noun.* the third month of the year

margarine *noun.* a fatty substance similar to butter but produced from vegetable fats

margin *noun.* a space with no writing along the edges of a page

marina *noun.* a special pier for yachts and private pleasure boats where services (such as repairs) are provided

marine *adj.* associated with water

maritime *adj.* relating to ships or commerce at sea

mark *noun.* 1. any spot, line, etc, on something that has nothing else on it 2. a spot or smear that makes something dirty 3. a grade in school

mark *verb.* (**marked, marking**) 1. make a mark on 2. spoil the way something looks 3. point out when something happened 4. correct exams, etc

market *noun.* 1. a place for buying and selling 2. the chances for selling a certain type of thing or getting a certain kind of job (no plural)

market *verb.* (**marketed, marketing**) try to sell something —**marketing** *adj.*

marketplace *noun.* a usually open area where market activity takes place

market research *noun.* collecting information about consumers in a particular area for a certain product or service

marriage *noun.* 1. married life 2. a wedding

married *adj.* 1. having a husband or wife 2. having each other as husband or wife

marry *verb.* (**married, marrying**) 1. become husband and wife 2. make two people husband and wife

Mars *noun.* the fourth closest planet to the sun that appears reddish in color

marsh *noun.* wet, soft land; a swamp

martyr *noun.* someone who dies or suffers for his/her beliefs

marvel *noun.* a wonderful and surprising thing

masculine *adj.* 1. of or like a man or boy 2. (grammar) relating to a certain group of nouns and pronouns (opposite **feminine**)

mask *noun.* a covering that hides or protects all or part of your face —**mask** *verb.* (**masked, masking**)

masked *adj.* wearing a mask

mass *noun.* a large amount of something without a specific shape

mass *adj.* for, by or connected with a large number of people

massacre *noun.* brutal murder of a group of people —**massacre** *verb.* (**massacred, massacring**)

massive *adj.* very big and heavy

massively *adv.* hugely; very large

mass media *noun.* TV, radio and newspapers

mass-produce *verb.* (**mass-produced, mass-producing**) produce in great quantities by using machines

mast *noun.* a post that supports the sail of a boat or a ship

master *noun.* 1. a man who owns or controls 2. someone who is especially good at something 3. an original document, recording, etc, used to make copies — **master** *adj.*

master *verb.* (**mastered, mastering**) learn something thoroughly or become good at it

masterpiece *noun.* an outstandingly

good piece of writing, painting, sculpture, etc

mat noun. 1. a small rug 2. a thick pad on the floor that is used in wrestling, exercises, or gymnastics

match noun. 1. something that you strike to get fire 2. a game between two teams or two players 3. things that go well together —**match** verb. (**matched, matching**)

matching adj. having the same color, style, etc

mate noun. 1. someone's husband or wife 2. an animal's sexual partner

mate verb. (**mated, mating**) have sex in order to reproduce

material noun. 1. stuff that other things are made of 2. things that you use for doing a job 3. cloth —**reading material** noun. books, articles, etc, used for information about something (no plural)

material adj. 1. connected with what you can touch 2. of the body, not of the mind or spirit —**materially** adv.

materialism noun. valuing only the things that money can buy, not things of the mind or the spirit (no plural)

materialist noun. someone who believes that possessions and money are more important than things of the mind or values

materialize verb. (**materialized, materializing**) happen; become true or a fact

maternal adj. of or like a mother (of or like a father = **paternal**)

maternity noun. adj. 1. the state of being pregnant or a mother 2. a hospital department that cares for women just before and just after giving birth

math noun short for **mathematics**

mathematical adj. connected with mathematics

mathematics noun. the study of numbers, shapes, etc, like arithmetic, algebra, geometry and trigonometry (short form **math**)

matter noun. 1. some problem that you have to discuss with someone; an issue 2. what everything is made of (no plural)

matter verb. (**mattered, mattering**) make a difference

mattress noun. a long, thick pad on a bed that you lie on to be comfortable (plural **mattresses**)

mature adj. 1. fully grown; adult; no longer a child 2. suitable for an adult person

mature verb. (**matured, maturing**) become mature

maturity noun. being mature

maximize verb. (**maximized, maximizing**) make something in the best, biggest, etc, possible way, size or amount (opposite **minimize**)

maximum noun. the largest possible number or amount —**maximum** adj. (opposite **minimum**)

may verb. (**might**) 1. perhaps; possibly yes, possibly no 2. a word that asks for and gives permission 3. even if something is true 4. a word that means I wish for you

May noun. the fifth month of the year

maybe adv. possibly; perhaps (written as one word; see **may**)

mayonnaise noun. a creamy yellowish spread made of oil, vinegar or lemon juice, eggs yolks and spices that are whipped together

mayor noun. the head of a city or town

maze noun. a system of turning and twisting lines, sometimes leading nowhere, whose aim is to reach a certain point

MBA abbr. = Master of Business Administration (a higher university degree)

MD abbr. = Doctor of Medicine (a higher university degree)

me pron. (grammar) the object form of I; the first person singular

meadow noun. an open field with grass and flowers

meal *noun*. the food that you eat at a particular time

mean *verb*. **(meant, meaning) 1.** be in other words **2.** translate into **3.** be a symbol for **4.** intend to say; be trying to say **5.** intend to do something

mean *adj*. **1.** unkind; nasty **2.** not generous; stingy; wanting to keep everything for yourself **3.** average

meaning *noun*. what a word means

meaningful *adj*. having important meaning or value

means *noun plural*. **1.** way **2.** money

meant *verb*. past and past participle of **mean**

meantime *noun*. meanwhile

meanwhile *adv*. in the time between; meantime

measles *noun*. a disease where small red spots appear on the body

measure *noun*. the size or amount of something

measure *verb*. **(measured, measuring) 1.** find out the size of something **2.** be a certain height or size **3.** show the amount or take a certain amount of something

measurement *noun*. **1.** the act of measuring (no plural) **2.** the size of someone or something

meat *noun*. the flesh of an animal or bird that people eat

mecca *noun*. **1.** a place many people want to go to **2.** **(Mecca)** the holiest of cities in the Islamic religion, in Saudi Arabia

mechanic *noun*. someone who makes or repairs machines or vehicles (**auto mechanic**)

mechanical *adj*. **1.** of or by a machine **2.** like a machine

mechanics *noun*. **1.** the study of how machines work (no plural) **2.** the way in which something works (plural)

mechanism *noun*. **1.** the working parts of the machine **2.** the way that anything made up of parts works (no plural)

mechanize *verb*. **(mechanized, mecha-** nizing) bring in machines to do work that people used to do

medal *noun*. a prize that looks like a metal coin

media *noun plural*. TV, radio, newspapers and magazines

mediate *verb*. **(mediated, mediating)** act as a negotiator between two parties in order to reach a settlement

mediation *noun*. negotiation

medical *adj*. connected with medicine or doctors

medication *noun*. a medicine; a drug

medicinal *adj*. used as a medicine

medicine *noun*. **1.** the study of how to prevent illnesses and how to cure them (no plural) **2.** a drug that helps you when you are ill or in pain

medieval, mediaeval *adj*. relating to or typical of the Middle Ages (between the years 1100 and 1500)

meditate *verb*. **(meditated, meditating)** clear your mind and enter into complete calm

Mediterranean *noun*. **1.** the body of water surrounded by southern Europe, northern Africa and the Middle East **2.** someone or something from or of this area —**Mediterranean** *adj*.

medium *adj*. not big and not small

meet *noun*. a sports competition

meet *verb*. **(met, meeting) 1.** come together or join together (with someone) **2.** come together or join (with something) **3.** get to know someone for the first time

meeting *noun*. **1.** a group of people coming together by plan **2.** a coming together of two or more people

megabyte *noun*. (computers) one million bytes (short **MB**)

melancholy *noun*. deep sadness, lasting a long time (no plural) —**melancholic** *adj*.

mellow *adj*. **(mellower, mellowest)** ripening and softening through age or experience

melody noun. a line of music; a tune (plural **melodies**)

melon noun. a large round sweet fruit that grows along the ground with dense flesh and small seeds in its center

melt verb. **(melted, melting)** change from a solid into a liquid

member noun. someone who belongs to a group or an organization —**membership** noun.

memo noun. a memorandum; a short note to remind someone to do something; a short note to someone in the same company

memoir noun. a record of events or of a person's experiences

memoirs noun plural. a famous person's story of his/her life

memorabilia noun plural. things that once belonged to someone famous and are interesting

memorable adj. so special that you cannot easily forget it

memorandum noun. **1.** (law) a written agreement **2.** a memo

memorial noun. something built or put up in a place to remind people of an event or a person

memorize verb. **(memorized, memorizing)** learn by heart

memory noun. **1.** the ability to keep information in your mind (no plural) **2.** specific things from the past that you remember (plural **memories**)

men noun. plural of **man**

menace noun. a danger; a threat

menacing adj. dangerous; threatening

mend verb. **(mended, mending) 1.** repair something **2.** do sewing repairs

menstrual period, menstruation noun. the monthly flow of blood from a woman's body

menstruate verb. **(menstruated, menstruating)** have a menstrual period

mental adj. of or in the mind

mentality noun. **1.** an attitude; an outlook; a manner of thinking **2.** the degree of intellectual ability

mentally adv. connected with the mind

mention verb. **(mentioned, mentioning) 1.** say something about **2.** say or write someone's name in connection with something

menu noun. **1.** a list of the different foods that you can get at a particular restaurant **2.** a list of choices in a computer program, shown on the screen

merchandise noun. things that people buy and sell; goods (no plural)

merchandise verb. **(merchandised, merchandising)** sell goods using advertising

merchant noun. **1.** someone who buys and sells goods; a trader **2.** a storekeeper

merciless adj. having no mercy

mercy noun. willingness to forgive or not to punish

mere adj. not more than

merely adv. only

merge verb. **(merged, merging)** bring or combine two or more things together —**merger** noun.

merit noun. what is good about someone or something

merit verb. **(merited, meriting)** deserve something

merry adj. cheerful; happy (but Happy Easter, Happy Birthday)

merry-go-round noun. a machine in an amusement park that carries riders around and around

mess noun. **1.** disorder; everything out of place **2.** dirt —**mess** verb. **(messed, messing)** —**messy** adj.

message noun. **1.** information passed from one person to another **2.** the important idea of something

messenger noun. someone who brings a message

met verb. past tense and past participle of **meet**

metal noun. a hard, shiny substance found in nature —**metal** adj.

metallic adj. like metal

metaphor noun. words that describe something but used to mean something else

meter noun. 1. a measure of length 2. a machine that counts or measures something

method noun. a way of doing something

meticulous adj. paying extreme attention to detail

metric adj. measuring by units of ten, such as 1 meter = 100 centimeters

metro adj. 1. metropolitan 2. the underground railroad system in Paris and some other cities

metropolis noun. a big important city that is a center of activity

metropolitan adj. relating to a big city or the behavior of someone from a big city

mews noun. where horses used to be kept behind a house in the city (singular)

Mexican noun. adj. someone or something from Mexico

mg abbr. = milligram

mice noun. plural of **mouse**

microchip noun. See **chip**

microphone noun. an electrical instrument that makes sound louder

microscope noun. an instrument with a lens that makes things look bigger

microscopic adj. so small that you need a microscope to see it

microwave noun. a type of very short electrical wave used for transmitting radio signals, radar or for cooking food —**microwave** adj.

midday noun. noon

middle noun. the center (of) —**middle** adj.

middle age noun. the years (usually around 45–60) when a person is not young anymore but not yet old

middle-aged adj. no longer young but not yet old

middle class noun. the social class between the upper class and the working class

midnight noun. at night

might verb. 1. may possibly happen 2. past tense of **may** 3. (might have + past participle of verb) a word that shows that something in the past did not happen

might noun. power; strength

mighty adj. (**mightier, mightiest**) powerful; strong

migrate verb. (**migrated, migrating**) go from one place to another for a time — **migrating** adj. —**migration** noun.

mike abbr. microphone

mild adj. 1. not hot or cold; pleasant 2. gentle

mile noun. a measure of distance (=5,280 ft or 1.6 km)

mileage noun. the distance something or someone has traveled in miles

militant adj. extremist; supporting the use of violence for social or political purposes

military noun. connected with the army or navy —**military** adj.

milk noun. the white liquid from cows, sheep, etc, that people drink (no plural)

milk verb. (**milked, milking**) take milk from an animal

milk adj. with milk in it

mill noun. 1. a building for making flour from grain 2. a type of factory

million noun. a thousand times one thousand (1,000,000) (plural **million**)

millionaire noun. a rich person who has more than a million dollars, pounds, etc

mime noun. acting without using words —**mime** verb. (**mimed, miming**)

mimic verb. (**mimicked, mimicking**) copy the way somebody does something

mind noun. the part of our brain that we think with; the brain

mind *verb.* **(minded, minding)** take care of; look after

mine *pron.* belonging to me (plural **ours**)

mine *noun.* **1.** a place where minerals are taken out of the ground **2.** a small bomb that is placed on the ground or under water

mine *verb.* **(mined, mining) 1.** take minerals from a mine **2.** put bombs in a place where they will do harm

miner *noun.* someone who works in a mine

mineral *noun.* stuff that comes from inside the earth

mineral water *noun.* water that comes from a spring and is good for your health

mingle *verb.* **(mingled, mingling)** move among guests of a party; become one of a crowd; mix

mini *noun.* (also **miniskirt**) a very short skirt

miniature *adj.* very small

minibus *noun.* a kind of van or small bus (plural **minibuses**)

minimal *adj.* smallest in amount or degree; the least possible

minimize *verb.* **(minimized, minimizing)** lessen to the smallest possible size or degree; make appear as not serious

minimum *noun.* the lowest number possible; the smallest amount possible

minimum *adj.* least; lowest (opposite **maximum**)

minister *noun.* **1.** a government official **2.** a Protestant Christian priest

ministry *noun.* an office of government (plural **ministries**)

minor *noun.* **1.** someone under 18 years of age (opposite **adult**) **2.** a second subject studied at college

minor *adj.* **1.** not very important **2.** not serious (opposite **major**)

minority *noun.* **1.** the smaller part of a group **2.** a group that is smaller than the biggest group (plural **minorities**)

minus *prep. adj.* **1.** less **2.** less than zero

minute *noun.* **1.** 60 seconds **2.** a very short time; a moment

minute *adj.* very small

minutes *noun plural.* the official notes of what was said during a meeting, etc

miracle *noun.* something wonderful and unexpected that happens

miraculous *adj.* amazing; wonderful — **miraculously** *adv.*

mirror *noun.* a piece of glass or other material in which you can see yourself

mischief *noun.* behavior that causes trouble

miserable *adj.* **1.** very unhappy **2.** ill and uncomfortable **3.** too small —**miserably** *adv.*

misery *noun.* great unhappiness or suffering

misfortune *noun.* bad luck

misinterpret *verb.* **(misinterpreted, misinterpreting)** give a wrong meaning to something

misjudge *verb.* **(misjudged, misjudging)** judge wrongly; form a wrong or unfairly bad opinion of someone

mislead *verb.* **(misled, misleading)** cause someone on purpose to understand wrongly

misrepresent *verb.* **(misrepresented, misrepresenting)** give a wrong description (on purpose)

miss *noun.* **1.** failure to hit or throw the ball into the basket, goal, etc **2.** failure to hit the target (plural **misses**)

miss *verb.* **(missed, missing) 1.** feel sad because you are not with a certain person or cannot have a certain thing any more **2.** see that something is not there **3.** be too late for the train, bus, etc **4.** not hit **5.** not see something

Miss *noun.* a title before the name of a woman who is not married (compare with **Mrs., Ms**)

missile *noun.* a weapon that comes through the air

missing *adj.* not where someone or something should be

mission noun. 1. a group of people who are sent abroad for a special purpose 2. the purpose for which a person or group is sent somewhere 3. a place where a religious group teaches, provides services for the poor, etc

missionary noun. someone who goes to other countries to teach people about his/her religion (plural **missionaries**)

mist noun. a thin fog

mistake noun. error; something that you do or say wrongly

mistake verb. (**mistook, mistaken, mistaking**) think that someone is somebody else —**mistaken** adj. —**mistakenly** adv.

mister noun. = Mr.; a title before a man's name

mistress noun. 1. a head of household; a woman in control 2. a woman who is the lover of a usually married man

misty adj. full of mist

misunderstand verb. (**misunderstood, misunderstanding**) understand something incorrectly —**misunderstanding** noun.

mix verb. (**mixed, mixing**) 1. make a combination out of different things 2. combine to make one thing

mixed adj. having different kinds of things

mixer noun. a machine that mixes something

mixture noun. 1. a combination of different things 2. something that is made up of different substances

moan verb. (**moaned, moaning**) make a long, low sound of pain or suffering — **moan** noun.

mob noun. an angry group of people who behave noisily and dangerously

mob verb. (**mobbed, mobbing**) crowd around someone

mobile adj. not fixed in one place; able to move or be moved easily

mock verb. (**mocked, mocking**) make fun of someone by imitating him/her cruelly

modal adj. (grammar) a helping verb that comes together with the base form of another verb to convey an additional message and never has an **s** or -**ing** ending

model noun. 1. a small-sized copy of something big 2. one example of something that has many copies 3. someone whose job is to wear certain clothes, cosmetics, jewelry, etc, so that people will see and buy them 4. someone that an artist paints or that a photographer photographs 5. someone that you would like to copy in life

model verb. (**modeled, modeling**) 1. make something out of clay 2. work as a model 3. let an artist paint you or a photographer take pictures of you — **model** adj.

modem noun. the part of a computer that enables communication between computers by way of the telephone lines

moderate adj. not extreme —**moderately** adv.

moderation noun. being or acting within limits

modern adj. new; up-to-date; of our time

modernize verb. (**modernized, modernizing**) make something modern

modest adj. 1. not boasting 2. simple

modestly adv. 1. without boasting; in a way that does not show off 2. in a simple way

modify verb. (**modified, modifying**) change; make something simpler

modular adj. made of or based on modules

module noun. a separate part of something bigger

mogul noun. a very rich, powerful and important person

moist adj. a little bit wet

moisture noun. slight wetness (no plural)

mom, mummy *noun.* loving name for a mother

moment *noun.* a very short time

momentary *adj.* lasting a very short time

monarch *noun.* a king or a queen

monarchy *noun.* a country that has a king or a queen (plural **monarchies**)

monastery *noun.* a building where monks live (plural **monasteries**)

Monday *noun.* the second day of the week

monetary *adj.* concerning money

money *noun.* 1. dollars, pounds, etc, that you use for buying things 2. what a particular country uses for buying and selling

monitor *verb.* (**monitored, monitoring**) watch or listen closely

monk *noun.* one of a group of men who live in a monastery, do not marry and spend their lives serving God

monkey *noun.* a small animal that has a long tail and climbs trees

monologue, monolog *noun.* a speech by a single actor who is (often) alone on stage

monopoly *noun.* 1. control of something by one company, person, etc 2. the exclusive right to something

monotonous *adj.* unchanging and boring

monster *noun.* 1. a frightening, imaginary animal 2. a cruel person —**monstrous** *adj.*

month *noun.* one of the 12 divisions of the year

monthly *adj.* coming once a month

monument *noun.* a building, statue, stone, etc, that is put up so that people will remember something or someone; memorial

monumental *adj.* very large

mood *noun.* the way you feel at a particular time

moon *noun.* the bright body that gives light in the sky at night

moonlight *noun.* light from the moon

moonlight *verb.* (**moonlighted, moonlighting**) work (unofficially) at an additional job

moor *noun.* wide open land that cannot be farmed because of bad quality soil

mop *noun.* a tool with a long handle and strips of cloth or a sponge at one end for washing floors

moral *noun.* a lesson that tells what is right and what is wrong

morale *noun.* the way people feel about things

morality *noun.* standards and ideas about what is right and wrong

more *adj.* larger in number, size or amount (opposite **less** with uncountable nouns, **fewer** with countable nouns)

moreover *adv.* a word that shows that there is something more; in addition; besides

more (than) *adv.* 1. a word that shows that one thing is bigger, stronger, etc, than something else, added to: long adjectives; adjectives that end in -**ful**; adjectives that end in -**less**; adjectives that end in -**ing** 2. a word that compares how much

morning *noun.* the early part of the day —**morning** *adj.*

mortgage *noun.* a loan taken from a bank in order to buy a house

mosaic *noun.* small pieces of stone fitted together to form a picture

Moslem *noun.* see **Muslim**

mosque *noun.* a building where Muslims worship God

mosquito *noun.* a small flying insect that bites and sucks blood from someone and that can also carry diseases (plural **mosquitoes**)

moss *noun.* a green flat thick furry plant that grows on wet soil

most *adj. pron.* 1. the majority of 2. the biggest number 3. the largest amount

mostly *adv.* mainly; more than anything else

motel *noun.* a simple hotel for travelers with cars where the rooms often face the parking lot

mother *noun.* a female parent

mother-in-law *noun.* the mother of someone's husband or wife (plural **mothers-in-law**)

motif *noun.* 1. the main subject on which a work of art is based 2. an often repeated set of notes within a musical composition

motion *noun.* movement; activity (no plural)

motion *verb.* (**motioned, motioning**) indicate by moving your head, etc

motionless *adj.* not moving; still

motivate *verb.* (**motivated, motivating**) give someone a strong reason to do something

motivated *adj.* having motivation

motivation *noun.* what encourages someone to work hard for something (no plural)

motive *noun.* a reason for doing something

motor *noun.* a machine that makes another thing work or move

motorbike *noun.* a motorcycle

motorcycle *noun.* a vehicle with two wheels that looks like a large, heavy bicycle and has a motor

motorist *noun.* someone who drives a car; a driver

motto *noun.* a few words or a short sentence that someone uses as a guide for living

mound *noun.* 1. a pile; a heap 2. a place where the pitcher stands in the game of baseball

mount *verb.* (**mounted, mounting**) 1. get on a horse 2. climb to a higher place

Mount *noun.* a name that is used for a high mountain (usually written **Mt.**)

mountain *noun.* a very high hill — **mountainous** *adj.*

mourn *verb.* (**mourned, mourning**) be sad and grieve over a death

mourning *noun.* the formal show of sadness and grief after a death (no plural)

mouse *noun.* 1. a small animal that runs very fast and eats through things with its front teeth (plural **mice**) 2. (computer) a device that you move and press to make the computer do things (plural **mouses**)

mousse *noun.* 1. an airy sweet dessert 2. sticky stuff put on the hair that comes in a pressurized can

mouth *noun.* what we use for eating and talking

move *noun.* 1. moving 2. taking a turn in a game 3. acting on a decision

move *verb.* (**moved, moving**) 1. be in motion 2. walk, dance, etc 3. change your place 4. put a part of your body into motion 5. put something in a different place 6. get something out of the way 7. change your living place

movement *noun.* 1. the act of moving (no plural) 2. a group of people struggling for principles they believe in

mover *noun.* 1. someone who sets something in motion 2. someone who loads possessions into a truck, transfers them from one place to another and then unloads them there

movie *noun.* a series of moving pictures shown in a theater or on TV; a film

moving *adj.* in motion; not still

mow *verb.* (**mowed, mowing**) cut grass or crops with a machine

mower *noun.* a machine for cutting grass (also **lawn mower**)

MP *abbr.* Member of Parliament

mph, m.p.h. *abbr.* = miles per hour

much *adj.* (**more, most**) a large amount of something (used with uncountable nouns; in negative sentences and questions)

much *adv. pron.* a lot

muck *noun.* dirt; mess; sticky stuff (no plural)

mud *noun.* wet earth

muddy *adj.* **(muddier, muddiest)** full of mud

muffin *noun.* a small, round cake

mug *noun.* a big cup with a handle

mug *verb.* **(mugged, mugging)** attack and rob someone in the street

mule *noun.* an animal that was created from the mating of a horse and a donkey

multimedia *noun.* the use of more than one medium (sound, text, pictures in one program)

multinational *adj.* having offices, factories, operations, etc, in more than one country

multiple *noun.* a number that has a smaller number which divides it an exact number of times

multiple *adj.* having many parts

multiplication *noun.* times (x) in arithmetic

multiply *verb.* **(multiplied, multiplying)** 1. use multiplication in arithmetic 2. have young ones

mumble *verb.* **(mumbled, mumbling)** speak unclearly

munch *verb.* **(munched, munching)** chew on something hard and crunchy

municipal *adj.* concerning the government of a city or town

municipality *noun.* a local government (of a city or town)

mural *noun.* a large painting on a wall

murder *noun.* 1. the planned killing of another person (no plural) 2. a case of murder

murder *verb.* **(murdered, murdering)** kill another person on purpose

murderer *noun.* someone who has committed murder

murderous *adj.* 1. capable of murder 2. looking as if someone wanted to kill

murmur *noun.* 1. the sound of soft voices 2. the gentle sound of water flowing

murmur *verb.* **(murmured, murmuring)** speak very softly

muscle *noun.* the elastic parts inside your body that make it possible for you to move

muscular *adj.* having strong muscles

museum *noun.* a building where people can see pictures, statues, etc

mushroom *noun.* a fungus that can be eaten

music *noun.* 1. sounds that people make by singing or playing musical instruments 2. written notes that tell you how to play a song, tune, etc

musical *noun.* a play or a movie with a lot of singing and dancing

musical *adj.* 1. connected with music 2. good at music

musician *noun.* someone who writes or performs music

Muslim, Moslem *noun.* a believer in (the religion of) Islam

must *verb.* 1. be absolutely necessary 2. have to 3. ought to (because **must** has no future or past, use **have to** or **had to; must not** means **forbidden**, and is stronger than **don't have to** = not necessary)

mustache *noun.* the hairs above a man's lip

mustard *noun.* a thick, sharp, yellow sauce that many people like with meat

mustn't *abbr.* = must not 1. forbidden; do not! 2. shouldn't

mutiny *noun.* a rebellion of soldiers or sailors against their officers or their captain (plural **mutinies**)

mutter *verb.* **(muttered, muttering)** speak or complain in a low or unclear voice so that people do not understand you

mutual *adj.* 1. having the same feelings for one another 2. one for the other 3. shared in common by two or more people —**mutually** *adj.*

mutual fund *noun.* a company where someone can buy shares of many other different companies

muzzle *noun.* 1. the mouth and nose of a dog 2. a guard that you put over the face of a dog so that it cannot bite

my *adj.* belonging to me (compare with mine)

myself *pron.* **1.** a word that tells that you are the person whom you are talking about **2.** I and no other person

mysterious *adj.* **1.** strange; difficult or impossible to explain **2.** secretive

mysteriously *adv.* **1.** in a strange way **2.** in a secretive way

mystery *noun.* **1.** something that is not known or understood **2.** a story about a crime that someone tries to solve

myth *noun.* **1.** a very old story about the history and ancient beliefs of a people **2.** something that is not a fact but which many people believe is true

mythology *noun.* all the myths of a people (plural **mythologies**)

N

nag *verb.* **(nagged, nagging)** ask for something again and again

nail *noun.* **1.** the hard substance at the ends of your fingers and toes **2.** a thin piece of metal that holds things together or that you can hang things on

nail *verb.* **(nailed, nailing)** fasten with nails

naive *adj.* without knowledge or experience of life; not suspecting dishonesty

naked *adj.* without clothes

name *noun.* **1.** the special words for a particular person, animal or place **2.** the title of a book, play, poem, etc **3.** what people say about you; reputation

name *verb.* **(named, naming) 1.** give a name to a person, place, animal, etc **2.** know the name of something

named *adj.* having the name; by the name of

namely *adv.* that is to say; i.e.

nanny *noun.* a woman who takes care of the children in a family (plural **nannies**)

nap *noun.* a short sleep in the daytime

napkin *noun.* a piece of cloth or paper for wiping your mouth

narcotic *noun.* **1.** something that takes away pain or makes you sleep **2.** an illegal drug

narrator *noun.* a person who tells what is happening in a book, play, TV program, etc

narrow *adj.* small from side to side (opposite **wide, broad**)

narrow *verb.* **(narrowed, narrowing)** become or make narrow

narrowly *adv.* only just

nasty *adj.* **1.** disgusting **2.** rude; ill-mannered **3.** difficult and troublesome

nation *noun.* a large group of people who feel a sense of belonging together and usually live in one country and speak the same language

national *adj.* **1.** of a country **2.** for a whole country

national anthem *noun.* the national song of a country

nationality *noun.* **1.** belonging to a particular country **2.** citizenship (plural **nationalities**)

nationalize *verb.* **(nationalized, nationalizing)** take governmental control of a business or industry

nationwide *adj.* all over the nation

native *noun.* someone who was born in a certain place —**native** *adj.*

Native American *noun.* a member of the original people living in North America who used to be called an American Indian

natural *adj.* **1.** made by nature, not by people **2.** the same as in nature **3.** normal **4.** from birth **5.** without artificial help

naturally *adv.* **1.** from nature **2.** of course **3.** in a normal way

nature *noun.* **1.** everything that exists and was not made by people (no plural) **2.** the way that something is **3.** someone's character or temperament

naughty *adj.* **(naughtier, naughtiest)** behaving badly; making trouble (usually used for a child)

naval *adj.* connected to the navy

navigate *verb.* **(navigated, navigating) 1.** control the direction of a ship or an aircraft **2.** find the right direction by using a map, compass, etc —**navigation** *noun.*

navigator *noun.* the officer who navigates a ship or an aircraft

navy *noun.* the military force that defends a country at sea (plural **navies**)

Nazi *noun.* a member of Adolf Hitler's National Socialist party in Germany in the 1930s and 1940s —**Nazi** *adj.*

NB *abbr.* (in writing) pay special attention

NE *abbr.* northeast

near *prep.* close to

near *adj. adv.* not far; close

nearby *adj. adv.* not far

nearly *adv.* almost

neat *adj.* orderly; tidy —**neatly** *adv.*

necessarily *adv.* as an unavoidable result

necessary *adj.* needed; that must be done (opposite **unnecessary**)

necessity *noun.* **1.** things that people need (plural **necessities**) **2.** a very strong need (no plural)

neck *noun.* the part of your body where your head sits

necklace *noun.* a decoration worn around the neck

need *noun.* **1.** necessity (no plural) **2.** the things that are necessary

need *verb.* (**needed**) **1.** must have **2.** be necessary; require

needle *noun.* a sharp, pointed piece of metal for sewing clothes, etc

needless *adj.* not necessary

needn't *verb.* = need not

needy *adj.* poor

negate *verb.* (**negated, negating**) **1.** stop something from having an effect **2.** deny

negative *noun.* **1.** (grammar) a sentence that means **no** and has words like **not, no** or **never 2.** a film in which light things appear dark and dark things appear light **3.** no

negative *adj.* **1.** the opposite of positive **2.** less than zero —**negatively** *adv.*

neglect *verb.* (**neglected, neglecting**) not take care of; not do what is necessary —**neglect** *noun.* —**neglected** *adj.*

negligence *noun.* failure to use the carefulness that a sensible person usually uses

negligent *adj.* careless; not taking enough care

negotiable *adj.* that can be talked about in order to reach an agreement

negotiate *verb.* (**negotiated, negotiating**) talk to another person, or group of people, with the intention of reaching an agreement —**negotiator** *noun.*

negotiation *noun.* the act or process of negotiating

neither *pron.* not one and not the other of two things

neither *adv.* also not; not either (use a positive verb)

neither *adj.* not one of two things (use **none** for more than two things)

neoclassical *adj.* something (usually) in the Greek or Roman classical style (of architecture, art, music, etc) but done recently

nephew *noun.* the son of your brother or sister

nerve *noun.* a kind of thread that carries messages between the brain and other parts of your body

nervous *adj.* **1.** worried; tense **2.** not calm; jumpy **3.** connected with the nerves —**nervousness** *noun.*

nervous breakdown *noun.* deep depression; inability to manage your life (a kind of mental illness)

nervously *adv.* in a way that shows worry

nervous system *noun.* all the nerves in your body

nest *noun.* **1.** the home that a bird makes in a tree, etc **2.** a protected place where groups of animals or insects live

nest *verb.* (**nested, nesting**) build and live in a nest —**nesting** *noun.*

net *noun.* **1.** a cloth made out of threads or strings twisted together with spaces between them (no plural) **2.** an item made from net **3.** (computers) **the Net**; the Internet (no plural)

net *verb.* (**netted, netting**) **1.** catch fish in a net **2.** earn money after paying tax

net *adj.* **1.** made of net **2.** left after paying taxes

network noun. **1.** a system of many lines, roads, etc, that cross each other **2.** different radio or TV stations that belong to the same company and use the same programs **3.** a set of computers that are connected to each other so that they can share information —**network** verb. **(networked, networking)**

neutral adj. not taking sides —**neutrality** noun.

neutralize verb. **(neutralized, neutralizing)** stop something from having an effect; cancel out the value or force of something

never adv. not ever; not at any time (when **never** comes at the beginning of the sentence, the verb changes its place)

nevertheless adv. in spite of that fact; however; anyway (use a comma after **nevertheless** if it is the first word in a sentence)

new adj. **1.** that has just been bought; not used **2.** different **3.** not known to you before **4.** that has just begun to exist

newborn noun. adj. a recently-born baby

newcomer noun. someone new in a place

newly adv. recently

news noun. **1.** information about what is happening **2.** the news; a radio or TV program that reports what is happening

newsletter noun. a (printed) publication meant for people who are interested in the same things

newspaper noun. (also **paper**) sheets of printed paper with news, articles, advertisements, sports, etc

newsroom noun. the office of a newspaper, a radio station, TV station, etc, where news comes in and then it is decided what should be published

newsstand noun. a place on the street or in a building that sells newspapers, magazines, etc

New Year's Day noun. January 1st, the first day of the new year

New Year's Eve noun. December 31st, the last day of the old year

next adj. **1.** the one just after; the following one **2.** the one that is closest

next adv. **1.** after that; then **2.** the second

next door adj. adv. in the house or apartment beside yours

nice adj. **1.** pleasant and kind **2.** sunny and pleasant **3.** kind and generous **4.** polite **5.** pleasant and entertaining **6.** pretty; lovely

nicely adv. in a good or pleasant way

nickname noun. **1.** a special or funny name that your friends or family call you **2.** a short form of someone's real name

niece noun. the daughter of your brother or sister

night noun. **1.** the hours of darkness **2.** evening

nightclub noun. a place where people go at night to drink, eat, dance and sometimes watch a show

nightmare noun. **1.** a frightening dream **2.** something so terrible that it seems like a bad dream

nine noun. adj. the number 9

nineteen noun. adj. the number 19

nineteenth adj. = 19th

ninetieth adj. = 90th

ninety noun. adj. the number 90

ninth adj. = 9th

nip verb. **(nipped, nipping)** pinch; catch between two sharp points

nitrogen noun. a gas without smell or color that is a large part of the air we breathe

no excl. a negative answer (opposite **yes**)

no adj. not any (opposite **some**)

no adv. not any

noble adj. **1.** brave; unselfish; correct **2.** aristocratic; of high rank or high birth

nobody *pron.* not anybody; no one (use a positive verb)

nod *verb.* **(nodded, nodding)** move your head up an down to show agreement or give a signal to someone — **nod** *noun.*

noise *noun.* **1.** loud unpleasant sound (no plural) **2.** any sound

noisy *adj.* **(noisier, noisiest)** loud; full of noise (opposite **quiet**) —**noisily** *adv.*

nominate *verb.* **(nominated, nominating)** name someone as a candidate for a job, etc —**nomination** *noun.*

nominee *noun.* someone who is nominated as a candidate

non, non- *prefix.* = not, that does not, without

none *pron.* not any; not one

nonetheless *adv.* nevertheless; however; in spite of that

nonsense *noun.* foolish things (no plural)

nonsmoker, non-smoker *noun.* someone who does not smoke

nonstop, non-stop *noun. adj. adv.* without stopping

noon *noun. adj.* midday; 12:00 in the day

no one *pron.* nobody (use a positive verb; in the present tenses, add **s** to the base form of the verb; opposite **everyone**)

nor *conj.* **1.** neither/nor; not ... and not **2.** neither; also not

normal *adj.* not unusual; expected; standard

normally *adv.* **1.** usually **2.** in a normal way

north *noun.* one of the four directions —**north** *adj.*

north *adv.* toward the north (opposite **south**) —**northeast** *noun. adj.* (short form **NE**) —**northwest** *noun. adj.* (short form **NW**)

northern *adj.* of the north (opposite **southern**)

northward, northwards *adv.* to the north (opposite **southward, southwards**)

Norwegian *noun. adj.* someone or something from Norway; the language spoken in Norway

nose *noun.* **1.** the part of the face for smelling and breathing **2.** the front part of a car, ship, etc, that looks like a nose

not *adv.* a negative word that gives the opposite meaning to a verb (can be shortened to **n't** when attached to helping verbs, such as **cannot** = **cannot**)

notch *noun.* a V-shaped cut

note *noun.* **1.** a short message **2.** a short letter **3.** a mark on a sheet of music to show what sound to sing or play **4.** paper money; a bill

note *verb.* **(noted, noting)** notice something

notebook *noun.* a school book with a soft cover and pages for writing things down

notes *noun plural.* writing on a piece of paper to help you remember something

noteworthy *adj.* deserving attention, especially an event or things

nothing *pron.* not anything (use a positive verb)

notice *noun.* a written announcement

notice *verb.* **(noticed, noticing) 1.** happen to see **2.** see that something is happening **3.** pay attention to something or someone

noticeable *adj.* significant; attracting attention

notify *verb.* **(notified, notifying)** give someone information about an event —**notification** *noun.*

notion *noun.* an idea, a belief, or concept

notoriety *noun.* being famous for something bad —**notorious** *adj.* —**notoriously** *adv.*

noun *noun.* (grammar) the name of a thing, a person, an animal, a quality, or an idea

Nov. *abbr.* = November

novel *noun.* a long story about imaginary people or historical people

novelist *noun.* someone who writes novels

November *noun.* the eleventh month of the year

now *adv.* **1.** at once **2.** at this time **3.** at present

nowadays *adv.* these days

no way *interj.* not under any circumstances

nowhere *adv.* **1.** not anywhere; not in any place **2.** not anywhere; not to any place

nuclear *adj.* atomic

nucleus *noun.* **1.** the central part of an atom **2.** the central part of a living cell

nude *adj.* naked; not wearing clothes

nuisance *noun.* something or someone that annoys you or gives you trouble

null *adj.* invalid; without value; being equal to zero

numb *adj.* unable to feel anything because of cold, fear, etc

number *noun.* a word or a figure such as one (1) or ninety nine (99) —**number** *verb.* **(numbered, numbering)**

numerous *adj.* many (use with countable nouns)

nun *noun.* a religious woman who lives apart from society and devotes her life to serving God

nurse *noun.* **1.** someone who is trained to take care of sick people and help doctors **2.** a woman who looks after young children

nurse *verb.* **(nursed, nursing) 1.** take care of a sick person **2.** breast-feed a baby

nursery *noun.* **1.** a room for babies or small children **2.** a place where young plants and trees are grown and then sold (plural **nurseries**)

nut *noun.* **1.** the hard fruit of a tree or a bush that grows inside a shell **2.** a small piece of metal that screws onto a bolt

nutrition *noun.* eating foods that are good for your health (no plural) —**nutritional** *adj.* —**nutritious** *adj.*

nutritionist *noun.* someone who studies food and its effects on health

nylon *noun.* a strong man-made elastic material that is used to make material for clothing, string, brushes, etc

O

O *excl.* = Oh; a word that shows surprise, pain or suddenly remembering something

oak *noun.* **1.** a big tree that gives shade **2.** the light-colored wood of an oak tree (no plural)

oak *adj.* made of oak

oar *noun.* a long, flat pole for rowing a boat

oasis *noun.* a place with water and trees in a desert (plural **oases**)

oath *noun.* **1.** a very serious promise **2.** a formal statement that something is true

obedience *noun.* doing what you are told to do (no plural; opposite **disobedience**) —**obedient** *adj.* (opposite **disobedient**)

obey *verb.* **(obeyed, obeying)** do what someone tells you to (opposite **disobey**)

object *noun.* **1.** a thing that you can touch **2.** (grammar) something or someone that receives the action of the verb **3.** a reason for doing something; a purpose

object *verb.* **(objected, objecting) 1.** be against **2.** think that something is wrong; not allow something

objection *noun.* disagreement with something

objective *noun.* a goal; a purpose

objective *adj.* fair; able to see more than one side of a question —**objectivity** *noun.*

objectively *adv.* fairly

obligation *noun.* something that you have to do

obligatory *adj.* compulsory; not a matter of choice

oblige *verb.* **(obliged, obliging)** make someone do something

observance *noun.* going according to the law; keeping/following a religious ceremony, law or custom

observation *noun.* **1.** careful watching (no plural) **2.** remark

observatory *noun.* a building that is designed for watching the stars, the moon, and the sky (plural **observatories**)

observe *verb.* **(observed, observing) 1.** watch carefully **2.** notice something **3.** keep/obey religious laws or customs

observer *noun.* a person who watches but does not take part

obsession *noun.* something that a person cannot stop thinking about or doing —**obsessed** *adj.* —**obsessive** *adj.*

obsolete *adj.* something that is not used any more

obstacle *noun.* **1.** something that stands in your way; a barrier **2.** something that prevents you from doing what you want or plan

obstinate *adj.* not willing to do what someone else wants; stubborn

obstruct *verb.* **(obstructed, obstructing)** be in someone's way

obstruction *noun.* something that gets in the way

obtain *verb.* **(obtained, obtaining)** get something you want

obvious *adj.* clear

obviously *adv.* clearly

occasion *noun.* **1.** event; happening **2.** a time when something happens

occasional *adj.* happening from time to time

occasionally *adv.* once in a while; now and then

occupant *noun.* someone who lives in a place, but is not necessarily the owner of it

occupation *noun.* **1.** a profession or

job; how you earn a living **2.** conquering and keeping a territory in war

occupational *adj.* about or caused by someone's work

occupied *adj.* **1.** taken; not vacant **2.** busy

occupy *verb.* **(occupied, occupying) 1.** conquer and hold a country or territory **2.** keep someone busy **3.** take up one's thoughts

occur *verb.* **(occurred, occurring)** happen; take place (use **take place** for planned events)

occurrence *noun.* (formal) an event

ocean *noun.* one of the great seas of the Earth

o'clock *adv.* the time; the hour

Oct. *abbr.* = October

October *noun.* the 10th month of the year

odd *adj.* **1.** strange; not usual **2.** not even (number); that you cannot divide exactly by two **3.** supposed to be part of a pair

oddly *adv.* in a strange way

odds *noun plural.* the probability that something can happen

odor *noun.* a smell, usually an unpleasant one

of *prep.* **1.** belonging to **2.** from something bigger **3.** a word that tells an amount **4.** containing something **5.** written or painted by **6.** showing **7.** about **8.** made from **9.** a word that tells direction **10.** a word that tells when **11.** a word that tells place

of course *adv.* **1.** certainly **2.** not surprisingly; naturally; understandingly

off *prep.* **1.** down from **2.** away from **3.** a word that tells how far away from

off *adv. adj.* **1.** away **2.** distant **3.** not operating

offend *verb.* **(offended, offending)** insult; hurt someone's feelings

offender *noun.* someone who does something wrong or breaks the law

offense *noun.* **1.** breaking the law **2.**

something that hurts your feelings and makes you angry (no plural) **3.** an attack **4.** the players on a team whose job is to score goals or baskets

offensive *noun.* an attack

offensive *adj.* **1.** rude and disgusting **2.** aggressive; attacking

offer *noun.* a proposal

offer *verb.* **(offered, offering)** suggest that you will do something for someone

office *noun.* **1.** a room or rooms for taking care of business or professional work **2.** an important job

officer *noun.* **1.** a person who commands soldiers in the army or navy **2.** member of a police force **3.** someone who has an important job in government or in business

official *noun.* someone who holds a high position in government or in business

official *adj.* **1.** from someone who has authority **2.** made known to everyone

officially *adv.* **1.** with authority **2.** publicly

offspring *noun.* a child; children; young of animals

often *adv.* many times

oil *noun.* **1.** a thick, fatty liquid from plants or animals **2.** the liquid from under the ground that is necessary for industry

oil *verb.* **(oiled, oiling)** put oil on something

oil well *noun.* a well that oil comes out of

oily *adj.* **(oilier, oiliest)** having too much oil

ointment *noun.* something creamy or oily that you can put on a burn or a sore to heal it

okay, OK, O.K. *interj. adv. adj.* yes; all right

okay *verb.* **(okayed, okaying)** approve (a plan, etc)

old *adj.* **1.** not young **2.** not new **3.** known for a long time **4.** not recent

old age *noun.* the state of being old

old-fashioned *adj.* not modern

olive *noun.* **1.** a small, sharp-tasting, green or black fruit with a pit inside **2.** the dull green color of an olive (no plural) —**olive** *adj.*

Olympic Games, Olympics *noun.* international sporting event held every four years —**Olympic** *adj.*

omelet, omelette *noun.* eggs that are beaten and sometimes cooked with some kind of filling

omen *noun.* a sign of what will happen in the future

omission *noun.* something left out, left undone or neglected

omit *verb.* **(omitted, omitting)** not include; leave out

on *prep.* **1.** a word that tells what place **2.** a word that tells what day **3.** a word that tells about belonging to something **4.** by means of **5.** about

on *adv.* **1.** working; operating (opposite **off**) **2.** farther away in place **3.** being shown

once *adv.* **1.** one time **2.** when; after **3.** in the past

one *noun.* the number 1

one *pron.* **1.** a person; any person **2.** a word that you can use instead of a noun

one *adj.* **1.** a single thing **2.** the same

one another each other

one-off *adj. noun.* something done once only

one-on-one, one-to-one *adj.* between two people only

oneself *pron.* (formal) used instead of himself, herself, yourself, etc, when we do not mean a specific person

one-way *adj.* going in one direction only

on-going *adj.* being in the process; continuing

onion *noun.* a round bulb with a sharp taste that is eaten as a vegetable

on-line, online *adj.* (computers) connected to the Internet or to a central computer network

only *adj.* **1.** with no others **2.** the one that is possible

only *adv.* **1.** no more than **2.** just

only *conj.* but; however

onto *prep.* from one place to the top of another

onward, onwards *adv.* **1.** forward **2.** into the future

ooze *verb.* **(oozed, oozing)** flow out of something slowly as a thick liquid or cream

open *verb.* **(opened, opening) 1.** make something not closed **2.** move so it is not closed **3.** unfasten **4.** unfold (or change the shape of) something **5.** begin something

open *adj.* **1.** not closed; not shut **2.** not covered **3.** ready for business **4.** not for a special group **5.** known to everyone

open-air *adj.* out-of-doors

opener *noun.* an instrument that you use for opening things

opening *noun.* **1.** a space where you can get inside or outside of something **2.** beginning something (no plural) **3.** a chance to compete for something **4.** the first night of a play

openly *adv.* not secretly

open-minded *adj.* ready to hear all the facts before making a decision

opera *noun.* a play in which almost all the words are sung rather than spoken

operate *verb.* **(operated, operating) 1.** make something work **2.** work; function **3.** run a business **4.** cut into the body of a person or an animal (for healing purposes)

operation *noun.* **1.** starting to work; coming into force (no plural) **2.** an action involving a number of people **3.** cutting into a patient to take out or repair something

operational *adj.* ready to be used

operative *adj.* working; producing effects

operator *noun.* **1.** someone who works a telephone switchboard **2.** someone who makes something work

opinion *noun.* someone's idea about something

opponent *noun.* **1.** someone who plays against you in a match or runs against you in an election **2.** someone who is against something

opportunity *noun.* a chance to do something

opportunities *noun plural.* advantages

oppose *verb.* **(opposed, opposing)** be against something

opposite *prep.* across from; facing

opposite *adj.* **1.** completely different **2.** the one facing **—opposite** *noun.*

opposite sex *noun.* the other sex

opposition *noun.* **1.** disagreement with; being against something **2.** (Opposition) in politics, the parties that are not in power **3.** someone in a competition that you are competing against

oppress *verb.* **(oppressed, oppressing)** treat cruelly and take away rights and freedom **—oppression** *noun.*

opt *verb.* **(opted, opting)** choose (usually one of two things)

optical *adj.* connected with seeing

optics *noun.* the scientific study of light

optimism *noun.* the tendency to see the good side of and to expect good results from a situation (opposite **pessimism**) **—optimistic** *adj.* (opposite **pessimistic**)

optimist *noun.* someone who believes that good things will happen (opposite **pessimist**)

option *noun.* a choice

optional *adj.* not compulsory

or *conj.* **1.** a word that shows choice **2.** if not

oral *adj.* spoken; not written

orange *noun.* **1.** a round, sweet citrus fruit with a thick peel **2.** the color between yellow and red **—orange** *adj.*

orbit *noun.* the path of one thing around another thing

orchard *noun.* a field of fruit trees

orchestra *noun.* a large group of musicians who play together

ordeal *noun.* a difficult and/or painful experience

order *noun.* **1.** a command **2.** something that you ask for at a restaurant or store **3.** the way that one thing comes after another (no plural) **4.** neatness; everything having a place

order *verb.* **(ordered, ordering) 1.** command **2.** ask for something at a restaurant **3.** ask for a store to send you something

orderly *noun.* someone who helps patients in a hospital (plural **orderlies**)

orderly *adj.* **1.** neat and tidy **2.** well-organized and systematic

ordinarily *adv.* unusually

ordinary *adj.* not special; usual (opposite **strange, unusual**)

ore *noun.* rock or earth in which there is metal

organ *noun.* **1.** a musical instrument that looks like a piano with pipes **2.** an internal part of the body

organic *adj.* **1.** connected with living things **2.** (fruit, vegetables, meat, milk, etc) produced without using chemicals

organism *noun.* a living thing

organization *noun.* **1.** a group of people who work or meet together for a special purpose **2.** arranging; organizing (no plural) **—organizational** *adj.*

organize *verb.* **(organized, organizing) 1.** make a plan and carry it out **2.** put something in order

organized *adj.* **1.** neat and efficient **2.** well run **3.** official; with a strong organization

organizer *noun.* **1.** someone who organizes **2.** a diary (calendar) and appointment book for arranging your affairs

orient *verb.* **(oriented, orienting) 1.** to

become familiar with a new situation **2.** find the place on a map, by a compass, etc

Orient noun. (old fashioned) the Far East (= East Asia), especially China and Japan

Oriental adj. of or from the Orient (use **Asian** for people)

orientation noun. **1.** a program to help someone become familiar with a new activity, situation, job, etc **2.** a person's beliefs

oriented adj. being directed toward a certain purpose

origin noun. **1.** the place where something began; the source **2.** the way that something began

original adj. **1.** not copied from anyone **2.** authentic; not a copy of something famous **3.** imaginative and creative **4.** the first one of something

original noun. not a copy

originality noun. (no plural) being new and different from the usual

originally adv. at first

originate verb. **(originated, originating)** start; begin

ornament noun. something that makes someone or something look pretty

ornamental adj. decorative; adding beauty (opposite **plain**)

ornate adj. with a lot of decoration

orphan noun. a child whose parents are dead

orphanage noun. a building where orphans live

orthodox adj. **1.** officially accepted; generally observed (customs, etc) **2.** observing a religion in a strict way

other adj. **1.** not this thing, time or place **2.** different; not yourself

others noun plural. other people

otherwise conj. if not

otherwise adv. **1.** differently **2.** except for that

ounce noun. a unit of weight (short form oz)

our adj. belonging to us

ours pron. the thing that belongs to us

ourselves pron. us (if the speakers mean themselves)

ourselves adv. we and not anyone else; emphatically

oust verb. **(ousted, ousting)** force someone out of an office, a position, a job, etc

out adv. **1.** away from the inside **2.** not at home, at the office, etc **3.** away from home **4.** for everyone to see **5.** open **6.** not in the game anymore **7.** outside the limits in a game **8.** aloud; using your voice **9.** forward

out prep. from the inside to the outside

outbreak noun. the sudden appearance of an illness in large numbers of people

outcast noun. someone who was rejected

outcome noun. a result

outcry noun. a public protest

outdated adj. not modern; old-fashioned; out-of-date

outdo verb. **(outdid, outdoing)** be better than; do more than

outdoor adj. done or played outside (opposite **indoor**)

outdoors noun. adv. outside (opposite **indoors**)

outer adj. belonging to the outside of something (opposite **inner**)

outer space noun. the universe beyond the earth's atmosphere

outfit noun. **1.** a set of things, especially clothes, which go together **2.** (informal) a military unit; an organization — **outfit** verb. **(outfitted, outfitting)**

outgoing adj. **1.** friendly; someone who mixes well socially with other people **2.** something or someone who is leaving an office

outgrow verb. **(outgrew, outgrown, outgrowing)** become too big or old for something

outing noun. a short trip

outlaw *noun*. a dangerous person who lives outside the law; a criminal

outlay *noun*. money spent for a particular purpose

outlet *noun*. a way to get to something

outline *noun*. 1. something general that you see without the details 2. the main points of something

outline *verb*. **(outlined, outlining)** point out the important things

outlive *verb*. **(outlived, outliving)** live longer than

outlook *noun*. how you feel about life

outnumber *verb*. **(outnumbered, outnumbering)** be more in number than

out of *prep*. 1. not in; away from 2. from 3. out

out-of-date *adj*. 1. not modern; outdated 2. not up-to-date

out-of-the-way *adj*. not near any main road

out-of-town *adj. adv*. coming from or happening in a different town

out of work *adj*. unemployed

outpatient *noun. adj*. a person who goes to a hospital for treatment but does not stay there

output *noun*. 1. what is produced 1. data output by computer (= the information is supplied by the computer) (no plural)

output *verb*. **(output, outputting)** supply information by computer

outrage *noun*. 1. strong anger 2. something that causes you to feel strong anger

outrageous *adj*. 1. very offensive 2. extremely unusual; shocking

outright *adj*. clear; without any doubt

outset *noun*. the beginning of something (no plural)

outside *noun*. the outer part of something

outside *adv*. to the outside —**outside** *adj*. —**outside** *prep*. (opposite **inside**)

outsider *noun*. someone who doesn't belong to a particular group

outskirts *noun plural*. the parts of a city that are farthest from the center

outstanding *adj*. excellent

outstrip *verb*. **(outstripped, outstripping)** 1. do better than 2. be more than; surpass 3. run faster than

outward, outwards *adj. adv*. toward the outside (opposite **inward, inwards**)

outweigh *verb*. **(outweighed, outweighing)** be more important or valuable than (something)

oval *noun. adj*. having the shape of an egg

oven *noun*. the place where you cook food or bake

over *prep*. 1. higher than 2. on top of 3. on the other side of 4. to the other side of 5. across 6. more than

over *adv*. 1. more 2. again; from beginning to end 3. to a place 4. finished

overalls *noun plural*. thick pants with a piece that covers the chest and two shoulder straps

overboard *adv*. over the side of a ship and into the water

overcharge *verb*. **(overcharged, overcharging)** charge too much money

overcoat *noun*. a winter coat that you wear over your other clothes

overcome *verb*. **(overcame, overcoming)** 1. succeed in spite of difficulties 2. be stronger than

overcrowded *adj*. with too many people —**overcrowding** *noun*.

overdo *verb*. **(overdid, overdone, overdoing)** 1. do more than you should 2. cook too much

overdose *noun*. too much of a medicine or drug

overdraft *noun*. the amount of money owed to a bank because more money was taken out of an account than there was in it

overdrive *noun*. 1. a gear in a car that lets it go faster than the engine speed 2. (informal) a state of intense activity

overdue *adj.* **1.** late **2.** not yet paid or returned

overestimate *verb.* **(overestimated, overestimating)** consider someone or something above their real value (opposite **underestimate**)

overflow *verb.* **(overflowed, overflowing)** rise over the edge

overhang *verb.* **(overhung, overhanging) 1.** stick out over something **2.** threaten

overhaul *verb.* **(overhauled, overhauling)** repair so that something (such as an engine) is almost like new

overhead *adv.* above you

overhead *noun.* costs and expenses of running a business, like rent, electricity, and salaries

overhear *verb.* **(overheard, overhearing)** hear something without meaning to

overland *adj. adv.* by, across or on land (instead of by sea or air)

overlap *verb.* **(overlapped, overlapping) 1.** cover part of something else and sometimes go past it **2.** have something in common with something else

overlook *verb.* **(overlooked, overlooking) 1.** look down on something from above **2.** not notice something **3.** forgive; excuse

overly *adv.* too much (usually used in negative sentences)

overnight *adj.* including the night

overnight *adv.* **1.** for the night **2.** suddenly

overpower *verb.* **(overpowered, overpowering)** be too strong for

overrule *verb.* **(overruled, overruling)** decide against something

overrun *verb.* **(overran, overrun, overrunning) 1.** conquer and occupy **2.** speak or last longer than is planned

overseas *adv. adj.* across the ocean; from abroad

oversee *verb.* **(oversaw, overseen, overseeing)** supervise; be responsible for work being done by others

overshadow *verb.* **(overshadowed, overshadowing)** make something or someone else seem less important

oversight *noun.* something that was accidentally left out or done by mistake

overtake *verb.* **(overtook, overtaken, overtaking) 1.** catch up with **2.** reach and pass a car, etc, on the road

overthrow *verb.* **(overthrew, overthrown, overthrowing)** conquer and get rid of a ruler or a government

overtime *noun. adv.* extra time that someone works

overturn *verb.* **(overturned, overturning)** make something fall over

overview *noun.* a general picture of a situation, program, etc

overweight *adj.* weighing too much; too heavy

overwhelm *verb.* **(overwhelmed, overwhelming)** be too much for

overwhelming *adj.* too large to oppose

overwork *verb.* **(overworked, overworking)** work too much or make someone else work too much

owe *verb.* **(owed, owing)** have a debt to someone

own *verb.* **(owned, owning)** have; possess

own *adj.* **1.** belonging to you **2.** a word that makes the meaning stronger — **own** *pron.*

owner *noun.* the person who owns something

ownership *noun.* the legal possession of something

ox *noun.* **1.** a fully grown male of cattle does heavy work on a farm **2.** (slang) a clumsy person (plural **oxen**)

oxygen *noun.* a gas in the air that we need for breathing

ozone *noun.* a bluish gas that is outside the atmosphere and protects the Earth from harmful radiation

P

pa *noun.* father

pace *noun.* **1.** speed **2.** a step

pace *verb.* **(paced, pacing)** walk backward and forward

pacemaker *noun.* a small electronic instrument put in the body to regulate an uneven heartbeat

pacifism *noun.* the belief that all war is bad and that people should not take part in war

pacifist *noun.* a believer in pacifism

pack *noun.* **1.** a bundle **2.** a group of things that go together; a package **3.** a group of people that do something bad together **4.** a group of certain animals that stay together

pack *verb.* **(packed, packing) 1.** put things into suitcases for a trip **2.** put things into boxes, cartons, etc **3.** press something down until it is tight — **packer** *noun.*

package *noun.* **1.** one thing or a group of things that are put in a box **2.** a pack

package *verb.* **(packaged, packaging)** put things into boxes, cartons, etc

package tour *noun.* a holiday with trips, hotels, meals, etc, arranged and paid for in advance

packed *adj.* **1.** full **2.** ready for a trip **3.** put inside boxes or cartons

packet *noun.* a small package

packing *noun.* putting things into suitcases (no plural)

pact *noun.* a treaty; an agreement between opposing nations, groups, etc

pad *noun.* **1.** something soft and thick that protects a person or a thing **2.** a block of paper to write on **3.** (computers) a square of plastic to place the mouse on

pad *verb.* **(padded, padding)** protect something by putting something thick and soft on it

padded *adj.* with pads or padding

padding *noun.* something thick that you put around something to protect it (no plural)

paddle *noun.* a small oar that you hold in both hands for rowing a canoe

padlock *noun.* a hanging lock for a door, luggage, etc —**padlock** *verb.* **(padlocked, padlocking)**

page *noun.* **1.** a piece of paper with writing in a book, newspaper, magazine, etc **2.** a piece of paper for writing on

pageant *noun.* a magnificent parade with people in costumes, sometimes depicting a historical event, often outdoors

paginate *verb.* **(paginated, paginating)** put numbers on pages

pagoda *noun.* a temple in the Far East (China etc) that is a number of stories high with a decorated roof at each level

paid *verb.* past tense and past participle of **pay**

pail *noun.* a bucket

pain *noun.* something that hurts you —**pain in the neck** (slang) an event or a person that is very annoying

painful *adj.* hurting you in the body or the mind —**painfully** *adv.*

painless *adj.* not giving pain

painlessly *adv.* without causing pain

paint *noun.* a liquid that you spread with a brush to give color to something

paint *verb.* **(painted, painting) 1.** make a picture using paint **2.** cover something with paint

paintbrush *noun.* a brush used for spreading paint on a wall or a picture (plural **paintbrushes**)

painter *noun.* **1.** someone who paints

pictures; an artist **2.** someone whose job is to paint houses, etc

painting *noun.* **1.** a picture that is done in paints **2.** a job using paint (no plural) **3.** making pictures by using paints (no plural)

paints *noun plural.* a set of paints for children

pair *noun.* **1.** a set of two things that go together **2.** a thing that has two parts **3.** a couple

pajamas *noun plural.* special clothing for wearing to bed

pal *noun.* (informal) a friend

palace *noun.* a large building where a king or queen lives

pale *verb.* **(paled, paling)** cause to turn a lighter shade of color

pale *adj.* **1.** without color **2.** light in color **3.** of a light shade —**paleness** *noun.*

pallet *noun.* a wooden frame or metal platform on which something heavy is placed to make transporting or storing it easier

—**pallet** *verb.* **(palleted, palleting)** = palletize

palletize *verb.* **(palletized, palletizing)** place goods on a pallet for transporting or storage

pallor *noun.* paleness of the face

palm *noun.* **1.** the flat open part of your hand **2.** a tall, narrow tree that grows in hot places

palpitate *verb.* **(palpitated, palpitating)** (referring to the heart) throb; beat fast —**palpitation** *noun.*

pamphlet *noun.* a thin paperback booklet on a subject of public interest

pan *noun.* a flat dish or pot

pancake *noun.* a kind of flat, round cake made from batter that you fry in a frying pan

panda *noun.* a black and white animal native to China that resembles a bear

pandemonium *noun.* disorder and confusion because of fear, excitement, anger, etc

pane *noun.* a flat piece of glass

panel *noun.* **1.** something narrow and flat along the edge of something **2.** one part of something that folds up **3.** a board with controls, dials and switches **4.** a group of people who discuss a certain subject —**panel** *adj.*

panic *noun.* wild, excited fear (no plural)

panic *verb.* **(panicked, panicking)** become wildly frightened —**panicky** *adj.*

panic-stricken *adj.* terrified

panorama *noun.* a very wide view of a landscape

pant *verb.* **(panted, panting)** breathe with short, quick breaths

panther *noun.* a black leopard; a large, black, quick, meat-eating member of the cat family

panties *noun plural.* underpants for women

pantomime *noun.* acting without speaking

pantry *noun.* a cupboard or a small room next to the kitchen for keeping food (plural **pantries**)

pants *noun plural.* **1.** a piece of outer clothing for the legs **2.** underpants

pantyhose *noun plural.* long nylon stockings that are also underpants, like tights

papa *noun.* child's word for father

paper *noun.* **1.** what we write on **2.** a piece of work that someone writes **3.** a newspaper

paperback *noun. adj.* a book with a paper cover

paper clip *noun.* a metal clip for holding sheets of paper together

papered *adj.* covered with paper or wallpaper

papers *noun plural.* documents, such as an identification card, a passport, etc

paperwork *noun.* work involving writing

parachute *noun.* a device that enables you to jump from an airplane, etc, and land safely

parachute verb. **(parachuted, parachuting)** jump from an aircraft using a parachute —**parachutist** noun.

parade noun. an organized, colorful march, usually to celebrate something

parade verb. **(paraded, parading)** march together for show

parade ground noun. a place for holding parades

paradise noun. 1. heaven 2. a place where you feel happy

paragraph noun. 1. a group of sentences in a written text that contain one main idea 2. a small item in the newspaper

paragraph verb. **(paragraphed, paragraphing)** arrange in paragraphs

parallel adj. 1. always the same distance from one another 2. the same as

paralysis noun. loss of function, movement or feeling in a part of the body

paralyze verb. **(paralyzed, paralyzing)** make someone or some part of the body unable to move

paralyzed adj. unable to move

paramedic noun. someone who is trained to give first aid, to help a doctor, etc, but is not a doctor or nurse

paraphernalia noun. 1. small personal items 2. equipment needed for a certain activity (no plural)

parcel noun. a wrapped package (see **package**)

pardon noun. 1. forgiving someone 2. a paper that proves that you are free from punishment

pardon verb. **(pardoned, pardoning)** 1. excuse someone for doing something 2. free someone from punishment

pare verb. **(pared, paring)** 1. cut away the thin outer covering (of a fruit) 2. decrease as if by cutting away

parent noun. a mother or a father

parent verb. **(parented, parenting)** be or act as a parent —**parental** adj.

park noun. a place in a city where there are grass and trees

park verb. **(parked, parking)** leave a car after you turn off the motor —**parking** noun.

parking lot noun. a special place for leaving cars in the city

parliament noun. the part of some governments that makes the laws

Parmesan noun. a sharp tasting hard yellow cheese that is often grated and sprinkled over pasta

parole noun. letting someone out of prison before he/she serves the whole time on the condition of good behavior

parrot noun. a colorful tropical bird that is often kept as a pet and can sometimes be taught to mimic human speech

parsley noun. a plant with small flavorful green leaves used in cooking or for decorating food

part noun. 1. some but not all of something 2. a role in a play 3. someone's role in doing something

part verb. **(parted, parting)** 1. separate 2. separate one person from another 3. make a separation in your hair

partial adj. 1. not total 2. biased; favoring one side more than the other (opposite **impartial**) —**partially** adv.

participant noun. one of the people who participates or takes part in something

participate verb. **(participated, participating)** take part

participation noun. taking part in

particle noun. a tiny piece of something

particular adj. 1. special; specific 2. fussy

particularly adv. more than anything else

parting noun. 1. separating from someone that you care about 2. (of hair) where someone's hair is parted

partition noun. 1. something that separates one thing from another 2. division into separate parts

partly *adv.* not completely

partner *noun.* **1.** one of two people who do or share something together **2.** a person who you dance with **3.** someone you are married to or live with as lovers

partnership *noun.* being partners

part-time *adj. adv.* less than the usual working hours; not full-time

party *noun.* **1.** an event where people get together to have fun **2.** a large group of people with the same ideas **3.** a group of people who go somewhere together

party *verb.* **(partied, partying)** give or attend a party

pass *noun.* **1.** a narrow passage through the mountains **2.** a piece of paper that shows that you are allowed to go somewhere **3.** a ball that you throw, kick or hit to someone in certain games, like football or hockey

pass *verb.* **(passed, passing) 1.** go by something else **2.** go by **3.** overtake another car, etc **4.** do as well as you need to in a test, a course, etc **5.** hand something to someone **6.** spend time

passage *noun.* **1.** a narrow space that connects two places **2.** a short article **3.** going from one place to another by boat

passenger *noun.* **1.** a person who travels with someone else **2.** someone who pays to travel by bus, taxi, train, plane, etc

passing *noun.* **1.** going by **2.** death

passing *adj.* **1.** good enough **2.** going past

passion *noun.* **1.** strong love **2.** a strong emotion, like anger or hate

passionate *adj.* full of emotion

passive *adj.* not aggressive; letting things happen to you

passive *noun. adj.* (grammar, also **passive voice**) the form of the verb in which something is done to the subject (opposite **active**)

passport *noun.* a special identification card for traveling outside one's own country

password *noun.* **1.** a secret word which shows that you are not an enemy or an outsider **2.** a secret word which allows you to read information or go on-line in a computer

past *noun.* **1.** the time that has gone by **2.** an earlier time in someone's life **3.** (grammar) a verb tense to show a completed action (usually), often with an adverb of time (no plural)

past *adj.* recent

past *prep.* **1.** after **2.** by

past *adv.* by

pasta *noun.* a food made from flour and water, rolled into thin dough, cut into different shapes and then cooked in boiling water

paste *noun.* something that we use for sticking one thing to another

pastime *noun.* a hobby; a way of spending time enjoyably

pastry *noun.* **1.** a dough for making certain cakes and pies (no plural) **2.** a cake made from pastry dough (plural **pastries**)

pat *verb.* **(patted, patting)** touch someone or something gently a few times with your hand —**pat** *noun.*

patch *noun.* **1.** a piece of cloth that you put over a hole in material **2.** a place where the color is different from the rest **3.** a piece of ground that is used for planting something

patch *verb.* **(patched, patching)** sew a patch on something

patent *noun.* an invention protected by law to prevent others from copying it

paternal *adj.* of or like a father (of or like a mother = **maternal**)

path *noun.* **1.** a narrow way for walking **2.** the way from one place to another

pathway *noun.* a place for walking

patience *noun.* the ability to wait calmly and to deal with annoying or difficult things without becoming angry or nervous (no plural; opposite **impatience**)

patient *noun.* someone who receives medical or dental treatment

patient *adj.* having patience; tolerant; not quick to lose your temper (opposite **impatient**) —**patiently** *adv.* (opposite **impatiently**)

patriot *noun.* someone who loves and supports his/her country —**patriotic** *adj.* —**patriotism** *noun.*

patrol *noun.* **1.** going around a place to see if everything is all right (no plural) **2.** a group of people who are on patrol

patrol *verb.* (**patrolled, patrolling**) go around a place to see if everything is all right

patron *noun.* **1.** (formal) a customer, a client, etc **2.** someone who supports (gives money to) an organization, a museum, a charity, etc

patronize *verb.* (**patronized, patronizing**) **1.** buy regularly at a certain store, restaurant, etc **2.** behave with a superior manner toward someone

pattern *noun.* **1.** shapes on something **2.** a model for making something **3.** something that you do again and again

pause *noun.* a short break in an activity

pause *verb.* (**paused, pausing**) stop doing something for a moment

pave *verb.* (**paved, paving**) make a road smooth for driving or walking

paved *adj.* covered with a smooth surface (opposite **unpaved**)

pavement *noun.* a sidewalk

pavilion *noun.* **1.** a building constructed for short-term use **2.** a number of separate or attached buildings in a hospital, museum, etc

paw *noun.* the foot of a four-legged animal

pawn *noun.* **1.** the simplest piece in a chess game **2.** someone who is used by someone else

pay *noun.* the money that you get for working (no plural)

pay *verb.* (**paid, paying**) **1.** give money for something that you buy or for a service **2.** be worthwhile **3.** give good value for what you do

payable *adj.* that must be paid

payment *noun.* **1.** paying (no plural) **2.** an amount that you pay at one time

payoff *noun.* (informal) a bribe

payroll *noun.* a list of workers who get salaries or the money to be paid to workers

PC *abbr.* **1.** personal computer **2.** politically correct

pea *noun.* one of a number of round green seeds that grow together in a pod and that can be eaten as a vegetable

peace *noun.* **1.** freedom from fighting and war **2.** quiet

peaceful *adj.* **1.** calm and quiet **2.** without anger or fighting

peacefully *adv.* without making trouble

peach *noun.* a soft, round juicy fruit with a pit in the center (plural **peaches**)

peak *noun.* **1.** the top of a mountain **2.** the top point of something

peak *verb.* (**peaked, peaking**) reach a high point

peanut *noun.* a type of nut that grows in a shell under the ground; a groundnut

pear *noun.* a sweet, juicy, green fruit that has small seeds inside and is wider at the bottom than at the top

pearl *noun.* a silvery-white hard round mass formed inside the shell of an oyster used to make jewelry

peasant *noun.* a farmer (not using modern agriculture) (used for underdeveloped countries or in the past)

pebble *noun.* a very small stone

peculiar *adj.* strange; not usual

pedal *noun.* something that you move with your foot

peddle *verb.* (**peddled, peddling**) travel about, selling things

pedestrian *noun.* someone who is walking in or near the street

peel *noun.* the skin of fruits, such as oranges, apples, or bananas

peel *verb.* **(peeled, peeling) 1.** take the peel off a fruit or a vegetable **2.** come off in flakes or strips

peep *verb.* **(peeped, peeping)** look at something quickly and secretly

peg *noun.* **1.** a kind of hook that you can hang things on **2.** a kind of pin made of wood for fastening things

pen *noun.* **1.** a tool for writing that has ink inside **2.** a place with a fence around it for keeping farm animals

penal *adj.* of or connected to the law

penalize *verb.* **(penalized, penalizing)** punish a player or a team

penalty *noun.* a punishment (plural **penalties**)

pence *noun.* British money (plural of **penny**)

pencil *noun.* a tool for writing or drawing made of wood with lead inside it

pending *prep.* (formal) waiting for or until something happens

penetrate *verb.* **(penetrated, penetrating) 1.** manage to pass into or through something **2.** go in or force one's way in —**penetration** *noun.*

penguin *noun.* a black and white seabird that can swim but cannot fly and is native to the Antarctic

peninsula *noun.* a piece of land that has water on three sides

penny *noun.* **1.** American money; one cent (plural **pennies**) **2.** British money (plural **pence**)

pen pal *noun.* someone in a different country with whom you correspond by writing letters to each other

pension *noun.* a regular payment to a person no longer working because of old age or illness

pension *verb.* **(pensioned, pensioning)** pay a pension

pensioner *noun.* someone receiving a pension

people *noun.* **1.** human beings (men, women, boys and girls) (plural) **2.** a nation or ethnic group

pepper *noun.* **1.** a sharp-tasting powder that gives taste to food (no plural) **2.** a green or red vegetable for salads or cooking

per *prep.* for each

per annum *adv.* in or for each year

perceive *verb.* **(perceived, perceiving)** understand; be aware of or know by using your senses, especially through sight or the mind —**perception** *noun.* —**perceptive** *adj.*

percent *noun.* = (%); out of a hundred

percentage *noun.* a part out of a whole

perch *noun.* **1.** a (usually high) place where a bird sits **2.** a spiny finned fish that lives in lakes or rivers

perfect *verb.* **(perfected, perfecting)** make something as good as possible —**perfection** *noun.*

perfect *adj.* without mistakes or defects

perfectly *adv.* **1.** in a perfect way **2.** completely

perform *verb.* **(performed, performing) 1.** carry out an action **2.** have a role in a play **3.** do something in front of an audience

performance *noun.* **1.** a show **2.** playing something in front of an audience **3.** how well you do something (no plural)

performer *noun.* someone who does something in front of an audience

perfume *noun.* **1.** something sweet-smelling that people put on their bodies **2.** any sweet smell

perfume *verb.* **(perfumed, perfuming)** put on perfume

perhaps *adv.* maybe; possibly

peril *noun.* **1.** (no plural) danger **2.** a specific danger

perilous *adj.* dangerous

period *noun.* **1.** a certain amount of time **2.** a dot at the end of a sentence **3.** a lesson at school **4.** (also **menstrual**

period or **menstruation**) the monthly flow of blood from a woman's body

periodical noun. a magazine that comes out regularly every week or month, but not every day

peripheral adj. 1. on the outer edge 2. not important; not central

perish verb. (**perished, perishing**) die

permanent adj. for always; for good (opposite **temporary**)

permanently adv. for always (opposite **temporarily**)

permission noun. allowing someone to do something (no plural)

permit noun. a document confirming the right to do something or go somewhere

permit verb. (**permitted, permitting**) allow

permitted adj. allowed

perpendicular adj. at an angle of 90 degrees

perplexed adj. confused; having difficulty understanding something

persecute verb. (**persecuted, persecuting**) treat someone cruelly because of his/her race or beliefs

persecution noun. cruel treatment because of race or beliefs

persist verb. (**persisted, persisting**) continue

persistence noun. determination to do something (no plural) —**persistent** adj.

persistently adv. again and again

person noun. 1. a human being (man, woman, boy or girl) (plural **people**) 2. (grammar) whom a verb or pronoun refers to

persona noun. the personality someone presents in public

personal adj. 1. private; not for everyone to know 2. your own

personality noun. 1. the kind of person that you are 2. someone who is well known

personalize verb. (**personalized, personalizing**) 1. indicate that something

belongs to one person 2. refer to people rather than politics

personally adv. 1. speaking for myself 2. closely; as a person

personnel noun. the people who work at a certain place (no plural; do not to confuse with **personal**)

perspective noun. 1. drawing in a way that the relationship between things looks real (no plural) 2. a point of view 3. a sense of what is really important and what is not (no plural)

persuade verb. (**persuaded, persuading**) succeed in getting someone to do something; convince —**persuasion** noun. (no plural)

persuasive adj. 1. good at persuading 2. convincing

pessimism noun. the belief that things will come out badly (no plural; opposite **optimism**)

pessimist noun. a person who usually expects things to come out badly (opposite **optimist**) —**pessimistic** adj.

pest noun. 1. someone who bothers you constantly 2. an insect or animal that is harmful or troublesome

pet noun. 1. an animal that you love 2. someone that you love more than the rest

pet verb. (**petted, petting**) 1. touch lovingly; caress an animal 2. kiss and embrace —**pet** adj.

petition noun. a letter from a group of people asking for something

petty adj. 1. not important; minor 2. having narrow interests

pharmacy noun. a store that sells medicines; a drugstore (plural **pharmacies**)

phase noun. a stage of development; a period

phenomenon noun. 1. something that happens in nature 2. an unusual happening (plural **phenomena**)

philharmonic adj. a name used in connection with a symphony orchestra

philosopher noun. someone who studies philosophy; a great thinker

philosophy noun. 1. the study of life, knowledge, right and wrong, etc (no plural) 2. a person's outlook on life

phobia noun. a fear or dislike of something that is too strong for you to control

phone noun. a telephone —**phone** verb. (**phoned, phoning**)

phone call noun. a call on the telephone

phony adj. 1. false; fake 2. to describe someone who pretends to be something that he/she is not —**phony** noun.

photo noun. short for photograph

photocopy verb. (**photocopied, photocopying**) make a photographic image

photograph noun. a picture that you take with a camera

photograph verb. (**photographed, photographing**) take a picture with a camera —**photographic** adj.

photographer noun. someone who takes pictures with a camera

photography noun. 1. taking pictures with a camera 2. work done with a camera

phrase noun. 1. (grammar) a group of words in a sentence 2. a short, suitable way of saying something

phrase verb. (**phrased, phrasing**) say something in a certain way

physical adj. connected with the body

physically adv. in the body

physician noun. medical doctor (do not confuse with **physicist**)

physicist noun. an expert in physics

physics noun. the study of matter and energy (light, heat, sound, etc) (used with a singular verb)

physiotherapy noun. treatment of patients through exercise, heat, massage, water, etc —**physiotherapist** noun.

pianist, piano player noun. someone who plays the piano

piano noun. a big musical instrument with white and black keys

pick noun. 1. choice 2. a tool with a pointed end that is used to break up soil, ice, etc

pick verb. (**picked, picking**) 1. take fruit, vegetables or flowers from a tree, plant, etc 2. choose from among many

pickle noun. a cucumber or other vegetable that has a special, sharp taste from being kept in salt water or vinegar

picnic noun. a light meal that you take somewhere and eat out of doors

picnic verb. (**picnicked, picnicking**) have a picnic

picture noun. 1. a drawing or painting 2. a photograph 3. a movie 4. something that you see in your mind

picture verb. (**pictured, picturing**) see something in your mind; imagine

pie noun. two pieces of flaky, baked crust with a filling (usually fruit) in between

piece noun. 1. a part of something larger 2. a broken part of something 3. a single thing 4. one of a set 5. something that you play on a musical instrument

pier noun. a place on the shore for tying up a boat

pierce verb. (**pierced, piercing**) stick something sharp through something else

pierced adj. with tiny holes

pig noun. 1. a fat farm animal with a little curly tail 2. someone who is greedy, eats too much or behaves in a disgusting way

pigeon noun. a gray bird with a small head, a plump body and short legs

pike noun. a large fish eating fish that is found in lakes and rivers

pile noun. a lot of things one on top of another without any order; a heap —**pile** verb. (**piled, piling**)

pilgrim noun. someone who travels to a holy place

pilgrimage noun. a trip to a holy place

pill *noun.* a small, hard piece of medicine

pillar *noun.* something strong and tall that holds up a building

pillow *noun.* something soft to put your head on when you sleep

pilot *noun.* 1. someone who flies an aircraft 2. someone who guides a ship through a passage of water

pilot *verb.* (**piloted, piloting**) 1. fly an aircraft 2. guide a ship

pin *noun.* 1. a thin, sharp piece of metal that holds things together 2. a piece of jewelry with a pin on one side for a dress, coat, etc

pin *verb.* (**pinned, pinning**) fasten something with a pin

pinch *noun.* 1. a small, hard squeeze 2. the amount that you can hold between your thumb and first finger

pinch *verb.* (**pinched, pinching**) 1. squeeze someone or something between your thumb and first finger 2. cause pain by pressing 3. (slang) take something that is not yours

pine *noun.* a tall evergreen tree with sharp narrow leaves called needles, or the wood from this tree

pineapple *noun.* a sweet juicy yellow tropical fruit

pink *noun. adj.* the light color that you get when you mix red and white

pinpoint *verb.* (**pinpointed, pinpointing**) locate a place very specifically

pint *noun.* a measure of liquid

pioneer *noun.* 1. someone who goes to a new, undeveloped place to live 2. someone who works at something that is new

pioneer *verb.* (**pioneered, pioneering**) develop something new

pipe *noun.* 1. a tube that carries liquids or gas from one place to another 2. a tool for smoking tobacco 3. a musical instrument that you play by blowing

pirate *noun.* a sailor who robs other ships

pistol *noun.* a hand gun

pit *noun.* 1. a deep hole in the earth 2. a coal mine 3. the large seed of a fruit

pitch *noun.* 1. a throw 2. how high or low a sound is

pitch *verb.* (**pitched, pitching**) throw something

pitcher *noun.* 1. a tall jug with a handle for pouring cold drinks 2. in baseball, the player who stands in the center and throws the ball to the batter

pitiful *adj.* 1. making you feel pity 2. ridiculous; not worth respect

pity *noun.* a feeling of sadness because of the suffering of someone else (no plural)

pity *verb.* (**pitied, pitying**) feel sorry for

pizza *noun.* an Italian food made from bread dough covered with tomato sauce and cheese

place *noun.* 1. a particular area, location or spot 2. space 3. a seat 4. a street or square 5. a home 6. where someone finishes in a contest 7. a setting at a table

place *verb.* (**placed, placing**) 1. put something somewhere 2. finish in a contest

placement *noun.* the act of placing someone or something in a certain spot

plague *noun.* 1. a fatal disease that spreads quickly 2. an attack by enormous numbers of animals or insects

plain *noun.* a large area of flat land

plain *adj.* 1. not decorated 2. simple; ordinary; not fancy 3. without a pattern 4. clear; easy to understand 5. not pretty 6. with nothing on it —**plainly** *adv.*

plaintiff *noun.* (law) the one who brings a complaint against someone else in a lawsuit

plan *noun.* 1. an idea or arrangement for doing something 2. a diagram for a building, a machine, etc

plan *verb.* (**planned, planning**) make an arrangement for the future

plane *noun*. **1.** an airplane **2.** a tool for making wood smooth

planet *noun*. a body in the sky that moves around a star such as the sun

plank *noun*. a long, flat, thin piece of wood

planner *noun*. **1.** someone who makes plans **2.** a diary or list where your write your plans for the day, etc; an organizer

plant *noun*. **1.** a living thing that grows in the earth **2.** a factory

plant *verb*. **(planted, planting)** put a seed or a young plant in the ground so that it will grow

plantation *noun*. a very large farm for growing crops in tropical and semitropical areas where workers both work and live

plaster *noun*. **1.** something smooth for covering the walls of a building before you paint them **2.** a substance for covering and holding a broken arm, leg, etc, to help the bone heal —**plaster** *verb*. **(plastered, plastering)**

plastic *noun*. *adj*. (made of) a light, strong material made of chemicals

plastic surgery *noun*. medical operations to change a person's appearance or to repair injuries

plate *noun*. **1.** a round almost flat dish that you eat from **2.** a thin, flat piece of metal or glass

platform *noun*. **1.** a place where you get on or off a train **2.** a place that is higher than the rest, like a stage, where you stand to make a speech or receive an award

platinum *noun*. a very expensive gray-white metal used in jewelry making

play *noun*. **1.** a game; fun; what is not work (no plural) **2.** a theater show with actors and actresses

play *verb*. **(played, playing) 1.** do something for fun **2.** take part in a game **3.** make music on an instrument **4.** take part in a play **5.** not be serious

player *noun*. **1.** someone who takes part in a game **2.** someone who plays a musical instrument

playful *adj*. loving to play

playground *noun*. a place with swings, slides, etc, where children can play

playhouse *noun*. **1.** a theater **2.** a small house for children to play in

playing field *noun*. a grassy place for playing a game

playwright *noun*. someone who writes plays

plaza *noun*. an (often big) open public square or marketplace in a city or town

plea *noun*. **1.** an urgent request **2.** a statement in court by the defendant, guilty or not guilty

plead *verb*. **(pleaded/pled, pleading) 1.** beg someone for something **2.** say in court that you are guilty or not guilty

pleasant *adj*. **1.** nice to be with **2.** sunny and warm **3.** enjoyable

pleasantly *adv*. in a nice way (opposite **unpleasantly**)

please *verb*. **(leased, pleasing) 1.** make someone glad **2.** want; like (opposite **displease**)

please *interj*. *adv*. a polite way of asking for something or giving an order

pleased *adj*. glad, satisfied (opposite **displeased**)

pleasing *adj*. pleasant; giving satisfaction

pleasure *noun*. **1.** enjoyment (no plural) **2.** something that gives you enjoyment

plentiful *adj*. being more than enough

plenty *noun*. a large quantity; more than enough (no plural)

plot *noun*. **1.** the connected happenings in a story **2.** a small piece of land **3.** a secret plan

plot *verb*. **(plotted, plotting)** make a secret plan

plow *noun*. a heavy instrument for breaking up and turning over the earth for planting

plow *verb*. **(plowed, plowing)** work with

a plow to prepare the earth for planting

plug noun. **1.** something that stops water from going down the drain **2.** something at the end of an electrical cord that you put into the outlet — **plug** verb. **(plugged, plugging)**

plum noun. a small, juicy, dark red, purple or yellow fruit with a pit inside

plumber noun. someone who puts in or repairs water pipes **—plumbing** noun.

plump adj. **1.** pleasantly fat **2.** round and juicy

plunge verb. **(plunged, plunging)** fall suddenly downward **—plunge** noun.

plural noun. adj. (grammar) a form of a noun, pronoun or verb that means more than one

plus prep. more than; in addition to (opposite **minus**)

plus noun. something good; an advantage (plural **pluses**)

p.m., P.M. abbr. between noon and midnight

PM abbr. Prime Minister

pocket noun. a small bag or space sewn into your trousers, coat, shirt, etc, that you can put things in

pocketbook noun. a handbag that a woman carries with her to hold money, cosmetics, etc; a purse

pocket money noun. money for spending on small things

poem noun. a piece of writing in verse, often with a special rhythm (a poem is spoken, not sung; a poem with music is a **song**)

poet noun. someone who writes poetry

poetic adj. referring to or typical of poetry

poetry noun. **1.** poems **2.** writing in the form of poems

point noun. **1.** a sharp tip **2.** moment **3.** the main idea **4.** a place **5.** a purpose or a reason for doing something **6.** a dot **7.** part of a score in sports or an exam **8.** an idea for consideration

point verb. **(pointed, pointing) 1.** use your finger to show where something is **2.** show direction

pointed adj. sharp

pointless adj. without a useful purpose

point of view noun. the way you look at a problem (plural **points of view**)

poised adj. **1.** self-assured; having self-confidence; dignified **2.** hanging in the air above a certain spot; in an uncertain situation or condition **3.** prepared for action

poison noun. something dangerous that will kill you or make you very ill if you eat or drink it

poison verb. **(poisoned, poisoning)** kill a person or an animal with poison — **poisoned** adj.

poisonous adj. **1.** able to kill you because it contains poison **2.** very unfriendly and insulting

poke verb. **(poked, poking)** push sharply and quickly into something

poker noun. **1.** a metal rod used to move burning logs in a fireplace **2.** a card game often played for money

polar adj. connected with the North Pole or the South Pole

polarize verb. **(polarized, polarizing) 1.** divide into two definite camps **2.** cause (light) waves to move up and down and go in a one direction.

pole noun. **1.** a tall piece of wood or metal, with one end in the ground, that holds something up **2.** the opposite end of a magnet

police noun plural. the people whose job is to enforce the law by catching criminals

police verb. **(policed, policing)** keep watch over something

police force noun. an organization of police officers

policeman, policewoman noun. a man who works in the police force (plural **policemen, policewoman**)

police officer noun. a policeman or policewoman

police station *noun.* a building where the police work

policy *noun.* **1.** the plan or program of a government or political party **2.** a standard of behavior **3.** a printed agreement with an insurance company

policyholder *noun.* the name of the person, company, etc, on an insurance form

policy-making *noun.* the process of deciding on a plan or program that is to be followed by others

polio *noun.* a disease that affects the nervous system and can cause muscles to stop functioning or bones to become out of shape

polish *noun.* a substance for polishing something (plural **polishes**)

polish *verb.* **(polished, polishing) 1.** make something shiny by rubbing it or putting something special on it **2.** make something better

Polish *noun.* **1.** the language spoken in Poland **2. (the Polish** or **Poles)** the people of Poland **—Polish** *adj.*

polished *adj.* **1.** shiny and clean **2.** smooth; nearly perfect **3.** charming and polite

polite *adj.* having good manners (opposite **impolite, rude**) **—politely** *adv.*

politeness *noun.* good manners (no plural)

political *adj.* connected with politics **— politically** *adv.*

politician *noun.* someone in politics

politics *noun.* **1.** the affairs of government (no plural) **2.** someone's political opinions (usually with plural verb)

poll *noun.* **1.** a survey that asks a number of people their opinion about something (often a political question) in order to decide what the general public thinks **2.** the process of voting in an election or counting the votes

polling station *noun.* where you vote in an election

pollute *verb.* **(polluted, polluting)** make the air or water dirty

polluted *adj.* dirty; contaminated

pollution *noun.* dirty air or water; contamination (no plural)

polo *noun.* a game played on horseback where two teams try to hit a small ball with sticks into the opponent's goal

polyester *noun.* a man-made material used to make cloth

pond *noun.* a small lake

pony *noun.* a type of small horse (plural **ponies**)

poodle *noun.* a dog with thick, curly hair which people keep as a pet

pool *noun.* **1.** a place that is made for swimming **2.** a small circle of water **3.** an arrangement to do things together

poor *adj.* **1.** having little money **2.** unfortunate **3.** weak **4.** bad (opposite **rich**)

poorly *adv.* badly (opposite **well**)

pop *noun.* **1.** popular music (no plural) **2.** (informal) father **3.** the sound of a very small explosion

pop *verb.* **(popped, popping)** burst

popcorn *noun.* dried grains of corn that burst open and turn white when you heat them (no plural)

Pope *noun.* the head of the Roman Catholic Church

poppy *noun.* **1.** a flower with bright red petals and a black center **2.** a black seed used as a filling in baking or for decoration **3.** the plant from which opium comes

popular *adj.* that many people like

popularity *noun.* being popular (no plural)

popularize *verb.* **(popularized, popularizing)** make popular

populate *verb.* **(populated, populating)** live in a certain place; inhabit

population *noun.* the number of people who live in a certain area

porch *noun.* **1.** an open area with walls and a roof at the side of a house or an apartment; veranda **2.** a doorway with a roof

pork *noun.* meat from a pig (no plural)

port *noun.* **1.** a harbor **2.** a city with a port

portable *adj.* that you can carry from place to place

porter *noun.* **1.** someone who carries baggage at a hotel, a station, etc **2.** someone who takes care of passengers in the sleeping car of a train

portfolio *noun.* **1.** a (usually large and flat) case or file containing (loose) drawings, business papers, etc **2.** stocks and shares owned by someone or by a company **3.** the office and duties of a government minister

portion *noun.* the amount of food that one person gets

portrait *noun.* a painting or photograph of a person

Portuguese *noun. adj.* someone or something from Portugal; the language spoken in Portugal and Brazil

pose *verb.* (**posed, posing**) **1.** sit for a painting or a photograph **2.** pretend to be something that you aren't

position *noun.* **1.** the way that someone stands or sits **2.** situation **3.** where something is placed; a location **4.** a job **5.** an attitude; a viewpoint —**position** *verb.* (**positioned, positioning**)

positive *noun.* (math) a number that is more than zero

positive *adj.* **1.** sure; certain **2.** optimistic; confident **3.** replying **Yes** to a question

positively *adv.* really; definitely

possess *verb.* (**possessed**) **1.** have as your own **2.** have as a part of you —**possessive** *adj.*

possession *noun.* **1.** something that you own **2.** having or owning something (no plural)

possessive *noun.* (grammar) a word that tells that something belongs to a person or a thing

possibility *noun.* something that can happen (plural **possibilities**)

possible *adj.* **1.** that someone or something can do **2.** that can be arranged (opposite **impossible**)

possibly *adv.* **1.** in any possible way **2.** maybe; perhaps

post *noun.* **1.** a wooden pole that supports something or marks a spot **2.** a job **3.** a place where a soldier or a diplomat serves

post *verb.* (**posted, posting**) **1.** send a person somewhere to do a job **2.** put up a notice

postage *noun.* what it costs to send something by mail (no plural)

postal *adj.* connected with the mail service or post office

postcard *noun.* a card that you send in the mail without an envelope

poster *noun.* **1.** a large notice for advertising something that you put up where people can see it **2.** a large printed picture

postgraduate *noun. adj.* **1.** a student who continues studies after graduation (usually from college) **2.** a course, etc, connected to such studies

post office *noun.* a place where you can buy stamps, send packages or telegrams, etc

postpone *verb.* (**postponed, postponing**) do something at a later time than you had planned; put off —**postponement** *noun.*

postwar *adj. adv.* happening or being present after a war, especially World War I or World War II

pot *noun.* **1.** a deep dish that you cook things in **2.** a jar for keeping food **3.** (slang) marijuana

pot *verb.* (**potted, potting**) put into a pot (especially a young plant into an earthenware pot)

potato *noun.* a vegetable that grows under the ground

potential *adj.* **1.** a possibility or capability of becoming **2.** hidden abilities —**potentially** *adv.*

potter *noun.* a person who makes clay pots by hand

pottery *noun.* **1.** dishes made of baked clay **2.** making dishes from baked clay

poultry *noun.* chickens, turkeys and other birds that people raise for food (no plural)

pound *noun.* **1.** a unit of weight **2.** a unit of money in certain countries, like Great Britain

pound *verb.* **(pounded, pounding) 1.** beat something over and over again **2.** beat something until you crush it **3.** beat heavily

pour *verb.* **(poured, pouring) 1.** move liquid from one container to another **2.** rain heavily

poverty *noun.* being poor (no plural; opposite **wealth**)

powder *noun.* small, crushed pieces of something

powder *verb.* **(powdered, powdering)** put powder on something

powdered *adj.* in the form of a powder

power *noun.* **1.** control over people (no plural) **2.** the strength to do something (no plural) **3.** a right to do something **4.** how powerful something is **5.** a powerful country **6.** physical ability **7.** energy (no plural)

power *verb.* **(powered, powering)** work; supply energy

powerful *adj.* having a lot of power; strong —**powerfully** *adv.*

powerhouse *noun.* **1.** a very strong person **2.** a person who has powerful ideas, thoughts, etc, or does things with great strength and energy

powerless *adj.* not having the power

power plant, power station *noun.* a large building for making electricity

practical *adj.* **1.** useful **2.** sensible; workable **3.** good at dealing with real problems

practicality *noun.* reality (not theories) (plural **practicalities**)

practically *adv.* almost; nearly

practice *noun.* **1.** doing something again and again to be good at it **2.** the business of a doctor, a dentist or a lawyer

practice *verb.* **(practiced, practicing) 1.** do something again and again to be good at it **2.** work as a doctor, dentist, or lawyer

praise *verb.* **(praised, praising)** say that you think something or someone is good —**praise** *noun.* (no plural)

prank *noun.* a small practical joke

pray *verb.* **(prayed, praying)** speak to God

prayer *noun.* **1.** praying to God **2.** what someone says when he/she prays

preach *verb.* **(preached, preaching)** give a religious talk in a church, mosque, temple, or synagogue

preacher *noun.* someone who preaches to others

precaution *noun.* something that you do to prevent something else from happening

precede *verb.* **(preceded, preceding)** come before

preceding *adj.* coming before

precious *adj.* **1.** dear; much loved **2.** of great value; worth a lot of money

precise *adj.* exact

precisely *adv.* exactly

precision *adj. noun.* exactness, accuracy

predecessor *noun.* a person doing the job before you

predicament *noun.* an uncomfortable situation

predict *verb.* **(predicted, predicting)** say what is going to happen

predictable *adj.* easy to predict

prediction *noun.* a forecast

preface *noun.* an introduction at the beginning of a book or speech

prefer *verb.* **(preferred) 1.** like one thing more than another **2.** want or not want to do something

preferable *adj.* better; that you would prefer —**preferably** *adv.*

preference *noun.* what you like more than other things —**preferential** *adj.*

pregnant *adj.* going to have a baby

prehistoric *adj.* happening before written history

prejudice *noun.* a dislike of something or someone that is not based on facts or reason —**prejudice** *verb.* **(prejudiced, prejudicing)**

prejudiced *adj.* having a prejudice

premier *noun.* (often capitalized) a prime minister; the leader of the government in some countries

premiere *noun.* the first performance in public of a play, etc

premise *noun.* (law) an idea or statement on which reasoning is based

premises *noun.* a piece of property with a building on it and the surrounding area

premium *noun.* **1.** the money paid to an insurance company **2.** a bonus

premium *adj.* of the best quality

preparation *noun.* being ready for something

prepare *verb.* **(prepared, preparing) 1.** make something ready **2.** make someone ready

pre-school *noun. adj.* a nursery school (for ages 3-5)

prescribe *verb.* **(prescribed, prescribing)** say what medicine someone should take

prescription *noun.* something written that tells what medicine to give someone

presence *noun.* being at a place (no plural; opposite **absence**)

present *noun.* **1.** a gift **2.** the time happening now **(the present)** —**the present** *noun.* now

present *verb.* **(presented, presenting) 1.** give formally, especially at a ceremony **2.** show a document **3.** introduce or appear in a TV or radio program **4.** broadcast

present *adj.* **1.** at a certain place (opposite **absent**) **2.** existing or happening now **(the present)**

presentation *noun.* **1.** the way something is presented **2.** a talk or demonstration given to a group of people

present-day *adj.* current, modern

presently *adv.* **1.** soon **2.** now

preserve *noun.* **1.** fruit cooked in sugar, something like jam **2.** a place where animals are kept for private use (as in hunting or fishing) **3.** a place to keep safe from harm or injury

preserve *verb.* **(preserved, preserving) 1.** keep something from spoiling **2.** keep something safe —**preservation** *noun.* —**preservative** *adj.*

presidency *noun.* the position or job of president

president *noun.* someone who is elected to be the head of something —**presidential** *adj.*

press *noun.* **1.** **(the press)** newspapers and newspaper people (no plural) **2.** a push with your finger **3.** (also **pressing**) ironing

press *verb.* **(pressed, pressing) 1.** push down (on) **2.** push heavily (against) **3.** iron clothing **4.** urge someone to do something

press conference *noun.* a meeting in which an important person gives a statement to the press

pressure *noun.* **1.** weight or force on something **2.** things that you need to do (no plural)

pressure *verb.* **(pressured, pressuring)** try to influence someone to do something

prestige *noun.* the respect someone or something has or gets because of being connected with high quality, success, etc —**prestigious** *adj.*

presumably *adv.*

presume *verb.* **(presumed, presuming)** suppose to be true or a fact without having actual proof

pre-tax *adj.* before tax has been taken off

pretend *verb.* (**pretended, pretending**) **1.** try to make something appear to be true **2.** imagine that something is true

pretension *noun.* a claim to have importance, qualities, abilities, etc, without justification —**pretentious** *adj.*

pretext *noun.* a pretended reason given for doing something in order to hide the real reason

pretty *adj.* **1.** nice looking **2.** beautiful to look at (used for women and girls; compare with a **handsome** man, a **good-looking** boy)

pretty *adv.* somewhat but not completely; fairly

prevail *verb.* (**prevailed, prevailing**) **1.** be widespread **2.** win, succeed

prevalent *adj.* common

prevent *verb.* (**prevented, preventing**) not let something happen

prevention *noun.* not letting something happen (no plural)

preventive *adj.* that prevents something bad from happening

previous *adj.* earlier; from before

previously *adv.* earlier; before that

prey *noun.* an animal that is hunted and eaten by another animal (no plural)

price *noun.* the cost of something — **price** *verb.* (**priced, pricing**)

priceless *adj.* worth too much to put a price on

price tag *noun.* a small card attached to an item in a store that tells its price

prick *verb.* (**pricked, pricking**) stick with something sharp

prickly *adj.* covered with sharp points

pride *noun.* **1.** being proud of something or someone **2.** self-respect; the feeling that you are worth something **3.** thinking too highly of yourself

priest *noun.* a member of the clergy; in some religions, a person who performs ceremonies in places of worship

priestess *noun.* a woman priest (plural **priestesses**)

primarily *adv.* mainly

primary *adj.* **1.** the first; the earliest **2.** the most important

primary school *noun.* elementary school; grade school

prime *adj.* **1.** the most important or of the best quality **2.** of a number that can only be divided by one and itself; 3, 5, 7 and 11 are all prime numbers

prime minister *noun.* the head of the government in certain countries

prime-time, prime time *noun. adj.* the most popular hours during the day for watching TV (generally in the evening)

primitive *adj.* **1.** at an early stage of social development **2.** simple in technology

prince *noun.* the son of a king or a queen

princess *noun.* the daughter of a king or a queen (plural **princesses**)

principal *noun.* the head of a school; a headmaster or headmistress (do not confuse with **principle**)

principal *adj.* the most important

principally *adv.* mainly; chiefly

principle *noun.* a standard for what is right or wrong; a guiding rule

print *noun.* **1.** letters or words that a machine makes (no plural) **2.** a mark that something makes **3.** a kind of copy of a painting **4.** a copy of a photograph

print *verb.* (**printed, printing**) **1.** write with letters that are not in handwriting **2.** make many copies of a book, etc, using a machine

printed *adj.* **1.** written in print, not handwriting **2.** written by machine

printer *noun.* **1.** someone whose business is printing **2.** a machine that prints

printing *noun.* **1.** the business of making copies of written material (no plural) **2.** an edition of a book

prior *adj.* before; coming first

priority *noun.* what you think is more important and less important (plural **priorities**)

prison noun. a building where criminals are locked up

prisoner noun. 1. someone who is in prison for a crime 2. someone who is captured and held

privacy noun. being by yourself without anyone disturbing you or interfering in your affairs (no plural)

private noun. a soldier of the lowest rank

private adj. 1. personal; not for everyone to know 2. belonging to someone; not public 3. where nobody can go without permission 4. not belonging to the government

privately adv. in private

privatize verb. (**privatized, privatizing**) sell a government owned company, industry, etc, to private people —**privatization** noun.

privilege noun. 1. a special right that only certain people have 2. a chance to do certain things in life; an advantage 3. something that gives pleasure (no plural)

prize noun. something that you get for winning a contest or a game

prize adj. that won a prize

pro abbr. = professional; someone who gets paid for doing something; not an amateur (opposite **amateur**)

probability noun. a reasonable chance; likelihood (plural **probabilities**)

probable adj. likely to happen

probably adv. almost certainly

probation noun. 1. the testing of someone's character, abilities, etc; a trial period 2. allowing a criminal (usually a first time offender) not to go to jail under condition that he/she does not break the law again

problem noun. 1. a situation that is difficult 2. a question that you have to answer

problematic adj. with problems

procedure noun. a way of doing things —**procedural** adj.

proceed verb. (**proceeded, proceeding**) keep on doing something; continue

proceeds noun plural. profits; the amount of money gained from a sale

process noun. 1. the way that you do something 2. connected happenings in nature

process verb. (**processed, processing**) 1. print film that has been exposed 2. put information into a computer 3. deal with something (like an application) by following a certain established procedure —**processor** noun.

procession noun. a number of people, cars, etc, that move along one after another in an orderly way

proclaim verb. (**proclaimed, proclaiming**) announce —**proclamation** noun.

prodigy noun. someone who has extraordinary talent or ability

produce noun. fruits and vegetables (no plural)

produce verb. (**produced, producing**) 1. manufacture something 2. grow a crop or have in nature 3. cause; be the reason for; give results 4. give birth to young ones 5. arrange the preparation of a play, a film, etc 6. take something out and show it

producer noun. 1. a manufacturer 2. a grower 3. someone who is in charge of a film or a show and provides the money

product noun. something that is produced

production noun. 1. manufacturing (no plural) 2. growing something 3. a movie or a show

production line noun. an assembly line; the arrangement of workers and machines in a factory so that the manufacture of a product follows one stage after another

productive adj. bringing good results —**productivity** noun.

profession noun. work that needs special studies

professional *noun. adj.* **1.** for money, not as a hobby **2.** with the necessary training —**professionally** *adv.*

professionalism *noun.* the behavior of a professional (no plural)

professor *noun.* **1.** a top teacher at a college or university **2.** any member of the teaching staff

profile *noun.* **1.** a side of someone's face **2.** a short biography of a person

profit *noun.* **1.** the money that you make if you sell something for a higher price than you paid for it **2.** advantage (no plural)

profit *verb.* **(profited, profiting)** gain something

profitable *adj.* bringing in money — **profitability** *noun.*

profound *adj.* deep; beyond the obvious

program *noun.* **1.** something that is broadcast on radio or TV **2.** information about a performance **3.** a plan **4.** a list of instructions for a computer

program *verb.* **(programmed, programming)** **1.** plan something **2.** give instructions to a computer —**programmed** *adj.*

programmer *noun.* someone who writes software programs for computers

programming *noun.* the job of writing programs for computers

progress *noun.* moving in a forward direction; becoming better (no plural)

progress *verb.* **(progressed, progressing)** move forward; become better

progression *noun.* gradual development

progressive *adj.* in favor of reforms

prohibit *verb.* **(prohibited, prohibiting)** not allow; forbid

project *noun.* **1.** a big plan that will take a lot of work **2.** a big piece of practical work that a student does

project *verb.* **(projected, projecting)** **1.** stick out beyond a ledge **2.** throw forward; propel

projection *noun.* **1.** something that sticks out **2.** an estimate; a calculation **3.** the act of projecting a picture, etc

projector *noun.* a machine for showing movies or slides

proletariat *noun.* the working class

prologue *noun.* an introduction to a book, play, poem, etc

prolong *verb.* **(prolonged, prolonging)** stretch out; make longer

prom *noun.* a formal dance that is held at a school

promenade *noun.* a wide path for walking near the sea

prominent *adj.* **1.** important and well-known; influential **2.** easily seen

promise *noun.* **1.** something that you tell someone you will certainly do **2.** the possibility of being excellent in the future (no plural)

promise *verb.* **(promised, promising)** tell someone that you will do something for certain

promising *adj.* **1.** showing promise **2.** likely to be good

promo *abbr.* = promotion; promotional

promote *verb.* **(promoted, promoting)** **1.** give someone a higher job or status **2.** try to make something happen **3.** sell —**promoter** *noun.*

promotion *noun.* **1.** going up in rank **2.** trying to sell something (no plural) — **promotional** *adj.*

prompt *adj.* **1.** on time **2.** quick

promptly *adv.* **1.** as quickly as possible **2.** exactly

prone *adj.* **1.** having a tendency to; likely to **2.** (formal) lying with your face to the floor

pronoun *noun.* (grammar) a word that comes instead of person, place, thing or idea

pronounce *verb.* **(pronounced, pronouncing)** **1.** say something in a certain way **2.** say something

pronounced *adj.* strong; that you can see or hear

pronouncement *noun.* a serious announcement

pronunciation *noun.* the way that you say something

proof *noun.* something that shows what is true

prop *noun.* things that are on the stage in a play

prop *verb.* **(propped, propping)** support something

propaganda *noun.* information, often untrue, that is spread to make people think a certain way (no plural)

propeller *noun.* a blade that goes around and around to make something move

proper *adj.* suitable; correct

properly *adv.* correctly; in a suitable way

property *noun.* 1. what belongs to you (no plural) 2. land 3. what is natural to a thing

prophecy *noun.* the telling of things that will happen in the future (no plural)

prophet *noun.* 1. someone who believes that God has sent him/her to teach people 2. a person who claims to know what is going to happen in the future

proponent *noun.* someone who argues in favor of something (opposite **opponent**)

proportion *noun.* 1. the relationship between the sizes of different things 2. the relationship between a part of a thing and the whole thing

proposal *noun.* 1. a suggestion 2. asking someone to marry you

propose *verb.* **(proposed, proposing)** 1. suggest; offer 2. ask someone to marry you

proprietor *noun.* the owner of a business, especially a store, restaurant, or hotel

prose *noun.* speaking or writing that is not poetry (no plural)

prosecute *verb.* **(prosecuted, prosecuting)** charge someone with committing a crime (opposite **defend**)

prosecution *noun.* 1. the people who bring a criminal case against someone to court (no plural; opposite **defense**) 2. a criminal process against someone

prospect *noun.* 1. expectations for the future 2. something that looks hopeful for the future

prospective *adj.* possible

prosper *verb.* **(prospered, prospering)** do well; become bigger or richer

prosperity *noun.* a time when business is good and the economy of the country is in good condition (no plural)

prosperous *adj.* successful in matters of money

prostitute *noun.* someone who has sexual relations for payment

prostitution *noun.* sexual relations in return for payment (no plural)

protect *verb.* **(protected, protecting)** keep from harm

protection *noun.* keeping something from harm (no plural)

protectionism *noun.* a system of protecting the trade of one's own country by preventing the import of goods from a foreign country (usually through high import taxes)

protective *adj.* keeping from harm

protest *noun.* a strong complaint

protest *verb.* **(protested, protesting)** complain that something is wrong or unfair

Protestant *noun. adj.* a member of a Christian religion that broke away from the Roman Catholic Church

protester, protestor *noun.* someone who protests

proud *adj.* 1. feeling pride in something or someone 2. feeling self-respect 3. feeling that you are better than other people

proudly *adv.* 1. with pride 2. with self-respect

prove verb. (**proved, proven, proving**) show that something is true

provide verb. (**provided, providing**) give what is needed

provider noun. someone who supports his/her family

province noun. a division of a country

provincial adj. from the provinces, not from the big cities

provision noun. 1. the act of providing 2. preparation for the future 3. a condition in an agreement or in the law; a stipulation

provisions noun plural. food supplies

provocation noun. making someone angry on purpose (**no plural**)

provoke verb. (**provoked, provoking**) annoy on purpose

proxy noun. an agent; the power given to someone to vote, sign, act, etc, in your name (especially at a stockholders meeting) (plural **proxies**)

prune noun. a dried plum

pry verb. 1. open something using a lever 2. ask too many questions about other people's business

PS, P.S. abbr. = postscript; something that you write at the end of a letter if you want to add something after you have signed it

psychiatrist noun. a medical doctor who deals with the diagnosis and treatment of diseases of the mind and of mental disorders

psychologist noun. someone who studied and works in psychology

psychology noun. 1. the study of the human mind 2. a clever approach to someone —**psychological** adj. —**psychologically** adv.

pub noun. public house; a place where people go to drink beer and meet with friends

public noun. people in general

public adj. 1. for everyone 2. for large numbers of people —**publicly** adv.

publication noun. adj. 1. publishing (no plural) 2. a magazine

publicity noun. adj. being seen by everyone (no plural)

publicize verb. (**publicized, publicizing**) make public; bring to public attention; advertise

public relations noun plural. something a company, organization, institution, individual, etc, does in hopes of creating a good impression on the public

public school noun. a school that is paid for by the government and provides education for all children

publish verb. (**published, publishing**) 1. put out in printed form for people to buy 2. have something that you wrote appear in a publication 3. announce to the public

publisher noun. a person or a company that publishes books or magazines

pudding noun. a soft, sweet dessert

puddle noun. a small pool of dirty water

puff verb. (**puffed, puffing**) 1. breathe in short, heavy breaths 2. let out short bursts of air, smoke, steam, etc

pull verb. (**pulled, pulling**) use force to make something move in your direction (opposite **push**) —**pull** noun.

pump noun. a machine or a tool that moves air or water through something

pump verb. (**pumped, pumping**) use a pump

pumpkin noun. a very large yellow vegetable with thick orange flesh and white seeds in the center, used for making lanterns for Halloween or for cooking

pun noun. a play on words; humorously using words that can be understood two ways

punch noun. 1. a blow with the fist 2. a drink that you make by mixing fruit juice, sugar and sometimes alcohol

punch verb. (**punched, punching**) 1. hit someone with your fist 2. use a special tool to make a hole in something

punctual adj. on time —**punctually** adv.

punctuate verb. (**punctuated, punctu-**

ating) (grammar) use marks in writing, such as a comma (,), a period (.), a hyphen (-), a semicolon (;), etc

punctuation noun. the way that you punctuate something that you write

puncture noun. a small hole

punish verb. **(punished, punishing)** make someone suffer because of something that he/she did

punishment noun. **1.** the price that you must pay for doing something that is wrong **2.** hard use (no plural)

punk noun. **1.** a young person who during the 1970s and 1980s expressed anger against society through loud violent music and an aggressive appearance and behavior **2.** (slang) a worthless young man who, in general, fights and hangs around

pup noun. a puppy

pupil noun. someone who studies at school or with a certain teacher

puppet noun. adj. a doll, toy animal, etc, that moves if you put your hand inside it or pull strings from above

puppy noun. a young dog (plural **puppies**)

purchase noun. something that you buy

purchase verb. **(purchased, purchasing)** buy (the usual word)

purchaser noun. a buyer

pure adj. **1.** not having anything else mixed with it **2.** not polluted —**purity** noun.

purely adv. only; merely

purify verb. **(purified, purifying)** make pure

purple noun. adj. the combination of the colors red and blue

purpose noun. a reason for doing something

purr verb. **(purred, purring)** make a noise like a cat when something feels good

purse noun. **1.** a handbag **2.** any small bag where you keep money

pursuant adj. (formal) in accordance with

pursue verb. **(pursued, pursuing) 1.** follow someone or something in order to catch him/her/it **2.** keep on with something

pursuit noun. a chase

push noun. hard pressure on something (opposite **pull**)

push verb. **(pushed, pushing) 1.** use force to move something away from yourself (opposite **pull**) **2.** put pressure on someone

pussy, pussy cat noun. child's name for a cat

put verb. **(put, putting) 1.** set something down in a certain place **2.** say something in a certain way

put out verb. **1.** kill a fire **2.** turn off a light

puzzle noun. **1.** (also **jigsaw puzzle**) a picture made from separate pieces that you have to join together **2.** a question that you don't know the answer to; a mystery

puzzled adj. not understanding something

puzzling adj. confusing; not clear

pyramid noun. a solid figure (usually) with a square base and four triangular sides that go upward and meet at a peak

Q

quack *noun.* the sound that a duck makes —**quack** *verb.* **(quacked, quacking)**

quad- *prefix.* = four

quadrangle *noun.* 1. (math) a flat figure with four straight sides and four equal angles; a square 2. a four-sided open area surrounded by buildings as in a campus

quadruped *noun.* a four-legged animal

quadruplets *noun plural.* four children born at the same time from the same mother

quail *noun.* a small bird with a round body and a short tail

quaint *adj.* old fashioned but attractive and charming

quake *verb.* **(quaked, quaking)** shake; tremble

qualification *noun.* the necessary training (with a diploma, degree, etc) for a certain kind of work

qualified *adj.* having qualifications

qualify *verb.* **(qualified, qualifying)** be allowed to do something

quality *noun.* 1. how good something is (no plural) 2. a special thing about someone or something; a characteristic

quality control *noun.* checking goods as they are produced, to make sure they are of the right quality

quantity *noun.* how much of something; amount

quarrel *noun.* an angry argument with someone

quarrel *verb.* **(quarreled, quarreling)** argue angrily

quarry *noun.* a place from where stone is dug out (for use in building)

quart *noun.* a unit of measurement for liquid

quarter *noun.* 1. one fourth of the whole thing (= 1/4) 2. a special part of a town 3. a coin worth 25 cents

quarter-final *noun.* (sports) one of the set of four games, whose winners then compete in the semi-finals

quarterly *noun.* a magazine that comes out every three months

quarterly *adv.* four times a year; every three months

quarters *noun plural.* a place where people live

quartet *noun.* four people making music together, either singing or playing instruments

quay *noun.* a place where boats or ships take on or unload cargo or passengers

queen *noun.* 1. a woman who rules a country 2. the wife of a king 3. a woman or girl who is first of something 4. a playing card with the picture of a queen

queer *adj.* **(queerer, queerest)** 1. odd; strange 2. sick —**queerly** *adv.*

question *noun.* 1. a sentence that asks for information 2. a problem; an issue 3. doubt; uncertainty (opposite **answer**)

question *verb.* **(questioned, questioning)** 1. ask someone questions 2. have doubts or uncertainties about

questionable *adj.* uncertain; possibly not true; possibly not honest —**questionably** *adv.*

question mark *noun.* a punctuation mark (?) at the end of a question

questionnaire *noun.* a printed list of questions asking for information about something

queue *noun.* a line of people waiting for something —**queue** *verb.* **(queued, queuing)**

quick *adj.* **(quicker, quickest)** fast

quickly *adv.* fast

quick-tempered *adj.* easily made angry

quiet *adj.* **1.** without noise **2.** with a low sound; soft **3.** without excitement **4.** not talking much —**quiet** *noun.*

quietly *adv.* **1.** without making a noise **2.** in a soft voice **3.** calmly

quilt *noun.* a warm blanket with stuffing inside

quin- *prefix.* = five

quit *verb.* **(quit/quitted, quitting) 1.** stop **2.** leave a job or school

quite *adv.* **1.** very **2.** completely; entirely **3.** somewhat, but not completely
—**quite a bit/lot** a lot
—**quite a few** many; a large number

quiver *verb.* **(quivered, quivering)** shake; tremble

quiz *noun.* **1.** a short test on a particular item **2.** a competition in which you have to answer questions

quiz show *noun.* a quiz game on radio or TV

quorum *noun.* the minimum number of participants necessary (of a committee, etc) in order to hold a meeting and make decisions

quota *noun.* **1.** a limit on something **2.** a minimum

quotation *noun.* words from a book, an article, etc

quotation marks *noun plural.* punctuation marks " " that show that those are the exact words, not a report

quote *noun.* a quotation

quote *verb.* **(quoted, quoting)** repeat the exact words that someone else said

R

rabbi *noun.* a teacher of Jewish religious law

rabbit *noun.* a small, furry animal that has long ears and eats vegetables, sometimes kept as a pet

rabies *noun.* an illness that comes from the bite of a sick dog or other animal

race *noun.* 1. a contest of speed 2. a group of people with the same skin color or the same physical features 3. a group of people with the same history, customs, culture, etc; a people

race *verb.* **(raced, racing)** compete in a race against someone

racecourse *noun.* a racetrack

racehorse *noun.* a horse specially raised and trained for horse racing

racetrack *noun.* a wide path or road, usually going around in an oval, for horse racing, auto racing, or athletics

racial *adj.* connected with race (meanings 2 and 3)

racism *noun.* the belief that all people of a certain race are inferior (no plural)

racist *noun. adj.* someone who believes or practices racism

rack *noun.* 1. a shelf or frame with bars for holding things 2. an overhead shelf for suitcases in a bus or train

racket *noun.* 1. something that you use in games for hitting a ball 2. loud noise (no plural)

radar *noun.* an instrument for finding the position of things that you cannot see (no plural)

radiant *adj.* 1. sending out rays of light; shining 2. sending out a feeling of happiness

radiate *verb.* **(radiated, radiating)** send out light and heat

radiation *noun.* sending out light or heat (sometimes harmful) (no plural)

radiator *noun.* 1. an instrument for heating a room 2. an instrument for cooling the motor of a car

radical *adj.* 1. complete; drastic 2. in favor of extreme change

radio *noun.* 1. an instrument for listening to broadcasts that come over electromagnetic waves 2. communication by radio (no plural)

radio *verb.* **(radioed, radioing)** send a message by radio

radioactive *adj.* having radioactivity

radioactivity *noun.* harmful radiation that comes from the breaking up of certain atoms (no plural)

radius *noun.* the distance from the center of a circle to the side (plural **radii, radiuses**)

raft *noun.* something flat and open that floats on water

rag *noun.* a small piece of cloth

rage *noun.* extreme anger (no plural) — **rage** *verb.* **(raged, raging)**

ragged *adj.* 1. shabby and worn out 2. wearing old, shabby, worn-out clothes

raging *adj.* angry and violent

rags *noun plural.* old, shabby, worn-out clothes

raid *noun.* 1. a surprise attack 2. a sudden attack for the purpose of robbing

raid *verb.* **(raided, raiding)** 1. make a surprise attack 2. make a sudden attack in order to rob —**raider** *noun.*

rail *noun.* 1. a bar that you can hold on to 2. a metal track on the ground 3. railroad (no plural)

railroad, railway *noun.* 1. tracks for trains 2. everything connected with the running of trains (no plural)

railroad, railway *adj.* connected with trains

rain *noun.* 1. water that comes from clouds in the sky (no plural) 2. a period of rain —**rain** *verb.* **(rained, raining)**

rainbow *noun.* a big half-circle of different colors that appears in the sky when the sun starts to come out after a rain

raincoat *noun.* a coat that keeps you dry in the rain because water doesn't go through the material

rainfall *noun.* the amount of rain or snow that falls in a certain place at a certain time

rainy *adj.* **(rainier, rainiest)** with rain

raise, rise *noun.* an increase in salary, taxes, etc

raise *verb.* **(raised, raising) 1.** move something to a higher place **2.** make a curtain or a shade go up **3.** make something bigger **4.** increase prices, taxes, etc **5.** grow a crop **6.** keep animals for food, etc **7.** bring up children

raisin *noun.* a dried grape

rake *noun.* a garden tool with a long handle and teeth at one end

rally *noun.* a large meeting to show that the people support or are against something; a demonstration

rally *verb.* **(rallied, rallying)** hold a rally; demonstrate

RAM *noun.* (computers) random access memory; computer memory in which data can be stored, used or changed

Ramadan *noun.* the month during which Muslims do not eat or drink during the daylight hours

ramp *noun.* a slope for walking instead of stairs

rampage *noun.* wild, dangerous, irresponsible behavior

ran *verb.* past of **run**

ranch *noun.* a large farm for raising cattle or sheep

rancher *noun.* the owner of a ranch

random *adj.* done without a plan or order —**randomly** *adv.*

rang *verb.* past of **ring**

range *noun.* **1.** the limits from one end to the other **2.** the different things in a group **3.** the distance that someone can see, hear, shoot, etc

range *verb.* **(ranged, ranging)** have high and low limits

ranger *noun.* **1.** a person who supervises and cares for a forest, a national park, etc **2.** (especially in Texas) a police officer who rides through open country areas to make sure that the law is obeyed

rank *noun.* **1.** a grade in the army or the police force **2.** a line of soldiers standing or marching next to each other

rank and file *noun.* the ordinary members of an organization (not the leaders)

ranks *noun plural.* large numbers of people

ransack *verb.* **(ransacked, ransacking)** search wildly and violently through a house, apartment, store, etc, leaving the place a terrible mess

ransom *noun.* money that is paid to free someone who is held by criminals

rap *noun.* **1.** a sharp, quick knock **2.** a punishment **3.** type of music where words are spoken, not sung, to a rhythm

rap *verb.* **(rapped, rapping)** knock sharply and quickly

rape *noun.* forcing a person to have sexual relations

rape *verb.* **(raped, raping)** force someone to have sexual relations

rapid *adj.* fast; quick

rapidly *adv.* quickly

rapids *noun plural.* a place in a river where the water moves fast over rocks

rapist *noun.* someone who has committed the crime of rape

rare *adj.* **1.** unusual; not happening often **2.** (of meat) undercooked and still red inside

rarely *adv.* not often

rarity *noun.* something rare or extremely uncommon; something that does not happen often

rash *noun.* spots that appear on your body

rash *adj.* too quick; done without thinking

raspberry *noun.* a small, sweet, red or black juicy fruit

rat *noun.* an animal that looks like a big mouse and carries diseases

rate *noun.* 1. speed 2. a way of measuring one number against another number

rate *verb.* (rated, rating) estimate; judge the value/character/size of someone or something

rather *adv.* 1. to some degree 2. (with would or had) showing preference 3. more accurately

ratio *noun.* a relationship between two amounts

ration *noun.* a limited measured portion (of food, gasoline, etc) for a limited period of time (for example, during a war)

rational *adj.* 1. sensible 2. being able to understand and make decisions

rationalize *verb.* (rationalized, rationalizing) make excuses for bad or unreasonable things or behavior —rationalization *noun.*

rationally *adv.* sensibly; using the power of reason

raven *noun.* a big noisy bird with shiny black feathers

raw *adj.* 1. not processed, not cooked, etc 2. harsh 3. painful

ray *noun.* a beam of light

razor *noun.* a very thin short blade inside a holder used for shaving hair

Rd. *abbr.* road

reach *verb.* (reached, reaching) 1. stretch far enough to touch something 2. arrive at a place 3. get in touch with someone

react *verb.* (reacted, reacting) act in response to something

reaction *noun.* 1. how you react to something 2. what someone thinks about something

reactive *adj.* happening as a result of something else; changing when mixed with another substance (especially chemicals)

reactor *noun.* 1. a nuclear reactor; a building for the production of nuclear energy 2. someone who reacts 3. a device that causes something else to react

read *verb.* (read, reading) look at written or printed words and say them aloud or understand them

reader *noun.* 1. someone who reads 2. a book for pupils

readership *noun.* the number and type of readers of a certain newspaper, magazine, journal, etc

readily *adv.* without hesitation

reading *noun.* 1. the activity of reading 2. books, magazines, etc 3. understanding

ready *adj.* 1. prepared 2. willing

ready-made *adj.* ready to wear

real *adj.* 1. genuine; not false or imitated 2. from life; not made up 3. true; not a lie

real estate *noun.* land and property (no plural)

realism *noun.* 1. dealing (with life) in a practical way without emotions 2. art that shows things the way they really are

realist *noun.* a person who believes in, and acts according to, realism; a realistic person

realistic *adj.* 1. seeing a situation as it is 2. seeming to be real —realistically *adv.*

realities *noun plural.* facts

reality *noun.* what is true and a fact (no plural)

realize *verb.* (realized) 1. understand; be aware of 2. make into real facts 3. be sold

really *adv.* 1. truly; not a lie 2. truly; very much 3. actually

reap *verb.* (reaped, reaping) 1. cut and gather crops, etc; harvest 2. win; gain

reappear verb. (**reappeared, reappearing**) appear again

rear noun. the back

rear adj. in the back

reason noun. 1. why you do or feel something 2. why something happens; a cause 3. understanding; the ability to think

reasonable adj. 1. logical 2. willing to listen to logical reasons 3. fair; moderate

reasonably adv. 1. sensibly; with fairness 2. rather; quite

reasoning noun. arguments; the use of someone's ability to think and form opinions

reassure verb. (**reassured, reassuring**) remove someone's fears

rebate noun. money that is returned

rebellion noun. 1. a fight against someone who is in power with hopes of overthrowing him/her 2. opposition to authority; refusal to obey orders

rebuild verb. (**rebuilt, rebuilding**) build again

recall verb. (**recalled**) remember

receipt noun. a piece of paper that shows you have paid for something

receive verb. (**received, receiving**) 1. get 2. greet guests

receiver noun. the part of a telephone that you pick up and talk into

receivership noun. the administration of someone else's property (especially if that other person has become bankrupt)

recent adj. from a short time ago

recently adv. lately

reception noun. 1. a party to celebrate something 2. the receiving of radio and TV programs (no plural)

receptionist noun. someone who deals with the public at an office, a hotel, a restaurant, etc

receptive adj. open to new ideas

recession noun. an economic slowdown; a period of reduced business activity

recipe noun. a set of instructions for cooking or baking something

recipient noun. someone who receives something

recital noun. a (usually musical) performance by one performer or the students of one teacher

recite verb. (**recited, reciting**) say something that you have learned by heart

reckless adj. 1. very careless; irresponsible 2. not worrying about the result

reckon verb. (**reckoned, reckoning**) think; consider; suppose

reclaim verb. (**reclaimed, reclaiming**) make land (especially if it was covered by the sea) fit for use

recognition noun. 1. acknowledgement; public thanks 2. identifying something or someone 3. the act of recognizing or being identified

recognize verb. (**recognized**) 1. know who someone or something is 2. know what something is 3. accept that something exists

recollection noun. memory of something

recommend verb. (**recommended, recommending**) 1. suggest 2. tell someone that something or someone is good or worthwhile

recommendation noun. a suggestion that something or someone is good in your opinion

reconcile verb. (**reconciled, reconciling**) 1. become friends again after a quarrel 2. (with oneself) accept an unpleasant situation

reconciliation noun. 1. acceptance of something you do not really desire 2. becoming friendly again after quarreling

reconsider verb. (**reconsidered, reconsidering**) consider again —**reconsideration** noun.

reconstruct verb. (**reconstructed, reconstructing**) construct again —**reconstruction** noun.

reconvene verb. (reconvened, reconvening) meet again

record noun. 1. a disk that you play on a record player; an album 2. written notes about something that has happened 3. things that someone has done 4. something that was done better or faster than ever before

record verb. (recorded, recording) 1. make a disk that you can play on the phonograph 2. put a film on tape by a video recorder, etc 3. write down what is happening

recorder noun. 1. a person who records 2. an instrument that records 3. a musical instrument of the flute family made from wood or plastic with eight holes and a whistle-like mouthpiece

recording noun. a record

recover verb. (recovered, recovering) get well from an illness or an operation; get over a shock

recovery noun. getting well (plural recoveries)

recreation noun. a relaxing or enjoyable activity as a pastime —**recreate** verb. (recreated, recreating) —**recreational** adj.

recruit verb. (recruited, recruiting) 1. find people who want to join an organization, a company, etc 2. enlist or draft new soldiers into the armed services —**recruitment** noun.

rectangle noun. a four-sided figure that has two longer parallel sides and two shorter parallel sides

rectangular adj. with the shape of a rectangle

rectify verb. (rectified, rectifying) make right; correct

recur verb. (recurred, recurring) 1. happen again 2. come to mind again

recycle verb. (recycled, recycling) take something that was already used for some other purpose and make it usable for a new purpose

red noun. adj. (redder, reddest) the color of blood, tomatoes, etc

reddish adj. rather red

redecorate verb. (redecorated, redecorating) decorate again —**redecoration** noun.

redesign verb. (redesigned, redesigning) design again

reduce verb. (reduced, reducing) make less or smaller; decrease (opposite increase) —**reduction** noun.

redundancy noun. 1. something done by something else; extra and unnecessary 2. something or someone no longer needed (plural redundancies) — **redundant** adj.

redwood noun. a very tall tree (height up to 300 feet or 90 meters) with red-colored wood, native to California

reef noun. a line of sharp coral, rocks, sand, etc, underwater but near the surface that sometimes can cause a shipwreck

reel verb. (reeled, reeling) 1. bring in by winding 2. be unsteady

refer verb. (referred, referring) 1. speak about someone or something 2. be used instead of another word

referee noun. a judge in some sports

reference noun. 1. an explanation 2. written information 3. something that tells a reader where the information came from 4. a mention

referral noun. sending to another person or place

refine verb. (refined, refining) make pure

refinery noun. a place where raw materials (such as petroleum, sugar cane, etc) are refined

reflect verb. (reflected, reflecting) 1. throw back an image 2. think about 3. show —**reflection** noun. —**reflective** adj.

reflex noun. a sudden physical movement done without thinking in reaction to a stimulus

reform verb. (reformed, reforming) improve by changing —**reformation** noun.

refrain verb. (refrained, refraining) hold someone back from doing something

refresh verb. (refreshed, refreshing) bring back to strength; make less tired; make fresh again

refreshments noun plural. light food that is served at a party or a meeting

refrigerator (short form fridge) noun. a machine for keeping food cold and fresh —refrigerate verb. (refrigerated, refrigerating)

refuge noun. a place of shelter or protection

refugee noun. someone who has left his/her country to escape danger and needs to find a new place to live

refund verb. (refunded, refunding) give money back because of damage or dissatisfaction —refund noun.

refurbish verb. (refurbished, refurbishing) make clean and fresh again

refusal noun. saying no to a request or an offer

refuse noun. garbage; waste; trash

refuse verb. (refused, refusing) 1. say that you will not do something 2. not accept something

regain verb. (regained, regaining) get something back; take back into your possession

regal adj. royal; suitable for a king or queen

regard verb. (regarded, regarding) think of someone or something in a certain way

regarding prep. concerning; about

regards noun plural. good wishes that you send through another person

regent noun. someone who rules in the name of a king or queen, especially if the king or queen is ill or very young

region noun. an area without specific limits —regional adj.

register verb. (registered, registering) 1. put someone's name on a list 2. put your name on a list

registration noun. putting a name on a list

regret noun. something that you are sorry about

regret verb. (regretted, regretting) 1. be sorry 2. a polite way of refusing

regular adj. 1. happening again and again at fixed times 2. usual 3. (grammar) obeying a rule

regularly adv. at fixed times

regulate verb. (regulated, regulating) control the amount of something so that it stays regular

regulation noun. 1. a rule 2. a law —regulatory adj.

rehabilitate verb. (rehabilitated, rehabilitating) 1. make a person healthy and/or useful again 2. bring back to good condition —rehabilitation noun.

rehearsal noun. practicing something again and again so that you can perform in front of an audience —rehearse verb. (rehearsed, rehearsing)

reign noun. the time when a king or a queen rules

reign verb. (reigned, reigning) rule a country as a king or a queen

reimburse verb. (reimbursed, reimbursing) pay someone back for expenses; repay —reimbursement noun.

rein noun. a strap for controlling a horse

reinforce verb. (reinforced, reinforcing) strengthen; make stronger —reinforcement noun.

reject verb. (rejected, rejecting) not accept; not consider something

rejection noun. not accepting

relate verb. (related, relating) 1. tell about something 2. have a connection

relation noun. 1. connection 2. a love affair (not marriage) 3. a relative; a member of your family

relations noun plural. dealings between countries or people

relationship noun. 1. the type of connection between two people or groups of people 2. a family connection

relative *noun.* someone who is related to you; a member of your family

relative *adj.* not absolute; in relation to or compared to something else —**relatively** *adv.*

relax *verb.* **(relaxed, relaxing)** 1. become less tense; take it easy 2. make something become less tense or tight

relaxation *noun.* 1. rest; not working or worrying 2. loosening something; making something less tense or tight

relaxed *adj.* not tense or worried

relaxing *adj.* making you feel less tense; soothing

relay *verb.* **(relayed, relaying)** 1. lay again 2. send out (radio, TV) signals; pass a message

release *noun.* setting free

release *verb.* **(released, releasing)** 1. set free 2. let part of a machine move

relevance *noun.* connection with the subject (no plural)

relevant *adj.* connected with the subject (opposite **irrelevant**)

reliable *adj.* that you can depend on (opposite **unreliable**) —**reliability** *noun.* (opposite **unreliability**)

relief *noun.* 1. the stopping of pain 2. the stopping of worry 3. food, clothes, money, medicines, etc, that you send to help in an emergency

relieve *verb.* **(relieved, relieving)** 1. make less painful 2. make less worried 3. take over work from someone

religion *noun.* 1. belief in God or a god 2. a set of beliefs and ways of worshipping; faith —**religious** *adj.*

relish *noun.* 1. enjoyment (especially if connected to food) 2. olives and/or pickles

relocate *verb.* **(relocated, relocating)** move or be moved to a new place

relocation *noun.* moving people somewhere else

reluctance *noun.* not wanting to do something (no plural)

reluctant *adj.* not willing to do something —**reluctantly** *adv.*

rely *verb.* **(relied, relying)** depend; trust

remain *verb.* **(remained, remaining)** 1. stay in the same place 2. stay the same way 3. be left after something happens

remainder *noun.* 1. the rest 2. what is left when you take one number away from another number

remains *noun plural.* what is left

remark *noun.* a comment

remark *verb.* **(remarked, remarking)** say; comment about something

remarkable *adj.* 1. amazing 2. excellent; outstanding

remarkably *adv.* amazingly

remarry *verb.* **(remarried, remarrying)** marry again

remedy *noun.* something that makes you well or makes you feel better (plural **remedies**)

remember *verb.* **(remembered)** 1. keep past things in your mind; recall 2. have something come into your mind suddenly 3. not forget 4. send greetings (to someone)

remind *verb.* **(reminded, reminding)** make someone remember something

reminder *noun.* a way of reminding someone to do something

reminisce *verb.* **(reminisced, reminiscing)** talk or write pleasant things about one's past

reminiscent *adj.* bringing back memories; suggesting

remnant *noun.* something that is left over

remote *adj.* **(remoter, remotest)** distant; far away —**remote control** *noun.*

remove *verb.* **(removed, removing)** 1. take something away 2. take something out of something else —**removal** *noun.*

remunerate *verb.* **(remunerated, remu-**

nerating) pay back; reimburse; compensate; reward someone for his/her trouble —**remuneration** *noun.*

Renaissance *noun.* the period in Europe between the 14th and 17th centuries when art, literature, music, philosophy, etc, prospered

renew *verb.* **(renewed, renewing)** begin again —**renewal** *noun.*

renovate *verb.* **(renovated, renovating)** rebuild or redecorate a place to make it in good condition

renowned *adj.* famous especially for a particular thing

rent *verb.* **(rented, renting)** **1.** pay to live in a place or use something that you do not own **2.** (also **rent out**) let someone use something of yours in return for payment

rent, rental *noun.* money that you pay to live in a place that you do not own

reorganize *verb.* **(reorganized, reorganizing)** organize again

repaid *verb.* past tense and past participle of **repay**

repair *verb.* **(repaired, repairing)** fix or mend something —**repair** *noun.*

repay *verb.* **(repaid, repaying)** **1.** pay someone back **2.** show your thanks for something that someone has done for you —**repayment** *noun.*

repeat *verb.* **(repeated, repeating)** **1.** say something again **2.** say exactly what someone else says **3.** say the same thing over and over again **4.** pass on information **5.** do something a second time

repeatedly *adv.* again and again

repellent *noun. adj.* causing strong disgust or distaste; a substance that drives away by force

repetition *noun.* saying or doing the same thing more than once (no plural)

repetitive *adj.* over and over

replace *verb.* **(replaced, replacing)** **1.** take the place of **2.** put something back in its place **3.** buy something that

is exactly the same as something else

replacement *noun.* **1.** buying or putting one thing in place of another (no plural) **2.** a substitute

replay *verb.* **(replayed, replaying)** play a game/disk again —**replay** *noun.*

reply *noun.* an answer

reply *verb.* **(replied, replying)** answer a question, request, letter, etc

report *noun.* a description of something that happened

report *verb.* **(reported, reporting)** **1.** write or publish an article about something that happened **2.** make a complaint to someone in authority

reporter *noun.* someone whose job is doing news reports for a newspaper, magazine, radio or TV

repossess *verb.* **(repossessed, repossessing)** take back goods

represent *verb.* **(represented, representing)** **1.** speak or act for a country, an organization, a business or some other group **2.** show or be something **3.** be a symbol for something (meanings 2 and 3 not used in the progressive tenses) —**representation** *noun.*

representative *noun.* someone who represents someone else

reprimand *noun.* an expression of strong disapproval —**reprimand** *verb.* **(reprimanded, reprimanding)**

reprint *verb.* **(reprinted, reprinting)** print again —**reprint** *noun.*

reproduce *verb.* **(reproduced, reproducing)** **1.** have young ones **2.** make something that is just like something else

reproduction *noun.* **1.** having young ones **2.** something that is like the original

reptile *noun.* cold-blooded animals that crawl

republic *noun.* a country in which the people elect their government and the head of state is a president

Republican *noun.* a supporter of the Republican Party

reputable *adj.* having a good reputation

reputation *noun.* what other people say and think about someone

request *verb.* **(requested, requesting)** 1. ask for something in a polite way 2. ask someone to do something — **request** *noun.*

require *verb.* **(required)** 1. need something 2. be necessary (time, money, help, etc) 3. demand; insist on having something

requirement *noun.* something that you need

reschedule *verb.* **(rescheduled, rescheduling)** replan

rescue *verb.* **(rescued, rescuing)** save someone or something from harm or danger — **rescue** *noun.*

research *noun.* finding out as much as you can about something (no plural) — **research** *verb.* **(researched, researching)** — **researcher** *noun.*

resemblance *noun.* looking or being like someone or something else

resemble *verb.* **(resembled)** look or be like

resent *verb.* **(resented, resenting)** be angry or hurt about something done to you — **resentful** *adj.* — **resentment** *noun.*

reservation *noun.* an arrangement that you will get a room, a seat, a table, etc; a booking

reserve *noun.* 1. something that you keep for a later time 2. a place for protecting something from harm

reserve *verb.* **(reserved, reserving)** 1. make a reservation 2. keep something aside

reserved *adj.* not showing your feelings easily

reserves *noun plural.* soldiers who are not on active duty but who can be called up in an emergency

reservoir *noun.* a place for storing water

reset *verb.* **(reset, resetting)** 1. set again for a second time (such as a broken bone that was incorrectly treated the first time) 2. change so that a counter shows a different number 3. take a stone from one piece of jewelry and place it in another one 4. restart a computer without turning off the electricity

reshuffle *verb.* **(reshuffled, reshuffling)** change the job of people in an organization — **reshuffle** *noun.*

residence *noun.* 1. the place where you live 2. living in a place (no plural)

resident *noun.* someone who lives in a certain place

residential *adj.* having houses or apartments but no factories or offices

residual *adj.* left over

resign *verb.* **(resigned, resigning)** quit a job

resignation *noun.* a statement that you are quitting a job (no plural)

resist *verb.* **(resisted, resisting)** 1. try to stop something that is happening 2. control yourself

resistance *noun.* 1. trying to stop an attack 2. natural ability to stay healthy (no plural)

resistant *adj.* able to remain unharmed by something

resolution *noun.* decision

resolve *verb.* **(resolved, resolving)** 1. find an answer to a problem 2. decide something

resort *noun.* 1. a place where people go on vacation 2. use of something that can help you (no plural)

resort *verb.* **(resorted, resorting)** turn to after other ways have failed

resource *noun.* 1. something of value that is found in nature 2. things that you own, like money and property

resourceful *adj.* clever at finding solutions to practical problems

respect *noun.* 1. admiration for or having a high opinion of someone (no plural) **2.** consideration **3.** a part of a situation (no plural)

respect *verb.* **(respected, respecting) 1.** admire; have a high opinion of **2.** show consideration

respectable *adj.* proper; doing things correctly

respectful *adj.* showing respect — **respectfully** *adv.*

respective *adj.* of each particular one

respond *verb.* **(responded, responding) 1.** (formal) answer a letter or an advertisement **2.** react

response *noun.* **1.** (formal) an answer **2.** a reaction —**responsive** *adj.*

responsibility *noun.* a duty (to take care of someone or something)

responsible *adj.* reliable; careful (opposite **irresponsible**)

rest *noun.* **1.** a time when you are not working **2.** something that you lean your head, arms, etc, on

rest *verb.* **(rested, resting) 1.** lie down for a while in the daytime **2.** stop working for a certain time **3.** let your legs, muscles, etc, relax **4.** lean on something **5.** lean one thing on something else

restate *verb.* **(restated, restating)** state again

restaurant *noun.* a place where you buy and eat a meal

restaurateur *noun.* the owner and usually the manager of a restaurant

restless, restive *adj.* unable to stay still because of boredom, impatience, etc

restore *verb.* **(restored, restoring) 1.** return a situation to the way it was before **2.** fix something up so that it looks like new **3.** put someone back in the same job or place

restrict *verb.* **(restricted, restricting)** limit

restriction *noun.* **1.** a limit **2.** something that you are not allowed to do

restrictive *adj.* something that is limiting

restructure *verb.* **(restructured, restructuring)** (drastically) change the way an organization, company, etc, is organized, managed, etc

result *noun.* **1.** what happens because of something else **2.** the answer to a problem in arithmetic **3.** the way that something ends —**result** *verb.* **(resulted, resulting)**

resume *verb.* **(resumed, resuming)** begin again after a stop

retail *noun. adj. adv.* the sale of things to individual customers (not meant to be sold again to others)

retailer *noun.* a storekeeper

retain *verb.* **(retained, retaining) 1.** hold in place **2.** keep **3.** employ a lawyer, consultant, adviser, etc

retarded *adj.* slow; backward

rethink *verb.* **(rethought, rethinking)** think again; reconsider

retire *verb.* **(retired, retiring) 1.** stop working because you are old enough **2.** go to bed **3.** go someplace private —**retired** *adj.*

retiree *noun.* a pensioner; a retired person

retirement *noun.* leaving your job because you are old enough (no plural)

retort *verb.* **(retorted, retorting)** reply quickly, angrily or humorously

retrace *verb.* **(retraced, retracing)** go back the way you came

retrain *verb.* **(retrained, retraining)** teach or learn new skills

retreat *verb.* **(retreated, retreating)** move back —**retreat** *noun.*

retrospective *noun.* a collection of an artist's works over a period of time

retrospective *adj.* thinking about something that happened in the past (and understanding its meaning in the present)

return *noun.* **1.** coming back or going back **2.** giving or paying something back

return *verb.* **(returned, returning) 1.** come back; go back **2.** give or pay something back

return *adj.* coming back

returns *noun plural.* results

reunion *noun.* a gathering of old friends, a family, etc

revalue *verb.* **(revalued, revaluing) 1.** estimate the value of something again (and give a higher value) **2.** increase the exchange value of a country's currency (in comparison to another country's currency) (opposite **devalue**)

reveal *verb.* **(revealed, revealing) 1.** tell about something that had been a secret **2.** show something —**revelation** *noun.*

revenge *noun.* harm in return for harm that was done to you —**revenge** *verb.* **(revenged, revenging)**

revenue *noun.* income (especially from taxes paid to a government)

reverence *noun.* deep respect, admiration and love —**reverent** *adj.*

Reverend *noun.* a title for a Christian priest

reversal *noun.* **1.** something reversed **2.** bad luck

reverse *noun.* **1.** the opposite **2.** the gear that makes a car, etc, travel backward —**reverse** *verb.* **(reversed, reversing)**

reverse *adj.* opposite

review *noun.* **1.** going over material again **2.** thinking about something carefully **3.** a critique; an article that gives the writer's opinion of a book, play, etc

review *verb.* **(reviewed, reviewing) 1.** go over what you learned before an exam **2.** think about something carefully **3.** write an opinion about a book, a play, etc —**reviewer** *noun.*

revise *verb.* **(revised, revising)** make changes

revised *adj.* with changes and corrections

revision *noun.* a change

revitalize *verb.* **(revitalized, revitalizing)** give new life (strength and power) into something

revival *noun.* **1.** a new performance of a play that was performed some time in the past **2.** a gathering to encourage and strengthen religious feelings

revive *verb.* **(revived, reviving)** bring someone back to life

revoke *verb.* **(revoked, revoking)** cancel; take away

revolt *noun.* a fight against a ruler or a government by a large number of people

revolt *verb.* **(revolted, revolting)** fight against someone in power

revolting *adj.* disgusting and very unpleasant

revolution *noun.* **1.** a change of government by force **2.** a complete change **3.** turning

revolutionary *noun.* someone who works for total change (plural **revolutionaries**)

revolutionary *adj.* complete and dramatic

revolutionize *verb.* **(revolutionized, revolutionizing)** change something completely

revolve *verb.* **(revolved, revolving)** spin around

revolver *noun.* a hand gun

revolving door *noun.* a door that goes around instead of in or out

revue *noun.* a (theater) performance made up of short separate songs, dances and skits

reward *noun.* a gift or money for doing something for someone

reward *verb.* **(rewarded, rewarding)** give a reward

rewrite *verb.* **(rewrote, rewritten, rewriting)** write something again

rhododendron *noun.* an evergreen bush with colorful flowers

rhyme *noun.* **1.** words where the endings sound the same **2.** a kind of short poem

rhythm *noun.* a regular beat —**rhythmic** *adj.*

ribbon *noun.* a strip of colored cloth for tying something to make it look pretty

rice *noun.* grains that grow in wet earth (no plural)

rich *adj.* having a lot of money; wealthy (opposite **poor**)

riches *noun plural.* wealth

rid *verb.* (**rid/ridded, ridding**) make yourself free of something

ridden *verb.* past participle of **ride**

riddle *noun.* a trick question that you have to find the answer to

ride *noun.* 1. a journey in a vehicle 2. going somewhere on the back of an animal 3. a trip on a bicycle, etc 4. a trip to a particular place with someone else; a lift

ride *verb.* (**rode, ridden, riding**) 1. travel as a passenger in a vehicle (car, bus, train) 2. travel on the back of an animal 3. travel by bicycle, motorcycle, etc — **riding** *noun.* (no plural)

rider *noun.* someone who rides a bicycle, motorcycle, etc, or on the back of an animal

ridge *noun.* a (high) long narrow edge, especially on the top of a mountain

ridicule *verb.* (**ridiculed, ridiculing**) make fun of something or someone

ridiculous *adj.* absurd; silly —**ridiculously** *adv.*

rifle *noun.* a gun with a long barrel

right *noun.* 1. the opposite of the left hand side 2. what is good; fair; correct 3. something that the law says you can have or do; a just claim 4. (the Right) the political group strongly in favor of private enterprise and nationalism, and against social welfare (opposite the Left)

right *adj.* 1. opposite of left 2. correct; not wrong 3. good; proper 4. suitable

right *adv.* 1. to the opposite of left 2. correctly; without mistakes 3. exactly 4. suitably 5. directly; straight

right angle *noun.* an angle of 90 degrees; a corner

right-hand *adj.* on the right

right-handed *adj.* preferring the right hand

rightly *adv.* correctly; with good reason; justly

rigid *adj.* stiff; not flexible; fixed; strict

rigorous *adj.* 1. thorough 2. severe; harsh

rind *noun.* the covering of certain fruits, especially citrus fruits and cheeses

ring *noun.* 1. a piece of jewelry that you usually wear around your finger 2. a circle 3. a telephone call (no plural) 4. an enclosed space for boxing matches, circus performances, etc

ring *verb.* (**rang, rung, ringing**) 1. make a sound like a bell or a telephone 2. make something ring 3. call someone on the phone

rink *noun.* a place especially for skating

rinse *noun.* washing out soap

rinse *verb.* (**rinsed, rinsing**) 1. wash the soap out of something 2. wash lightly with water or some other liquid

riot *noun.* wild, uncontrolled behavior in a crowd —**riot** *verb.* (**rioted, rioting**)

rip *verb.* (**ripped, ripping**) tear (sometimes with force)

ripe *adj.* ready for picking and eating

ripen *verb.* (**ripened, ripening**) become ripe

rise *noun.* becoming more; an increase

rise *verb.* (**rose, risen, rising**) 1. move upward 2. get out of bed 3. go up 4. stand up 5. come up (the sun or moon)

rising *adj.* 1. going up 2. becoming more; increasing

risk *noun.* a danger that you take on yourself —**risk** *verb.* (**risked, risking**)

risky *adj.* dangerous

ritual *noun. adj.* a ceremony or customary act that is always done the same way; a rite

rival *noun.* someone who competes against you —**rival** *adj.*

rivalry noun. competition (plural **rivalries**)

river noun. a large body of water that flows into the sea

riverside noun. land near the banks of a river

road noun. 1. a wide street 2. the way to a place

roam verb. (**roamed, roaming**) wander or travel around without going anywhere special

roar noun. a loud, impressive noise — **roar** verb. (**roared, roaring**)

roast noun. a large piece of roasted meat

roast verb. (**roasted, roasting**) 1. cook something in an oven or over an open fire 2. heat coffee beans, peanuts, etc, in an oven

rob verb. (**robbed, robbing**) steal from a person or a place —**robbery** noun.

robber noun. someone who robs

robe noun. 1. a long, loose piece of clothing 2. a dressing gown

robot noun. a machine that does things which people normally do

rock noun. 1. a very large stone 2. a piece of stone 3. a kind of pop music

rock verb. (**rocked, rocking**) move something gently from side to side

rock and roll noun. pop music with a heavy beat (no plural)

rock bottom noun. adj. the lowest point

rocker noun. a rocking chair

rocket noun. 1. a spacecraft; a missile that carries a spacecraft 2. a smaller missile used as a weapon

rocky adj. (**rockier, rockiest**) full of rocks

rod noun. a straight thin stick

rode verb. past of **ride**

rodeo noun. a presentation of cowboy skills in front of an audience

rogue noun. adj. dishonest; not following the accepted rules and behavior

role noun. 1. a part in a play 2. your connection with something 3. an important thing that you do in life

role model noun. a person that you respect and want to copy

roll noun. 1. bread in the shape of a small, round cake 2. something that is folded over and over into the shape of a cylinder

roll verb. (**rolled, rolling**) 1. turn over and over 2. make something into the shape of a ball 3. move on wheels

roller noun. a type of tube

ROM abbr. Read-Only Memory; computer memory that contains data and instructions that cannot be changed

Roman noun. adj. of or connected with ancient or modern Rome

Roman Catholic noun. adj. someone who is a member of a church whose head is the Pope in Rome

romance noun. 1. love between two people (no plural) 2. a love relationship 3. a novel about being in love

romantic adj. 1. about love 2. not practical; full of dreams

roof noun. the top of the outside of a building, a car, etc

room noun. 1. a space inside four walls 2. space (no plural)

room verb. (**roomed, rooming**) share a rented room or apartment with someone

root noun. the part of a plant that grows inside the earth

roots noun plural. strong feelings of connection with a place where your family originally comes from

rope noun. a thick, strong cord

rope verb. (**roped, roping**) tie with a rope

rose noun. 1. a flower with a strong, sweet smell 2. a dark pink color (no plural)

rose verb. past of **rise**

rosy adj. (**rosier, rosiest**) pink; healthy looking

rot verb. (**rotted, rotting**) spoil; become bad

rotten adj. **1.** spoiled; gone bad **2.** cruel; nasty **3.** bad; unpleasant; unfortunate

rough adj. **1.** not smooth **2.** not calm **3.** not gentle **4.** difficult **5.** not exact; not in detail **6.** coarse and unpleasant to listen to

roughly adv. **1.** not gently **2.** more or less; not exactly

round noun. a part of a game or match

round adj. having the shape of a circle or a ball

round adv. moving in a circle; around

round prep. **1.** in a circle **2.** on all sides of **3.** on the other side of

roundabout noun. a crossroads or a junction with a circular area in the middle

route noun. **1.** a way of getting somewhere **2.** a main road in the U.S.

routine noun. things that you do regularly every day

routine adj. happening regularly

row noun. **1.** a line of something **2.** a loud quarrel **3.** an unpleasant noise

row verb. **(rowed, rowing)** make a small boat move by using oars **—rowing** noun. (no plural)

rowdy adj. noisy and rough

royal adj. connected with a king or queen

royalties noun plural. payments given to a writer, musician, etc, from the sales of copies of his/her work

royalty noun. kings, queens, princes and princesses; members of a royal family (no plural)

rub verb. **(rubbed, rubbing)** move something hard back and forth against something else

rubber noun. an elastic material made from the liquid of certain trees (no plural) **—rubber** adj.

rubbish noun. **1.** trash; garbage **2.** silly ideas; nonsense (no plural)

ruby noun. **1.** a precious red stone **2.** a red color like the stone (plural **rubies**)

rude adj. ill-mannered; inconsiderate; impolite

rug noun. a covering for a floor or part of a floor

rugby noun. a game similar to football played by two teams with 13 players each

rugged adj. **1.** strongly built **2.** with an uneven surface

ruin noun. **1.** destruction (no plural) **2.** what is left of a place that was destroyed or fell apart long ago

ruin verb. **(ruined, ruining)** spoil or destroy completely

rule noun. **1.** a regulation (in a game, school, etc) **2.** a principle that tells what is correct and what is not **3.** control over a country

rule verb. **(ruled, ruling) 1.** control a country **2.** make a decision in court or in a sport **3.** make lines on paper

ruled adj. with lines

ruler noun. **1.** someone who rules a country **2.** something flat and straight for drawing lines

ruling noun. a decision by a judge or a referee

rum noun. a strong alcoholic drink that is made from the juice of the sugar cane

rumble noun. a long, deep, uneven noise

rumor noun. something that people talk about which may not be true

run noun. **1.** moving fast on your feet **2.** a tear in a stocking **3.** the time that something continues

run verb. **(ran, running) 1.** move very fast on your feet **2.** leave in a hurry **3.** manage a business **4.** operate a machine **5.** operate **6.** flow **7.** be performed many times **8.** be a candidate in an election **9.** appear in different members of a family

runaway noun. someone who escapes from a place

run-down adj. shabby; in bad condition

rung *noun.* a step on a ladder

rung *verb.* past participle of **ring**

runner *noun.* someone who runs

runner-up *noun.* the person who comes in second in a contest

running *adj.* (water) coming out of a pipe

run-up *noun.* **1.** a sudden increase **2.** the time leading up to an event (such as an election) **3.** the speed or distance needed in order to do a particular action

runway *noun.* a paved road where a plane takes off or lands

rural *adj.* of or in the countryside; not of or in the city (opposite **urban**)

rush *noun.* a hurry (no plural)

rush *verb.* **(rushed, rushing) 1.** move quickly **2.** hurry **3.** make someone do something fast

rush hour *noun.* the hours when everyone is traveling to or from work

Russian *noun.* someone from Russia; the language spoken in Russia — **Russian** *adj.*

rust *noun.* the reddish brown covering that air or water makes on some metals

rustle *noun.* a soft, whispering kind of sound

rusty *adj.* **(rustier, rustiest)** covered with rust

ruthless *adj.* cruel; without pity —**ruthlessly** *adv.*

rye *noun.* a type of grain used for making bread and whiskey

S

S *abbr.* south; southern

Sabbath *noun.* the day of rest in many religions

sabotage *verb.* **(sabotaged, sabotaging)** destroy or damage something on purpose

sack *noun.* a big bag that is made of strong cloth

sack *verb.* **(sacked, sacking)** fire someone from her/his job; dismiss

sacred *adj.* connected with God or someone's religion; holy

sacrifice *noun.* **1.** giving up something that is important to you for the good of someone or something else **2.** an offering to the gods, usually an animal that has been killed

sacrifice *verb.* **(sacrificed, sacrificing) 1.** give up something that is very precious to you for the good of someone or something else **2.** make an offering to the gods

sad *adj.* **1.** unhappy **2.** making you unhappy **—sadden** *verb.* **(saddened, saddening) —sadly** *adj.* (opposite **happily) —sadness** *noun.* (opposite **happiness)**

saddle *noun.* **1.** a leather seat put on the back of a horse in order to make riding easier **2.** a bicycle seat

safari *noun.* a trip (in eastern Africa) into wild open country in order to observe, hunt, photograph, etc, animals in their natural surroundings

safe *noun.* a metal container with a special lock where you can keep money, jewels, etc

safe *adj.* **1.** free from harm or danger; protected **2.** where nobody can find you **3.** not dangerous **4.** without harm

safely *adv.* **1.** not dangerously **2.** out of the way of harm **3.** without harm **4.** where nobody can find it

safety *noun.* being safe (no plural)

sage *noun. adj.* very wise

said *verb.* past tense and past participle of **say**

sail *noun.* **1.** a big piece of cloth that catches the wind and makes a boat move **2.** a trip on a sailboat (no plural)

sail *verb.* **(sailed, sailing) 1.** travel by boat or ship **2.** begin a journey by ship **3.** control a sailboat **—sailing** *noun.* (no plural)

sailor *noun.* **1.** a member of the crew of a ship **2.** someone who is in the navy

saint *noun.* **1.** a person who is recognized (after his/her death) as particularly holy by the Christian church **2.** (informal) a very good, kind and unselfish person

sake *noun.* **1.** for the good of someone or something **2.** in order to get

salad *noun.* raw vegetables that are cut, sliced or grated

salary *noun.* money that you get regularly (usually weekly or monthly) for work that you do

sale *noun.* **1.** selling **2.** selling a certain thing (no plural) **3.** a time when stores sell at a lower price

salesclerk *noun.* someone who sells things in someone else's store

salesman, salesperson, saleswoman *noun.* a person whose job is selling (plural **salesmen, salespeople, saleswomen)**

salmon *noun.* a large fish with pink meat that swims upstream in order to lay its eggs and is native to the northern oceans

salon *noun.* **1.** a living room in a large house **2.** a fashionable place where services are given **3.** a gallery for exhibiting artwork

saloon *noun.* **1.** (identified with the Wild

West in America) a bar for selling alcohol **2.** a large room used by many passengers on a ship for general purposes

salsa *noun*. **1.** a Latin American dance **2.** a hot sauce

salt *noun*. the small white grains that we use on food (no plural)

salt *verb*. **(salted, salting)** put salt in or on (food)

salty *adj*. having salt

salute *noun*. lifting your hand formally as a sign of respect

salute *verb*. **(saluted, saluting)** lift your hand to your forehead to show respect

salvage *verb*. **(salvaged, salvaging)** save something from disaster, damage or harm

same *adj*. identical; not different

sample *noun*. a small part or one piece that shows what the whole thing is like

sample *verb*. **(sampled, sampling)** try a small part or piece to see what the rest is like

sanctuary *noun*. **1.** a safe place **2.** the holiest of places in a religious building

sand *noun*. **1.** very small, powdery grains of rock (no plural) **2.** the beach

sandal *noun*. an open shoe, usually with straps

sandstone *noun*. stone that is composed of sand mixed with a natural cement

sandwich *noun*. slices of bread or a sliced roll with something in between

sandy *adj*. full of sand

sane *adj*. mentally healthy; not crazy (opposite **insane**)

sang *verb*. past of **sing**

sanitary *adj*. clean; not harmful to your health (opposite **unsanitary**) **—sanitation** *noun*.

sanity *noun*. being sane (no plural)

sank *verb*. past of **sink**

sarcastic *adj*. saying the opposite of what you mean in order to hurt or insult someone **—sarcasm** *noun*.

sat *verb*. past tense and past participle of **sit**

satellite *noun*. a spacecraft that moves around the Earth in space

satin *noun*. a shiny smooth material

satire *noun*. making fun of something or someone to make it/them seem absurd or stupid (especially in a play or in writing) **—satirical** *adj*.

satisfaction *noun*. **1.** being pleased because of what you do or what someone else does (no plural) **2.** pleasure from a certain thing

satisfactorily *adv*. giving satisfaction sufficient to meet a demand or requirement; adequate (opposite **unsatisfactorily**)

satisfactory *adj*. good enough; adequate (opposite **unsatisfactory**)

satisfied *adj*. pleased (opposite **dissatisfied**)

satisfy *verb*. **(satisfied, satisfying) 1.** be good enough for someone **2.** be enough for

satisfying *adj*. making you feel good (opposite **unsatisfying**)

Saturday *noun*. the 7th day of the week

sauce *noun*. a liquid that you pour over food to make it taste better

saucepan *noun*. a small pot with a long handle

saucer *noun*. a small plate to put under a cup

savage *noun*. **1.** someone who is very primitive **2.** a person or an animal who is very cruel

savage *adj*. **1.** brutal; fierce **2.** cruel

save *verb*. **(saved, saving) 1.** keep someone from dying **2.** keep something from harm or destruction **3.** put money aside **4.** keep something for later **5.** avoid waste of money, time, etc **6.** keep information in a computer's disk

savings *noun plural*. the money that you have saved

saw *noun*. a metal tool with teeth that

you use for cutting wood or other hard materials —**saw** verb. **(sawed, sawn, sawing)**

saw verb. past of **see**

say verb. **(said, saying)** 1. speak a word or words 2. show something 3. tell someone something

saying noun. a well-known statement that people say to prove a point or give advice

scale noun. 1. a machine for measuring weight 2. a series of numbers or marks for measuring things from the lowest to the highest

scale verb. **(scaled, scaling)** 1. climb 2. make a copy according to a certain scale

scan verb. **(scanned, scanning)** 1. look at something with great attention 2. read quickly to look for a certain detail

scandal noun. something shocking that has happened —**scandalous** adj.

scanner noun. a machine that scans

scar noun. a mark that remains on your skin after an injury or an operation

scar verb. **(scarred, scarring)** leave a scar

scarce adj. hard to get; not easily available

scarcely adv. 1. almost none; hardly 2. just barely

scare noun. something that frightens you

scare verb. **(scared, scaring)** frighten — **scary** adj. **(scarier, scariest)**

scared adj. frightened

scarf noun. 1. a long, narrow piece of cloth that you wear around your neck 2. a piece of cloth that a woman ties over her head; a kerchief

scarred adj. having scars

scatter verb. **(scattered, scattering)** 1. run off in different directions 2. make people, animals or things go off in different directions 3. spread something in different places

scenario noun. a description of what could happen

scene noun. 1. something pleasant to look at 2. a part of an act of a play 3. a part of a movie 4. where something happened —**scenic** adj.

scenery noun. 1. beautiful sights 2. the things on a stage that make a play seem real

scent noun. 1. a pleasant smell 2. a particular perfume 3. any smell

scent verb. **(scented, scenting)** 1. smell something 2. make something smell sweet

schedule noun. 1. a timetable 2. a program or plan for a certain period of time

schedule verb. **(scheduled, scheduling)** plan something for a certain time

scheme noun. a secret, dishonest plan —**scheme** verb. **(schemed, scheming)**

scholar noun. someone who has studied and knows a great deal

scholarship noun. 1. money that is given to a student so that he/she can study at a university, college, etc 2. studying and learning (no plural)

school noun. 1. a place where children and young people get an education 2. attending school (no plural) 3. people with the same opinions, style, etc

schooling noun. formal education (no plural)

schoolteacher noun. someone whose work is teaching at a school

science noun. 1. the study of what happens in nature (no plural) 2. a subject that relates to science 3. all sciences (no plural) —**scientific** adj. —**scientifically** adv.

science fiction noun. stories about other worlds or what may happen in our world in the future

scientist noun. someone who works in the sciences

scissors noun plural. a tool for cutting things which has two blades that move and two holes for your fingers

scold verb. **(scolded, scolding)** tell

someone angrily that he/she did something bad; tell off

scone *noun.* a quickly baked light cake

scoop *noun.* 1. a kind of deep spoon 2. a big, round spoonful of something 3. a big news story that nobody else has printed —**scoop** *verb.* (**scooped, scooping**)

scope *noun.* how far something's activity or influence extends

score *noun.* the number of points that each one has in a match or competition

score *verb.* (**scored, scoring**) make a point, goal, etc, in a competition or a match

scorn *noun.* a feeling that someone or something doesn't deserve respect; contempt

Scot *noun.* someone from Scotland

Scotch, Scottish *adj.* from or belonging to Scotland

Scotsman, Scotswoman *noun.* a man or woman from Scotland (plural **Scotsmen, Scotswomen**)

scout *noun. adj.* someone who goes ahead of the soldiers to get information about the enemy

scowl *verb.* (**scowled, scowling**) look angry; frown

scramble *verb.* (**scrambled, scrambling**) mix things up

scrap *noun.* a small piece of something

scrap *verb.* (**scrapped, scrapping**) 1. throw away something 2. decide not to do something

scrape *noun.* 1. a scratch that takes off some skin 2. trouble

scrape *verb.* (**scraped, scraping**) 1. remove something from something else with an instrument or by scratching against something 2. hurt yourself by rubbing off skin

scratch *noun.* a small wound or marks on the surface

scratch *verb.* (**scratched, scratching**) 1. rub an itch 2. use nails or claws to injure someone 3. make a cut that is not deep

scratchy *adj.* 1. marked with scratches 2. making a scratching noise 3. itchy

scream *noun.* a loud cry

scream *verb.* (**screamed, screaming**) 1. shout loudly out of fear 2. raise your voice; shout

screen *noun.* 1. where a film, information, etc, is shown 2. something that you put around a place for privacy 3. a frame with wires for keeping insects, etc, out of the house

screen *verb.* (**screened, screening**) protect something from light, wind, dust, etc

screenplay *noun.* a script used when making a movie

screw *noun.* a type of nail that you twist into wood, metal, etc, to fasten something

screw *verb.* (**screwed, screwing**) fasten with screws

screwdriver *noun.* a tool for turning screws

scribble *verb.* (**scribbled, scribbling**) 1. make meaningless marks on paper 2. write quickly

script *noun.* 1. handwriting; a system of writing in which the letters are joined (no plural) 2. the written form of a play, broadcast, etc

Scriptures *noun plural.* the Bible

scrub *verb.* (**scrubbed, scrubbing**) rub something with something else to get it clean —**scrub, scrubbing** *noun.*

scrutinize *verb.* (**scrutinized, scrutinizing**) check very closely and carefully

sculpt *verb.* (**sculpted, sculpting**) shape, mold, or fashion especially with artistry or precision

sculptor *noun.* an artist who makes figures (sculptures) out of stone, clay, metal, etc

sculpture *noun.* 1. making figures from stone or other materials (no plural) 2. a piece of sculpture

SE *abbr.* southeast

sea *noun.* 1. a large body of salt water 2. the seashore (no plural)

seafood *noun.* fish, especially shellfish (no plural)

seal *noun.* 1. a sea mammal that usually lives in cold water 2. an official stamp that presses an emblem into a piece of paper 3. something that prevents something from being opened

seal *verb.* **(sealed, sealing)** 1. close with melted wax or some other means that guarantees a tight closing 2. place an official mark on a document 3. close tightly, using something sticky

seam *noun.* a line where two pieces of cloth, leather, etc, were put together

search *verb.* **(searched, searching)** try to find something; look for something —**search** *noun.*

seaside *noun.* the seashore; the beach (no plural)

season *noun.* 1. one of the four parts of the year 2. a time of year when something happens

season *verb.* **(seasoned, seasoning)** add salt or spices to give taste to food

seasonal *adj.* connected to the seasons

seasoning *noun.* the spices that you put in food to give it a better taste

seat *noun.* a place to sit

seat *verb.* **(seated, seating)** 1. tell someone to sit in a certain place 2. have enough space to sit

seat belt *noun.* a safety belt in a car or on an airplane

second *noun.* 1. 1/60 of a minute 2. a very short time; a moment

second *adj. pron.* after the first and before the third

secondary *adj.* not the most important

second-class *adj.* not of the best quality; not first-class

second-hand *adj.* used; that belonged to someone else

secondly *adv.* the second of a number of details, facts, etc

second-rate *adj.* not so good; pretty poor

secrecy *noun.* the condition of being secret; the capability of keeping a secret

secret *noun.* something that you don't want other people to know

secret *adj.* that people don't know about

secretarial *adj.* connected with the work of a secretary

secretary *noun.* 1. someone who takes care of the paper work in an office 2. a government official; a minister 3. someone who keeps the records of the meetings of an organization

secretive *adj.* not telling about yourself

secretly *adv.* without other people knowing about it

sect *noun.* a group of people with special beliefs and practices that separate them from the main group

section *noun.* a part of something larger

sector *noun.* 1. a part of the population or economy 2. part of a circle with two straight lines that meet at a point and an arc 3. a special area

secure *verb.* **(secured, securing)** 1. shut something firmly 2. get something after trying

secure *adj.* 1. safe; firm 2. safe from danger 3. safe for the future

securely *adv.* firmly; tightly (opposite **insecurely**)

securities *noun plural.* stocks and bonds

security *noun.* 1. safety 2. protecting other people

sedan *noun.* a car with room for five passengers that has two or four doors and a permanent roof

see *verb.* **(saw, seen, seeing)** 1. use your eyes 2. notice 3. find out 4. understand 5. meet someone 6. go with someone; escort someone 7. make certain that something gets done

seed *noun.* **1.** a small thing from which a plant grows if you put it in the earth **2.** the beginning of an idea

seed *verb.* **(seeded, seeding)** plant seeds in the ground

seek *verb.* **(sought, seeking)** (formal) search for something

seem *verb.* **(seemed)** appear to be

seeming *adj.* appearing to be, but may not be so; apparent

seemingly *adv.* giving the wrong impression

seen *verb.* past participle of **see**

segregate *verb.* **(segregated, segregating)** separate by force (opposite **integrate**) —**segregation** *noun.*

segregated *adj.* kept separate (opposite **integrated**)

seize *verb.* **(seized, seizing)** **1.** grab something with both hands **2.** capture **3.** capture and keep

seldom *adv.* not often

select *verb.* **(selected, selecting)** choose

selection *noun.* **1.** things to choose from **2.** choosing (no plural) **3.** a choice

self *noun.* that person and no other; what makes a person different from other people (plural **selves**)

self- *prefix.* = alone; not by others; not for others

self-confidence *noun.* belief in yourself (no plural)

self-conscious *adj.* aware of what other people may be thinking about you; shy; embarrassed

self-control *noun.* the ability to control your behavior

self-employed *adj.* not working for anyone else

self-image *noun.* the way someone sees himself/herself

selfish *adj.* caring only about yourself; wanting everything for yourself (opposite **generous**)

self-respect *noun.* respect for yourself; knowing that you are worth something

self-sufficient *adj.* able to do everything alone

sell *verb.* **(sold, selling)** **1.** give something for payment **2.** carry a certain product for sale **3.** have people buy something; be in demand

seller *noun.* someone who sells something

selves *noun.* plural of **self**

semantics *noun.* the study of meaning (in language)

seminal *adj.* **1.** connected to the seed and fluid which is produced by males **2.** very important and having a strong influence on the future

seminar *noun.* **1.** a small group of students and a teacher who discuss ideas **2.** a short course of study

senate *noun.* one of the law-making bodies is some countries

senator *noun.* a member of a senate

send *verb.* **(sent, sending)** **1.** put something in the mail **2.** deliver a message without going yourself **3.** make someone go somewhere

sender *noun.* someone who sends something

senior *adj.* **1.** older in age **2.** higher in rank **3.** (with a capital letter) the father, if he is alive and if the son has the same name

senior *noun.* someone who is older than someone else (opposite **junior**)

senior citizen *noun.* a retiree; an old-age pensioner; someone above the age of 60–65

sensation *noun.* **1.** feeling (no plural) **2.** a feeling **3.** big excitement

sensational *adj.* **1.** very exciting **2.** causing a scandal **3.** terrific

sense *noun.* **1.** seeing, hearing, touch, smell, and taste (the five senses) **2.** practical intelligence (no plural) **3.** a feeling about something (no plural) **4.** the point or practical reason (no plural) **5.** meaning

sense *verb.* **(sensed, sensing)** have a feeling about something

senseless adj. **1.** pointless; having no meaning **2.** unconscious

sensible adj. having good sense

sensibly adv. using common sense

sensitive adj. **1.** quick to understand other people's feelings **2.** easily insulted or embarrassed **3.** quick to feel pain **4.** easily damaged **5.** allergic **6.** painful and embarrassing

sensitivity noun. **1.** consideration of the feelings of others; tact (no plural) **2.** an allergy

sent verb. past tense and past participle of **send**

sentence noun. **1.** (grammar) a group of words with a subject and verb that you put together in a certain order to say or ask something **2.** a punishment by a court

sentence verb. **(sentenced, sentencing)** send to prison

sentimental adj. **1.** emotional **2.** nostalgic about your past

separate verb. **(separated, separating) 1.** divide something **2.** keep something divided **3.** part **4.** move apart **5.** be moved apart

separate adj. **1.** apart **2.** different **3.** not joined together

separately adv. **1.** apart **2.** alone; not with all the rest

separation noun. **1.** a division into separate parts (no plural) **2.** time apart **3.** a space between two things

Sept. abbr. September

September noun. the ninth month of the year

sequel noun. something (usually a film, book, etc) that comes after another one, but also continues it

sequence noun. the order of things as they happen, one following the other

sergeant noun. rank in the army or police

series noun. things that come one after another (singular and plural)

serious adj. **1.** hard-working and responsible **2.** important; not funny **3.** difficult to solve or cure **4.** doing a lot of harm **—seriously** adv.

seriousness noun. importance (no plural)

servant noun. a person who does the work in someone else's house

serve verb. **(served, serving) 1.** put food on a table **2.** take care of the needs of customers **3.** work for someone or something **4.** be in the armed forces

server noun. **1.** someone who is the one to start a game of volleyball, tennis, etc **2.** a dish or tool used for serving food **3.** a main computer that provides services for or controls other computers

service noun. **1.** attention to the needs of customers (no plural) **2.** something that you do for people as part of a job **3.** a complete set of dishes **4.** organized prayers

service verb. **(serviced, servicing)** make fit for use; adjust, repair, or maintain

session noun. a meeting of an organized group for working purposes

set noun. **1.** a group of things that go together **2.** the place where a movie is filmed (no plural) **3.** a group of people with similar intentions who often meet each other

set verb. **(set, setting) 1.** put something down **2.** prepare a clock, timer, alarm, etc, to do what you want **3.** fix something firmly in place **4.** become firmly fixed **5.** go down

set adj. **1.** firmly fixed in your ways; unwilling to do things differently **2.** fixed in advance

setback noun. **1.** a delay **2.** bad luck; difficult times **3.** becoming worse

setter noun. **1.** a dog with long hair **2.** someone or something that sets

setting noun. **1.** going down (no plural) **2.** where a play takes place **3.** places at a table

settle verb. (**settled, settling**) **1.** make your new home in a place **2.** be the first ones to make a home in or to colonize a place **3.** put an end to something

settlement noun. **1.** a group of houses where people live **2.** an agreement about money

settler noun. someone who makes a home in a new country or area

seven noun. adj. the number 7

seventeen noun. adj. the number 17

seventeenth noun. adj. = 17th

seventh noun. adj. = 7th

seventieth adj. = 70th

seventy noun. adj. the number 70

several adj. some but not many

several pron. more than one

severe adj. **1.** harsh (opposite **mild**) **2.** strict **3.** bad

severely adv. **1.** harshly; without humor or pity **2.** seriously

severity noun. harshness (no plural)

sew verb. (**sewed, sewn, sewing**) make stitches with a needle and thread — **sewing** noun. (no plural)

sewer noun. a pipe under the ground for carrying away water and waste

sewing machine noun. a machine that sews

sewn verb. past participle of **sew**

sex noun. **1.** being male or female **2.** sexual activity —**sexual** adj. —**sexually** adv.

sex appeal noun. sexual attraction

sexism noun. the opinion that one sex (usually the male) is superior to the other —**sexist** noun. adj.

sexy adj. very attractive

sh, shh excl. a sound that you make to tell someone to be quiet

shade noun. **1.** protection from the sun (no plural) **2.** something that keeps out light **3.** lighter or darker tones of the same color **4.** small differences in meaning

shade verb. (**shaded, shading**) give shade or protection against light

shadow noun. **1.** a dark shape on a surface caused by something or someone blocking the light **2.** places that a painter makes darker **3.** a dark area under your eye

shadowy adj. **1.** not clear because of the darkness **2.** felt in the background but not seen

shady adj. **1.** in the shade **2.** not honest

shaggy adj. having a lot of loose hair

shake verb. (**shook, shaken, shaking**) **1.** tremble **2.** move something forcefully up and down or from side to side

shaky adj. not steady

shall verb. (**should**) **1.** will (with I or we) **2.** asking for a suggestion (with I or we) **3.** should (with I or we in a question) **4.** a word that makes an offer (with I or we in a question) **5.** (formal) a word that gives an order or tells an intention

shallow adj. not deep

shambles noun. complete disorder; a total mess (no plural)

shame noun. a feeling of deep embarrassment (no plural)

shame verb. (**shamed, shaming**) bring dishonor or disgrace on

shameful adj. disgraceful

shameless adj. not feeling shame

shampoo noun. a liquid soap used for washing hair

shape noun. **1.** a form **2.** a condition

shape verb. (**shaped, shaping**) give form to

shaped adj. having the shape of

share noun. **1.** the part that belongs to you **2.** the amount that is fair **3.** being part owner and dividing profits in a business

share verb. (**shared, sharing**) **1.** divide something up with other people **2.** use something with another person

shareholder noun. someone who has invested money in a business that sells shares to the public

shark noun. a (usually) large gray fish that lives in warm sea water, which has many teeth and can be dangerous

sharp *adj.* **1.** with an edge that cuts **2.** with a narrow point **3.** clever and quick **4.** with strong contrast **5.** loud and quick **6.** able to see, hear or smell well **7.** very spicy **8.** severe and cutting **9.** quick and unkind **10.** cold and cutting **11.** changing direction suddenly **12.** in music, a half-note above a tone — **sharply** *adv.* —**sharpness** *noun.*

sharpen *verb.* **(sharpened, sharpening)** make sharp

shatter *verb.* **(shattered, shattering) 1.** break into many small pieces **2.** break something into many pieces

shave *verb.* **(shaved, shaving)** take the hair off with a razor (such as from a man's face) —**shave** *noun.*

shaver *noun.* an electric razor

she *pron.* (third person singular subject) that woman or girl

shed *noun.* **1.** a simple wooden building **2.** a building for farm animals

she'd *abbr.* **1.** she would **2.** she had

sheen *noun.* a gloss; a shine; a gleam

sheep *noun.* a farm animal that gives wool and whose meat people eat (singular and plural)

sheepish *adj.* embarrassed and uncomfortable especially because of doing something stupid

sheer *adj.* **1.** absolute **2.** very steep **3.** very thin and almost transparent (material)

sheet *noun.* **1.** a piece of cloth that you put on a bed **2.** a thin flat piece of something

shelf *noun.* a flat piece of wood or metal for putting things on (plural **shelves**)

shell *noun.* **1.** sea shell; the hard covering of some small sea animals **2.** the covering of an egg **3.** the hard covering of a nut or a peanut and certain grains **4.** a metal case with explosive material inside **5.** the outside walls of a ship or a building

shell *verb.* **(shelled, shelling) 1.** remove the hard covering **2.** attack with explosive shells

she'll *abbr.* she will

shelter *noun.* **1.** a place to live (no plural) **2.** a place where you are safe

shelter *verb.* **(sheltered, sheltering) 1.** protect **2.** hide someone from the police, etc

sheltered *adj.* very protected

shepherd *noun.* someone who looks after or raises sheep

sheriff *noun.* an elected law officer in the U.S. who is in charge of an area and whose job is to carry out directions from the courts and to keep law and order

shield *noun.* something to protect a part of the body from being hit or injured

shift *noun.* **1.** a group of people who start work when another group leaves **2.** a change; a switch

shift *verb.* **(shifted, shifting) 1.** change to a different place or position **2.** move into a different position **3.** switch from one to another

shifting *adj.* constantly moving

shine *noun.* brightness (no plural)

shine *verb.* **(shone, shining) 1.** give bright light **2.** look bright and polished

shine *verb.* **(shined, shining)** polish or rub something so that it looks bright —**shining** *adj.*

shiny *adj.* bright; new-looking

ship *noun.* a big boat that sails on the sea

ship *verb.* **(shipped, shipping)** send (goods); deliver

shipment *noun.* a load of goods

shipyard *noun.* a place where ships are built

shirt *noun.* a piece of clothing for the upper half of the body

shiver *noun.* a trembling from cold or fear

shiver *verb.* **(shivered, shivering)** shake with cold

shock *noun*. **1.** a sudden, unpleasant surprise **2.** an electric shock; an electric current coming into your body **3.** weakness and confusion after an accident, loss of blood, tragic news, etc (no plural) —**shock** *verb*. **(shocked, shocking)**

shocking *adj*. causing shock or surprise

shoe *noun*. something that you wear on your foot for walking

shone *verb*. past tense and past participle of **shine**

shook *verb*. past of **shake**

shoot *verb*. **(shot, shooting) 1.** fire a gun **2.** use a bow and arrow **3.** move very fast **4.** use a camera

shooting *noun*. **1.** the use of a gun to kill or wound **2.** the use of a camera to make a movie

shop *noun*. a place where you buy things; a store

shop *verb*. **(shopped, shopping)** go out to buy something

shopping *noun*. the things you buy in stores

shopping mall *noun*. a covered area where there are many stores and restaurants and sometimes movie theaters

shore *noun*. the land at the edge of a sea or lake

short, short circuit *noun*. (electricity) a bad connection or other fault that stops the flow of electricity to a machine, etc, or causes fire

short *adj*. **1.** not long **2.** not lasting long **3.** not taking long **4.** not tall

shortage *noun*. not enough; a lack

shorten *verb*. **(shortened, shortening)** make shorter (opposite **lengthen**)

shorthand *noun*. a way of writing faster by writing signs instead of whole words

shortly *adv*. soon; before long

shorts *noun plural*. **1.** short pants (trousers) **2.** men's underpants

short-term *adj*. for a short period

shot *noun*. **1.** the sound that a gun makes when you fire it **2.** a photograph **3.** an injection **4.** a try **5.** a kick (in soccer); a throw (in basketball); a stroke (in golf, tennis, etc)

shot *verb*. past tense and past participle of **shoot**

should *verb*. **1.** ought to; have a duty to; be the right thing to do **2.** advise **3.** probably will **4.** (grammar) past of shall in reported speech **5.** by chance

shoulder *noun*. the place where a person's arm is connected to the main part of the body

shouldn't *abbr*. should not

shout *verb*. **(shouted, shouting)** call or talk loudly —**shout** *noun*.

shove *noun*. a hard push

shove *verb*. **(shoved, shoving)** push someone or something roughly

shovel *noun*. a tool for digging; a spade

show *noun*. **1.** a play; a performance **2.** a showing of a movie **3.** an exhibit

show *verb*. **(showed, shown, showing) 1.** let someone see something **2.** demonstrate how to do something **3.** appear; be seen **4.** lead someone to a certain place

show business *noun*. the world of entertainment, including the theater, movies, etc (no plural)

showcase *noun*. a large glass box where something is put on display either in a store or in a museum

shower *noun*. **1.** a light rain **2.** a place where you can get washed under water that falls from above

shower *verb*. **(showered, showering)** take a shower

shown *verb*. past participle of **show**

showroom *noun*. a place where examples of products are put on display in order to interest buyers

shrewd *adj*. good at judging people or things

shrimp *noun*. a small sea animal with a stiff outer covering and a long tail, that has ten legs

shrine *noun*. a holy place

shrink *verb*. **(shrank, shrunk, shrinking)** **1.** become less **2.** become smaller

shrub *noun*. a small bush

shrug *verb*. **(shrugged, shrugging)** move your shoulders up and down to show that you do not know or care — **shrug** *noun*.

shudder *verb*. shake for a moment from cold, fear or disgust

shut *verb*. **(shut, shutting)** **1.** close something **2.** block the way (opposite **open**)

shut *adj*. closed (opposite **open**)

shuttle *noun*. **1.** a vehicle (airplane, bus, train, etc) that goes back and forth on a short route at regular times **2.** a spacecraft that can be used a number of times

shy *adj*. easily embarrassed; not comfortable with people

sick *adj*. ill; not well (opposite **well, healthy**)

sicken *verb*. **(sickened, sickening)** make someone feel sick — **sickening** *adj*.

sickly *adj*. weak and unhealthy

sickness *noun*. ill health; illness (no plural)

side *noun*. **1.** one of the lines that make up a figure **2.** the part that is away from the middle, the front or the back **3.** one of the parts that enclose something **4.** a long surface that goes up and down **5.** a surface of paper **6.** things to consider **7.** opposing groups — **side** *adj*.

sidewalk *noun*. a paved place for walking along the side of a street

sideways *adv*. from the side; turned to the side

sigh *verb*. **(sighed, sighing)** take a deep breath because of a feeling that you have — **sigh** *noun*.

sight *noun*. **1.** eyesight; the ability to see (no plural) **2.** something that you see

sight *verb*. **(sighted)** see something suddenly

sights *noun plural*. famous and interesting places for tourists to visit

sightseeing *noun*. going around a place to see the sights (no plural)

sign *noun*. **1.** a notice that gives information or tells what to do **2.** a movement that you make to show what to do or how you feel **3.** a symbol in mathematics or in writing **4.** something that shows what may happen or be true; an indication

sign *verb*. **(signed, signing)** **1.** write your name **2.** write your name on something to make it legal

signal *noun*. a sign that gives a certain message — **signal** *verb*. **(signaled, signaling)**

signature *noun*. the special way that you sign your name

significance *noun*. meaning; importance (no plural)

significant *adj*. meaningful; important (opposite **insignificant**) — **significantly** *adv*.

signify *verb*. **(signified, signifying)** mean; be a sign of

silence *noun*. **1.** complete quiet (no plural) **2.** a period of time when there is no sound

silent *adj*. without noise; completely quiet — **silently** *adv*.

silk *noun*. cloth that is smooth and fine

silk *adj*. made of silk

silky *adj*. soft like silk

silly *adj*. foolish; without sense

silver *noun*. **1.** a shiny, white metal that is used for coins, jewelry and other things **2.** silverware; forks, knives and spoons that are made of silver

silver *adj*. **1.** made of silver **2.** of the color of silver

silver medal *noun*. the medal for second place in a competition

similar *adj*. **1.** the same or almost the same **2.** of the same type but not exactly the same

similarity *noun*. being alike or having

something in common (plural **similarities**)

similarly adv. in the same way

simple adj. **1.** easy to understand or do (opposite **difficult**) **2.** plain (opposite **complicated**) **3.** (grammar) having only one part **4.** (grammar) relating to a verb tense that does not include a participle (such as -ing, -en, etc) **5.** stupid and slow

simplified adj. made simpler

simplify verb. (**simplified, simplifying**) make easier

simply adv. **1.** without a lot of decoration **2.** really

simultaneous adj. happening, doing or present at the same time; parallel — **simultaneously** adv.

sin noun. an evil act or the breaking of a law of God

since adv. conj. prep. **1.** from that time until now **2.** from a time in the past until a later time in the past

since conj. because

sincere adj. **1.** honest **2.** truthful

sincerely adv. honestly; truthfully

—**Sincerely, Sincerely yours, Yours sincerely** endings to a formal letter

sing verb. (**sang, sung, singing**) use your voice to make music

singer noun. someone who sings

single adj. **1.** only one **2.** not even one (in negative sentences) **3.** not married **4.** for one

single-handed adj. adv. alone; without help

singular noun. adj. (grammar) the form of a word that means **one thing** or **one person** (opposite **plural**)

sink noun. a place for washing your hands, washing dishes, etc

sink verb. (**sank, sunk, sinking**) **1.** go down to the bottom **2.** make something go down to the bottom

sip noun. a very small drink of something

sip verb. (**sipped, sipping**) drink in small sips

sir noun. **1.** a title of respect for a man **2.** (Sir) a British title before the name of a knight

siren noun. a kind of whistle that makes a long, high noise to warn people

sister noun. **1.** a girl or woman with the same parents as yours **2.** (Sister) a title for a nun

sister-in-law noun. the sister of your husband or wife; your brother's wife (plural **sisters-in-law**)

sit verb. (**sat, sitting**) **1.** not stand or lie down; rest your weight on your bottom **2.** have a regular place **3.** rest in a certain place

sitcom noun. a situation comedy; a humorous TV program with the same characters appearing in each episode

sit-down noun. adj. a stoppage of work by the workers who refuse to leave the office, factory, etc, until their demands are met

site noun. a place

situate verb. (**situated, situating**) put in a certain location or position

situation noun. **1.** the way things are **2.** someone's medical condition **3.** job; post; position

six noun. adj. the number 6

sixteen noun. adj. the number 16

sixteenth noun. adj. 16th

sixth noun. adj. = 6th

sixtieth noun. adj. **1.** = 60th **2.** = 1/60

sixty noun. adj. the number 60

size noun. **1.** how big something is (no plural) **2.** a measurement of how big something is

size verb. (**sized, sizing**) give or mark a size

skate noun. a shoe with wheels or a blade fastened to it

skate verb. (**skated, skating**) move smoothly on ice skates or roller skates

skeletal adj. like a skeleton

skeleton noun. the bones that form the framework of the bodies of people and animals

skeptical adj. not trusting; doubtful

sketch verb. **(sketched, sketching)** draw something quickly without details

sketch noun. a quick drawing

ski noun. a long, thin piece of wood, plastic or metal that is attached to a boot for moving smoothly and fast over snow

ski verb. **(skied, skiing)** move on skis

skid verb. **(skidded, skidding)** slide sideways without control

skiing noun. the sport of moving on skis (no plural)

skill noun. something special that you know how to do (from practice and training)

skilled adj. **1.** very good at what you do **2.** trained to do a certain job

skim verb. **(skimmed, skimming) 1.** remove fat from a liquid, such as fat from soup after it has cooled, cream from milk, etc **2.** quickly read through something to find the main facts

skin noun. adj. **1.** the outer covering of the body of a person or an animal **2.** the fur of an animal **3.** the smooth covering of some fruit and vegetables

skin verb. **(skinned, skinning)** remove the skin

skinhead noun. a young hooligan who shaves off her/his hair, especially one who is a racist

skinny adj. too thin

skip verb. **(skipped, skipping) 1.** leave something out **2.** run with a little hop on each foot **3.** talk and keep on changing the subject

skipper noun. (informal) the captain of a ship

skirt noun. women's or girls' clothing for the lower part of the body

skull noun. the bone of the head which covers the brain

sky noun. the blue that you see above you (plural **skies**)

skyline noun. the shape buildings or hills make against the background of the sky as seen from a distance

skyscraper noun. a very tall building

slack adj. **1.** loose; not tight **2.** without much business; slow

slacks noun plural. long pants (trousers) for informal wear

slam verb. **(slammed, slamming)** shut with force —**slam** noun.

slang noun. very informal words that are used for talking to friends or by a particular group, but not for formal writing or when talking to people that we don't know well

slant verb. **(slanted, slanting)** be higher on one side than on the other

slap noun. a blow with the open hand

slap verb. **(slapped, slapping)** hit with the open hand

slaughter noun. mass killing (no plural)

slaughter verb. **(slaughtered, slaughtering) 1.** kill large numbers of people or animals **2.** kill an animal for food or sacrifice

slave noun. someone who is the property of another person and must work for that person

slave verb. **(slaved, slaving)** work very hard at something that you have to do

slavery noun. having slaves or being a slave (no plural)

sled noun. a vehicle for traveling on snow which moves on strips of wood or metal

sleek adj. smooth and shiny

sleep verb. **(slept, sleeping)** close your eyes and get total rest —**sleep** noun. (no plural)

sleeping bag noun. a kind of warm sack for sleeping in when you go on a camping trip

sleepless adj. without sleep

sleepy adj. wanting to sleep

sleeve noun. the part of a shirt, jacket, dress, etc, that covers all or part of your arm

slender adj. attractively thin; slim (opposite **fat**)

slept verb. past tense and past participle of **sleep**

slice *noun.* a piece of bread, cake, meat, cheese, etc —**slice** *verb.* **(sliced, slicing)** —**sliced** *adj.*

slick *adj.* **1.** good at persuading people and sometimes dishonest **2.** smooth and slippery **3.** well-polished

slide *noun.* **1.** the act of sliding (no plural) **2.** a photograph that you show on a screen

slide *verb.* **(slid, sliding) 1.** move smoothly **2.** move something smoothly

slight *adj.* **1.** small; not important or serious **2.** some but not much

slightly *adv.* a little bit

slim *adj.* **1.** attractively thin (opposite **fat**) **2.** small; very slight

slip *noun.* **1.** a sliding fall; slipping **2.** a small piece of paper **3.** a mistake

slip *verb.* **(slipped, slipping) 1.** slide and fall on something smooth **2.** fall out of place **3.** move quietly so that nobody will see you **4.** move something secretly into place

slipper *noun.* a soft shoe

slippery *adj.* **1.** smooth; hard to catch **2.** smooth; easy to fall or skid on

slogan *noun.* a short catchy phrase, used in advertising, a political campaign, etc

slope *noun.* ground going up or down

slope *verb.* **(sloped, sloping)** be at a slant —**sloping** *adj.*

sloppy *adj.* **1.** messy; untidy **2.** carelessly done

slot *noun.* a narrow opening for putting something in

slow *verb.* **(slowed, slowing)** make slow —**slow down** *verb.* move more slowly

slow *adj.* **1.** not fast **2.** not bright or clever **3.** not able to keep correct time **4.** not active —**slow** *adv.* **(slower, slowest)** —**slowly** *adv.* (opposite **fast, quickly**)

slow motion *noun.* the appearance of very slow speed on film

sluggish *adj.* slow-moving; not very quick; not very active

slum *noun.* a poor, crowded neighborhood

slump *noun.* a severe economic depression

slump *verb.* **(slumped, slumping)** drop (suddenly)

sly *adj.* clever and cunning

smack *verb.* **(smacked, smacking)** hit with something that makes a noise (especially an open hand) —**smack** *noun.*

small *adj.* **1.** not large in size **2.** young

smart *adj.* **1.** clever; intelligent (opposite **stupid**) **2.** elegant and stylish **3.** quick and painful

smartly *adv.* elegantly and stylishly

smash *verb.* **(smashed, smashing) 1.** break into many small pieces **2.** break something into small pieces

smear *verb.* **(smeared, smearing) 1.** spread a sticky substance on something **2.** make something dirty by leaving marks

smell *noun.* **1.** one of the five senses that you learn with your nose (no plural) **2.** odor; aroma

smell *verb.* **(smelled/smelt, smelling) 1.** use your nose **2.** sense through your nose **3.** give off a smell **4.** stink

smelly *adj.* with a bad smell

smelt *verb.* **(smelted, smelting)** heat up ore in order to separate the metal

smile *noun.* a happy look on your face

smile *verb.* **(smiled, smiling)** show happiness or pleasure by moving your lips —**smiling** *adj.*

smog *noun.* a combination of smoke and fog that makes the air look brown (no plural)

smoke *noun.* **1.** a gray or black gas that comes from something burning (no plural) **2.** smoking a cigarette, a cigar or a pipe

smoke *verb.* **(smoked, smoking) 1.** inhale the smoke of a cigarette, pipe or cigar **2.** give off smoke —**smoking** *noun.* (no plural)

smoked *adj.* preserved with smoke

smoky *adj.* full of smoke

smooth *verb.* **(smoothed, smoothing)** take the wrinkles or bumps out of something

smooth *adj.* 1. not rough on the surface 2. not bumpy

smoothly *adv.* 1. without bumps or roughness 2. without difficulties or mistakes

smudge *noun.* a smear; a dirty mark that does not have clear edges, usually made from rubbing

smug *adj.* too pleased with yourself

smuggle *verb.* **(smuggled, smuggling)** bring a person or an object into or out of a place secretly —**smuggling** *noun.* (no plural)

smuggler *noun.* someone who brings goods or people into a country illegally

snack *noun.* a small, quick meal

snag *noun.* an unexpected problem

snail *noun.* a slow-moving small creature with a shell on its back

snake *noun.* a long, cold-blooded animal that moves on its belly

snake *verb.* **(snaked, snaking)** move like a snake

snap *verb.* **(snapped, snapping)** break something sharply —**snappy** *adj.*

snapshot *noun.* a photograph

snatch *verb.* **(snatched, snatching)** grab roughly

sneak *verb.* **(sneaked, sneaking)** 1. come to a place quietly and secretly so as not to be seen 2. bring someone or something into a place without anyone seeing you

sneaker *noun.* a sports shoe

sneer *verb.* **(sneered, sneering)** smile in a way that shows you have a low opinion of someone

sneeze *verb.* **(sneezed, sneezing)** let out a loud burst of air through the nose

sniff *verb.* **(sniffed, sniffing)** smell something to find out about it —**sniff** *noun.*

snob *noun.* someone who thinks that he/she is much better than other people

snobbery *noun.* the behavior of snobs

snore *verb.* **(snored, snoring)** make a loud noise while you are sleeping — **snore** *noun.*

snow *noun.* white flakes that fall from the clouds when the weather is cold (no plural) —**snow** *verb.* **(snowed, snowing)**

snowball *noun.* a ball of snow

snowy *adj.* with snow

snuff *verb.* **(snuffed, snuffing)** put out a candle

snug *adj.* 1. feeling warm and comfortable 2. giving a feeling of warmth and comfort

so *adv.* 1. a word that tells how big, small, good, bad, important, etc, something is 2. very 3. as much or as many as this 4. also; too 5. a word that shows that you agree 6. a word that shows that you think or don't think that something is the case 7. that

so *conj.* that is why; therefore

soak *verb.* **(soaked, soaking)** leave something in water

soaked *adj.* very wet

soap *noun.* something that you use for bathing or washing things (no plural)

soap *verb.* **(soaped, soaping)** put soap on something

soar *verb.* **(soared, soaring)** 1. go high into the air 2. go up fast

sob *verb.* **(sobbed, sobbing)** cry very hard

sober *adj.* 1. not drunk 2. serious

so-called *adj.* a word that shows that you don't agree with what people say

soccer *noun.* a game played by two teams with 11 players each who try to score goals by kicking the ball

sociable *adj.* friendly

social *adj.* connected with people — **socially** *adv.*

socialism *noun.* an economic and social system of state ownership of the means of the economy and of equality of all the people

socialize *verb.* **(socialized, socializing)** be with people

social security *noun.* social welfare; a program where the government provides benefits for old-age, unemployment, health, etc

social worker *noun.* a person who is trained to help people who need special help

society *noun.* **1.** all the people (no plural) **2.** a particular group of people **3.** a group of people with a particular interest; a club (plural **societies**)

sociology *noun.* the study of the organization, function and development of human society and of social relations —**sociological** *adj.*

sock *noun.* something you wear on your foot under your shoe

socket *noun.* power point; outlet; where you plug in electrical equipment

soda *noun.* **1.** carbonated water; water with bubbles in it (no plural) **2.** a carbonated and flavored cold drink

sofa *adj.* a couch; a long piece of furniture for sitting on

soft *adj.* **1.** not firm; not hard **2.** light in color **3.** not loud **4.** smooth **5.** not firm enough **6.** pleasant; not harsh

soft drink *noun.* a drink that does not have alcohol in it

soften *verb.* **(softened, softening) 1.** become softer **2.** make soft

softly *adv.* **1.** with a low sound (opposite **loudly**) **2.** gently

softness *noun.* being soft (no plural)

software *noun.* programs used in operating a computer and directing it to do what the user wants

soggy *adj.* heavy with water

soil *noun.* earth

soil *verb.* **(soiled, soiling)** make dirty

solar *adj.* of or from the sun

sold *verb.* past tense and past participle of **sell**

soldier *noun.* someone who serves in the army

sole *noun.* **1.** the bottom of a foot **2.** the bottom of a shoe **3.** a flat fish that is good to eat

sole *adj.* only

solely *adv.* the only one

solemn *adj.* serious —**solemnly** *adv.*

solicit *verb.* **(solicited, soliciting) 1.** ask for; request; petition **2.** offer to have sex for money

solicitor *noun.* **1.** someone who goes from place to place selling things; a peddler **2.** a lawyer (in England) who gives advice and can represent clients in lower courts

solid *noun.* something that is not a liquid or a gas

solid *adj.* **1.** hard; firm **2.** strong; not easily broken **3.** firm; committed **4.** not mixed with anything else —**solidly** *adv.*

solidarity *noun.* loyalty and support among a group of people, especially when they struggle for something (no plural)

solitary *adj.* alone; without other things or people

solo *noun.* music that only one person plays or sings

solo *adv.* alone

soloist *noun.* someone who plays or sings a solo

solution *noun.* **1.** the answer to a problem **2.** a mixture of something with a liquid

solve *verb.* **(solved, solving)** find an answer to a problem, a mystery, etc

solvent *noun.* something that can cause something else to dissolve

solvent *adj.* being able to pay your debts

some *adj.* **1.** a little; a few; a certain amount of something (it does not matter exactly how much) **2.** part of **3.** unknown **—some** *pron.* (use **any** in a negative sentence or a question)

somebody, someone *pron.* a person; any person (use **anybody** in a negative sentence)

somehow *adv.* **1.** in any way that is possible **2.** a word that shows that you don't know how something was done

someone *pron.* somebody

someplace *adv.* a word that tells that you are not sure where

something *pron.* **1.** a word that you use if you do not know what a thing is **2.** a word that you use if it doesn't matter what the thing is

sometime *adv.* at an unknown time in the future or past

sometimes *adv.* not often but now and then

somewhat *adv.* to some extent; not very much; slightly; a little

somewhere *adv.* see **someplace**

son *noun.* someone's male child

song *noun.* music that you sing

songwriter *noun.* someone who writes the music (and sometimes also the words) of a song

son-in-law *noun.* the husband of your daughter (plural **sons-in-law**)

soon *adv.* **(sooner, soonest)** a short time from now

—sooner or later used to say something must happen, although possibly not soon

—the sooner the better used to say something should happen as soon as possible

soot *noun.* the black powder left over from burning

soothe *verb.* **(soothed, soothing) 1.** make calmer **2.** make less painful

soothing *adj.* making less angry, excited, frightened or painful

sophisticated *adj.* **1.** not naive; worldly; cultured **2.** complicated (especially modern and high-tech)

soprano *noun.* the highest singing voice (of a woman or child) or an instrument that makes music with a high range of notes (plural **sopranos**)

sore *noun.* a small, painful wound

sore *adj.* **1.** painful **2.** (slang) angry

sorely *adv.* badly; very much

sorrow *noun.* sadness (opposite **joy**)

sort *noun.* **1.** things that are very much alike **2.** a type; a kind

sort *verb.* **(sorted, sorting)** separate into types

so-so *adj. adv.* not so good and not so bad

sought *verb.* past tense and past participle of **seek**

soul *noun.* **1.** a person's spirit **2.** a person

sound *noun.* **1.** what you hear (no plural) **2.** something that you hear **3.** the impression that something makes (no plural)

sound *verb.* **(sounded, sounding) 1.** give a certain impression; seem **2.** give a signal by making a noise with something **3.** make a noise

sound *adj.* **1.** healthy; in good condition **2.** thorough

soundtrack *noun.* the music from a movie

soup *noun.* a liquid cooked food that you eat with a spoon

sour *adj.* **1.** having a sharp taste, like lemon juice or vinegar (opposite **sweet**) **2.** spoiled; gone bad

source *noun.* where something comes from

south *noun.* one of the four directions (no plural; opposite **north**)

south *adj.* southern

southeast *noun. adj.* the direction between south and east

southern *adj.* of or from the south (opposite **northern**)

southerner *noun.* someone from the south

souvenir *noun.* a thing that brings memories of a place or a person

soviet, Soviet *adj. noun.* connected to the former USSR (= the Soviet Union)

sow *verb.* (**sowed, sown, sowing**) plant seeds in the earth

spa *noun.* a resort with mineral springs; a place where someone can get health treatment (such as a massage)

space *noun.* 1. the universe (no plural) 2. room (no plural) 3. a place 4. the distance between two things

space *verb.* (**spaced, spacing**) place things or people with spaces between

spacecraft, spaceship *noun.* a machine that travels in outer space

space shuttle *noun.* a reusable spacecraft

spacious *adj.* big; with a lot of room

spade *noun.* 1. a tool for digging; a shovel 2. one of the four shapes on playing cards appearing like a pointed leaf

spaghetti *noun.* an Italian food made from flour and water, that is cut into thin strands and then cooked in boiling water

span *noun.* 1. a period between two points in time 2. the distance between two points or sides

Spaniard *noun.* someone from Spain

Spanish *noun.* the language spoken in Spain, and most of South and Central America —**Spanish** *adj.*

spare *verb.* (**spared, sparing**) 1. not give trouble or pain when you could 2. afford to give

spare *adj.* 1. extra; that you can use if necessary 2. free; not busy

spark *noun.* a tiny piece of fire

sparkle *verb.* (**sparkled, sparkling**) be bright; send out light —**sparkling** *adj.*

sparrow *noun.* a small brownish bird that is found in many places of the world

spat *verb.* past tense and past participle of **spit**

spawn *verb.* (**spawned, spawning**) (of fish) lay large numbers of eggs

speak *verb.* (**spoke, spoken, speaking**) 1. use words 2. know a language 3. talk in a certain way 4. give a speech 5. have a conversation

speaker *noun.* 1. someone who makes a speech 2. someone who knows a certain language 3. the part of a radio, etc, where the sound comes from

special *adj.* 1. important and different from the usual 2. your best or closest 3. important to you 4. better than the ordinary —**specialty** *noun.* (plural **specialties**)

specialist *noun.* 1. an expert 2. a doctor who is an expert in a particular thing

specialize *verb.* (**specialized, specializing**) 1. carry a certain kind of product 2. be an expert in something —**specialization** *noun.*

specially *adv.* for the particular reason

species *noun.* a group of living things that are the same in many ways (no plural)

specific *adj.* 1. one in particular 2. detailed and exact

specifically *adv.* in particular —**specification** *noun.*

specify *verb.* (**specified, specifying**) give exact details

specimen *noun.* 1. an example of a certain type of thing 2. a small piece of something for testing to see what the rest is like

speck *noun.* a tiny spot or piece

spectacle *noun.* a big show for many people

spectacles *noun plural.* specs; glasses; eyeglasses (**glasses** is much more usual)

spectacular *adj.* 1. wonderful; unusual; exciting 2. great; much more than expected

spectator *noun.* someone who watches a sports event

speculate *verb.* (**speculated, speculating**) make a guess without having facts

speculative *adj.* 1. based on guesses 2. theoretical

sped verb. past tense and past participle of **speed**

speech noun. 1. the ability to talk (no plural) 2. a talk that someone gives in front of other people

speed noun. 1. how fast something moves 2. drive fast (no plural)

speed verb. **(sped/speeded, speeding)** 1. move fast 2. drive too fast

speeding noun. driving faster than the speed limit allows (no plural)

speed limit noun. the maximum legal speed for a car, etc

speedy adj. fast; quick (opposite **slow**)

spell noun. a magic effect

spell verb. **(spelled/spelt, spelling)** put together a word by using the right letters

spelling noun. 1. writing correctly (no plural) 2. the correct way to write something

spend verb. **(spent, spending)** use money for payment

spice noun. something that gives taste to food

spicy adj. sharp-tasting; full of spices

spider noun. a very small eight-legged creature with a body that is divided into two parts and that spins a web

spill verb. **(spilled/spilt, spilling)** pour liquid or salt, sugar, etc, out of something by accident

spin verb. **(spun, spinning)** 1. go around and around 2. turn around suddenly 3. make something go around and around 4. make thread 5. make something with threads 6. tell people good things about yourself or a politician or businessperson; engage in public relations work

spinach noun. a soft dark green leafy vegetable

spine noun. the backbone

spin-off noun. 1. something that is a by-product of something else 2. a TV program that is based on characters or an idea from a different (pre-existing) TV program

spiral noun. something with a screw shape; a coil; a curved line winding around a central point

spire noun. a tall pointed roof (on top of a church)

spirit noun. 1. the part of a person that is not the body; the mind; the soul (no plural) 2. a ghost

spirit noun. an alcoholic drink, like whiskey or vodka

spirited adj. full of liveliness

spirits noun plural. someone's mood

spiritual adj. connected with the mind and the feelings, not the body

spit noun. the natural liquid in your mouth; saliva (no plural)

spit verb. **(spat, spitting)** throw saliva out of your mouth

spite noun. a wish to annoy or harm the plans of another person (no plural) — **spite** verb. **(spited, spiting)**

splash verb. **(splashed, splashing)** 1. throw water 2. make liquid jump up 3. play in water

splendid adj. 1. very grand 2. wonderful; excellent

split noun. a division

split verb. **(split, splitting)** 1. break something into two pieces 2. separate into two parts 3. divide something among people —**splitting** adj.

spoil verb. **(spoiled/spoilt, spoiling)** 1. go bad; become rotten or sour 2. ruin something 3. give too much; not be firm enough —**spoiled, spoilt** adj.

spoke, spoken verb. past tense and past participle of **speak**

spoken adj. as people speak; not written

spokesperson noun. someone who speaks in the place of someone else or in the name of a group, a business, an organization, a government office, etc (also for a man **spokesman**, for a woman **spokeswoman**)

sponge noun. something soft and full of holes that we use for bathing or washing things

sponge *verb.* (**sponged, sponging**) use a sponge for bathing or washing something

sponsor *noun.* 1. someone who supports or takes the responsibility for the efforts of someone else 2. a business that pays for a sports event, a performance, a broadcast, etc —**sponsor** *verb.* (**sponsored, sponsoring**)

sponsorship *noun.* money collected from sponsors

spontaneous *adj.* not planned in advance —**spontaneously** *adv.*

spool *noun.* something round that you can wind thread, film or wires on

spoon *noun.* a round tool with a handle that you use for stirring or for eating soft foods or liquid

spoonful *noun.* the amount that a spoon holds (plural **spoonfuls**)

sport *noun.* a game or exercises that you do with your body

sport *verb.* (**sported, sporting**) wear proudly

sports *noun plural.* all sports

sports car *noun.* a fast low car that has a removable roof and can seat only two people

sporty *adj.* showy and brightly-colored, especially informal clothes

spot *noun.* 1. a round mark of a different color from the rest 2. a small, dirty mark 3. a place

spot *verb.* (**spotted, spotting**) see something or someone

spotlight *noun.* a light on an actor in the theater

spotted *adj.* with spots

spouse *noun.* someone's husband or wife

spout *noun.* 1. a pipe that water comes out of 2. a short pipe on the side of a kettle

sprang *verb.* past of **spring**

sprawl *verb.* (**sprawled, sprawling**) lie with your body stretched out

spray *noun.* 1. water that falls in small drops 2. something that comes out of a bottle or a machine in a stream of small drops 3. a small bunch of flowers

spray *verb.* (**sprayed, spraying**) use a bottle or a machine to make a spray

spread *noun.* 1. an increase; becoming more and more (no plural) 2. something that you put on bread or crackers with a knife 3. something soft that you use for a covering

spread *verb.* (**spread, spreading**) 1. become bigger and bigger 2. become more and more 3. open something that was folded 4. cover something with something else 5. put butter, jam, etc, on bread or crackers with a knife

spreadsheet *noun.* a page used by accountants to keep track of accounts and/or finances

spring *noun.* 1. one of the four seasons (no plural) 2. a stream of clear water under the ground 3. a piece of metal that is twisted so that it jumps back into place if you push or pull it 4. a sudden long jump

spring *verb.* (**sprang, sprung, springing**) jump suddenly

sprinkle *verb.* (**sprinkled, sprinkling**) 1. fall lightly in small drops 2. scatter small drops or small bits of something

sprout *verb.* (**sprouted, sprouting**) begin to grow

spruce *adj.* clean and neat in appearance

sprung *verb.* past participle of **spring**

spun *verb.* past tense and past participle of **spin**

spur *noun.* 1. an incentive meant to encourage someone to go forward 2. an attachment to boots worn by horseback riders meant to force a horse to go faster

spy *noun.* someone who tries to find out your secrets for somebody else

spy *verb.* (**spied, spying**) try secretly to find out things

squabble *verb.* (**squabbled, squab-**

bling) quarrel over something unimportant

squad noun. a group of people who are trained to work together as a team

square noun. 1. a figure with four equal sides and four equal angles 2. a large, open area in a city, sometimes in the form of a square or circle 3. when you multiply a number by the same number

square adj. with the shape of a square

squash noun. 1. a hard-skinned vegetable, usually eaten cooked 2. a sport in which a racket is used to hit a ball against four walls of an indoor court

squash verb. (squashed, squashing) 1. crush and break something 2. crush something out of its shape 3. squeeze

squeak verb. (squeaked, squeaking) make a short, high sound

squeeze noun. a press

squeeze verb. (squeezed, squeezing) 1. press something to get juice from it 2. press between two things

squint verb. (squinted, squinting) make your eyes narrow to look at something

squirt verb. (squirted, squirting) 1. make liquid burst out of something 2. burst out in a sudden flow

stab noun. 1. a sharp cut in the body 2. a sudden sharp pain

stab verb. (stabbed, stabbing) stick a knife or another sharp weapon into someone

stabbing noun. killing or injuring with a knife

stable noun. a building where horses live

stable adj. steady; not changing (opposite **unstable**) **—stability** noun. **—stabilize** verb. (stabilized, stabilizing)

stack noun. a neat pile

stack verb. (stacked, stacking) make a neat pile of something

stadium noun. an outdoor area for sports that has seats all around it

staff noun. a group of people who work

at the same place (singular and plural) **—staff** verb. (staffed, staffing)

stage noun. 1. a place where actors, dancers, etc, appear in front of an audience 2. the theater (no plural) 3. a certain point in time while something is happening 4. a certain period in someone's development

stagger verb. (staggered, staggering) walk very unsteadily

stagnant adj. 1. (of water) standing; not flowing 2. not developing

stain noun. a dirty mark on something that is hard to get out

stain verb. (stained, staining) make a stain

stained glass noun. different pieces of colored glass used to make a decorative window especially of a church

stainless adj. not easily marked by dirt, rust, etc

stainless steel noun. steel that does not rust

stair noun. one of a series of steps

staircase, stairway noun. stairs inside a building, usually with a railing at the side

stake noun. 1. a pointed stick pushed into the ground to hold ropes of a tent in place 2. in olden times, the pole someone was tied to before being burned to death 3. something (like money, a reputation, etc) that is at risk **—stake** verb. (staked, staking)

stale adj. not fresh

stalk noun. a long stem

stall noun. 1. a small, open shop where you can buy things in the street 2. a narrow space with walls inside a building or a room

stall verb. (stalled, stalling) do something more slowly than you need to

stammer verb. (stammered, stammering) repeat the same sounds when you speak; stutter

stamp noun. 1. a small sticker that you stick on a letter, etc, for sending it 2. a certain mark that gives information 3. a small tool that you press down to make a mark on something

stamp verb. **(stamped, stamping)** 1. hit your foot hard on the ground 2. put a postage stamp on something 3. use a small press that makes a certain mark

stand noun. 1. a small outdoor shop 2. something that holds a certain thing 3. your opinion on an issue

stand verb. **(stood, standing)** 1. be on your feet 2. get up from a sitting position 3. lean something against something else 4. put something in a standing position

standard noun. a level that is good enough

standard adj. usual; ordinary

standardize verb. **(standardized, standardizing)** make everything according to the same standard

standard of living noun. the level at which someone lives

star noun. 1. one of the points of light that shine in the sky 2. something in the shape of a star 3. a famous performer

star verb. **(starred, starring)** have the leading role in a play or movie

stare noun. a long, fixed look

stare verb. **(stared, staring)** look at someone or something for a long time

start noun. 1. a beginning 2. the beginning of a trip 3. a small jump of surprise

start verb. **(started, starting)** 1. begin 2. begin to do something 3. make something begin to work or move 4. jump suddenly because you are surprised

starter noun. a device that makes a motor start working

startle verb. **(startled, startling)** surprise someone suddenly

start-up, start up noun. 1. a new company needing investment funds 2. starting in motion; the act of starting something

starvation noun. extreme hunger (no plural)

starve verb. **(starved, starving)** 1. suffer from hunger 2. not let someone have food 3. (informal) be very hungry

starving adj. dying of hunger

state noun. 1. a country 2. a part of a country 3. the condition that something or someone is in

state verb. **(stated, stating)** say something definitely

statement noun. what someone says clearly or definitely

state-of-the-art adj. the latest and most modern (especially technology)

statewide adj. throughout the state

static adj. noun. 1. not moving 2. electrical interference

station noun. 1. a place where passengers get on and off a train or a bus that goes from one city to another 2. a place where buses begin and end their route 3. a building for a certain kind of work

stationery noun. paper for writing letters (no plural)

statistic noun. a number in a collection of data that represent facts

statistics noun plural. a collection of numbers that represent facts

statue noun. a figure made of stone, metal, wood, etc

status noun. someone's position in society, at work, etc (no plural)

stay noun. the time that you spend visiting a certain place

stay verb. **(stayed, staying)** 1. live somewhere for a short period 2. remain 3. not move 4. be a guest at a place

steadily adv. without stopping

steady adj. 1. firm 2. regular 3. not shaking

steak noun. a thick piece of meat that you cook on a grill

steal verb. **(stole, stolen, stealing)** take something that does not belong to you —**stolen** adj.

steam *noun.* **1.** the gas that rises from boiling water (no plural) **2.** the power that steam produces

steam *verb.* **(steamed, steaming) 1.** let out steam **2.** cook over steam

steamed *adj.* cooked over steam

steaming *adj.* very hot

steel *noun.* a strong metal that is made of iron and carbon

steep *adj.* **1.** sloping sharply **2.** very expensive

steer *verb.* **(steered, steering)** move something in a certain direction

steering wheel *noun.* a wheel that you turn to move a car, bus, etc, in the direction that you want

stem *noun.* the tall part of a plant that the flowers grow from

step *noun.* **1.** one movement of the foot in walking **2.** a stair **3.** a stage in doing something

step *verb.* **(stepped, stepping)** move one foot in a certain direction

stepfather *noun.* a man who is married to your mother but is not your real father

stepmother *noun.* a woman who is married to your father but is not your real mother

stereo *noun.* a record or compact disc player that has sound coming from two speakers

stereotype *noun.* a fixed oversimplified opinion about what a group of people or something is like —**stereotype** *verb.* **(stereotyped, stereotyping)**

sterile *adj.* free from germs

sterling *noun.* British money

stern *adj.* **1.** strict; demanding obedience **2.** without humor; showing that you do not approve

stew *noun.* meat that you cook slowly in a pot with water

steward, stewardess *noun.* **1.** someone who looks after another's property or finances **2.** a person who takes care of passengers on a plane; a flight attendant

stick *noun.* a thin piece of wood

stick *verb.* **(stuck, sticking) 1.** stay fastened to something **2.** glue two things together **3.** push a sharp point into something

sticker *noun.* a small piece of paper that you stick on something

sticky *adj.* covered with something that sticks

stiff *adj.* **1.** not easy to bend or move **2.** not soft —**stiffly** *adv.*

still *adv.* **1.** up to this time or that time **2.** nevertheless; anyway; even so **3.** even more so

still *adj.* without motion

stimulate *verb.* **(stimulated, stimulating)** activate; encourage —**stimulation** *noun.*

stimulus *noun.* something that stimulates (plural **stimuli**)

sting *noun.* **1.** the pricking of a bee or other insect **2.** a sharp pain

sting *verb.* **(stung, stinging) 1.** cause pain by pricking **2.** give sharp pain to the skin **3.** feel sharp pain —**stinging** *adj.*

stink *verb.* **(stank, stunk, stinking)** smell terrible —**stinking** *adj.*

stipulate *verb.* **(stipulated, stipulating)** make a condition (in order to reach an agreement)

stir *noun.* unusual excitement

stir *verb.* **(stirred, stirring) 1.** move a liquid around, usually with a spoon **2.** move

stitch *noun.* **1.** a piece of thread that shows one in-and-out movement of a needle **2.** a loop of wool on a knitting needle

stitch *verb.* **(stitched, stitching)** sew; put stitches in something

stock *noun.* **1.** a large amount of something in reserve **2.** a share in owning a business

stockbroker *noun.* someone whose job is to buy and sell stocks, bonds and shares for someone else

stockholder *noun.* the owner of stocks, bonds and shares

stocking *noun.* a long covering for the leg

stock market, stock-exchange *noun.* a place where stocks, bonds and shares are bought and sold

stockpile *verb.* **(stockpiled, stockpiling)** collect something (such as food, arms, etc) in case it is necessary in the future **—stockpile** *noun.*

stole, stolen *verb.* past tense and past participle of **steal**

stomach *noun.* 1. the organ in the middle of your body that digests food 2. your belly

stone *noun.* 1. the hard material that rocks are made of (no plural) 2. a small piece of rock 3. a kind of rock that is worth a lot of money and is used for jewelry 4. a seed inside a fruit; a pit

stone *verb.* **(stoned, stoning)** throw stones at someone or something

stone *adj.* made of stone

stony *adj.* full of stones

stood *verb.* past tense and past participle of **stand**

stool *noun.* a chair with no back

stoop *verb.* **(stooped, stooping)** bend down

stooped *adj.* bent over

stop *noun.* 1. standing still after moving (no plural) 2. a bus stop; a place where a bus picks up and lets off passengers

stop *verb.* **(stopped, stopping)** 1. (+ verb + -ing) quit doing what you were doing 2. (+ to + verb) stand still in order to do something 3. quit moving 4. make something quit moving 5. end; finish 6. prevent

stoppage *noun.* the state of being stopped

storage *noun.* keeping something in a place while not in use (no plural)

store *noun.* 1. a place where you buy things; a shop 2. a large amount of something that you keep in reserve

store *verb.* **(stored, storing)** 1. keep a supply of something in reserve 2. keep something in a place where it is not used

storekeeper *noun.* someone who owns a store

storm *noun.* a heavy rain with thunder, lightning and wind **—storm** *verb.* **(stormed, storming) —stormy** *adj.*

story *noun.* 1. a description of events that are usually imagined or made up 2. a level of a building; a floor (plural **stories**)

storyteller *noun.* 1. someone who tells a story 2. someone who tells little lies

stove *noun.* a machine for cooking or for keeping a room warm

straight *adj.* 1. not crooked or curved 2. not curly

straight *adv.* 1. directly 2. without bending over

straight away, right away *adv.* at once

straighten *verb.* **(straightened, straightening)** make something straight

straightforward *adj.* direct; honest

strain *noun.* too much pressure

strain *verb.* **(strained, straining)** 1. try very hard to do something 2. make something work too hard 3. pull too tightly 4. injure by pulling too tightly 5. use a device to separate liquid from solid pieces **—strainer** *noun.*

strait *noun.* a narrow passage of water connecting two larger bodies of water

straits *noun.* a very bad situation, especially because of no money

strand *noun.* a single hair, thread, etc

strange *adj.* 1. not usual; odd 2. not known **—strangely** *adv.*

stranger *noun.* 1. someone that you do not know 2. someone in a new place

strangle *verb.* **(strangled, strangling)** kill by pressing someone's throat

strap *noun.* a strip of leather or other strong material that holds something in place

strap *verb.* **(strapped, strapping)** hold something in place with a strap

strategist *noun.* an expert in strategy

strategy *noun.* **1.** a particular plan or the art of planning in advance, especially war tactics **2.** an overall plan — **strategic** *adj.* —**strategically** *adv.*

straw *noun.* **1.** dried stalks of wheat or other plants (no plural) **2.** a piece of straw **3.** a thin tube that you can use for drinking from a bottle, can, etc

straw *adj.* made of straw

strawberry *noun.* a small soft red juicy fruit that has little seeds on its outside (plural **strawberries**)

stray *noun.* a homeless animal

stray *adj.* **1.** not having a home **2.** that has lost its way

streak *noun.* **1.** a thin band that is different in color or quality from its surrounding **2.** a short period **3.** a quality that is different from the rest

stream *noun.* **1.** a small river **2.** a flow of water or other liquids

stream *verb.* **(streamed, streaming)** flow steadily

streamline *verb.* **(streamlined, streamlining) 1.** make narrow and smooth in order to allow water or air to pass around something more easily **2.** make an organization, business, etc, simpler and therefore more efficient

street *noun.* **1.** a road inside a town **2.** a road with buildings

strength *noun.* being strong (no plural)

strengthen *verb.* **(strengthened, strengthening)** make or become strong

stress *noun.* **1.** a sound that is heavier than the others in a word **2.** too much pressure **3.** too many worries

stress *verb.* **(stressed, stressing) 1.** make a sound heavier than the rest **2.** say that something is important — **stressful** *adj.*

stretch *verb.* **(stretched, stretching) 1.** become longer **2.** make something longer **3.** make something wider **4.** cover a space

stretcher *noun.* a kind of bed for carrying a sick or wounded person

stricken *adj.* showing the negative effect of an illness, misfortune, sorrow, etc

strict *adj.* **1.** insisting on obeying the rules; stern **2.** that must be obeyed

strictly *adv.* completely; absolutely

stride *noun.* **1.** a long step in walking **2.** an advancement in development

strike *noun.* **1.** a time when workers refuse to work **2.** an attack

strike *verb.* **(struck, stricken, striking) 1.** hit someone hard **2.** attack **3.** refuse to work (in order to get better conditions) **4.** make an impression

striker *noun.* **1.** a worker who is on strike **2.** (soccer) a player in an attacking position who tries to score goals

striking *adj.* **1.** good-looking **2.** unusual and showing style **3.** remarkable

string *noun.* **1.** a thin rope for tying things (no plural) **2.** a line of things connected together on a string or thread **3.** a piece of wire, plastic, etc, for certain musical instruments

string *verb.* **(strung, stringing)** put things on a string

stringent *adj.* strict and severe (rules, laws, limits, etc)

strip *noun.* something long and narrow

strip *verb.* **(stripped, stripping) 1.** take something off something else **2.** take clothes off

stripe *noun.* a line of color

striped *adj.* with stripes

stroke *noun.* **1.** a cutting blow **2.** the sound of the bell of a clock **3.** a sudden illness of the brain which can cause loss of speech, paralysis or death

stroke *verb.* **(stroked, stroking)** move your hand gently over something

stroll *noun.* an unhurried walk —**stroll** *verb.* **(strolled, strolling)**

strong adj. 1. physically powerful 2. not easy to break; able to carry heavy weight 3. having great force 4. with the power to do things 5. sharp in smell or taste 6. easily remembered

stronghold noun. 1. a place where an army is strongly in position 2. a center for a group with certain opinions

strongly adv. very much

struck verb. past tense and past participle of **strike**

structure noun. 1. a building 2. (grammar) the way that a sentence is built

structure verb. (**structured, structuring**) arrange in an organized way — **structural** adj.

struggle noun. a fight

struggle verb. (**struggled, struggling**) make a very great effort to do something

strung verb. past tense and past participle of **string**

stubborn adj. refusing to obey or listen to advice; obstinate; determined — **stubbornly** adv.

stuck verb. past tense and past participle of **stick**

stuck adj. not able to move

stud noun. 1. a small button-like item that can be attached to shoes, tires, clothing, etc 2. a horse kept for breeding —**studded** adj.

student noun. 1. someone who goes to school 2. someone who studies or has studied a particular subject

studies noun plural. the things that you are learning

studio noun. 1. a room where a painter or a photographer works 2. a place where radio or TV broadcasts are recorded

study noun. 1. learning about a certain thing 2. a small, private room where you can work (plural **studies**)

study verb. (**studied, studying**) 1. do school work 2. learn everything that you can about something or someone

3. learn by using something (compare with **learn: studying** is an activity, **learning** is the result)

stuff noun. 1. substance 2. things

stuff verb. (**stuffed, stuffing**) 1. fill with something 2. put a filling into food before you cook it

stuffed adj. filled with something else

stuffing noun. something you fill food with

stuffy adj. too warm and without fresh air

stumble verb. (**stumbled, stumbling**) 1. walk unsteadily 2. hit against something and fall

stumbling block noun. a problem or situation that prevents progress

stump noun. a small piece of something that is left when the rest is gone

stun verb. (**stunned, stunning**) 1. temporarily stop someone by causing him/her to be momentarily unconscious 2. shock; surprise

stung verb. past tense and past participle of **sting**

stunt noun. a trick (especially showing great skillfulness or daring) to attract attention

stupid adj. 1. not clever or bright 2. foolish; done without thinking

stupidity noun. foolishness (no plural)

stutter verb. (**stuttered, stuttering**) repeat a sound several times when you talk; stammer

style noun. 1. fashion 2. a way of doing something 3. a certain appearance

style, stylize verb. (**styled/stylized, styling/stylizing**) design hair, clothing or furniture in a certain way; give a distinctive style

stylish adj. fashionable —**stylistic** adj.

stylist noun. 1. someone who develops styles of fashion, hairdressing, etc 2. someone who develops a good writing or speaking style

subcommittee noun. a part of a committee, formed to deal with a particular subject within the work of the committee

subconscious *adj.* feelings and thoughts that are in the mind but that you are not fully aware of

subject *noun.* 1. something that people talk or write about 2. something that you study at a school 3. (grammar) a noun or a phrase that tells who or what performs the action 4. a citizen of a country that has a king or queen

subject *verb.* **(subjected, subjecting)** 1. conquer 2. force someone to experience something

subjective *adj.* 1. influenced by personal feelings (opposite **objective**) 2. (grammar) connected to the subject of a sentence

submarine *noun.* a boat that can stay under the water

submission *noun.* the act of submitting or being submitted

submit *verb.* **(submitted, submitting)** 1. give in an application, plan, proposal, etc, to be considered by someone else 2. admit defeat; accept another's rule over you

subordinate *noun. adj.* someone less important or lower in rank (opposite **superior**)

subscribe *verb.* **(subscribed, subscribing)** 1. pay money to have a newspaper or magazine sent to you regularly 2. hold an opinion or belief

subscription *noun.* 1. having a newspaper or magazine sent to you regularly 2. payment in advance for a certain number of shows, sports events, etc

subsection *noun.* a subdivision of a section

subsequent *adj.* following in time, order or place —**subsequently** *adv.*

subsidiary *noun.* a company that is owned and controlled by a different company

subsidiary *adj.* 1. meant to help or add to something 2. secondary

subsidy *noun.* financial help to keep

costs down —**subsidize** *verb.* **(subsidized, subsidizing)**

substance *noun.* a type of thing; a material; stuff

substantial *adj.* of real importance or value; quite large in amount

substantiate *verb.* **(substantiated, substantiating)** bring proof that something is true

substitute *noun.* 1. a thing that replaces something else 2. someone who replaces someone else for a certain period of time

substitute *verb.* **(substituted, substituting)** 1. use one thing instead of another thing 2. do something in place of the usual person

subtle *adj.* 1. not obvious; not easy to notice 2. clever and devious 3. delicate —**subtly** *adj.*

subtlety *noun.* 1. a complicated detail 2. a fine distinction, difficult to understand

subtract *verb.* **(subtracted, subtracting)** take one number away from another number (opposite **add**)

suburb *noun.* an area just outside a big city —**suburban** *adj.*

subway *noun.* an underground train system, usually in a city

succeed *verb.* **(succeeded, succeeding)** 1. come after 2. do what you intended to do

success *noun.* 1. achieving what you hoped to do; succeeding in what you are trying to do (no plural) 2. something that has come out well (plural **successes**)

successful *adj.* 1. having success; doing well 2. able to do what you tried to do —**successfully** *adv.*

succession *noun.* one after the other

such *adj. pron.* 1. of that kind 2. a word that tells how much

suck *verb.* **(sucked, sucking)** 1. pull on something with your lips 2. let something melt inside your mouth

sudden *adj.* quick; without any warning —**suddenly** *adv.*

sue *verb.* **(sued, suing)** bring legal action against someone else

suffer *verb.* **(suffered, suffering)** feel pain or misery

sufferer *noun.* someone who suffers

suffering *noun.* pain or misery (no plural)

suffice *verb.* **(sufficed)** (formal) be enough

sufficient *adj.* enough (opposite **insufficient**) —**sufficiency** *noun.* —**sufficiently** *adv.* (opposite **insufficiently**)

suffocate *verb.* **(suffocated, suffocating)** 1. not have enough air 2. die from not having enough air

sugar *noun.* what you put into food to make it sweet (no plural)

suggest *verb.* **(suggested, suggesting)** say what you think is a good idea

suggestion *noun.* what someone says is a good idea

suicide *noun.* killing yourself (no plural)

suit *noun.* 1. two or more pieces of clothing that go together; a jacket and trousers or a jacket and skirt 2. one of the four sets of playing cards (hearts, diamonds, spades, clubs)

suit *verb.* **(suited, suiting)** 1. be what you like or what you want 2. look good on someone

suitable *adj.* appropriate or right for something (opposite **unsuitable**) —**suitability** *noun.*

suitably *adv.* in the correct way (opposite **unsuitably**)

suitcase *noun.* something that you carry your clothes in when you travel

suite *noun.* 1. a number of joined rooms in a hotel 2. a piece of music with loosely connected parts

sum *noun.* 1. the answer when you add two or more numbers 2. an amount of money —**sum** *verb.* **(summed, summing)**

summarize *verb.* **(summarized, summa-rizing)** give the main points about something

summary *noun.* a short description of something

summer *noun.* 1. the hot season of the year (no plural) 2. a particular summer —**summer** *adj.*

sun *noun.* 1. the big star in the sky that gives us light and heat during the daylight hours 2. light or heat from the sun

Sunday *noun.* the first day of the week

sunflower *noun.* a big, yellow flower with a dark center that grows in the sun

sung *verb.* past participle of **sing**

sunglasses *noun plural.* dark glasses to protect your eyes from the sun

sunk *verb.* past participle of **sink**

sunken *adj.* of something that has sunk

sunlight *noun.* light from the sun (no plural)

sunny *adj.* with sunshine

sunrise *noun.* the coming up of the sun

sunscreen *noun.* cream or oil for the skin to prevent sunburn

sunset *noun.* the going down of the sun

sunshine *noun.* light from the sun (no plural)

super *noun.* short for superintendent; a janitor in an apartment house

super *adj.* (informal) great; excellent

superb *adj.* excellent; outstanding —**superbly** *adv.*

superficial *adj.* 1. not deep; on the surface only 2. not thorough or complete

superfluous *adj.* extra and unnecessary

superior *noun.* someone who is above you in position or rank

superior *adj.* 1. above you in rank 2. better —**superiority** *noun.*

superlative *noun.* (grammar) the form of an adjective or adverb that tells you that something is the most

supermarket *noun.* a very big store where you can buy food and other things

supermodel *noun.* a very highly paid model who is very much in demand

supernatural *adj.* something beyond what is explainable by nature

superpower *noun.* a nation that is very powerful economically, politically and militarily with worldwide influence

supersede *verb.* **(superseded, superseding)** take the place of someone or something usually because it is an improvement over something older

superstar *noun.* someone in show business, sports, etc, who is extremely popular

superstition *noun.* a belief in things that bring good luck, bad luck, etc (no plural)

superstitious *adj.* having superstitions

superstore *noun.* a very large store (sometimes located on the outskirts of a city) with a lot of parking space and usually very cheap prices, selling food, clothing, electrical goods, etc

supervise *verb.* **(supervised, supervising)** be in charge of a group of people

supervision *noun.* inspecting the work or behavior of other people (no plural)

supervisor *noun.* someone who supervises the work of other people **supervisory** *adj.*

supper *noun.* the last meal of the day

supplement *noun.* something in addition (in order to complete it)

supplies *noun plural.* the things that you need

supply *noun.* the amount of something that you have

supply *verb.* **(supplied, supplying)** provide —**supplier** *noun.*

support *verb.* **(supported, supporting)** 1. bear the weight of something; keep something from falling 2. give someone money to live on 3. say that something is good or right 4. encourage someone

supporter *noun.* 1. someone who thinks that a certain idea is good 2. a fan; someone who wants a certain team, candidate, etc, to win

supportive *adj.* giving encouragement

suppose *verb.* **(supposed, supposing)** 1. think; guess; believe 2. imagine

suppose, supposing *conj.* what if

supposedly *adv.* it is believed to be (possibly wrongly)

supreme *adj.* the most important

surcharge *noun.* an additional charge or tax

sure *adj.* certain; having no doubt

surely *adv.* 1. certainly; without doubt 2. it must or cannot be so

surf *verb.* **(surfed, surfing)** 1. ride the waves of an ocean on a special board 2. move around the Internet looking at different sites

surface *noun.* 1. the part that is on the outside 2. the smooth top of liquid

surgeon *noun.* a doctor who operates on people or animals

surgery *noun.* a medical operation (no plural)

surgical *adj.* used in surgery

surname *noun.* a last name; a family name

surpass *verb.* **(surpassed, surpassing)** go beyond in amount, quality or degree; exceed

surplus *adj.* an amount that is more than used or needed

surprise *noun.* 1. the feeling that you get when you see or hear something unexpected (no plural) 2. an unexpected present

surprise *verb.* **(surprised, surprising)** be or do something unexpected

surprising *adj.* not expected; giving a feeling of surprise —**surprisingly** *adv.*

surrender *noun.* a declaration that you have lost a war

surrender *verb.* **(surrendered, surrendering)** 1. give up fighting; declare you have lost a war 2. hand something over to someone

surround *verb.* **(surrounded, surrounding)** be or go all around something

surroundings *noun plural.* everything that is around you; environment

survey *noun.* a study that is made by asking people questions or by making a detailed inspection —**survey** *verb.* **(surveyed, surveying)**

surveyor *noun.* someone whose profession is to measure and record the exact dimensions of a tract of land or to professionally examine a piece of property

survival *noun.* staying alive (no plural)

survive *verb.* **(survived, surviving)** stay alive

surviving *adj.* still alive

survivor *noun.* someone who is still alive after something terrible has happened

suspect *noun.* someone that the police believe is guilty

suspect *verb.* **(suspected, suspecting)** have a feeling that something bad has happened

suspend *verb.* **(suspended, suspending)** **1.** hang above **2.** postpone **3.** stop **4.** prevent from taking part **5.** hold in the air or a liquid —**suspension** *noun.*

suspense *noun.* excitement about how something is going to end (no plural)

suspicion *noun.* **1.** believing bad things about people (no plural) **2.** a feeling that someone is doing something bad or that something bad happened

suspicious *adj.* **1.** feeling suspicion **2.** seeming dishonest **3.** making you think that something is wrong

suspiciously *adv.* **1.** feeling that harm may come to you **2.** making you feel suspicion

sustain *verb.* **(sustained, sustaining) 1.** keep, hold, or support **2.** suffer **3.** (law) accept as being correct —**sustainable** *adj.*

swallow *noun.* **1.** the act of swallowing **2.** a kind of small bird with a forked tail

swallow *verb.* **(swallowed, swallowing)** pass food or liquid down your throat

swam *verb.* past of **swim**

swamp *noun.* soft, muddy land

swan *noun.* a long-necked, usually white but sometimes black, bird from the duck family that lives on rivers and lakes

sway *verb.* **(swayed, swaying) 1.** move slowly from side to side **2.** influence a person

swear *verb.* **(swore, sworn, swearing) 1.** make an absolute promise; promise in the name of God; take an oath **2.** use bad language

sweat *noun.* drops of water that come out through your skin; perspiration (no plural) —**sweat** *verb.* **(sweat/sweated, sweating)**

sweater *noun.* a warm piece of clothing usually made of wool or acrylic

sweatshirt *noun.* a kind of shirt made of thick cotton cloth that you wear for sports

sweaty *adj.* **1.** covered with sweat **2.** full of sweat; smelling of sweat

Swedish *noun.* the people of Sweden; the language spoken in Sweden —**Swedish** *adj.*

sweep *verb.* **(swept, sweeping)** use a broom to clean the floor —**sweep, sweeping** *noun.* —**sweeper** *noun.*

sweet *adj.* **1.** having the taste of sugar or honey **2.** pleasant and kind **3.** cute

sweeten *verb.* **(sweetened, sweetening)** make sweet

sweetener *noun.* stuff that makes food taste sweet but is not made of sugar

sweetheart *noun.* **1.** someone of the opposite sex that you love **2.** a name that you call someone you love

sweets *noun plural.* candies and sweet food in general

swell *verb.* **(swelled, swollen, swelling)** become bigger than the normal size —**swelling** *noun.*

swept *verb.* past tense and past participle of **sweep**

swerve *verb.* **(swerved, swerving)** turn sharply

swift adj. 1. that can move fast 2. quick; prompt

swiftly adv. quickly; fast

swim verb. (swam, swum, swimming) move yourself through water —**swim, swimming** noun.

swimmer noun. someone who swims

swimming pool noun. a place that is filled with water for swimming

swimsuit noun. a special piece of clothing for a woman or girl to wear for swimming or lying on the beach; a bathing suit

swindle verb. (swindled, swindling) cheat someone in order to get money from them —**swindle** noun.

swine noun. a pig; pigs

swing noun. a seat that hangs on a rope or a chain which you can ride back and forth on

swing verb. (swung, swinging) 1. move back and forth from a fixed place 2. ride on a swing 3. make something move back and forth

Swiss noun. the people of Switzerland —**Swiss** adj.

switch noun. 1. a kind of button that you press to turn something on or off 2. an exchange

switch verb. (switched, switching) 1. exchange 2. change

switchboard noun. a unit where numerous telephones are connected and can be controlled

swollen adj. bigger than the normal size

sword noun. a weapon with a long, sharp blade

swore, sworn verb. past tense and past participle of **swear**

swung verb. past participle of **swing**

syllable noun. a part of a word that has one vowel sound

syllabus noun. a curriculum; an outline of a course of studies (plural **syllabuses** or **syllabi**)

symbol noun. 1. a picture or mark that has a meaning 2. something that represents an idea

symbolize verb. (symbolized, symbolizing) be a symbol

symmetry noun. a pleasing balance; the exact likeness in size, shape, etc — **symmetrical** adv.

sympathetic adj. feeling or showing sympathy —**sympathetically** adv.

sympathize verb. (sympathized, sympathizing) share someone else's feelings of sadness, worry, etc; have sympathy with/for

sympathy noun. sharing or understanding the sad feelings of others (no plural)

symphony noun. music written to be played by an orchestra, with four main parts

symptom noun. a sign of illness

symptomatic adj. showing a certain bad condition or symptom

synagogue noun. a Jewish place of worship

synonym noun. a word with the same meaning —**synonymous** adj.

synthesis noun. 1. the combination of different ideas, etc 2. the production of sound, music, etc, by electronic means

synthesizer noun. an electric musical instrument with a keyboard that can make many different types of sounds

synthetic adj. artificial; not produced naturally

syrup noun. a thick, sweet liquid

system noun. 1. a group of parts that work together 2. a method for doing something

systematic adj. doing things in an orderly way —**systematically** adv.

T

table *noun*. **1.** a piece of furniture for eating on **2.** a set of facts or figures arranged in a certain order

tablespoon *noun*. a large spoon for eating soup

tablet *noun*. **1.** a pill **2.** something hard and flat with writing on it

tabloid *noun*. a newspaper that is mainly made up of pictures and short news articles

tack *noun*. thumbtack; a small nail that is wide and flat at one end

tackle *noun*. a running jump to bring someone down

tackle *verb*. **(tackled, tackling) 1.** try to take the ball from a player (especially in football) **2.** jump on someone who is moving in order to bring the person down **3.** try to do something difficult

tag *noun*. a piece of paper, metal, etc, that gives information

tail *noun*. **1.** the part of an animal that sticks out or hangs down in the back **2.** the back part of an airplane

tail *verb*. **(tailed, tailing)** (informal) follow someone

tailor *noun*. someone who sews men's clothes (compare with **dressmaker**)

tailor *verb*. **(tailored, tailoring) 1.** sew a piece of clothing so that it fits you **2.** custom design a program, etc

take *verb*. **(took, taken, taking) 1.** get hold of something **2.** bring something with you **3.** bring someone to a certain place **4.** carry something for someone **5.** eat or drink something **6.** travel in something **7.** go by a certain road **8.** steal **9.** last a certain amount of time **10.** measure

—**take apart** *verb*. separate into pieces

—**take care** *verb*. be careful; watch out

—**take care of** *verb*. **1.** look after **2.** handle; deal with; be responsible for something

—**take down** *verb*. **1.** write something **2.** get something from a high place **3.** pull to pieces; take apart

—**take heart** *verb*. get courage

—**take hold** *verb*. **1.** grab **2.** stick

—**take in** *verb*. **1.** bring into your home to stay **2.** fool someone

—**take off** *verb*. **1.** go up into the air (opposite **land**) **2.** leave suddenly

—**take on** *verb*. **1.** accept (a challenge) **2.** start to employ **3.** change in some way and appear to be something else **4.** carry

—**take up** *verb*. **1.** occupy **2.** start to do something as a hobby **3.** continue something after you stopped

taken *verb*. past participle of **take**

takeover *noun*. the act of gaining control of a company especially if someone buys most of the shares

tale *noun*. a story

talent *noun*. something that someone is good at

talented *adj*. having talent

talk *noun*. **1.** a speech **2.** a rumor that may or may not be true (no plural)

talk *verb*. **(talked, talking) 1.** speak **2.** tell about something

talks *noun plural*. discussions

tall *adj*. **1.** high (a person) (opposite **short**) **2.** high (a building) (opposite **low**)

tan *noun*. **1.** a light brown color **2.** a suntan

tangible *adj*. something that can be touched, felt or seen (opposite **intangible**)

tank *noun*. **1.** a large metal container **2.** a very large army vehicle with guns, which moves on belts instead of wheels

tanker *noun.* a ship or other vehicle for carrying large amounts of oil

tap *noun.* 1. a light knocking 2. a faucet; a handle for controlling the flow of water from a pipe

tap *verb.* (tapped, tapping) 1. knock lightly 2. get information by listening secretly

tape *noun.* 1. a narrow strip of something that is sticky on one side 2. a special magnetic strip that records sound or pictures

tape *verb.* (taped, taping) 1. use strips of tape for keeping something shut or mending something 2. record on special magnetic tape

target *noun.* something that you aim at —**target** *verb.* (targeted, targeting)

tariff *noun.* 1. a tax paid on goods coming into a country 2. a set price, especially for meals and rooms at a hotel

task *noun.* a job that you have to do

taste *noun.* 1. one of the senses; the ability to feel or recognize something in your mouth (no plural) 2. flavor 3. what you like and what you do not 4. suitability (or unsuitability) for a given situation 5. small amount of food or drink

taste *verb.* (tasted) 1. have a certain flavor 2. take a very small amount of something in your mouth to feel the flavor

taught *verb.* past tense and past participle of **teach**

tax *noun.* money that you have to pay to the government —**tax** *verb.* (taxed, taxing) —**taxation** *noun.*

taxi *noun.* cab; a car with a driver that will take you where you want to go for payment

tea *noun.* 1. a brown liquid that is made from leaves (no plural) 2. a cup of tea 3. a light meal between lunch and supper

teach *verb.* (taught, teaching) 1. pass on knowledge to someone else 2. show someone how to do something 3. have a job as a teacher

teacher *noun.* 1. someone whose job is teaching 2. someone who teaches a person something

teaching *noun.* the job of being a teacher (no plural)

team *noun.* 1. a group of people who work together at something 2. a group of players

tear *noun.* a drop of water that comes out of your eye

tear *verb.* (tore, torn, tearing) 1. split open; get a hole 2. split something open or make a hole in something 3. open something or remove something in a hurry

tease *verb.* (teased, teasing) 1. laugh at someone; make fun of someone 2. annoy an animal 3. joke; not be serious

teaspoon *noun.* a small spoon (compare with **tablespoon**)

tech *abbr.* 1. (informal) technical school or college 2. technical 3. technology

technical *adj.* 1. for a special, practical purpose 2. connected with a specific subject; not general —**technically** *adv.*

technician *noun.* someone trained to make, fix, or plan electrical, electronic, mechanical equipment, etc

technique *noun.* a way of doing something

technology *noun.* knowledge or machinery connected to scientific methods and their use in industry —**technological** *adj.*

teddy *noun.* a stuffed toy bear

tedious *adj.* repetitive, tiring and boring

teenage, teenaged *adj.* between the ages of 13 and 19

teenager *noun.* someone between the ages of 13 and 19; an adolescent

teeth *noun.* plural of **tooth**

telecommunications *noun.* (also **telecommunication**) the business (or process) of getting or sending messages by telephone, radio, television, etc

telephone *noun.* **1.** phone; a way of talking over electrical wires (no plural) **2.** an instrument for talking —**telephone** *verb.* **(telephoned, telephoning)** (also **phone**)

telescope *noun.* an instrument that you look through to make very distant things look very close and big

televise *verb.* **(televised, televising)** broadcast on television

television *noun.* TV; a way of making programs with pictures and sound

tell *verb.* **(told, telling)** **1.** give information **2.** give an order (compare with **say:** She told me that ... (with me, us, etc); She said that ... (without me, us, etc)

temper *noun.* mood

temperature *noun.* **1.** how hot or cold something is **2.** body heat that is too high; a fever

temple *noun.* a building where people come to pray or worship

temporarily *adv.* for now; for the time being

temporary *adj.* that will last for only a short time; not permanent

tempt *verb.* **(tempted, tempting)** **1.** make you want **2.** try to make someone do something wrong

temptation *noun.* the desire to do something that you should not

ten *noun. adj.* the number 10

tenant *noun.* someone who pays rent to live in a place

tend *verb.* **(tended, tending)** usually be a certain way or do a certain thing

tendency *noun.* **1.** something that usually happens in a particular situation **2.** something that happens more and more often

tender *adj.* **1.** gentle and loving **2.** soft and easy to chew **3.** sore

tender *verb.* **(tendered, tendering)** give or offer something

tender *noun.* an offer to supply goods or do a job for an agreed price

tennis *noun.* a game played by two or four players with rackets and a small bouncy ball within a bordered court, back and forth across a low net

tense *adj.* **1.** not relaxed **2.** pulled tightly

tense *noun.* (grammar) a form of a verb that tells you about time

tension *noun.* being tense; being under strain

tent *noun.* a shelter that campers or soldiers make from strong, thick cloth

tentative *adj.* **1.** not definite or certain **2.** hesitant; not confident

tenth *noun. adj.* 10th

term *noun.* **1.** a division of time in the school year **2.** a fixed period of time **3.** a technical word used in a particular profession or activity

terminal *noun.* **1.** the end of a bus or railroad line **2.** a building at an airport where passengers begin or end their journey **3.** a computer keyboard and screen connected to a main computer somewhere else

terminate *verb.* **(terminated, terminating)** finish; come or bring to an end

terminology *noun.* particular vocabulary connected with a certain field

terms *noun plural.* **1.** a kind of relationship **2.** conditions

terrace *noun.* a place with a floor or grass for sitting outside the house

terrible *adj.* very bad; awful

terribly *adv.* very

terrific *adj.* **1.** wonderful **2.** very big

terrify *verb.* **(terrified, terrifying)** frighten

territory *noun.* land that a government owns or controls

terror *noun.* **1.** very strong fear or violence (no plural) **2.** something that you are terribly afraid of

terrorism *noun.* using violence to get what you want by making everyone afraid (no plural) —**terrorist** *noun. adj.*

terrorize verb. **(terrorized, terrorizing)** terrify and bully people

test noun. **1.** a way of finding out how well you know something; an exam **2.** a way of finding out how good something is **3.** a medical examination

test verb. **(tested, testing) 1.** give someone a test **2.** find out how good something is

testify verb. **(testified, testifying)** make a sworn statement; (in court) give evidence that you swear is true

testimony noun. an account of a situation that you pledge is absolutely true (as in a court of law)

text noun. something in writing

textbook noun. a book that you study from

textile noun. material that is made by weaving cotton, silk, synthetic, etc, threads

Thai noun. someone from Thailand; the language spoken in Thailand —**Thai** adj.

than conj. prep. a word that you use for comparing two things or types of things

thank verb. **(thanked, thanking)** tell someone that you appreciate what he/she did

thankfully adv. gratefully

thanks noun plural. (informal) gratitude; words that say you appreciate what someone did

that adj. **1.** the one over there **2.** the one that was just talked about **3.** the one then

that adv. to that extent; so

that pron. **1.** a certain thing, event or idea **2.** the one there (plural **those**) **3.** a time or place in the past **4.** a word that refers to someone or something that was just mentioned (who, whom, which, where, when) **5.** after an adjective in the superlative

that conj. **1.** a word that shows what **2.** a word that shows result

the def. art. **1.** a word that tells that you mean something or someone specific **2.** a word that is part of the name of a river, a mountain range, etc, or things that there is only one **3.** a word that is used with the name of a musical instrument **4.** for every; per **5.** a word that you use with superlative adjectives or adverbs such as tallest, best, worst, largest, most, least

thee pron. (dated) you

theft noun. stealing

their adj. belonging to them

theirs pron. belonging to them

them pron. those people or things

theme noun. the subject of a piece of writing or a tune on which a piece of music is based

themselves pron. **1.** the same people **2.** they and no others

then adv. **1.** after that; next **2.** at that time **3.** if so; in that case

theoretical adj. **1.** not tested; not based on practice or experience **2.** related to theory

theory noun. an idea that explains something (plural **theories**)

therapeutic adj. helping in therapy; having a positive effect

therapist noun. someone who specializes in a certain therapy

therapy noun. treatment of a physical or mental sickness (not by drugs or an operation)

there adv. **1.** in/at that place **2.** to that place

there pron. (+ to be) meaning that someone or something exists or happens

thereby adv. (formal) because of that

therefore adv. as a result

these adj. pron. the ones here (plural of **this**)

thesis noun. a long original piece of writing done in order to receive a master's or doctoral degree

they pron. **1.** plural of **he, she, it 2.** people in general

229

—**they'd** *abbr.* **1.** = they had **2.** = they would

—**they'll** *abbr.* = they will

—**they're** *abbr.* = they are

—**they've** *abbr.* = they have

thick *adj.* **1.** wide from one side to the other **2.** close together **3.** heavy and warm **4.** not flowing quickly

thickness *noun.* how thick something is

thief *noun.* someone who steals things (plural **thieves**)

thin *adj.* **1.** slim **2.** skinny; without enough fat **3.** narrow from one side to the other **4.** watery; runny **5.** not thickly grown —**thin** *verb.* (**thinned, thinning**)

thing *noun.* **1.** an object **2.** what you do or say **3.** a happening

things *noun plural.* belongings

think *verb.* (**thought, thinking**) **1.** use your brain **2.** believe **3.** have an opinion

third *noun. adj.* **1.** 3rd **2.** 1/3; one of three equal parts

Third World *noun.* the group of countries that are less industrially developed; the developing nations of Asia, Africa and South America

thirteen *noun. adj.* the number 13

thirteenth *noun. adj.* = 13th

thirties *noun.* **1.** between the ages of 30 and 40 **2.** in the 1930s

thirtieth *noun. adj.* = 30th

thirty *noun. adj.* the number 30

this *adj.* **1.** the one here **2.** the one now **3.** the one that has just past (plural **these**)

this *pron.* **1.** the one here **2.** a person **3.** a place **4.** something that you are explaining (plural **these**)

this *adv.* to such an extent; so

thorough *adj.* complete

thoroughly *adv.* not leaving anything out

those *adj.* **1.** the ones there (plural of that) **2.** the ones that

those *pron.* plural of **that**; the ones there

though *conj.* although; even though; in spite of the fact that

though *adv.* however; nevertheless

thought *noun.* **1.** whatever you are thinking (no plural) **2.** something that you think about or believe **3.** an idea

thought *verb.* past tense and past participle of **think**

thoughtful *adj.* **1.** thinking about other people **2.** showing that you have thought —**thoughtfully** *adv.*

thousand *noun.* **1.** the number 1,000 **2.** many

thread *noun.* a very thin piece of cotton, etc, that you sew with —**thread** *verb.* (**threaded, threading**)

threat *noun.* **1.** a danger **2.** something that you say you will do to harm someone

threaten *verb.* (**threatened, threatening**) **1.** be a danger to **2.** say that you will do something harmful to someone; make a threat

threatening *adj.* containing threats

three *noun. adj.* the number 3

threw *verb.* past of **throw**

thrill *noun.* **1.** a feeling of great excitement **2.** a sudden feeling that makes you shiver

thrill *verb.* (**thrilled, thrilling**) give suspense and excitement

thriller *noun.* a book or a movie that is full of suspense

thrive *verb.* (**throve/thrived, thriving, thrived/thriven**) be successful; be strong and healthy —**thriving** *adj.*

throat *noun.* **1.** a part of the body leading from the back of the mouth into the lungs or into the stomach **2.** the front of the neck

throb *verb.* (**throbbed, throbbing**) beat regularly (and usually with force)

throne *noun.* **1.** the chair of a king or queen **2.** the rank of king or queen

through *prep.* **1.** inside one end of something and out the other **2.** from one side to the other **3.** from the beginning of something to the end **4.** in between two parts of something **5.** by means of; because of

throughout *prep.* **1.** from the beginning of something to the end; through **2.** in every part

throw *verb.* **(threw, thrown, throwing)** send through the air with your arm — **throw** *noun.*

thrown *verb.* past participle of **throw**

thrust *verb.* **(thrust, thrusting)** forcefully push forward

thumb *noun.* the first of the five fingers on one hand

thunder *noun.* **1.** the loud, exploding noise that comes before a storm **2.** a loud, pounding noise —**thunder** *verb.* **(thundered, thundering)**

Thursday *noun.* the fifth day of the week

thus *adv.* **1.** in this way; so **2.** therefore; for this reason; so

tick *noun.* **1.** the sound that a clock makes **2.** a mark that you write at the side of something

tick *verb.* **(ticked, ticking) 1.** make the sound of a clock **2.** mark with a tick; check

ticket *noun.* **1.** a piece of paper that shows that you have paid to go somewhere **2.** a piece of paper that shows that you have broken a traffic law

tide *noun.* the rise and fall of waters according to the pull of the moon, occurring approximately every 12 hours

tidy *adj.* **(tidier, tidiest)** orderly

tidy *verb.* **(tidied, tidying)** make something tidy

tie *noun.* **1.** a long strip of cloth that a man wears around his neck under his shirt collar **2.** an equal score in a game; a draw

tie *verb.* **(tied, tying) 1.** use rope, string, etc, to fasten something **2.** make a knot or a bow

tiger *noun.* a large wild cat with yellow fur and black stripes, native of Asia

tight *adj.* **1.** firm **2.** fitting closely **3.** stretched as far as something will go

tighten *verb.* **(tightened, tightening)** make tighter

tightly *adv.* **1.** firmly or with force **2.** as far as something will go **3.** so that nothing can move inside

tights *noun plural.* stockings covering the lower half of the body, such as dancers wear

tile *noun.* a thin piece of baked clay for making roofs, floors, wall coverings, etc

till *prep. conj.* until; up to a certain time **(till** is spelled with two lls; but **until** with one l)

timber *noun.* wood or trees grown for building

time *noun.* **1.** the specific hour (no plural) **2.** the passing of all days, hours, etc (no plural) **3.** a limited period (no plural) **4.** an event in the past **5.** an experience **6.** an occasion **7.** how long something takes

time *verb.* **(timed, timing)** fix or measure the time for something

times *noun.* **1.** a period in the past **2.** a word that shows one number in relation to another number

times *prep.* multiplied by

timetable *noun.* **1.** a list of the times when planes, trains, etc, will arrive and leave **2.** a list of the hours of classes at school; a schedule

tin *noun.* **1.** a metal (no plural) **2.** a container made from this metal

tiny *adj.* **(tinier, tiniest)** very small

tip *noun.* **1.** the pointed end of something **2.** extra money that you give to a waiter, porter, taxi driver, etc; a gratuity **3.** a piece of useful advice

tip *verb.* **(tipped, tipping) 1.** raise something at one end **2.** give money for service to a waiter, etc

tired *adj.* **1.** wanting to sleep **2.** not having strength left

tissue *noun.* **1.** a group of cells in a living thing **2.** a paper handkerchief

title *noun.* **1.** the name of a book, article, story, poem, etc **2.** a word in front of a person's name

to *prep.* **1.** in a certain direction **2.** a word that tells what place **3.** from until **4.** for a certain reason; in order to **5.** a word that shows change **6.** a word that tells who receives something **7.** before the hour **8.** in; forming **9.** for each one; per **10.** a word that tells that something touches something else

to *adv.* into a closed position

toast *noun.* **1.** bread that was grilled quickly to make it crisp and brown (no plural) **2.** a good wish that you make when you raise a glass of wine before you drink it

toast *verb.* **(toasted, toasting) 1.** make toast **2.** raise your wineglass and make a good wish

tobacco *noun.* a plant with wide leaves that are dried and then used for making cigarettes, cigars, etc

today *noun.* this day —**today** *adv.*

toe *noun.* **1.** one of the five parts at the end of your foot that are like the fingers of your hand **2.** the front part of a shoe or sock

together *adv.* **1.** in a group **2.** with someone or something else **3.** so as to mix two (or more) things

toilet *noun.* **1.** a place in a bathroom with a seat where you get rid of waste material from your body **2.** the small room that has a toilet in it; a bathroom, a lavatory, a washroom, a restroom

token *noun.* **1.** a special coin that fits into a certain kind of machine **2.** a gift that you give to show respect or to be remembered

token *adj.* very small

told *verb.* past tense and past participle of **tell**

tolerate *verb.* **(tolerated, tolerating)** allow; put up with; accept even if you don't like it —**tolerance** *noun.* (opposite **intolerance**)

toll *noun.* **1.** a fee paid in order to use a certain privilege **2.** payment for making a long distance phone call **3.** the cost in terms of health, life, etc, of an accident, disaster, situation, etc

tomato *noun.* a round, juicy red plant that we eat in salads as a vegetable (plural **tomatoes**)

tomb *noun.* a large place where someone is buried that sometimes serves as a memorial

tomorrow *noun. adv.* the day after today

ton *noun.* **1.** a measure of weight **2.** any heavy weight

tone *noun.* **1.** how a musical instrument sounds **2.** how a voice sounds —**tone** *verb.* **(toned, toning)**

tongue *noun.* the moving part inside your mouth

tonight *noun. adv.* this night

too *adv.* **1.** also **2.** more than necessary (in negatives use **either** instead of **too**)

took *verb.* past of **take**

tool *noun.* something that you use for doing a job

tooth *noun.* the hard, white things in your mouth that you chew with (plural **teeth**)

top *noun.* **1.** a cover for a jar, bottle, box, etc **2.** the highest place —**top** *verb.* **(topped, topping)**

top *adj.* **1.** the highest **2.** the best

topic *noun.* a subject that you talk or write about

torch *noun.* a stick with fire at the end of it

tore *verb.* past tense and past participle of **tear**

torn *adj.* not whole; having tears

torture *verb.* **(tortured, torturing)** make another person suffer terrible pain —**torture** *noun.*

toss *verb.* **(tossed, tossing)** throw something without much force

total *noun.* the complete amount — **total** *verb.* **(totaled, totaling)**

total *adj.* complete

totally *adv.* completely

touch *noun.* 1. one of the five senses 2. the feel of something on your skin 3. a small amount of something (no plural)

touch *verb.* **(touched, touching)** 1. reach the surface of something 2. reach out to make contact with something

touches *noun plural.* details

touching *adj.* making you feel pleased and cared for

tough *adj.* 1. strong; able to live in difficult conditions 2. mean and dangerous 3. hard to chew 4. hard; difficult

tour *noun.* 1. a group of people who are traveling together 2. a visit around a place with a guide 3. a pleasure trip in which you travel around 4. check to see what is happening

tour *verb.* **(toured, touring)** 1. travel from place to place to see things 2. walk around a place

tourism *noun.* a business of supplying vacation packages, hotels, tours, etc, for tourists

tourist *noun. adj.* someone who visits a place for the pleasure of seeing it

tournament *noun.* a competition

tow *verb.* **(towed, towing)** pull something with a rope or a cable

towel *noun.* a piece of cloth for drying something

tower *noun.* a very tall, narrow building or part of a building

tower *verb.* **(towered, towering)** be taller than the people or things nearby

town *noun.* 1. a place with houses, businesses, etc (no plural) 2. a community smaller than a city, but larger than a village

toxic *adj.* poisonous

toy *noun.* something to play with

trace *noun.* some kind of sign that someone or something has been in a place

trace *verb.* **(traced, tracing)** 1. find out where something comes from 2. put a thin piece of paper over something to make an exact drawing

track *noun.* 1. metal rails for traveling on 2. a narrow path 3. footprints 4. a special area for a race

track *verb.* **(tracked, tracking)** try to find and catch

tractor *noun.* a big vehicle for farm work

trade *noun.* 1. buying and selling; commerce (no plural) 2. a particular business 3. a way of earning a living (no plural) 4. getting something in exchange for giving something

trade *verb.* **(traded, trading)** 1. buy and sell goods 2. buy and sell a certain thing 3. switch 4. get something in exchange for giving something

trader *noun.* someone who buys and sells goods

trade union *noun.* = labor union (see **union**)

tradition *noun.* something that you do the same way that your grandparents and their grandparents did —**traditional** *adj.* —**traditionally** *adv.*

traffic *noun.* cars, buses, etc, in the streets (no plural)

tragedy *noun.* 1. a terrible thing that happens 2. a play about terrible things that happen

tragic *adj.* terribly sad

trail *noun.* 1. a long mark or line that something leaves 2. a narrow path

trail *verb.* **(trailed, trailing)** follow someone

trailer *noun.* a home that you can attach to your car

train *noun.* a vehicle with an engine and railroad cars which moves along metal tracks

train *verb.* **(trained, training)** 1. teach someone how to do something well 2. teach an animal to do what you tell it to 3. learn how to do a job 4. do exercises to prepare for a match, race, etc

trainee *noun.* someone who is being taught to do a certain job while doing the job itself

trainer *noun.* someone who trains a person or an animal

training *noun.* 1. teaching; instruction 2. athletic practice

transaction *noun.* the act of carrying out (a business deal)

transfer *noun.* being moved or sent to another place

transfer *verb.* (**transferred, transferring**) move something from one place to another

transform *verb.* (**transformed, transforming**) make something completely different —**transformation** *noun.*

transit *noun.* moving goods or people from one place to another

translate *verb.* (**translated, translating**) put words into a different language

translation *noun.* a word, a statement, a piece of writing, etc, that is given in a different language

translator *noun.* someone who translates into another language

transmission *noun.* 1. a broadcast 2. the part of a motor vehicle that transfers the power of the engine to the wheels

transmit *verb.* (**transmitted, transmitting**) 1. broadcast 2. pass from one to another

transplant *verb.* (**transplanted, transplanting**) remove from one place and put in another place

transport *noun.* 1. carrying from one place to another (no plural) 2. transportation

transport *verb.* (**transported, transporting**) carry from one place to another

transportation *noun.* a way of going from one place to another (no plural)

trap *noun.* 1. a device for catching an animal 2. a trick to make someone say or do the wrong thing —**trap** *verb.* (**trapped, trapping**)

trash *noun.* things that you throw away; rubbish; garbage (no plural)

trash *verb.* (**trashed, trashing**) 1. break up; destroy 2. criticize very strongly; say something is very bad

travel *verb.* (**traveled, traveling**) 1. go from one place to another; take a trip 2. be on your way from one place to another

travels *noun plural.* all the traveling that someone has done

tray *noun.* a kind of big, flat dish for carrying things

tread *verb.* (**trod, trodden, treading**) 1. walk 2. step down hard on something

treasure *noun.* something that is very valuable —**treasure** *verb.* (**treasured, treasuring**)

treasurer *noun.* someone who looks after the money of an organization

treasury *noun.* the department of government that controls taxes and spending (no plural)

treat *noun.* something special —**my treat** = I'll pay

treat *verb.* (**treated, treating**) 1. behave in a certain way toward someone 2. take care of a patient or try to cure an illness

treatment *noun.* 1. the way someone behaves to someone else (no plural) 2. a way of curing an illness

treaty *noun.* an agreement in writing between different countries (plural **treaties**)

tree *noun.* a big, tall plant with a trunk, branches and leaves

tremble *verb.* (**trembled, trembling**) shake because of fear, weakness or excitement —**trembling** *adj.*

tremendous *adj.* 1. very big; enormous 2. wonderful; terrific

trend *noun.* 1. something that is temporarily fashionable 2. a direction in which something is moving

trial *noun.* 1. a hearing in court in which a judge or jury decides a case 2. a testing or trying out of something

triangle *noun.* a shape with three straight sides and three angles

tribal *adj.* connected with or belonging to a tribe

tribe *noun.* a group of people with the same beliefs, language and customs

tribute *noun.* an honor; a show of esteem; something done to show respect and admiration

trick *noun.* **1.** a dishonest action to make a person do what you want **2.** a sort of entertainment with cards, magic, etc

trick *verb.* **(tricked, tricking)** fool or cheat someone

tricky *adj.* **1.** dishonest **2.** full of difficulties

tried *verb.* past tense and past participle of **try**

trim *verb.* **(trimmed, trimming) 1.** cut a little **2.** decorate **3.** move a boat's sails into the right place to catch the wind

Trinity *noun.* (in the Christian religion) the Father, the Son and the Holy Spirit combined to make one God

trio *noun.* a group of three

trip *noun.* a journey

trip *verb.* **(tripped, tripping) 1.** fall over something that you catch your foot on **2.** make someone fall

triple *noun. adj.* **1.** something that is three times in amount or number; times three **2.** (in baseball) a hit that lets the batter get to third base

triple *verb.* **(tripled, tripling)** become or make something three times bigger

triumph *noun.* a victory —**triumph** *verb.* **(triumphed, triumphing)** —**triumphant** *adj.*

trivial *adj.* small and unimportant

trolley *noun.* **1.** a kind of bus that travels on rails **2.** a small table on wheels; a serving cart

troop *noun.* **1.** a group of soldiers **2.** a group of Scouts (youth movement) with an older leader

troop *verb.* **(trooped, trooping)** move together in a group

trophy *noun.* a prize for winning something especially in sports

tropical *adj.* of the hot parts of the world

trouble *noun.* **1.** difficulty (no plural) **2.** pain; sorrow **3.** bother; extra work (no plural)

trouble *verb.* **(troubled, troubling) 1.** ask a favor **2.** cause someone to worry

troubled *adj.* worried

trousers *noun plural.* pants

truce *noun.* an agreement to stop fighting

truck *noun.* a big vehicle for carrying goods

truck *verb.* **(trucked, trucking)** move something from one place to another by truck

true *adj.* **1.** the right information **2.** right; correct **3.** that you can trust

truly *adv.* really

trumpet *noun.* a musical instrument made from brass consisting of a long tube wound around once or twice, that has a mouthpiece at one end and widens out at the other

trumpet *verb.* **(trumpeted, trumpeting)** play the trumpet; promote

trunk *noun.* **1.** the main thick wooden stem of a tree **2.** a large box used to ship or store clothing and other things **3.** the long nose of an elephant **4.** the storage compartment of a car **5.** the central section of a human body (without the neck, head, arms or legs)

trunks *noun plural.* short pants worn by men for swimming, boxing, etc

trust *noun.* **1.** faith; a belief that someone is honest (no plural) **2.** a belief that someone will take care of you

trust *verb.* **(trusted, trusting) 1.** have faith in someone **2.** believe that something is safe **3.** feel sure that someone will do something **4.** hope

truth *noun.* the true facts (no plural)

try *noun.* seeing if you can do something; an attempt (plural **tries**)

try verb. **(tried, trying) 1.** make an effort **2.** see if you can do something **3.** see if you like something **4.** hear a case in court

T-shirt noun. a shirt with short sleeves and a round neck

tube noun. **1.** a long, soft container that you press on to get something out **2.** a hollow, round piece of rubber, metal, glass, etc, for carrying liquids

Tuesday noun. the third day of the week

tug verb. **(tugged, tugging)** pull hard

tumble verb. **(tumbled, tumbling)** fall

tune noun. a melody

tune verb. **(tuned, tuning)** put a musical instrument into the correct pitch

tunnel noun. a long, narrow underground passage

turkey noun. a large flightless bird whose meat is eaten

turn noun. **1.** a change of direction **2.** a change **3.** an act of turning something **4.** someone's time to do something

turn verb. **(turned, turning) 1.** move in a circle or part of a circle **2.** move something in a circle **3.** go around a corner **4.** become

turning noun. a place where one road branches off another road

turnover noun. **1.** how fast a certain thing is sold **2.** how much business someone has done **3.** how fast or how many workers leave a company and new workers are brought in to replace them

tutor noun. **1.** a private teacher **2.** someone who directs a student's studies at a university **—tutor** verb. **(tutored, tutoring)**

TV noun. **1.** television (no plural) **2.** a television set

twelfth noun. adj. = 12th

twelve noun. adj. the number 12

twenties noun plural. **1.** the years between 1920 and 1929 **2.** the ages between 20 and 29

twentieth noun. adj. = 20th

twenty noun. adj. the number 20

twice adv. two times

twin noun. a sister or brother born at the same birth with another sister or brother

twin adj. making up a pair

twist noun. a sharp turn

twist verb. **(twisted, twisting) 1.** wind around something **2.** turn in different directions **3.** wind something around something else **4.** turn something with a strong motion **5.** turn something in a way that injures you **6.** change the meaning of something in a deceitful way; distort

two noun. pron. the number 2

type noun. **1.** a kind **2.** printed letters made by a machine (no plural)

type verb. **(typed, typing)** write with a typewriter, a computer keyboard, etc

typical adj. **1.** being a strong example of something **2.** what you can expect of someone or something **—typically** adv.

U

ugly *adj.* **1.** unpleasant to look at **2.** unpleasant to hear

ulcer *noun.* a sore that can be found on the inside or outside of the body that may produce a poison so that the sore does not heal easily

ultimate *adj.* final

ultimately *adv.* in the end

ultimatum *noun.* a final word about what someone must do

umbrella *noun.* something that you carry to protect yourself from the rain

umpire *noun.* a judge in some sports, especially tennis, baseball, cricket or volleyball

unable *adj.* not able

unacceptable *adj.* that cannot be allowed or approved of; not acceptable

unanimous *adj.* with everyone agreeing —**unanimously** *adv.*

unarmed *adj.* without weapons

unavailable *adj.* **1.** unable to meet someone **2.** that cannot be obtained

unavoidable *adj.* that you cannot or could not avoid

unaware *adj.* not knowing about something

unbearable *adj.* that you cannot stand

unbelievable *adj.* difficult to believe; incredible

uncertain *adj.* **1.** not feeling sure **2.** not definite **3.** not sure —**uncertainty** *noun.*

uncle *noun.* the brother of your mother or father or the husband of your aunt

unclear *adj.* not clear

uncomfortable *adj.* **1.** giving an unpleasant feeling; not comfortable **2.** feeling embarrassed or not feeling comfortable or relaxed

uncommon *adj.* unusual; rare

unconditional *adj.* without conditions; not depending on anything

unconscious *adj.* **1.** not conscious; not knowing what is happening around you, as if asleep **2.** not knowing; not aware

unconsciously *adv.* without being aware of it

uncontrollable *adj.* that you cannot control

uncountable noun *noun.* (grammar) a noun that does not have a plural form and cannot take a or an before it

uncover *verb.* (**uncovered, uncovering**) **1.** take the cover off someone or something **2.** discover something that has been kept secret

uncovered *adv.* without a cover

undecided *adj.* **1.** without a clear or firm decision about **2.** not final

under *prep.* **1.** covered by something; beneath **2.** below **3.** in your charge **4.** less than **5.** classified

undercover *adj.* doing something in secret (for example, as a spy or police officer)

underdeveloped *adj.* not fully developed

underdog *noun.* the weakest contestant (in a competition, in an election, etc) who is expected to lose

underestimate *verb.* (**underestimated, underestimating**) not put enough value on someone or something (opposite **overestimate**)

undergo *verb.* (**underwent, undergone, undergoing**) have something done to you

underground *noun.* **1.** a place underneath the ground **2.** a political military organization against a government or occupying force

underground *adj. adv.* **1.** below the ground **2.** secretive; against the ruling establishment or mainstream

underline verb. **(underlined, underlining)** draw a line under a word, sentence, etc

underlined adj. with a line under it

underlying adj. a hidden reason or meaning; an explanation that is not obvious

undermine verb. **(undermined, undermining)** weaken (and possibly destroy) (often used regarding authority)

underneath prep. under; below

underpants noun plural. a piece of underwear that men and women wear on their bottom

underrate verb. **(underrated, underrating)** think something or someone is of less quality than it or he/she actually is (opposite **overrate**)

understand verb. **(understood, understanding)** 1. know the meaning or significance of something 2. hear or see words correctly 3. have knowledge of something 4. have practical knowledge 5. have sympathy for someone's feelings

understandable adj. reasonable

understandably adv. reasonably

understanding noun. having knowledge (no plural)

understanding adj. sympathetic to other people's problems

understatement noun. stating that something is less important or smaller than it really is

understood verb. past tense and past participle of **understand**

undertake verb. **(undertook, undertaken, undertaking)** take a responsibility on yourself

undertaker noun. someone whose job is to bury dead people and arrange funerals

undertaking noun. 1. a job 2. a promise to do something

underwater adj. beneath the surface of the water

underwear noun. clothes that you wear under other clothes, such as underpants or undershirt; underclothes (no plural)

underwent verb. past of **undergo**

underworld noun. the criminal part of society (no plural)

underwrite verb. **(underwrote, underwritten, underwriting)** 1. take financial responsibility (especially against failure) 2. take responsibility for paying for an insurance policy

undesirable noun. a person who is not liked or not welcome

undesirable adj.. not wanted

undo verb. **(undid, undone, undoing)** 1. open something that is tied, sewn or knit 2. make something go back to the way that it was

undone adj. 1. not finished 2. not closed (clothes)

undoubted adj. absolutely sure; certainly true

undoubtedly adv. certainly; without any doubt

undress verb. **(undressed, undressing)** 1. take off your clothes 2. take the clothes off someone else

undressed adj. without clothes on; naked

uneasy adj. **(more uneasy, most uneasy)** worried —**uneasily** adv.

unemployed adj. without a job

unemployment noun. 1. being unemployed 2. the number of people who are out of work

unexpected adj. not expected; surprising —**unexpectedly** adv.

unfair adj. not fair; not right —**unfairly** adv. —**unfairness** noun.

unfamiliar adj. not known to you

unfashionable adj. 1. not stylish 2. not popular

unfinished adj. not finished; not completed

unfit adj. not suitable

unfold verb. **(unfolded, unfolding)** open something that was folded

unforeseen adj. unexpected

unforgettable adj. that you will always remember

unfortunate adj. unlucky; too bad

unfortunately adv. 1. = I am sorry, but ... 2. unluckily

unfriendly adj. not friendly; not kind or encouraging

unhappy adj. 1. sad 2. not pleased; dissatisfied —**unhappily** adv. —**unhappiness** noun.

unhealthy adj. not in good health; ill

unhelpful adj. 1. not willing to help 2. not doing any good; not useful or constructive

unidentified adj. that nobody knows what or who it is

uniform noun. clothing that everyone in a specific job wears

unify verb. (**unified, unifying**) bring together different parts so as to make one whole unit

unimportant adj. not important

union noun. 1. the joining of two or more things (no plural) 2. people who join together to work as a group —**labor union** noun. (also **union**) a workers' organization for negotiating with employers about pay, working conditions, etc

unique adj. with no other like it; the only one —**uniquely** adv. —**uniqueness** noun.

unit noun. 1. something that is complete and also part of something bigger 2. a group of soldiers who train and fight together 3. a measurement

unite verb. (**united, uniting**) 1. join; come together 2. join two or more things to make one thing

united adj. joined together

United Kingdom noun. the UK; England, Scotland, Wales and Northern Ireland

unity noun. being one (no plural)

universal adj. for everyone in the world —**universally** adv.

universe noun. space and everything that exists in it

university noun. a place for higher studies after finishing high school

unjust adj. not fair —**unjustly** adv.

unjustified adj. without justification

unkind adj. not kind; not generous or considerate —**unkindly** adv. —**unkindness** noun.

unknown adj. 1. that nobody knows 2. not famous (opposite **known**)

unless conj. if not (do not use **will** after **unless**, use the present tense)

unlike prep. different from (opposite **like, similar to**)

unlikely adj. not expected

unload verb. (**unloaded, unloading**) take things out of a truck, ship, etc (opposite **load**)

unlock verb. (**unlocked, unlocking**) open a lock (opposite **lock**)

unlocked adj. open (opposite **locked**)

unlucky adj. 1. bringing bad luck 2. without luck 3. having bad luck

unmarried adj. not married; single

unmistakable adj. that you cannot be wrong about

unnatural adj. not natural; not normal; artificial

unnecessarily adv. unreasonably; without good cause.

unnecessary adj. not necessary

unnoticed adv. without being noticed

unpack verb. (**unpacked, unpacking**) take things out of a suitcase

unpaid adj. 1. without pay 2. that was not paid

unpleasant adj. 1. rude; nasty 2. not enjoyable 3. difficult; embarrassing

unpopular adj. that not many people like

unprepared adj. not ready

unqualified adj. not having a license to do something (opposite **qualified, licensed**)

unrealistic adj. not showing a sense of what is possible (opposite **realistic, practical**)

unreasonable *adj.* **1.** more than what is fair or reasonable **2.** that you cannot reason with; too demanding

unreliable *adj.* that you cannot depend on **—unreliability** *noun.*

unresolved *noun.* not finished; not settled; not decided

unsatisfactory *adj.* not good enough **— unsatisfactory** *adv.* **—unsatisfying** *adj.*

unsecured *adj.* unsafe; not locked

unseen *adj.* that you cannot see

unsettling *noun. adj.* upsetting

unskilled *adj.* without special training or skills

unsold *adj.* not sold

unsuccessful *adj.* **1.** not able to do something **2.** not successful; failing

unsuccessfully *adv.* without success

unsuitable *adj.* not appropriate; not suitable

untidy *adj.* **(untidier, untidiest)** messy; not orderly

untie *verb.* **(untied, untying)** open a knot or a bow

until *prep. conj.* till; up to the time that **(until** has one **l, till** has two **lls;** do not use **will** after **until;** use the present simple tense)

untouchable *noun.* **1.** someone or something that is beyond criticism; sacred **2.** something that cannot be touched either because it is too fragile, or because it is forbidden or too disgusting **3.** the lowest social group (caste) in India **—untouchable** *adj.*

untouched *adj.* unaffected

unused *adj.* brand new

unusual *adj.* not common

unusually *adv.* more than is usual

unveiled *adj.* revealed (as if by taking off a veil)

unwelcome *adj.* that you are not happy to receive

unwell *adj.* ill

up *noun.* **1.** someone or something in a high position **2.** a period of thriving and prosperity

up *adv.* **1.** in a higher place **2.** to a higher place or level **3.** as high as something will go **4.** louder **5.** out of bed **6.** finished; over **7.** completely; all there is of something

up *prep.* **1.** toward a higher place or the top **2.** along (in the direction of)

up *adj.* that goes up

upbeat *adj.* positive; optimistic

update *verb.* **(updated, updating)** give current information; bring something or someone up to date (about a situation)

upgrade *verb.* **(upgraded, upgrading)** raise or improve the level or quality of something

uphold *verb.* **(upheld, upholding)** give support to or defend against attack; stop from being taken away

upmarket *adj.* appealing to upper-class or richer clients

upon *prep.* on

upper *adj.* higher than something else (opposite **lower**)

upright *adj.* standing straight up

uprising *noun.* a rebellion; a revolt

uproot *verb.* **(uprooted, uprooting) 1.** take a plant out of the ground at the roots **2.** force people to leave their homes

upset *verb.* **(upset, upsetting) 1.** knock something over **2.** spoil someone's plans **3.** make someone feel unhappy, angry or worried

upset *adj.* unhappy, angry or worried about something

upside *noun.* an upper side; an upper trend; the positive aspect of a situation (opposite **downside**)

upside down *adv.* with the bottom on top

upstairs *adj.* on a higher floor

upstairs *adv.* to the top of the stairs (opposite **downstairs**)

up-to-date *adj.* **1.** knowing what is going on **2.** correct **3.** modern

upturn *noun.* a change for the better (usually an increase)

upward *adj.* going up (opposite **downward**)

urban adj. of or connected with the city

urge noun. a strong desire

urge verb. (urged, urging) suggest strongly to someone to do something

urgency noun. something of great and immediate importance

urgent adj. extremely important

urgently adv. immediately

urine noun. the water that leaves your body through your kidneys (no plural)

us pron. me and someone else; me and other people

usage noun. 1. (grammar) the accepted way of using a term in a language 2. how something is used

use noun. what you do with something

use verb. (used, using) do something with the help of something else

used adj. not new; second-hand (opposite **unused**)

useful adj. helpful; making things easier

useless adj. 1. without any chance of success 2. no good 3. not helpful

user noun. someone who uses something

user-friendly adj. easy to use and not needing special training

usher noun. someone who shows you where your seat is in a theater

usual adj. ordinary; normal

usually adv. most of the time

utensil noun. a household tool

utilize verb. (utilized, utilizing) make use of

utmost adj. of the greatest degree; to the best of someone's ability

utter verb. (uttered, uttering) (formal) say

utter adj. complete

utterly adv. completely

V

V the Roman number 5

vacancy *noun.* **1.** space at a hotel **2.** a job that needs filling

vacant *adj.* empty; not occupied; without anyone inside (opposite **occupied**)

vacate *verb.* **(vacated, vacating)** leave; stop using

vacation *noun.* **1.** a holiday **2.** a time when schools and law courts are closed or when an employee can take leave

vacation *verb.* **(vacationed, vacationing)** have a vacation

vaccinate *verb.* **(vaccinated, vaccinating)** put a substance (= a vaccine, usually by injection) into the body so that it will protect you against illness **—vaccination** *noun.* **—vaccine** *noun.*

vacuum *noun.* an empty space without air

vacuum *verb.* **(vacuumed, vacuuming)** use a vacuum cleaner

vacuum cleaner *noun.* a machine that cleans rugs, etc, by sucking up the dirt

vague *adj.* **1.** not clear **2.** not specific

vaguely *adv.* not clearly

vain *adj.* thinking very highly of yourself; conceited (opposite **modest**)

valid *adj.* that can still be legally used (opposite **invalid**)

validity *noun.* a legal reason or force; the basis of a claim that cannot be argued about; logic or truth of an argument

valley *noun.* low land between hills or mountains

valuable *adj.* **1.** worth a lot of money **2.** important to someone

valuables *noun plural.* things that are worth a lot of money

value *noun.* **1.** what something is worth **2.** great worth **3.** importance

value *verb.* **(valued, valuing) 1.** believe that something is important **2.** decide the worth of something

valued *adj.* with value

values *noun plural.* the principles that you believe are important in life

vampire *noun.* the character from folk tales who sucks the blood of (sleeping) people

van *noun.* a small truck or large car for transporting things or people

vandal *noun.* someone who destroys property for pleasure **—vandalism** *noun.* (no plural)

vanguard *noun.* **1.** the leading position in a development **2.** the soldiers at the head of an attack and leading it

vanish *verb.* **(vanished, vanishing)** disappear

vanity *noun.* thinking too highly of yourself (no plural)

variation *noun.* something that is basically similar to something else but with minor changes; a different form of something else

variety *noun.* **1.** a large choice; a number of things of different kinds (no plural) **2.** a type of something

various *adj.* different; diversified **—variously** *adv.*

varnish *verb.* **(varnished, varnishing)** cover something (usually wood) with a (usually clear) liquid substance to protect it; polish

vary *verb.* **(varied, varying) 1.** make things different **2.** be different **—varied** *adj.*

vase *noun.* a decorative pot for holding flowers

vast *adj.* very big; enormous; huge **— vastly** *adv.*

VAT *abbr.* value-added tax

vault *noun.* **1.** a room with a heavy door and strong locks to keep valuables safe **2.** a roof or ceiling made with a number of arches **3.** a jump made when using a tall pole to help you go higher

VCR *abbr.* video cassette recorder

vegetable *noun.* a plant that people eat

vegetarian *noun.* someone who does not eat meat —**vegetarian** *adj.*

vegetation *noun.* plants in general, especially in a certain area

vehicle *noun.* something that moves on wheels and carries people or goods

vein *noun.* **1.** a thin flexible tube-like vessel in a person's body that carries blood to the heart **2.** a thin line in a leaf (that carries food to the leaf) **3.** a line in rock that has (precious) metal **4.** a mood

vendor *noun.* someone who sells something, especially outside on the street

venture *noun.* a risk taken on something usually without knowing in advance how good it is

venue *noun.* somewhere that a meeting, conference, etc, is arranged to take place

verb *noun.* (grammar) a word that tells what someone or something does or is

verbal *adj.* **1.** connected with words **2.** spoken, not written

verbally *adv.* in spoken words

verdict *noun.* the decision of a jury in a law case

verify *verb.* **(verified, verifying)** check whether something is true or not — **verification** *noun.*

versatile *adj.* usable for many purposes; having many different abilities

verse *noun.* **1.** poetry; writing that has a beat (rhythm) and sometimes has rhyme; not ordinary language (no plural) **2.** one part of a song or a poem **3.** a group of lines in the Bible or the Koran

version *noun.* **1.** the way one person tells about an event **2.** a different form of the same thing

versus *prep.* against (short form **vs** or **v.**)

vertical *adj.* going straight up, not from side to side (opposite **horizontal**) — **vertically** *adv.* (opposite **horizontally**)

very *adv.* a word that makes other words stronger

very *adj.* the exact one

vessel *noun.* **1.** something that can hold something else inside of it (like a bucket or bowl) **2.** a ship **3.** a thin flexible tube inside the body that carries blood

vest *noun.* **1.** a jacket without sleeves **2.** an undershirt

vet *abbr.* veterinarian

veteran *noun. adj.* **1.** someone who was once in the army but is not any more **2.** someone with experience

veterinary *adj.* connected to the medical care of animals (usually pets or farm animals)

veto *noun.* a refusal to allow something to become law or to happen —**veto** *verb.* **(vetoed, vetoing)**

via *prep.* by way of; by going through

viable *adj.* **1.** able to develop into a living thing **2.** capable of becoming something real —**viability** *noun.*

vibrant *adj.* **1.** bright (colors) **2.** lively and exciting

vice *noun.* **1.** evil behavior, such as peddling drugs or prostitution (no plural) **2.** a bad habit

vice-president *noun.* second in position to the president

vice versa *adv.* the reverse; the opposite

vicious *adj.* cruel; wanting or able to harm

victim *noun.* someone who is killed or suffers harm or injury

victimize *verb.* **(victimized, victimizing)** treat someone unfairly, on purpose

victor *noun.* a winner (opposite **loser**)

Victorian *adj.* of or made during the time when Queen Victoria was in power in Great Britain (1837–1901)

victorious *adj.* winning

victory *noun.* the winning of a war, fight, game, etc (plural **victories**)

video *noun.* **1.** a film that you can show on a TV screen **2.** (also **video cassette recorder**) a machine for recording images on tape

videotape *verb.* (**videotaped, videotaping**) record material on tape to show on a TV screen

vie *verb.* (**vied, vying**) compete with someone (for something)

Vietnamese *noun.* someone from Vietnam; the language spoken in Vietnam —**Vietnamese** *adj.*

view *noun.* **1.** what you can see (no plural) **2.** something that is beautiful to look at in nature **3.** an opinion or ideas about something

view *verb.* (**viewed, viewing**) regard; look at; think about

viewer *noun.* someone who watches something, especially TV programs

viewpoint *noun.* point of view

vigorous *adj.* with or giving energy, strength or force

Viking *noun.* a Scandinavian who lived between the eighth and tenth centuries

vile *adj.* disgusting

villa *noun.* a house in the country

village *noun.* a very small town, usually in the country

villager *noun.* someone who lives in a village

villain *noun.* a very bad person in a story, movie, etc

vine *noun.* **1.** a climbing plant on which grapes grow **2.** any climbing or creeping plant

vinegar *noun.* a sour tasting liquid added to salads or used for pickling vegetables

viola *noun.* a string instrument that looks like a big violin and makes a deeper sound.

violate *verb.* (**violated, violating**) break a law, rule or principle

violation *noun.* breaking a law, rule or principle

violence *noun.* causing harm and pain (no plural)

violent *adj.* wild and dangerous —**violently** *adv.*

violet *noun.* **1.** a plant with small purple flowers **2.** a reddish blue color

violin *noun.* a string instrument played with a bow and held by the chin and shoulder —**violinist** *noun.*

virgin *noun.* someone who has never had sex

virtual *adj.* almost real; very near what is described

virtually *adv.* almost; very nearly

virtue *noun.* goodness of character; advantage

virus *noun.* **1.** a very tiny living thing that can cause (catching) diseases **2.** a computer code that infects programs and can bring down the system

visa *noun.* a stamp on a passport that shows that you are allowed to be in a certain country

visibility *noun.* what you can see (no plural)

visible *adj.* that you can see (opposite **invisible**)

vision *noun.* **1.** the ability to see **2.** the ability to anticipate or foresee things to come

visionary *noun.* a holy person who predicts the future

visionary *adj.* that is imaginary (and probably cannot happen)

visit *verb.* (**visited, visiting**) **1.** go to see a friend **2.** go to see a doctor, dentist, etc **3.** go to an interesting place — **visit** *noun.*

visitor *noun.* someone who visits another person; a guest

vista *noun.* **1.** a view through a narrow opening, such as between a row of trees, buildings, etc, (as in a perspective drawing) **2.** a far-reaching imaginary view of things to come **3.** a beautiful view

visual *adj.* relating to what is seen — **visually** *adv.*

visualize *verb.* **(visualized, visualizing)** form a mental picture; imagine

vital *adj.* very important; crucial

vitality *noun.* energy (no plural)

vitally *adv.* extremely

vitamin *noun.* substances found in very small amounts that give nutritional value to food

vivid *adj.* **1.** clear **2.** bright

vividly *adv.* clearly

vocabulary *noun.* **1.** words (no plural) **2.** the number of words that someone knows

vocal *adj.* of or for the voice

vocalist *noun.* a singer (with a band)

vocation *noun.* a profession; work someone does because she/he is particularly suited for that type of work

vocational *adj.* technical (education)

voice *noun.* the sound that a person makes when speaking or singing

voice *verb.* **(voiced, voicing)** express

void *adj.* null; without legal force

volcano *noun.* a mountain with an opening at the top that acts as a vent for melted rock (lava), steam and gases

volley *noun.* **1.** a pass back and forth of a ball (as in tennis) **2.** a firing of a number of missiles, etc, at the same time **3.** many things going out at the same time

volleyball *noun.* a game in which two teams of players hit a ball over a net with their hands

volt *noun.* a standard measure for electricity that is needed to create one amp

voltage *noun.* electrical energy measured in volts

volume *noun.* **1.** the space that something occupies (no plural) **2.** how loud something is (no plural) **3.** a book

voluntary *adj.* done of your own free will without being forced (opposite **compulsory**) — **voluntarily** *adv.*

volunteer *noun.* **1.** someone who offers to do something dangerous **2.** someone who offers a service without getting paid

volunteer *verb.* **(volunteered, volunteering)** offer to do something without payment

vomit *verb.* **(vomited, vomiting)** be sick; throw up your food

vote *verb.* **(voted, voting) 1.** choose someone by raising your hand or by putting a piece of paper into a box **2.** show that you support or are against a plan or a suggestion by raising your hand or putting a piece of paper into a box — **vote** *noun.*

voter *noun.* someone who votes

vow *noun.* a solemn promise — **vow** *verb.* **(vowed, vowing)**

vowel *noun.* (grammar) the letters **a, e, i, o, u**; the other letters are called **consonants**

voyage *noun.* a long journey by sea or in space

vs, v. *abbr.* versus (sport and law); against

vulgar *adj.* very rude; without elegance or taste

vulnerable *adj.* **1.** not protected **2.** easily hurt — **vulnerability** *noun.* (no plural)

vulture *noun.* a large wild bird that eats dead animals

W

W *abbr.* west

wage *noun. adj.* money that you get paid for working —**wages** *noun plural.*

wage *verb.* **(waged, waging)** fight a war or a battle

wagon *noun.* **1.** a cart pulled by an animal **2.** a small cart on wheels **3.** small table on wheels

waist *noun.* the middle part of the body

wait *verb.* **(waited, waiting)** stay until something happens —**wait** *noun.* (no plural)

waiter, waitress *noun.* a person who serves customers in a restaurant

wake *verb.* **(woke, woken, waking)** **1.** stop sleeping **2.** make someone stop sleeping

walk *noun.* **1.** moving on foot without running (no plural) **2.** a small journey on foot

walk *verb.* **(walked, walking)** move on foot; go on foot

walker *noun.* **1.** someone who walks **2.** a frame with wheels that helps someone to walk

wall *noun.* **1.** the side of a room or a building **2.** a kind of fence made of stones or bricks

wallet *noun.* a small folder for carrying money, a driver's license, etc

wallpaper *noun.* thick paper for covering walls, etc (no plural)

wander *verb.* **(wandered, wandering)** **1.** walk without any particular aim **2.** not concentrate and start thinking about other things

want *verb.* **(wanted)** **1.** feel like having or doing something **2.** need something **3.** wish for someone else to do something

want ad *noun.* an advertisement in a newspaper by someone wanting to buy or sell something or looking for work or workers

war *noun.* **1.** fighting, usually between two nations **2.** a struggle against something —**war** *verb.* **(warred, warring)**

ward *noun.* a department in a hospital where patients stay

wardrobe *noun.* **1.** a collection of clothes **2.** a clothes closet

warehouse *noun.* a building for storing things

warehouse *verb.* **(warehoused, warehousing)** store goods, etc, in a warehouse

warfare *noun.* **1.** a conflict; a war **2.** a method of fighting a war

warm *adj.* **1.** pleasantly hot; not too hot (opposite **cool**) **2.** friendly

warm *verb.* **(warmed, warming)** make warmer; heat

warmly *adv.* showing friendship

warmth *noun.* pleasant heat (no plural)

warn *verb.* **(warned, warning)** **1.** tell someone that there is danger **2.** tell someone not to do something; threaten someone

warning *noun.* **1.** an announcement of danger **2.** a threat

warrant *noun.* a piece of paper that shows that the police have the right to do something

warranty *noun.* a written guarantee given when someone buys a new car or appliance, stating that if something breaks during a limited period the manufacturer will fix it (plural **warranties**)

warrior *noun.* an old fashioned term for a soldier

wartime *noun.* a time of war (no plural; opposite **peacetime**)

wary *adj.* **(warier, wariest)** being alert and cautious; looking out for danger

was *verb.* past tense of be in the singular (I, he, she, it)

wash verb. **(washed, washing) 1.** take a shower or bath **2.** give someone else a bath **3.** make something clean with water

washing noun. clothes that you need to wash or have just washed; laundry (no plural)

wasn't abbr. = was not

waste noun. **1.** something that is not used as it should be **2.** what you cannot use (no plural)

waste verb. **(wasted, wasting)** not make good use of something

watch noun. an instrument you usually wear on your wrist to tell you what time it is

watch verb. **(watched, watching) 1.** look after; take care of **2.** look at something for a long time **3.** be careful of someone; be careful with something

water noun. the clear liquid of rain, rivers, etc (no plural)

water verb. **(watered, watering) 1.** give water to something **2.** fill with tears

watt noun. a unit of measurement of electricity

wave noun. **1.** a high sweep of water, especially on the sea **2.** a motion from side to side **3.** a sudden increase in something **4.** something that carries certain types of energy **5.** a curving shape

wave verb. **(waved, waving) 1.** move your hand back and forth in the air **2.** move back and forth gently **3.** go in curves

wax noun. a solid fatty substance that turns into a liquid when heated and disappears completely when burned

wax verb. **(waxed, waxing)** polish with wax

way noun. **1.** how to get to a place; a road; a route **2.** direction **3.** how to do something **4.** distance (no plural) **5.** someone's manner

way adv. far

way of life noun. the regular behavior or most important thing of someone's life

we pron. I and someone else

weak adj. **1.** not having a strong body **2.** not having a strong character **3.** not functioning well **4.** without a strong taste, smell, etc **5.** without much to support it

weaken verb. **(weakened, weakening)** make weak

weakness noun. **1.** being weak; not being strong (no plural) **2.** something that you cannot resist **3.** a defect in a system or in an argument (opposite **strength**)

wealth noun. a lot of money and possessions (no plural)

wealthy adj. **(wealthier, wealthiest)** rich (opposite **poor**)

weapon noun. something that you use to fight with

wear verb. **(wore, worn, wearing) 1.** have on your body (clothes, shoes, jewelry, lipstick, etc) **2.** have a certain hairstyle **3.** have a certain expression on your face **4.** last for a long time

weary adj. **(wearier, weariest)** very tired —**wearily** adv.

weather noun. cold, heat, sun, rain, snow, etc (no plural)

wed verb. **(wedded or wed)** marry

we'd abbr. **1.** = we would **2.** = we had

wedding noun. a marriage ceremony

wedge noun. a triangular shaped piece of wood put under a door to keep it open or placed between two things to push them apart

Wednesday noun. the fourth day of the week

weed noun. a wild plant that grows where you do not want it to

weed verb. **(weeded, weeding)** pull weeds out of the ground

week noun. **1.** seven days **2.** Monday through Friday; workdays

weekend noun. the days when you do not work at the end of the week

weekly *noun*. a magazine published every week (plural **weeklies**)

weekly *adj*. that you get every week

weekly *adv*. every week

weep *verb*. **(wept, weeping)** cry hard

weigh *verb*. **(weighed, weighing)** 1. have a certain weight 2. find the weight of something by using a scale

weight *noun*. 1. how heavy something is 2. something heavy that you lift

weird *adj*. very strange

welcome *noun*. a greeting

welcome *verb*. **(welcomed, welcoming)** greet someone at your house

welcome *adj*. that you are glad to have

welcoming *adj*. making you feel welcome

welfare *noun*. *adj*. 1. having good health, comfortable living conditions, etc 2. special economic help that a government gives to people who need it

well *noun*. a deep hole in the ground for getting water or oil

well *adj*. not ill

well *adv*. **(better, best)** (opposite **badly, poorly**) 1. in a good or satisfactory way 2. completely; thoroughly 3. a lot; to a considerable extent

well *interj*. 1. a word that shows that you are not sure 2. a word that shows surprise 3. a word that shows that you are annoyed

we'll *abbr*. = we will/shall

well known, well-known *adj*. 1. that everyone knows 2. famous

went *verb*. past tense of **go**

wept *verb*. past tense and past participle of **weep**

were *verb*. past tense of **be** in the plural (you, we, they)

we're *abbr*. = we are

weren't *abbr*. = were not

west *noun*. one of the four directions (no plural)

west *adj*. 1. from the west 2. in the west

west *adv*. toward or to the west (opposite **east**)

western *noun*. a book or movie about cowboys or the Old West in America

western *adj*. in the west (opposite **eastern**)

wet *adj*. **(wetter, wettest)** with water; full of water (opposite **dry**)

wet *verb*. **(wetted/wet, wetting)** make something wet

we've *abbr*. = we have

whale *noun*. a very large sea mammal that looks similar to a fish and has a flat tail

wharf *noun*. a pier; where ships load or unload cargo

what *adj*. *pron*. 1. a word for finding out about something 2. which one 3. the thing that 4. a word that you say when someone wants to talk to you 5. a word that you use to ask someone to repeat something 6. a word that shows surprise

whatever *adj*. *pron*. *adv*. 1. anything that 2. no matter what 3. whatsoever; at all 4. anything that works

whatsoever *adj*. *pron*. *adv*. at all; whatever

wheat *noun*. a grain whose flour is used to make bread, cakes, pasta, etc

wheel *noun*. something round that turns

wheel *verb*. **(wheeled, wheeling)** push something on wheels

wheelchair *noun*. a chair with wheels for a handicapped person to move around with

when *adv*. *conj*. 1. at what time 2. at the time 3. considering that 4. the moment that; as soon as

when *pron*. the time that

whenever *adv*. 1. at whatever time 2. every time that

where *adv*. 1. in what place 2. to what place 3. in the place(s) that

where *pron*. 1. the place in which, at which, etc 2. which place

whereabouts *noun*. where someone or something is (singular or plural)

248

whereas *conj.* but; in contrast

whereby *conj.* (formal) according to or by means of which

wherever *adv.* 1. in any place that 2. in all the places that

whether *conj.* if (only use **whether** (not **if**) before an infinitive, such as **whether to go**)

which *adj. pron.* 1. a word that asks about one among many 2. that 3. a word beginning a clause adding more information

whichever *adj. pron.* 1. any one of them 2. no matter which

while *conj.* 1. during the time that 2. although; even though

while *noun.* a short time

whip *noun.* 1. a long piece of leather or rope attached to a handle 2. the member of the U.S. Congress or British Parliament responsible for party discipline and attendance 3. a sweet dessert

whip *verb.* (**whipped, whipping**) 1. beat quickly in order to make (egg white or cream) stiff 2. hit with a whip

whiskey, whisky *noun.* a strong alcoholic drink made from a malted grain

whisper *verb.* (**whispered, whispering**) speak very softly so that people around you do not hear —**whisper** *noun.*

whistle *noun.* 1. a musical sound that you make by blowing air through your lips 2. the high sound that air makes when it goes through a small opening 3. a small instrument that makes a sharp noise when you blow into it —**whistle** *verb.* (**whistled, whistling**)

white *noun.* 1. the color of clean snow 2. the inside part of an egg that is not yellow —**white** *adj.*

who *pron.* 1. what person; which person or people 2. a word that begins a clause giving more information about someone 3. that

who'd *abbr.* 1. = who would 2. = who had

whoever *pron.* 1. anyone who 2. no matter who

whole *adj.* 1. complete or total; all of something 2. in one piece; not broken; uninjured

whole *noun.* 1. all of something 2. something complete (no plural)

wholesale *noun. adj.* a business that sells (especially to retail stores) in large quantities —**wholesale** *adv.*

wholly *adv.* completely; totally

whom *pron.* 1. (formal) a word that asks or tells which person 2. (formal) that 3. a word that introduces a clause giving more information about someone

who's *abbr.* 1. = who is 2. = who has

whose *pron.* 1. a word that asks what person something belongs to 2. a word that shows that one thing belongs to another

who've *abbr.* = who have

why *adv. pron.* 1. for what reason 2. that

wicked *adj.* bad; evil; cruel (opposite **good, kind**)

wide *adj.* 1. big from side to side; broad 2. how big something is from side to side (opposite **narrow**)

wide *adv.* completely —**widely** *adv.*

widen *verb.* (**widened, widening**) make wider

widespread *adj.* that exists in many places

widow *noun.* a woman whose husband died

width *noun.* how wide something is

wife *noun.* the woman that someone is married to (plural **wives**)

wig *noun.* a head covering that is made of false hair and that usually covers all of someone's own hair

wild *adj.* 1. not tame; living in nature 2. that grows in nature 3. violent; out of control; dangerous 4. strong in feeling —**wild** *adv.*

wilderness *noun.* a place, such as a desert, that is left in its natural state (without crops planted, etc) and where few or no people live

wildlife *noun*. wild animals and plants (no plural)

wildly *adv*. **1.** violently **2.** with great excitement or emotion **3.** without control

will *noun*. **1.** a piece of paper that tells who will get your money and property after you die **2.** the power to make your own choice (no plural) **3.** the desire to make something happen (no plural)

will *verb*. **(willed, willing)** leave something to someone in a will

will *verb*. **(would, willing) 1.** a word that tells that something is in the future **2.** a word that you use to offer something to someone **3.** a word that tells that you are determined to do what you want

willing *adj*. agreeing to something (opposite **unwilling**) **—willingness** *noun*.

win *noun*. a game that you won

win *verb*. **(won, winning) 1.** be the first; defeat the other side **2.** get money in a game of chance, at cards, etc **3.** get something good because you deserve it **4.** get people to feel a certain way about you

wind *noun*. air that is moving

wind *verb*. **(wound, winding) 1.** turn a key or a knob to make something work **2.** move something around and around something else **3.** have a path that curves (opposite **unwind**)

winding *adj*. going on a curved path; not straight

window *noun*. an opening in a wall, car, etc, that you can see out of

windy *adj*. **(windier, windiest)** with wind

wine *noun*. an alcoholic drink usually made from grapes

wing *noun*. **1.** the part of a bird or insect that moves up and down and lets it fly **2.** the part of an airplane that sticks out at the sides and helps it fly

wing *verb*. **(winged, winging)** (literary) fly

winner *noun*. the one who wins (opposite **loser**)

winning *adj*. **1.** that won (opposite **losing**) **2.** that makes people like you

winter *noun*. **1.** the coldest season of the year (no plural) **2.** a particular winter **—winter** *adj*.

wipe *verb*. **(wiped, wiping)** clean or dry something with a cloth **—wipe** *noun*.

wire *noun*. **1.** a metal thread **2.** a metal cord that carries electricity **3.** a telegram

wire *verb*. **(wired, wiring) 1.** put in electrical wires **2.** send a telegram

wireless *noun*. **1.** (old fashioned) a radio **2.** a system of sending and receiving signals without wires

wisdom *noun*. natural intelligence and understanding; good judgment; being wise (no plural)

wise *adj*. **1.** showing intelligence, understanding and good judgment **2.** right and sensible

wish *noun*. **1.** wanting; desire (no plural) **2.** what you want

wish *verb*. **(wished, wishing) 1.** want **2.** want something to be different **3.** want something that is impossible **4.** want someone to do something **5.** want to change something that has already happened **6.** say that you hope that something will happen to someone

wit *noun*. **1.** intelligence (usually **wits**) **2.** the ability to make jokes or say amusing things; a person with this ability **— witty** *adj*.

witch *noun*. in stories, a woman believed to have special magical powers. (plural **witches**) **—witchcraft** *noun*.

with *prep*. **1.** in the company of **2.** using **3.** having **4.** because of **5.** at **6.** in a way that shows **7.** the way that you handle something **8.** on the same side **9.** against **10.** at the same time as **11.** in the same direction as

withdraw *verb.* **(withdrew, withdrawn, withdrawing) 1.** leave something **2.** move back **3.** take something out of a place —**withdrawal** *noun.*

withhold *verb.* **(withheld, withholding)** refuse to give

within *prep.* **1.** inside of **2.** in not more than

without *prep.* **1.** not having **2.** not having the company of **3.** not doing something

witness *noun.* **1.** someone who sees something happen **2.** someone who testifies in a law court

witness *verb.* **(witnessed, witnessing)** see something happen

wives *noun.* plural of **wife**

woke, woken *verb.* past tense and past participle of **wake**

wolf *noun.* a wild animal that looks like a dog (plural **wolves**)

woman *noun. adj.* a grown-up female person (plural **women**)

won *verb.* past tense and past participle of **win**

wonder *noun.* **1.** a feeling of amazement (no plural) **2.** something that is difficult to explain (no plural) **3.** something marvelous

wonder *verb.* **(wondered, wondering) 1.** ask yourself a question **2.** be amazed **3.** a word that is used to ask for help in a polite way

wonderful *adj.* **1.** amazing **2.** excellent; marvelous —**wonderfully** *adv.*

won't *abbr.* = will not

wood *noun.* **1.** the material of a tree (no plural) **2.** (also **woods**) a place with a lot of trees; a small forest

wood *verb.* **(wooded)** gather wood; cover an area with trees

wooden *adj.* made of wood

woodland *noun.* an area of land covered with trees

wool *noun.* **1.** the hair of a sheep (no plural) **2.** thread made from wool

wool, woolen *adj.* made of wool

word *noun.* **1.** a unit of language that has meaning **2.** news or a message (no plural) **3.** a promise (no plural)

wore *verb.* past of **wear**

work *noun.* **1.** an activity that needs effort (no plural) **2.** a job (no plural) **3.** something that someone has created

work *verb.* **(worked, working) 1.** do something that takes effort **2.** have a job **3.** operate smoothly **4.** be successful **5.** function **6.** use

worker *noun.* **1.** someone who works **2.** someone who works for someone else; employee

workforce, work force *noun.* the total number of workers (in a factory, business, country, etc)

working *adj.* **1.** having a job **2.** operating the way it should **3.** used for work

working class *noun.* the industrial and agricultural workers as a social class

workload *noun.* how much work you have to do

workplace *noun.* the place (room, building, etc) where someone works

workshop *noun.* **1.** a place for making or repairing things **2.** a meeting in which people discuss or engage in a particular thing

world *noun.* **1.** the planet Earth; all the countries, oceans, etc (no plural) **2.** a planet with life on it **3.** people who do the same kind of work

worldwide *adj.* found everywhere in the world

worm *noun.* a small tube-like creeping creature

worn *verb.* past participle of **wear**

worn *adj.* old and used a lot

worried *adj.* feeling that something bad happened or may happen

worry *noun.* **1.** a nervous feeling (no plural) **2.** a problem

worry *verb.* **(worried, worrying) 1.** feel that something bad happened or may happen **2.** make someone feel worried

worse *adj.* **(bad, worse, worst) 1.** more

unpleasant, more terrible, etc **2.** more ill

worse adv. **1.** more **2.** more badly; more poorly

worsen verb. **(worsened, worsening) 1.** become worse **2.** make worse (opposite **improve**)

worship noun. a religious belief

worship verb. **(worshiped/worshipped, worshiping/worshipping) 1.** believe in; pray to **2.** love and respect someone

worst adj. worse than anything or anyone else

worth noun. value; quality (no plural)

worth prep. adj. **1.** having a certain price or value **2.** good enough to be worthwhile; deserving —**worthy** adj. **(worthier, worthiest)**

worthwhile adj. **1.** useful **2.** worth doing

would verb. **1.** past of **will 2.** a word that tells what is probably true **3.** a word that shows that you do not have or cannot do something **4.** a word that you use to ask someone to do something (more polite than will) **5.** a word that describes the past; used to **6.** (+ not) refuse

would-be adj. wanting or hoping to be or do something

wouldn't abbr. = would not

wound noun. a place where you are hurt; an injury

wound verb. **(wounded, wounding)** hurt or injure someone

wound verb. past tense and past participle of **wind**

wounded adj. hurt; injured

wrap verb. **(wrapped, wrapping)** (also

wrap up) cover something or someone completely with a paper, bag, cloth, blanket, etc

wreck noun. **1.** a serious accident involving a car, train, ship, etc **2.** a broken or destroyed ship, train, etc

wreck verb. **(wrecked, wrecking)** destroy completely —**wrecked** adj.

wretched adj. **1.** miserable **2.** poor; in very bad condition

wrist noun. the place where your hand joins your arm

writ noun. (law) a document from a court of law telling someone to do (or not to do) something

write verb. **(wrote, written, writing) 1.** put words on paper, etc, with a pen, pencil, etc **2.** send someone a letter **3.** compose a story, a poem, an article, etc **4.** compose music and put the symbols on paper

writer noun. someone who wrote a story, an article, etc; an author

writing noun. **1.** anything that is written (no plural) **2.** someone's handwriting (no plural) **3.** something that someone has composed

writings noun plural. all the things that someone has written

written verb. past participle of **write** — **written** adj.

wrong noun. what is bad

wrong verb. **(wronged, wronging)** treat or judge someone unfairly

wrong adj. **1.** not correct **2.** bad

wrong adv. not correctly

wrongly adv. **1.** not correctly **2.** unfairly; unjustly

wrote verb. past of **write**

X

xenophobia *noun.* hatred of foreigners
Xmas *noun.* Christmas

X-ray *noun.* a photograph of something inside your body (plural **X-rays**)

Y

yacht *noun.* **1.** a large private boat that belongs to a rich person **2.** a small sailing boat for racing

Yankee *noun.* **1.** (also **Yank**) an American **2.** someone who lived in the north and northeastern states during the American Civil War

yard *noun.* **1.** an area of ground beside a building **2.** a measurement of how long something is

yarn *noun.* **1.** long strands of synthetic material or wool used for knitting or weaving **2.** (informal) a long, exaggerated and incredible (often untrue) story

yawn *verb.* **(yawned, yawning)** open your mouth wide to take in air because you are tired or bored —**yawn** *noun.*

yeah *adv.* (informal) yes

year *noun.* **1.** a period of 365 days **2.** January 1 – December 31

yearly *adj.* coming once a year; annual

year-old *noun.* a person (usually a child or a teenager) of a certain age

yeast *noun.* a tiny plant from the mushroom family that is used to make bread rise, beer and alcohol

yell *noun.* a shout

yell *verb.* **(yelled, yelling)** talk or call someone in a loud voice; shout

yellow *noun.* the color of a lemon, the sun, gold, etc

yellow *adj.* **1.** of the color yellow **2.** (slang) afraid; cowardly

yen *noun.* **1.** a strong desire for something **2.** the currency of Japan

yes *interj. adv.* **1.** a word that shows that something is true or correct **2.** a word that shows that you agree to do something **3.** a word that shows that you agree with what someone says **4.** a word that shows that you disagree or that the opposite is true

yesterday *noun.* the day before today

yet *adv.* **1.** up till now **2.** up till then

yet *conj.* but; even so; in spite of that

yield *noun.* what a tree, plant, etc, gives

yield *verb.* **(yielded, yielding) 1.** give fruit, vegetables, flowers, etc **2.** give up; surrender

yoga *noun.* a method of exercising that teaches you to relax and gain control over your mind

yogurt *noun.* a soft, sour food that is made from milk

yolk *noun.* the yellow part of an egg

you *pron.* **1.** (singular and plural) the person that someone is talking to **2.** (singular and plural) the people that someone is talking to **3.** anyone

you'd *abbr.* **1.** = you would **2.** = you had

you'll *abbr.* = you will

young *adj.* **1.** not old **2.** not yet grown up —**young** *noun.* (no plural)

youngster *noun.* a child or a young person

your *pron.* someone or something that belongs to you (singular and plural; compare **This is your pen** and **Th͟** **is yours**)

you're *abbr.* = you are (singular and plural)

yours *pron.* **1.** belonging to you **2.** a way of closing a letter (singular and plural)

yourself *pron.* **1.** you; the person spoken to **2.** without any help **3.** you and nobody else

yourselves *pron plural.* **1.** without any help **2.** you and nobody else

youth *noun.* **1.** the years when someone is young (no plural; opposite **old age**) **2.** a young man —**youthful** *adj.*

you've *abbr.* = you have (singular and plural)

yuppie, yuppy *noun.* young upwardly mobile professional; a young ambitious educated person who earns a lot of money, likes to spend it and usually lives in the city

Z

zeal *noun.* great enthusiasm and eagerness —**zealous** *adj.*

zebra *noun.* an animal that looks like a horse with black and white stripes

zenith *noun.* **1.** the highest point (of your career, etc) **2.** the highest point that the sun or a star reaches in the sky

zero *noun. adj.* **1.** the number 0 (plural **zeroes**) **2.** (in games) no points scored (no plural) (for phone numbers you can also say **O**)

zigzag *noun.* a line that turns sharply one way and then the other, like a row of z's

zip *verb.* **(zipped, zipping)** close a zipper

ZIP code *noun.* numbers that you put next to the address on an envelope so that the letter will arrive faster

zipper *noun.* something that you pull up or down to fasten or unfasten a jacket, pants, a skirt, a suitcase, etc

zone *noun.* an area of land

zoo *noun.* a place where you can look at animals in cages

zoological *adj.* connected with animals

zoology *noun.* the study of animals

zoom *verb.* **(zoomed, zooming) 1.** (informal) move fast; go up sharply and quickly **2.** move a lens of a camera or microscope so that something small looks bigger **3.** move with a loud hum or buzz